THE TRUMPET SOUNDS

Printed in England by Clays Ltd, St Ives plc

About the author

Rev. David Gardner was born in Hasketon, Suffolk. He served in the Royal Navy during the Second World War, when an emergency on a submarine caused him to recognise the miraculous deliverance of God. This personal deliverance later helped him to understand what God had done for the people of Britain as a whole, many times in their history. He studied at Oakhill College and became a Chaplain of a Dockland settlement in East London. He was later the Chaplain and Evangelist for the Covenanter's Union. From the 1960s on, David recognised the signs of decline of Britain from its Christian heritage. He became a watchman who would write to leaders of the nation and publish pamphlets and books to call to remembrance God's past mercies on the nation. His desire was to see the leaders of Britain call the nation back to God through repentance and prayer. *The Trumpet Sounds for Britain* was probably David Gardner's central work. He died in the Spring of 2002 before the trilogy was republished.

Foreword

If a man was born for one central work, it is my opinion that *The Trumpet Sounds for Britain* comes from the central call from God on the life of the Rev. David Gardner. It was originally intended as a single volume but, like many of the Lord's prophets, David's path to publishing was not easy. Hence it was published as three volumes. Now it is put back together again and is printed as one volume. It is, however, printed without any changes, so that the three original volumes are bound together in their three original sections.

David Gardner died in April 2002, but negotiations were already underway for the republishing of the books. He would not countenance any changes, modifications or updating and his wishes have been respected. There would have been some minor advantages in sensitive modification, even if only to bring the message up-to-date. By keeping them in their original form, however, they retain their original thrust in the context in which they were written. It will fall on others to carry on where David left off.

Indeed, David's life and ministry, especially *The Trumpet Sounds for Britain*, has set a foundation from which others can minister. He has provided us with a unique analysis of the Christian heritage of Britain, one that would take an enormous amount of study to repeat, and he has led the way in alerting many in our nation to the dire consequences of continuing the path of rebellion against God. The foundational analysis of how Christianity came to Britain and took hold of the heart of the nation, and his description of God's hand of protection and deliverance still has the power to call the people of Britain to repentance. That is why it is being republished.

The strength of David's ministry was in his heart's

concern for his nation and how he brought his appeal from a sound biblical basis. He took the mantle of a prophet by understanding the message of the biblical prophets, seeing the signs of God's displeasure all around us, and he could foresee the nation being taken over by foreign armies just as Israel was at the time of Jeremiah. Perhaps one weakness was in his ability to predict how this might be. At the time of publishing the books, over fifteen years ago, the threat was from Russia and the subtler take-over by the powers of Europe were not so evident. In publishing the books again the reader will easily overlook this technical detail while retaining the thrust of the concern and warning in the otherwise excellent and inspired analysis.

Some of us have recognised that we come behind David in ministry, having benefited from his going before us to establish the foundations. I am among those who have been privileged to have known him personally and ministered with him for some years. I will continue to quote from what David has handed on to us, recognising also that the context for the ministry has moved on and we still need a contemporary witness to our nation. In the Spring of 2002 David and I were to be two of the speakers sharing a platform in London. David, though in hospital with, as it turned out, only days to live, had written his message and intended to give it. It was a message – his last – emphasising the true biblical call on the Christian disciple, a message that he wanted to leave behind him. It turned out that he could not make it to the meeting and so I had the privilege of reading out his message. I commented at the time, with the papers in my hand, that it felt as though the baton was passing. It was not long before I was writing his obituary for the National Council of Christian Standards, for which he had been a major writer. Now, with all seriousness I write this Foreword and exhort the next generation to learn from what David Gardner has left us and take on the work of contending

for the Gospel and raising the alarm bells in our nation.
Time is slipping away, and with it our Christian heritage.

Dr Clifford Denton
Director of Cambrian Bible College
Editor of the *Bulletin* for the
National Council of Christian Standards

The
Trumpet Sounds
for Britain

Volume 1
Revival or Perish

David E. Gardner

Contents

Foreword

by Sir Cyril Black, JP, DL, FRICS, FAI
(formerly MP for Wimbledon)

I am privileged to have been invited by my dear friend the Rev. David Gardner to contribute a foreword to Volume 1 of his latest book – *The Trumpet Sounds for Britain*, which is intended to be followed in due course by two further volumes.

This is, and is intended to be, a deeply disturbing book, and should most certainly be read by the increasing number of our fellow citizens who are deeply concerned at the obvious moral and spiritual decline of our nation, and its lessening influence in the world. Many such people cannot understand why our country, with its great history, and its triumph in 1945 (when in 1940 we had stood alone faced with what seemed to be certain defeat) has since suffered such unmitigated disasters.

The author makes clear that our decline has inexorably taken place over a very much longer period, and, for reasons which he clearly and carefully analyses, has brought us to the verge of disaster.

Some facile optimists still believe 'all's well with the world'. Such people have always existed since the days of Noah, but this attitude of mind and heart will not save them from impending disaster, any more than it saved mankind at the time of the flood.

This book is a careful analysis of the rises and falls in our nation's history since early times over long centuries, and explains the reasons why in some periods we have triumphed, and in others been cast down.

Not all readers, Christians and others, will totally agree in every particular with the author's reading of history, or with every detail of his stirring call. Our long island story contains episodes on which history seems clouded and doubtful, and of which the records are not clear. But this in no way invalidates the author's main conclusions which,

I am convinced, are soundly based.

On the main thesis I have no doubt.

Can we not all agree that God has shown great forebearance to our nation, and showered blessings upon us; that he has made it plain that he has a special purpose and destiny ordained for us; that at times when we have obeyed him and walked in the paths of righteousness he has blessed us; that when we have rebelled he has chastised us; that our profound influence in some periods of history has not been due to our wealth or power, but our faithfulness to God; that in this period of decline in which we live today our condition is grave, and due to our neglect of the laws of a just and righteous God, and our rejection of his Son, our Lord and Saviour Jesus Christ?

The day is dark, and the hour is late, but even at the eleventh hour it is still gloriously possible for us to turn defeat into victory.

God's faithful remnant has in days past wonderfully triumphed when all seemed lost.

The new birth, made possible by Christ's death on the cross, is offered to all 'without money and without price'. This is the 'one thing' that most of our people lack.

Through this book the trumpet has sounded its clarion call. Let us take courage and go forward in the name of the Lord, trusting in his strength.

This is the hour when in a special way the witness of every individual Christian counts. Readers of this book, by the very act of reading, will assume a new responsibility, for their duty will have been made clear and plain.

The crisis is desperate and the days are dark, but sometimes the darkest hour is just before the dawn.

My prayer for many years past, and today, is that I may be spared to behold the coming of revival to our beloved land.

May all readers work and pray for the early coming of that great day 'when the kingdoms of this world will become the kingdom of our Lord and of his Christ.'

Introduction

There is abundant evidence to show that the hand of God has been on the history of this country from its very earliest beginnings, and at work on its behalf in at least five ways by

1)   constituting us an island (or group of islands);
2)   giving us Christian foundations;
3)   preserving those Christian foundations whenever they have been in danger of being lost or destroyed;
4)   ensuring that our laws are based on the Bible; and
5)   bringing about mighty acts of deliverance.

These facts are quite irrefutable, and are explored in the first seven chapters of the book.

The author then moves to the present day. Since issuing his *A Warning to the Nation* in 1969, he has watched with concern and alarm Britain's spiritual and moral situation deteriorate unarrested. He warned then of the very real danger of a judgment of God falling upon Britain in terms of a 'takeover' by the enemy from without. He now sees this as imminent, and hence the urgent need to 'sound the trumpet' for Britain.

The author makes an assessment of Britain's present crisis from a study of similar situations which occur in the Bible. He finds that Britain's real trouble, as a nation which has been singularly blessed by God in past days, is not only that she has departed from God and is, in fact, now going directly against him and so is already incurring his judgments. He sees very clearly that Britain has also gone exactly the same way that the Old Testament nation of Israel went – if not further – and is therefore likely to suffer the same consequences which, in Israel's case, was a judgment of God at the hands of an invading enemy army. With the alarming increase in the Soviet military build-up forming the ingredients of that kind of judgment, the author considers that this is a very real possibility for Britain in the next few years, and sees the urgent need, like Ezekiel, 'to sound the trumpet and warn the people' (Ezekiel 33:1-7). With the enemy almost at the gates, the author's firm conviction is that the only answer to Britain's desperate situation is a heaven-sent Holy Spirit revival, but which may only come, as in the case of Joel chapter 2, when Britain is in such dire and desperate straits that she has to cry mightily to God for it.

The Trumpet Sounds For Britain is to be issued in a series of three volumes, of which this is Volume 1. The second volume will look at some of God's mighty acts of deliverance.

'Write the vision, and make it plain upon tables, that he may run that readeth it. For the vision is yet for an appointed time, but at the end it shall speak, and not lie: though it tarry, wait for it; because it will surely come, it will not tarry.'
Habakkuk 2:2,3

Chapter One
The Mighty Cleavage

Looking right back into the history of this country, there is every reason to say that it was due to an act of Almighty God that we ever became an island, or a group of islands – a fact which should not be allowed to go unmentioned in view of present-day developments.

For instance, not everybody will be aware that there was a period in our geological history when Britain was not an island; a period to which historians refer as 'pre-insular Britain'. At that time, this country was literally joined, in the geographical sense, to the continent of Europe and formed part of the European mainland. Therefore, when the very earliest prowling, primitive hunters came from Europe in those dim, distant days of our past, searching in our forests for the swine, reindeer and early mammoth which was their prey, they came *overland*. For the chalk downs of Dover were united in one long continuous range with the chalk cliffs of Calais, and there were no waters of the English Channel flowing in between. Furthermore, England and Holland were joined together by a wide marshy plain, and the Thames meandered majestically through it and merged into the lower Rhine.

Suddenly, a tremendous severance occurred. At some time in the far distant past, which experts on the subject say must have been even before the Pyramids were built, a violent earthquake caused an immense convulsion to take place in the region of the North Sea, and a great oceanic surge came sweeping round the northern coasts of Scotland and down towards the east coast of England. In the midst of this convulsion, the marshy plain sank a few hundred feet beneath the waves and thus admitted the mighty Atlantic Ocean to the North Sea and the Baltic. As a result, our islands were severed from the Continent at a point roughly between the Netherlands and what is now the coast of Norfolk and Suffolk; and today it is still the case that trawlers, whilst fishing off the Dogger Bank and over that part of the plain which now lies submerged under the North Sea, sometimes bring up in their nets the bones of mammoths or reindeer, and fragments of oak trees which tell their own tale.

Another violent earth tremor sundered the cliffs of Dover from the cliffs of Calais and Cap Gris Nez so that the Atlantic Ocean came surging through, gouging out with its strong tides what we now know as the English Channel. Ireland had already been cut adrift from England before the Dover Straits were pierced by the sea in this way, probably by a similar convulsion.

So Britain was constituted an island and a group of islands – for all time. Churchill, in the preface to his *History of the English-speaking Peoples,* says: 'No wanderings henceforth of little clans, in search of game or food-yielding plants, from the plains of France or Belgium, to the wooded valleys and downs of Southern England; no small ventures in dug-out canoes across narrow inlets at slack water. Those who come now must come in ships, and bold and wary they must be to face and master the Channel fogs and the Channel tides, and all that may lie beyond them.'

From then onwards, any would-be intruder into these islands would forever be confronted with this barrier of the sea, and would have those dangerous waters to cross.

And how often, since this mighty cleavage took place, have those twenty-five miles of water been the means of our national salvation!

They were, at the time of the Armada. They were again in Napoleon's day. And they were, more recently, immediately after the evacuation from Dunkirk and through the Battle of Britain.

I believe that this was all due to a mighty act of God. It was all part of God's plan; *God's* activity. How else do you explain that mighty under-water convulsion and the great act of severance, the result of which has played such a significant part in our history? What we need to understand above everything else is that at the back of all *visible* history is the *unseen* history – the thing that God is doing. I believe that what we see here, is the first of those great works which God has done for Britain. He had determined it all beforehand – even before creation and time began – and then he brought it to pass.

And there are strong biblical grounds for asserting this. For the Bible says that it is God who divided up the peoples of the world into nations, and who then divided to the nations their inheritance. Furthermore, it says that it is God who 'hath determined . . . the bounds of their habitation' – the borders of it, in other words. And the Bible gives the reason why: 'That they should seek the Lord, if haply they might feel after him and find him' (see Deuteronomy 32:7,8; Acts 17:26,27). Somehow or other, God's appointment of a nation's geographical position and boundaries – although it may be a mystery – is directly related to its people's, and maybe to other people's, eternal salvation.

For some reason known only to himself, when God Almighty was dividing to the nations their inheritances and setting the bounds of their habitations, he decreed that the people of this nation, – on whose behalf he was going to do so much – should dwell in a land that he himself had constituted an island.

Chapter Two
Christian Foundations

From all that we know, it is clear that the hand of God was at work at a very early stage in our history to ensure that this country was built on Christian foundations. In fact, the evidence shows that Christianity was here far earlier than most people realise.

I understand, for instance, that before Winston Churchill wrote his *History of the English-speaking Peoples* he employed an army of research workers, seeking to discover when it was that Christianity first came to these islands. They found their task was impossible. Christianity was already here when the first missionaries arrived.

It is quite wrong to think – as is popularly supposed – that everything began with Augustine, or with Augustine's particular branch of Christianity. This is most certainly not so. It is true that Augustine is frequently referred to as 'the Apostle of the English'. But Augustine did not arrive on these shores until the year AD 596, and Christianity had already been here long before that. It had probably been here over 500 years. And this means that it must have been a Christianity which was nearer to the pure New Testament form of Christianity than that which was brought here in AD 596.

Now it is most important to the theme of this book that

16

we look a little more closely into the matter. *When,* in fact, did Christianity first arrive here? *How* exactly did it come? And in what *form* did it come?

With regard to timing, it could have come direct from Pentecost, or very soon after, and I propose, a little further on, to give some good reasons why that could well have been the case.

This much can most certainly be established, that early Christianity in Britain dates at least as far back as the period of the Roman occupation of these islands, which can be dated quite definitely. Any history book will tell you that the Roman occupation of Britain began with the conquest of England by the Emperor Claudius who, incidentally, is the Claudius Caesar mentioned several times in the Acts of the Apostles (see, for instance, Acts 11:28; 18:2). That shows us how British history was running parallel with the events of the New Testament. It was in the year AD 43 that the Roman legions landed in Kent and, after several battles, achieved a decisive victory, with the result that Claudius returned to Rome from Britain with a long train of captives, and received from the Roman Senate the title of Emperor Britannicus.

From AD 43, therefore, Britannia became one of the forty-five provinces of the great Roman Empire, and remained so for four hundred years, until AD 407. That is a fact of history. No one can gainsay it.

The next thing which can be established is what the historians say of this period: 'The Roman occupation of Britain *gave time for the Christian faith to be planted.*' (my italics) Note that! It is very significant.

They also add that 'It was within that period that there arose a British Christian church which sent its bishops to the early councils.' This would seem to settle the matter pretty conclusively. Early Christianity would have had to be quite strongly established to be in a position to do that.

It is also of great interest to discover that G. M. Trevelyan, one of our most noted historians, places it on record that 'When the last of the Roman legions left these shores, and the Roman passed out of the story of Britain, they left behind them just three things of value, and the first of these was Welsh Christianity.'

I find that interesting, not only because it provides additional evidence to establish beyond any shadow of doubt that Christianity was already here well within this period of the Roman occupation, but also because Trevelyan's reference to 'Welsh' Christianity furnishes us with a clue as to what type of Christianity it was. The term 'Welsh' has a special significance in that respect, as we shall see a little later on.

Yet there are strong indications that Christianity was here even *earlier* than the period of the Roman occupation. And this is the point at which I shall examine the reasons why it could well have been here very soon after Pentecost.

First there is a need to put the entire subject into its proper context. What we are really talking about is not just the arrival of Christianity in Britain, but the arrival of Christianity in the world itself. And when we are considering the matter from that point of view, the most important thing to remember is that *God* planned it all. Indeed it is true to say that just as God had foreordained when and where his Son should come into the world to die for men's sins, so he had foreordained the ways by which the news concerning Jesus Christ should spread throughout the world, including just when it was to arrive in different places and countries, and by what means.

God had pre-arranged it all. He had designed it. He had drawn up the blue-print. And after our Lord had been crucified and had risen again, God began to put his predetermined plan into operation. Indeed he had been preparing the way long before the Saviour was born. And one of the means which he had purposed beforehand to put to his own use was the rise of the great Roman Empire which, when once Julius Caesar had planted its power firmly and widely on the north side of the Alps and into Gaul, stretched right across the world from East to West. And, in the providence of God, the roads which the Romans built across this great empire paved the way for the spread of the Gospel.

All the historians recognise the deep significance of this. For each in his turn gives testimony to the fact that 'The great Roman Empire, which arose after Julius Caesar, became the arena for the propagation of Christianity, which travelled to the four corners of civilisation in a very quick time by the roads built and guarded by the Roman soldiers.' And Churchill, when stressing this speedy means of communication, further enlarged upon the scene by telling us that 'The movement across this great Roman Empire was as rapid as when Queen Victoria came to the throne, and there were no obstructions of frontiers, laws, currency, or nationalism to hinder it.'

It needs to be repeated that, in all this, God was preparing the way, everywhere, for the arrival of Christianity.

In the context of all these developments which were taking place in the wider world at this time, something very significant began to happen *in Britain*.

Only a matter of fifty-five years before the birth of our Lord Jesus Christ in Bethlehem, Julius Caesar first landed in Britain, returning the following year. We are told that these two landings were but exploratory in nature; that they did not accomplish a great deal. What they *did* do, we are told, was to pave the way for the conquest of Britain under Claudius Caesar in AD 43.

However, I am intrigued to discover that the landings by Julius Caesar did something else besides pave the way for Britain's conquest under Claudius. They opened the way for the arrival of the Gospel. G. M. Trevelyan records that from the time of Julius Caesar's departure from these shores, a peaceful penetration of Britain by travellers from Rome and from other and more distant parts of the Roman Empire began (including all the Mediterranean countries), and continued throughout this interval of one hundred years between Julius Caesar's departure from Britain and the conquest by Claudius. All of which is very significant to our theme.

Why do I say this? The answer becomes apparent when we place the arrival and beginnings of Christianity in their historical setting. Christianity is based on fact – *historical* fact – a point which, in my own opinion, has not been stressed anywhere near sufficiently in past days, and is one which needs to be emphasised more and more today.

All the major events concerning its beginnings can be placed within a specific time-scale, including those which began to take place in the Roman province of Judea round about this time. We have already seen how God had been preparing the way beforehand for the spread of the Christian message. But, of course, it follows that before Christianity itself could be spread, the Saviour of the world had to come.

So we read: 'But when the fulness of the time was come, God sent forth his Son' (Galatians 4:4). This means that when everything was ready, when the way had been fully prepared, when the world scene had been well and truly set, when certain figures such as Pontius Pilate and Caiaphas were already on the stage – then God sent his Son. And he did this just fifty-four years after Julius Caesar's second landing in Britain.

Luke in his Gospel places this great event in its precise historical setting by telling us that the birth of our Lord Jesus Christ took place at Bethlehem in the days of the Roman emperor, Caesar Augustus – an historical figure. He was emperor from 31 BC to AD 14, and the birth of Jesus Christ took place during this time. You will remember the familiar words: 'And it came to pass in those days, that there went out a decree from Caesar Augustus, that all the world should be taxed.' (Luke 2:1)

To pin-point the time still further, Luke goes on to say

that 'This taxing was first made when Cyrenius was governor of Syria.' (Luke 2:2) Cyrenius was another historical figure. Everybody living in the region of Palestine in those days knew him. It is rather like saying that such-and-such an event took place when Sir Winston Churchill was prime minister of Great Britain, or when George VI was king of England.

This places the event in its historical setting, and within a definite time-scale. Luke does this kind of thing again when he begins to relate the arrival on the scene of John the Baptist at the beginning of his public ministry. 'Now in the fifteenth year of the reign of Tiberius Caesar, Pontius Pilate being governor of Judea, and Herod being tetrach of Galilee . . . Annas and Caiaphas being the high priests, the word of God came unto John the son of Zacharius in the wilderness.' (Luke 3:1–2)

There they all are. The historical figures – well-known figures – who were on the world scene at that time.

Christianity is based on *fact*. All the main events relating to its beginning can be placed against this specific time-scale. Caesar Augustus, who had been emperor of Rome at the time of the Saviour's birth, was succeeded by Tiberius Caesar. He reigned as emperor from AD 14 to AD 37. That is a fact. And to place the arrival of John the Baptist in its historical setting, as he came to prepare the way for our Lord's public ministry, Luke tells us that it was in the fifteenth year of Tiberius Caesar's emperorship.

Luke (3:1) even tells us who was in charge of the other regions of Palestine at this time. Philip, Herod's brother, was tetrach of Iturea and of the region of Trachonitis and Lysanias was 'tetrach of Abilene'. Both were well-known figures.

Then we read in this same third chapter of Luke's Gospel that our Lord began his earthly ministry when he was about thirty years of age (see Luke 3:23). We know that his crucifixion and resurrection took place three years later, followed, forty days after that, by his ascension into heaven, from whence he poured forth his Holy Spirit upon the original 120 disciples on the Day of Pentecost. And thus were the disciples empowered to take the Gospel throughout the world – beginning at Jerusalem.

What we are able to see from a review of this time-scale is that all the main events in our Saviour's life took place within the two historical points of Roman and British history to which we have referred earlier, namely, the landings in Britain by Julius Caesar on the one hand, and the invasion of Britain by the Emperor Claudius on the other. We also know that there were a few years to spare on either side.

So we can understand that if we place the crucifixion of our blessed Lord in the year AD 33, the gap in years between the world-shaking event on the Day of Pentecost and Claudius Caesar's invasion of Britain was very narrow indeed. Just a matter of ten years, in fact.

Why do I get so excited about all this?

Why, because from the point of view of discovering when Christianity first arrived in this country, I find it very exciting indeed to find that the historian Trevelyan has this to say about all these things: 'The hundred most important years in the history of the world' (note that perceptive phrase: it is an historian, not a theologian, who is using it) – 'The hundred most important years in the history of the world were not wholly blank, *even in Britain.*' (my italics)

A most significant statement indeed. What did he mean by it?

Well, he goes on to explain, by revealing what was happening in Britain within those vital and very crucial one hundred years. 'While Julius Caesar was being murdered and avenged, while the loves of Antony and Cleopatra were raising the question of the relation of East and West inside the Roman world, while Jesus Christ was preaching and while Paul was being converted – throughout all this period, far in the north, Roman traders and colonists, working from the base of the Romanised province of Gaul, were *establishing settlements in the interior of Britain* and gaining influence at the courts of its tribal kings.' (my italics)

You notice what he is telling us. They were doing this whilst all these things were happening within the Roman Empire. They were doing it *while Jesus Christ was preaching* and while Paul was being converted – establishing settlements in the interior of Britain. Roman traders and colonists were doing that, while Caesar Augustus was busy constructing the empire – the Caesar Augustus who features in the Bethlehem story.

This means that the Romans were establishing settlements in Britain even before Jesus Christ was born; on, after that, through the time of his childhood, earthly ministry, crucifixion and resurrection, up to Pentecost and beyond. Merchants and traders were travelling backwards and forwards between the Mediterranean countries and coming, with merchandise and produce, right into the interior of Britain, to the settlements which they had established there.

That is what I meant by saying that while all these other developments, such as the construction of roads, were taking place in the wider world and in the Middle-Eastern countries, something very significant and directly related to our theme began to happen in Britain. For I see in this the finger of God at work, preparing the way for an early arrival of the Gospel – a *very* early arrival of that Gospel. It was all happening according to the predeterminate counsel and foreknowledge of God.

Immediately Julius Caesar had landed in Britain, he had extended the trade routes from the Roman province of Gaul across to this country. Some fifty-five years before our Lord was born at Bethlehem, a way had begun to be opened up for any news about Jesus of Nazareth and the mighty miracles which he wrought – if not yet his teaching – to be carried, when the time was ready, from the Mediterranean, right across the Roman world via the trade routes into Britain. And the time between our Lord's birth and the beginning of his public ministry would have given a further thirty years for that route to be established by ever-increasing use. Altogether, there is a period of some eighty-five years involved.

This was God at work. When Gaius Julius Caesar, the proconsul of Gaul, first fixed his eyes upon Britain in the summer of 55 BC, he was about to accomplish more than he knew. Maybe in human eyes he was preparing the way for the later Roman conquest. But under the overruling providence of God he was preparing the way for the early arrival of Christianity. And in that sense he was God's instrument, although he would have been completely unaware of that fact.

The more I think and ponder about these things, the more I am persuaded that there is no reason whatsoever why faith in Christ, in terms of a personal belief in him, could not have been brought to Britain direct from Pentecost, or at least very soon after it. A study of history would seem to indicate that God was working to that end.

I am particularly convinced of this when I remember that there were gathered together in Jerusalem for the Feast of Pentecost, 'Jews, devout men, out of every nation under heaven.' (Acts 2:5) They could easily have included people from those settlements in Britain, especially if we are meant to take that phrase 'out of every nation under heaven' literally. For every nation under heaven included Britain.

And then, what happened? The Holy Spirit came down in tongues of fire upon the original disciples of Jesus. He was poured down upon them from heaven by the now enthroned Lord Jesus. Then this great multitude of devout Jews, who had come from so many nations, rushed together in the streets of Jerusalem to see what had happened. The disciples went out to them and Peter preached his first sermon. As a result 3,000 of them were converted to Jesus

Christ; then 5,000; and then a little later on, very many more.

But wait! What transpired when the Feast of Pentecost was over? Those who had arrived in Jerusalem from all these countries, returned to the various nations from which they had come; and when they did so, thousands who had been converted to Jesus Christ took their new-found faith with them – the Christian faith. Remember that it was no mere verbal belief or creed, not just a written formula or set of beliefs. These men went back *indwelt by the Spirit of Jesus Christ.* It is important to realise this, because it is what being converted to Jesus Christ really means; what makes a man a Christian. And if any of them had indeed come from Britain, they returned to Britain carrying the Spirit of the Lord within them.

In any case, in view of the numbers involved in these early Jerusalem conversions (there were not just hundreds of them, but thousands), some of them must have been merchants and traders who, in pursuit of their occupation, spent much of their time travelling backwards and forwards across the Roman world. It is quite inconceivable that this was not the case. After all, they were Jews! And for many of them, merchandise and trading was their means of livelihood, and travelling the caravan routes their very way of life. After the Feast of Pentecost was over, they would have continued to travel with their goods. But now they were new creatures in Christ Jesus, filled with the joy of the new life which they would have wanted to share with others. Because they had been so filled with the Holy Spirit, these people would surely have taken the Gospel wherever they went, to be discussed and talked about. And so faith in Christ Jesus would be carried very far afield. No doubt there was amongst them, too, the kind of trader who travelled backwards and forwards between the Mediterranean countries and the West, as far as those settlements in the very interior of Britain.

We need also to remember that many of those devout

people who had converged on Jerusalem for the festival had not come on their own. They had come in families and in groups – the Jew is noted for his family links. When they returned, they returned in families and in groups – but now, in many cases, as *Christian* groups. When they got back home, they used these Christian groups as nucleii for establishing Christian churches in the various countries, towns and cities from whence they had come. These cities and towns were situated all along the main highways and trade routes throughout the provinces of the Roman Empire, and that is one of the explanations why Christianity spread so quickly. This was God at work. There was a divine strategy involved at Pentecost, and here we see part of it in operation. God did not have to wait for 'missionaries', as we call them, to go into the various countries of the world and take the message of Christianity with them. Indeed, he did not do so. He brought together this great multitude 'out of every nation under heaven' and then, initially, used *them* to go back to their countries and provinces to plant Christian churches or groups of believers there. They were the forerunners, so to speak, which possibly explains why it was that when the apostle Paul came to Ephesus on his third missionary journey he found that there was already a nucleus of believers in that city (Acts 19:1,7). It may also explain the existence of a Christian church at a very early stage as far west as Rome.

We know that a group of Christians was already there during the time of Claudius Caesar (AD 41-54). For while the apostle Paul was in Corinth on his second missionary journey, he met Aquila and Priscilla who, we are told in Acts 18:2, had 'lately come from Italy . . . because that *Claudius* had commanded all Jews to depart from Rome'. Roman historians inform us that this expulsion was due to riots and disputes which had been levelled against the Christians by the Jewish communities, especially over the one who was called Christus or 'the Christ'.

A study of the Acts and one of the epistles makes it plain that the community of believers in Rome had already been in existence a number of years by the time the apostle Paul had completed his third missionary journey in the spring of AD 57. Whilst he was on that journey, Paul wrote to the Christians in Rome, telling them in advance that it was his intention to visit them shortly, on his way to Spain. The very existence of Paul's epistle to the Romans is evidence enough for the existence of this Christian community at an early stage. But in that letter he says that he had had a great desire 'these many years to come unto you' (see Romans 15:22-29), a statement which in itself proves that this group of believers in Rome had already been in existence a number of years.

It was not only 'in existence'. It was a very strong and influential Christian community at this early stage, for in his letter the apostle says: 'I thank my God through Jesus Christ *for you all*, that your faith is spoken of throughout the whole world.' (Romans 1:8) In other words, this group of believers was acting as a kind of 'sounding board' from which faith in Christ – their faith – was somehow or other being heard about, and indeed spoken of all over the Roman Empire. This, too, was God at work. The approximate time when this letter to the believers in Rome was written was AD 56, and Britain had already been a province of the Roman Empire for twelve years. So no doubt the faith of these Christians in Rome was being discussed at that time in Britain also. Do we now begin to see the significance of the statement regarding Winston Churchill's research workers? They had found it impossible to discover when it was that Christianity first came to Britain, because it was already here when the first missionaries arrived.

There is something very significant to learn from those early missionary journeys. The church at Antioch had been established well over a year before Claudius

Caesar's conquest of Britain. That is made plain from a reading of Acts 11:19-30 and by comparing relative dates. Paul then used Antioch as the base from which he set out on his missionary journeys. In fact, it was the Holy Spirit who sent him out from there (Acts 13:2-4).

A study of what followed, from the Acts of the Apostles, reveals that during his *second* missionary journey, when Paul and his party would have turned southwards, 'they were forbidden of the Holy Ghost to preach the word in Asia'; when they were intending to turn eastwards, again 'the Spirit suffered them not' (see Acts 16:6-8). From the remainder of Acts we read that thereafter the Gospel was brought *westwards* – ever westwards. I find that very significant, and particularly when it is very apparent that this movement westwards was all under the Holy Spirit's control. By AD 60, very much under the direction of the Lord himself, Paul had arrived at Rome, where he preached for two years (Acts 28:16-31).

It was his intention, as we have already seen, to go on as far as Spain. Indeed, some authorities claim that he was released from open imprisonment after those two years in Rome, and that between then and the time when he was martyred for his faith, he fulfilled his intention of taking the Gospel as far west as Spain. If that is indeed true, the Gospel could very quickly have reached Britain from Spain, either by the sea-route across the Bay of Biscay and round the coast of France, or overland through the Roman province of Gaul, and thence across the Channel to this country.

There were many ways by which the Gospel was being carried westwards along the roads which, by the providence of God, had been prepared beforehand. All that I have said so far does not even take into account the fact that, when persecution arose against the Christians in Jerusalem after the martyrdom of Stephen, 'they that were scattered abroad went everywhere preaching the word' (Acts 8:4) and, as later chapters reveal, planted churches wherever they went. Neither does it take into account that, when once Paul had planted churches along the trade routes of the eastern Mediterranean, he was able to say of more than one of them: 'From you sounded out the word of the Lord not only in Macedonia and Achaia, but also in every place your faith to God-ward is spread abroad; so that we need not to speak anything.' (1 Thessalonians 1:8) This was the amazing characteristic of the Thessalonian church; it was also the mark of the early Christians in Rome, not to mention many other Christian churches in those early days. In addition to all this, we have the evidence of the historian Eusebius (AD 260-340) who states that 'The apostles passed beyond the ocean to the isles called the Britannic Isles.'

The more I consider all this and dwell on the implications involved, the more I am led to believe that there is a strong case for saying that under the controlling influence and overruling direction of an Almighty God, Christianity could have arrived in Britain very early. All the evidence points that way. Whatever may be the truth concerning *how* it arrived, the facts, when taken together, point to an early arrival, not a late one. And some of the facts suggest that it *could* have arrived during the ten-year interval between Pentecost and Claudius Caesar's conquest, before Britain became a Roman province, and perhaps not very long after the Day of Pentecost. Those facts certainly suggest that Christianity came to Britain in apostolic times.

Or put it this way: I believe it is true to say that the Son of Righteousness had not long arisen from his grave on the day of his resurrection and ascended into the heavens, before the first transforming beams of his re-creative light began to penetrate the heathen darkness of some hearts in our islands.

The main reason for pursuing this theme is that it helps to establish the *type* of Christianity which was first brought to Britain. For if it came direct from Pentecost, or even twenty to thirty years after Pentecost, there is no doubt that it would have been the original New Testament form of Christianity, or something very closely akin to it.

After all, we know what type of Christianity was held by that original group of believers in Rome. We have only to read the sixteen chapters of Paul's epistle to the Romans to find out! For the purpose of that letter was to get them thoroughly grounded in the essentials of the Christian faith. And Paul leaves us in no doubt that it was original, genuine Christianity that he was teaching, and of the purest kind, because he makes it plain in his epistle to the Galatians that he received it direct from the Lord Jesus himself: 'I certify you, brethren, that the gospel which was preached of me is not after man. For I neither received it of man, neither was I taught it, but by the revelation of Jesus Christ.' (Galatians 1:11,12) He also made it plain that there were terrible consequences for preaching anything else. 'Though we, or an angel from heaven, preach any other gospel unto you than that which we have preached unto you, let him be accursed. . . . so say I now again, if any man preach any other gospel unto you than that ye have received, let him be accursed.' (Galatians 1:8,9)

It was *this* type of Christianity – received direct from the Lord himself – which all the apostles proclaimed and which was held in Rome by these early Christians between the years AD 60 and 62 when the apostle Paul was there preaching it. It was this type of Christianity which was being 'sounded forth' throughout the whole of the Mediterranean world. It was this type of Christianity which became embodied in the epistles and Gospels. And it would have been this type of Christianity which was carried to Britain, if the speed of travel in those days made it possible for it to arrive here at a very early date.

The fact of the matter is that it arrived! God had planned that it should, and had been preparing the way for its arrival from the time of Julius Caesar. And Christianity was definitely well established here at least as early as the Roman occupation in AD 43 – only ten years after Pentecost.

So God was at work very early in our history to ensure that these islands were well and truly built on Christian foundations. He must have had a very good reason for doing this.

Chapter Three
Three Great Landmarks

A study of the first one thousand years or so of British history will show that God so caused the Christianity which he had placed here to spread and grow, that under his guiding hand we were brought to three great landmarks.

First, a good two hundred years before the reign of King Alfred, God brought us to that point when, to quote the words of Winston Churchill: 'There was no kingdom in the realm in which *heathen* religions and practices now prevailed. The whole Island was now Christian.'

Here is a very significant statement which, in the light of what we see happening in our country today, confronts us with a tremendous challenge. It means that the island – which before the birth of our Lord Jesus Christ, and long before the days of Julius Caesar, had been the chief centre of ancient Druid worship; to which people from many a far-off land had come to receive instruction about this cult and to learn its dreadful heathen practices; where, in those days, human sacrifices were being made, and where human blood was being offered on heathen altars; where, later, temples to Mithras had been erected, and where, still later, the ancient gods of Thor and Woden held considerable sway – *that* island had so rallied to the Christian faith, that the great Venerable Bede was able to give this description of it: 'A Christian England . . . divided into seven kingdoms of varying strength, all professing the Gospel of Christ.'

It shows that God was so causing Christianity to grow, that all the regions and kingdoms in England which were under the sway of these heathen gods and practices had gradually, but perceptibly, submitted to the Lordship of Jesus Christ.

This is both an inspiring example and a clear demonstration of how certain statements of Scripture about the enthronement in heaven of our ascended Lord Jesus were being worked out in Britain at that time – such passages as those which say that God has 'raised him from the dead, and set him at his own right hand in the heavenly places, far above all principality, and power, and might, and dominion . . . and hath put all things under his feet . . . Sit on my right hand, until I make thine enemies thy footstool . . . For he must reign till he hath put all enemies under his feet.' (Ephesians 1:20-22; Hebrews 1:13; 1 Corinthians 15:25)

It is one of the glories of the Christian Gospel that all contestants, rival powers, gods and religions must, and will, be brought into subjection under the Lord Jesus Christ. As Christianity began to spread and grow, we see that truth being worked out in Britain on quite a considerable scale. Nobody can say that it was not God who was doing this, for whoever might have been the human instruments at the time, the Scriptures make it abundantly plain that one man plants and another waters, but it is *God* who gives the increase (1 Corinthians 3:6).

Then secondly, God brought us to that point during the twelfth century where – and I quote Winston Churchill again – 'After . . . years of being the encampment and battleground of an invading army, England became finally and for all time one coherent kingdom based on Christianity.'

This was at the time of Henry Plantagenet (Henry II,

1154-1189). We had reached another significant peak in our history which testifies to the fact that Christian growth and development has so continued under God that, by the time the British Isles had become *one* kingdom out of many kingdoms, the foundation of that one kingdom was the foundation of Christianity.

It was the rock on which the island kingdom had been built. You will notice that Churchill does not just say 'one coherent kingdom' but was at pains to stress that it was 'one coherent kingdom based on Christianity'.

'Finally and for all time', he wrote in a book first published in 1956 – a mere quarter of a century ago! For so he thought.

A united kingdom based on Christianity was a position which became so firmly established in the nation that eventually it became the position *constitutionally*.

This brings me to the *third* great landmark to which God Almighty brought us. The Christian faith – and here I need to stress that it was the *Protestant* Christian faith – became Britain's constitutional basis to such an extent that it was embodied by an act of Parliament in the Coronation Oath.

Many people will argue that our British Constitution is an unwritten one. The truth of the matter is that we have a *written* part of that constitution, and the written part happens to be Christian. It is, I repeat, embodied by Act of Parliament in the Coronation Oath. This still requires each Sovereign 'to uphold, to the utmost of my power, the Laws of God in the Realm; and the True Profession of the Christian Gospel.' The Sovereign, with a hand upon an open Bible, is on oath before Almighty God to do that, and Parliament pledges itself in the Coronation Service, through its senior peers, to support him or her. The position could not have been made more strong.

I need to emphasise this last point, because when the Christian position was embodied by Act of Parliament in the British Constitution, it made – or should have made –

those Christian foundations secure. Evidence abounds that Almighty God has been at work all down the years of our history to ensure that this nation was built on Christian foundations, and that the nation was to be governed by the laws of God, even to the point of ensuring that the Christian position became the British position constitutionally.

Chapter Four

Through Spiritual Darkness

There is overwhelming evidence to show that whenever those foundations have been in danger, either of being destroyed or of being eroded and gradually whittled away, God has been at work to ensure that they were either strengthened and buttressed or, where necessary, totally restored. We shall consider just a few of the outstanding examples.

It was true at the time of St Patrick, when this country was passing through one of its very early periods of great darkness.

The Christianity which God had so graciously brought to these islands so early, was taking root and spreading during the period of the Roman occupation of Britain to such an extent that Churchill, thrilled with excitement and caught up with the spirit of its onward march, proclaims with great exuberance: 'The new creed was winning victories everywhere.'

Then, at just about the time when Roman civilisation in this country was reaching its highest peak, a terrible and devasting menace of unprecedented proportions began to shake and convulse the nation. In the north, the Scots from Ireland and the Picts from Scotland were ferociously assaulting the defences of Hadrian's Wall, whilst at the same time the Saxons from Europe rowed across the

North Sea in their long boats and heavily attacked the east coast all the way from Dover to Newcastle. Thus, whilst the Romans were still in occupation, the inroads of these barbarian peoples began.

In the year 367, the Picts and the Scots and the Saxons all seemed to work in combination with one another, for all fell together on Britannia and circumstances of supreme and murderous horror beset our island. At that time also, the Roman Empire itself was being assailed by invading hordes, and was obliged to withdraw the legions from these shores in an attempt to defend the more immediate borders.

Less than forty years after the last of these legions had departed, in the year 442, there was added to the already devastating forces of the Saxons, Picts, and Scots, a mass migration of assaulting barbarians coming from north Germany across the North Sea to Britain. A period of terrible carnage and destruction began, and from this time onwards the curtains closed down on our history. The period called the Dark Ages had been ushered in, and a long, dark night fell upon Britannia.

What happened behind those curtains throughout these years is impossible to tell, for the darkness which closed in was so terrible that almost all records of events were completely obliterated, and the invaders kept none. Hence the next two hundred years of our history are left almost entirely blank. When those curtains lifted again it was revealed that an entire civilisation had been wiped out. The dawn broke on a scene of terrible devastation.

The well-planned Roman cities with their defensive walls had all been levelled to the ground with powerful battering rams. In place of the strong Roman-built stone houses, equipped with central-heating, baths, and many another 'modern' facility, there now stood only the wooden huts of the more primitive barbarians. All around, the roofless shells of Roman cities and villas stood starkly on the horizons. Their ruins were sprinkled over the entire land. Trevelyan says it is impossible to exaggerate in any way the injury which had been done to Roman-British civilisation in this two-century interval.

Our country was desolate; our towns and cities had been burned with fire. Strangers had devoured and over-thrown it in our presence. A complete way of life had perished, with all its culture. Four hundred years of law, order, craftsmanship, science and learning had been ruth-lessly swept away. The people had even lost the art of writing. Confusion and conflict reigned everywhere. As he surveys the appalling scene which emerged, Churchill laments: 'England was once again a barbarian island. It had been Christian, it was now heathen.'

It would seem, from such a grim description, that all lights had been entirely put out. Yet despite all that had happened, there was outstanding evidence that God had kept his hand on our history throughout the whole of this period, to retain our Christian foundations even in the midst of this great darkness.

In the first place, he had preserved and nurtured more than a remnant of that already existing Christian church. For in the face of the terrible barbarian onslaught, the British church had fallen back with other survivors upon the western parts of the island, and had taken refuge behind the Welsh mountains. There, under the hand of God, it continued to be spiritually fed, nurtured and encouraged, throughout this dark period, by Christian missionaries who kept coming over from the Continent to ensure that faith was sustained. It was a miracle of divine preservation.

It can be likened to the time of which Emperor Haile Selassie of Ethiopia spoke when he was last in Europe – the time when his early forefathers, on seeing how the onrush of Islam threatened to engulf the churches of the Middle East and so extinguish the light of the Gospel, determined that Ethopia, surrounded as she was by her mountain ranges, should remain an island site for the preservation of Christianity in the Middle East.

Something very similar happened here, preserving Christianity in the British Isles during the period of these barbarian invasions. As one historian has put it: 'There, far to the West, whilst the rest of Britain was being ravaged and shaken by these ferocious hordes – cut off from the rest of the world by the barbarian flood, but defended by its mountains – there remained this tiny Christian realm.'

I find it tremendously inspiring to think about this. Christians often sing:

> Crowns and thrones may perish,
> Kingdoms rise and wane,
> But the Church of Jesus
> Constant will remain.
>
> Gates of Hell can never
> 'Gainst that Church prevail,
> We have Christ's own promise
> And that cannot fail.

These lines are based on our Lord's own words: 'Upon this rock I will build my church; and the gates of hell shall not prevail against it.' Here, during the Dark Ages, is an outstanding example of his words being marvellously fulfilled.

It is also one of the occasions in history where we see meaning being given to some well-known words in Hebrews 12:26-27, and in quite a remarkable way. God says: 'Yet once more, I shake not the earth only, but also heaven. And this word...', says the writer of the epistle, 'signifieth the removing of those things that are shaken, as of things that are made, that those things which cannot be shaken may remain.' Which is exactly what happened.

If any preacher or Bible-class leader wants a living example to illustrate and explain what those words from the epistle to the Hebrews mean, he certainly has one here. For Britain was being violently shaken throughout

the whole of this two-hundred-year period, and during
that shaking there was a removal of the things that are
made by man. Walled cities, well-built Roman villas,
works of art, craftsmanship, an entire culture – all were
swept away and became obliterated. Yet there was one
thing that remained: the church of Jesus Christ. *That*
could not be shaken. It proved indestructible. It remained
intact.

Hebrews 12:28 goes on to say of Christians: 'Wherefore
we receiving a kingdom which cannot be moved'. When
Christians who were living at the time when this terrible
period of darkness had ended, saw how all else around
them had perished, those words must have had a profound effect upon them. And when we, who may well be
called to pass through a similar time of darkness, realise
the full force of the words in the context of all that
happened in those dark days, they should have a profound effect upon us too.

The preservation of the Christian church, then, was *one*
of the miracles which God wrought during this period.
History also reveals that God in his infinite goodness also
used this very darkness to do a work of consolidation. For
historians show how, all through this day of trouble, the
Christian faith – which was driven back behind the Welsh
mountains – got such a hold over the Welsh, that by the
fifth and sixth centuries they had come to regard Christianity as their distinguishing mark.

Almighty God was not only at work to ensure that
Christianity was nurtured and preserved all through this
long period. He was also at work to ensure that Christianity should once again be spread. We know this
because, as is so often the case in such a time, his eyes were
already upon a man. God usually works through *people*;
and certainly when he is purposing to turn the tide of
darkness.

The terrible time of trouble had not long begun, when a
band of raiders from Ireland came across to the Severn

valley, carried away captive a lad by the name of Patrick, the son of a Christian deacon, and sold him into slavery when they got back to Ireland. For six years he was obliged to tend and look after swine. But all this was of God: the hand of the Lord was upon him there, and during his long period of loneliness he was converted to Jesus Christ. He then received supernatural guidance that he should make his escape, which he did, and on reaching the coast managed to persuade a captain to take him on board his ship. After many wanderings, he found his way to some islands off Marseilles. His conversion must have been genuine, for during this time there began to well up within him an increasingly strong desire to go to his former captors in Ireland and return good for evil by sharing with them the good news of the Gospel. The guiding hand of God continued to rest upon him, for he came under the care of Bishop Germanus of Auxerre and, after fourteen years of preparation and training, sailed back to Ireland in 432.

By this time, the darkness was fast closing in over England. Just ten years later, the mass migration of barbarians from north Germany began. Britannia was plunged into night. These sombre words of Winston Churchill were uttered about that scene: 'Far away in the centre of the world where Christianity had had its origin, men remembered that Britain had been Christian once, and might be Christian again.'

But God had not been caught napping, not in any sense. He sees the end from the beginning, and even before the darkness finally fell, he had been preparing his instrument.

When the waves of barbarian Saxons from the Continent began to swarm over the east coast of England – to be followed in 442 by the migration from north Germany – Ireland, in the providence of God, was miraculously spared, and did not suffer any of these onslaughts. (The barbarians who had come from Ireland to the Severn

valley and captured Patrick were the native Scots from
Ireland, not continental invaders.) So God's eyes had not
only been fixed upon a man; they had also been fixed
upon a country. This was the country from which, in the
great plan and purposes of God, Christianity was once
again to be spread in the now darkened England.

Of God's chosen instrument who stepped back on the
scene in Ireland just ten years before the curtain finally
fell over England, we read: 'Then came Patrick, and
gathered together those Christians that remained, and
through them, proceeded to convert whole regions of
Ireland to Jesus Christ.' It was out of Ireland, then – when
Patrick's work of establishing churches there had been
accomplished – that the light of Christianity began to
shine once more like a gleaming beacon upon Britain. But
only, as yet, *upon* it.

From Ireland, the Gospel was carried over to the
northern part of Britain by Columba. When God's hour
of deliverance for Britain had come, this Columba,
imbued with the same fire and evangelistic zeal as Patrick,
set up his group of beehive huts on the island of Iona. In
563, and using Iona as his base, he led swarms of missionaries over western Scotland and northern Britain. An
ardent and vital movement of Christianity was therefore
set afoot in the north, which spread quickly to the kingdom of Northumbria in the east and the British kingdom
of Strathclyde in the west. Columba became the founder
of the Scottish Christian church.

In this way, therefore, the message which Patrick had
carried back to Ireland and had then proclaimed and
caused to be well established there, came across the sea to
these shores, and then spread widely through much of the
northern regions, dispelling the darkness everywhere.

And all this was still before the arrival of Augustine. He
was not to come for another thirty-three years! Indeed, in
the light of what we have seen in a previous chapter about
the early arrival of Christianity in Britain, it is important

to stress at this point that the history books do not refer to the time of Patrick and Columba as the *coming* of Christianity to Britain; rather, they refer to it as the *return* of Christianity to Britain.

It is important also to note at this point that there was a distinction between the form of Christianity which reached England through Columba, and that form of Christianity which, by then, existed throughout the Christianised countries of Europe.

Equally important is the fact that it is *historians* who tell us (and they have no particular axe to grind) that the form of Christianity which Columba brought, had travelled from its original source in the Middle East, through Northern Ireland, to its new home in Scotland and the north of England *without touching at any moment the centre at Rome*.

It was not until Pope Gregory the Great sent Augustine as a missionary in 596, that the Roman form of Christianity which had come to dominate Western Europe was introduced to Britain. Thereafter, two streams of Christianity flowed through the land: the one which had been brought by Columba, and the Roman form which had come with Augustine. As time went on, the latter sought to exercise a position of supremacy over the former.

* * * *

The time of King Alfred was another period when this country's Christian foundations were placed in great danger. We shall have cause to return, in Volume 2, to some of the great miracles of deliverance which God wrought on behalf of King Alfred when this country was being overrun by the Vikings.

How many people realise, however, that Alfred exerted a great Christian influence throughout the whole of his reign with lasting effect throughout these islands? Everybody has heard about King Alfred burning the cakes! But how many know that he said: 'There is only one way by which to build any kingdom, and that is on the sure and certain foundation of faith in Jesus Christ, and in Jesus Christ crucified, and it is on *that foundation* that I intend to build *my* kingdom'?

How many understand, too, with what great resolution and determination he sought to do this, as soon as God had given him final victory over the Vikings? He so painstakingly laid Christian foundations, that the effect of them has lasted to this day.

Chapter Five
The Reformation

We move now to the period of the English Reformation. This was certainly a time when the nation's Christian foundations were wonderfully restored, because the Reformation occurred when Britain was once again going through a period of intense spiritual darkness.

As we have already seen, the form of Christianity which came to Britain from Ireland had travelled with Patrick from its source in the eastern Mediterranean without reference to Rome. It is this which became known as 'Irish' or 'Celtic' Christianity, and in order to understand what happened subsequently, we need to look at the background more closely.

Under Patrick's leadership, this Celtic Christianity had taken the form of loosely-knit communities of devout Christians who separated themselves from the rest of mankind and lived in beehive huts made of wattle, clay, and turf, the huts often being grouped together in a fortified village or kraal under the supervision of an outstanding Christian leader on some rocky mountain or remote island.

The purpose of this separation was to so build themselves up in the faith that they could go out and convert whole areas and regions to Jesus Christ. These Christian communities were, by nature, missionary bases, and, in essence, this form of Christianity was independent. It was free from outside control. It was not, in this early period, associated in any way with the universal organisation of the papacy.

The devout life which these Christians lived, caused this Irish or Celtic form of Christianity to produce a rich crop of saints, of whom perhaps the greatest and most typical was Columba. He was born half a century after St Patrick's death and, was an offspring of his church. He founded his cluster of beehive huts on the small island of Iona off the west coast of Scotland round about 563, and from there, his missionaries had come over to northern Britain.

Now the papacy, from a very early stage, had followed with deep interest the results of St Columba's labour in Scotland and the north of England. It had seen, with thankfulness, that this was an ardent and zealous Christian movement which was breaking out in the northern parts of the far-off islands of Britain, and one which was full of fervour. Rome was also excited about the spread of the Gospel there. But she became deeply disturbed because the faith seemed to have been separately planted. She viewed with deep concern the fact that, from the very outset, it was independent of the papal throne.

Pope Gregory was the true founder of the medieval papacy and was the first of the great popes. These were the days when it was the first care of the Bishop of Rome to see that all Christians in every country should be brought under one earthly head. Therefore Gregory, and the ecclesiastical statesmen who were at that time gathered together in Rome, had sent Augustine to England in 596, not only to spread the Gospel in England further, but also to bring about an effective union between British Christians and what, in the Roman view, was the main body of the church.

Following the conversion of King Ethelbert of Kent, and after he had founded the see of Canterbury and made it the solid base for the subsequent spread of Roman Christianity over this island, Augustine set about this other task of bringing about the desired union of British Christians with Rome. From the outset, his attention became focused in a westerly direction, for his first attempt was directed towards the British church which, during the barbarian invasions, had been so miraculously preserved behind the Welsh mountains.

He summoned a conference of its British Christian bishops and Welsh representatives at the mouth of the river Severn. But the British bishops were in no mood for throwing themselves into the strong embraces of Rome. When Augustine claimed to have supremacy over all Christians in Britain by virtue of his Roman commission, they adamantly rejected his claim. They had defended the faith for so long against all the terrible cruelties and oppressions which the barbarians had levelled at them, and had remained independent, so why should they now subject themselves to being controlled from overseas? When Augustine threatened that if they did not submit, the Saxon armies in England would be used to bring the whole influence and prestige of Rome against them, they saw Rome in its true light.(It was one of the earliest indications that she intended to get what she wanted by force of arms if necessary.) That finished the matter as far as the British bishops and Welsh representatives were concerned, and the conference broke up in enmity. Augustine's attempt to bring about a union had totally failed and, with it, Rome's very first step in the direction of making Britain a Roman Catholic country. All further efforts by Augustine were virulently repulsed.

A second attempt was made by Rome more than half a century later, and this one was far more successful. It was levelled at the Celtic Christian missionaries operating in the north.

Once again Rome had become disturbed by the success of an ardent, evangelistic type of Christianity which was working independently of her. This time the leader was Aidan, Columba's successor. Aidan had founded the monastry of Melrose in east Scotland, and from there the surrounding districts of East, West, and Mid-Lothian beyond Northumbria were evangelised. The monastry of Lindisfarne on Holy Island off the Northumbrian and Lothian coast was also founded and Aidan became head of the Christian missionary community there. Then, at the invitation of King Oswald, Aidan began a mission to Oswald's kingdom of Northumbria in 635. This mission proved very successful. Indeed, strong bands of Celtic missionaries, under Aidan's dynamic leadership, not only reconverted Northumbria (which had relapsed) to the Christian faith, and not only evangelised the kingdom of Mercia which was just to the south, but they also continued in a southerly direction, penetrating to the south-east coast and bringing back East Anglia and Essex to Christianity. In fact, some of these Irish Christians even established groups of their missionary beehive huts as far south as Sussex, which was still heathen. They were winning victories wherever they went.

We are told that the ascetic yet cheerful life of these lovable, ardent, unworldly apostles of Jesus, who tramped the moors all day in order to preach to people in the evening, won the hearts of the men of the north. I am sure this was also true elsewhere. Indeed, it was said that Christianity had never, since its earliest years, appeared in a more attractive guise.

All this was undoubtedly a work of the Spirit. But it has always been true, all down the history of the Christian church from the Day of Pentecost, that wherever a genuine work of the Spirit breaks out, there are always those who want to bring it under control.

And so it proved to be in this case. The success of the Iona and Lindisfarne missions on English soil revived the dispute between the Celtic and Roman churches. So long as the Celtic church had remained in Celtic territory – beyond the border of Scotland – Rome could afford to overlook its remote existence. But when it broke out down south, and spread to the east and south-east coasts of England, in Rome's eyes a rivalry for the possession of Saxon England had begun.

Saxon England was Rome's preserve! Whatever happened, this independent Celtic church must submit to Rome. The issue could no longer be evaded. So once again the two streams of the Christian faith met in England and a struggle for supremacy began all over again. The tragedy was that all this was coming to a head at the very time when Anglo-Saxon England had turned away from the worship of Thor and Woden and had definitely rallied to the Christian faith. Indeed, this was the time of which it has been said: 'There was now no kingdom in which heathen practices prevailed. The whole Island was now Christian.'

The issue was no longer whether the island should be Christian or pagan, but whether the Roman or Celtic view of Christianity should prevail; whether British Christianity should conform with, and submit to, the Roman form of Christianity – which, by now, under the Bishop of Rome, dominated Christendom – or whether it should remain independent and free, and continue to be expressed through the type of Christianity on which the Celtic churches of the north had been founded.

To settle the matter, Oswy, King of Northumbria and brother of Oswald (now deceased), summoned the Synod of Whitby in 663. It hung for a long time in the balance but, in the end, King Oswy, who had championed the Celtic church of Iona since his brother's death, was tragically influenced by his wife, and gave his judgment that the church of Northumbria should be a definite part of the church of Rome and of the Catholic system.

This decision started a landslide. The church of Mercia conformed with it soon afterwards. Some of the outstanding Celtic Christians from Iona, like St Cuthbert, accepted the new order of things. The leader of the Celtic

church and the remainder of his followers returned to
Iona in disgust. When these Christians of Iona saw that
their Northumbrian friends had so tragically turned
against them, they realised they could no longer maintain
the struggle for their particular stream of Christianity in
England, and so they withdrew.

The synod's decision therefore meant that by far the
greater and more powerful part of the island was now to
be associated with the papacy. A major step had been taken
towards this country becoming Roman Catholic, and in
the course of succeeding generations Scotland, Wales and
Ireland gradually came into line with the rest of Roman
Catholic Western Europe. And this is the state of things
which we find just prior to the Reformation. It is only fair
to say, however, that the Irish clergy had originally
refused to submit.

Trevelyan saw some of the far-reaching results of all
this when he remarked: 'It cannot be denied that the
decision of Whitby contained the seeds of all the trouble
with Rome down the ages to come.' But there were consequences which were even worse than that.

Seeds sometimes have a habit of growing until they
develop into great trees whose branches reach out so that
they cover the whole land – indeed, many lands. To bring
under control a work of the Holy Spirit is to quench the
Spirit. To quench the Spirit – especially over a long period
of time – is to extinguish the light, and extinguishing the
light inevitably leads to darkness – sometimes to *great*
darkness. Which is exactly what happened in this case.

Even before the early Tudor period in England had
dawned, the original, pure, New Testament and biblical
form of Christianity had become so overlaid with non-
biblical and erroneous doctrine, and often with extra
teachings, requirements and practices introduced by the
popes and the Roman Catholic Church, that it became
entirely obliterated and lost. In consequence, a period of
great spiritual and moral darkness followed, not only in

Britain but also all over the continent of Europe, and wherever the Roman Catholic Church held sway. So by the time the Tudor period arrived, Britain had almost entirely lost her original – and essentially *biblical* – Christian foundations. Furthermore, she was a nation without a Bible in her own native tongue.

To understand that, is to understand what the Reformation was all about.

* * * *

God will not allow the light of his truth to be covered up and buried indefinitely. He always has a way of deliverance, and perhaps this is no more clearly demonstrated than in the English Reformation.

Far from being merely a political movement, as some may have been led to suppose, the Reformation was very much a spiritual revolution. It was, in fact, a revolution brought about by the Holy Spirit of God. When revealed in its true light, it can be seen as God moving to release his truth and to restore it as the only true foundation upon which people should build.

Darkness had closed in upon the land. But then the Spirit of God began to move upon the heart of a man, and this time, of a man on the Continent. The God who, at the time of creation, had caused the light to shine out of darkness, now shined in this man's heart. Martin Luther's eyes were suddenly opened to the glorious truth that rather than a man having to earn his salvation by his own personal efforts and merit, as Rome had taught, God's plan was that he could be saved eternally from the guilt, power, and eternal consequences of his sin by simply trusting in what the Lord Jesus Christ had done on the cross to atone for his sin. Luther suddenly saw that it was in *this* way that a man was made righteous in the sight of God, and could then be accepted by him.

When this brilliant light dawned upon Luther's soul, he believed it. He put his entire trust in it and the result was a new creation; he became 'a new creature' in Christ Jesus

(2 Corinthians 5:17). The scales had been removed from his eyes; old things had passed away, all things suddenly became new. His whole life and outlook were completely transformed and changed and he became filled with the Holy Spirit of God. In that way, there was a divine seal placed upon Luther that he was now God's son, and he knew it. He also knew that he had a mighty deliverance from bondage, and that he was now truly born again. This was, indeed, a revolutionary spiritual experience.

It was this experience of the new birth, in Luther's conversion, which sparked off that movement of the Spirit of God on the Continent which we now call the Reformation. The movement spread from Wittenberg to Geneva, began to take root in Scotland, and then came to England. In fact, historians record that the movement which Luther started was so dynamic, and spread so rapidly, that within the space of a mere ten years it had overrun the Continent. Right at its heart, all the time, was this basic *biblical* Christian teaching which had led to Luther's coversion – the doctrine of justification by faith in Jesus Christ, and only in Jesus Christ.

'It is *by faith*; it is *by faith*!', went up the cry. 'The just shall live by faith.' Luther had seen it, and it had revolutionised his life.

The rediscovery of this doctrine led to others, everywhere, entering into the self-same experience of the new birth. Very soon, thousands were being brought out 'from darkness to light, and from the power of Satan unto God' (Acts 26:18). Those who realised that they were estranged from God, found that they, too, could be reconciled and put right with him, simply by trusting in Jesus Christ in the same way that Luther had done and – as they later discovered – as the New Testament taught.

So countless lives were being miraculously changed and transformed, and that had a remarkable effect upon the Christian church. For the life of the church began to vibrate once again, first on the Continent, and then in *this* country. People everywhere were receiving this new life from God.

Furthermore, Luther's rediscovery of the vital doctrine of justification by faith led him to examine the whole question of authority in the church. For hundreds of years now, it was what the *church* said, that mattered. People must believe this and that because the church said so. They must always be guided by 'mother church', and the final court of appeal for settling matters in dispute was the pope.

Luther had received his revelation from the Bible. The Holy Spirit had lit up that vital verse: 'The just shall live *by faith'*, and he had believed it and was saved. He now saw that the *Bible* was the authority. So from now on the words of Scripture, not papal authority or the authority of the church, became his guiding light. When Luther made this truth known abroad, it sparked off a chain-reaction.

In the universities, the scholars of the day gave themselves to a re-examination of the Scriptures. This happened both on the Continent and here at home, leading to the Scriptures being translated from Latin into the common language of the day and being made available to the masses of the people so that, as we shall see, there was a great turning to the Bible amongst ordinary folk.

That is what the Reformation was all about.

It is well known that in 1517 Martin Luther denounced the Roman Catholic sale of Indulgences by nailing his thesis on this and other highly questionable matters to the door of Wittenberg Castle church. He began, therefore, by protesting against church practices, but his movement soon became a challenge to church doctrine – that is, to doctrine as it was being taught by Rome.

'Salvation by faith, not by works' was Luther's great theme. For the Bible says: 'A man is not justified by the works of the law . . . for by the works of the law shall no flesh be justified' – cleared of all sin in the sight of God – but it is 'by the faith of Jesus Christ' that he can be so cleared (Galatians 2:16).

The Lutheran doctrines had no sooner been proclaimed in Wittenberg, than they became a power in England. Although it is true that the Reformation *started* in this country with political issues, even those aspects proved to be of God. If we look a little more closely, we shall see why this was so. There had been a spirit of English nationalism abroad ever since Plantagenet times (from 1154 onwards) and it was now maturing. Men had been asking what British people are asking all over again today: 'Why should we look abroad for any part of our laws? Why not act through our own Parliament?'

In Henry VIII's day, the average Englishman retained the feeling of his Welsh and Celtic Christian ancestors against the pope's interference in England. So when Henry's divorce issue was at its height and was being strongly resisted by the pope, Henry himself, in his indignation, came to understand what many Englishmen had realised long before; that England, if she would be a nation indeed, must protect both spiritual and temporal jurisdiction from outside manipulation. As is so often the case in national affairs, it took a personal issue for Henry to see this so clearly.

Henry now found it intolerable that the interests of England should be subjected to the will of an outside power. The decisive moment had been reached. He made up his mind that England would no longer submit to being governed by a religious authority, or any other authority sitting hundreds of miles away, which judged English matters by Italian, Spanish, or French standards and interests, but never by English. To which we might well add the standards of Brussels and Moscow. These are the issues which have to be decided by this country today.

Henry therefore took measured steps until England was wholly independent of every kind of administration from Rome. When a Bill was finally passed through Parliament abolishing what still remained of papal authority in England, followed just a month later by a letter written personally by the king in which he described his position as 'King and Sovereign, recognising no superior in earth, but only God, and not subject to the laws of any earthly creature', the break between England and Rome was complete.

The way God used these political moves now becomes clear. At this stage the great revolution, called the English Reformation, freed the English church and state from the bonds of Rome, and ushered in the acceptance by England of the *Protestant* Christian religion. Christianity was now free to develop as it always should have been free to develop from the time of the Synod of Whitby, and the Reformation brought about a profound change. At the very time when the spiritual and moral darkness in England was most intense, God once again raised up a man. This time it was William Tyndale. Seeing the darkness with which his beloved country had become surrounded, Tyndale became gripped with the burning conviction that the entrance of God's Word into a man's heart brings light.

For centuries, the Scriptures had been denied to everyone but the priests, and even then they were in Latin. John Wycliffe, 'the Morning Star of the Reformation', and his Lollards had been instrumental in undertaking the work of translating the Bible into English earlier on. Now Tyndale was determined to see that the Bible was translated from the Latin into the Tudor English language of that day, in order that everybody should be able to understand it and that a copy should be placed in the hands of every man, woman and child in England. His desire was that even the poorest ploughboy should be able to read it.

He was hounded, harassed, and persecuted as he strove to get the work of translation and printing done, and was later driven to the Continent. There he resolutely and persistently continued his work and began shipping copies to England. It cost him his life, but just before he suffered martyrdom for his endeavours, he uttered this heart-rending prayer: 'O God: Open the King of England's eyes.'

God did not allow his servant's efforts to be thwarted; he answered his prayer. Within a year – at King Henry VIII's command – a copy of the Bible, translated into the language which everybody could read and understand, was chained to the lectern of every church in the land, and the king, backed by his government, enjoined the clergy to encourage Bible reading. Six copies of the Bible were set up in St Paul's Cathedral in the City of London, and multitudes thronged to the cathedral all day to read them, such was the hunger for the Word of God. Furthermore, when these people could find anybody with an audible voice to read aloud, their enthusiasm knew no bounds.

Tyndale, therefore, was used of God to fan the flame which Luther had already set alight. He was the first to give the Bible to England in Tudor English, and his heart-rending prayer is inscribed for all to see on a metal plaque in front of his statue in London's Thames Embankment Gardens.

Britain's foundations were being relaid. By 1535 the demand for complete printed Bibles was so great that copies of Tyndale's translation, and the one made by Coverdale, were running through several editions.

Under Henry, the Reformation continued apace in other directions as well. Having become (in the temporal sense) supreme head of the church, the heavy hand of his royal authority put away relic-worship, image-worship, paying sums of money for pardon to the priests, religious superstitions and such like. All over the country relics were destroyed, and 'miracle-working' images taken down. The cry went up: 'Dagon is everywhere fallen. Bel of Babylon is broken in pieces.'

The king also ordered fathers everywhere to teach their children the Lord's Prayer, the Ten Commandments, and the Articles of the Christian faith in English, *in their own homes*. Would that we could see this being done all over again today! And who says these things cannot be achieved by legislation?

But there was preaching involved in the Reformation as well. For we read that 'Hugh Latimer, preaching at St Paul's Cross to the citizens, and in the King's garden to the courtiers, by his rough, homely sermons, set the standard of that English pulpit oratory which, together with the Bible and the Prayer Book, effected the conversion of the people to Protestantism in the course of the next hundred years.'

It was the Bible, above all, which led to this profound spiritual and moral change in the nation. Historians say: 'We must credit the reign of Henry VIII with giving the English Bible to the people.' Trevelyan, in particular, comments: 'We talk much about Shakespeare and Shakespearian English, but our own historians proclaim that though Shakespeare may be in retrospect the greatest glory of his age, he was not in his own day its greatest influence. By the end of Elizabeth's reign, the Book of books for Englishmen was already the Bible.

'For every Englishman who had read Sidney or Spenser, or had seen Shakespeare acted at the Globe Theatre, there were hundreds who had read or heard the Bible with close attention as the Word of God. The effect of the continual domestic study of the Book upon the national character, imagination or intelligence for nearly three centuries to come, was greater than any literary movement in our annals, or any religious movement since the coming of St Augustine.'

As to the Bible's effect on people's language and thinking, Trevelyan goes on to say: 'New worlds of history and poetry were opened up in its pages to a people that had little else to read. Indeed it created the habit of reading and reflection in whole classes of the community, and turned a tinker into one of the greatest masters of the

English tongue.

'Through the Bible, the deeds and thoughts of men who had lived thousands of years before in the eastern Mediterranean, translated into English during the period when our language reached its brief perfection, coloured the daily thought and speech of Britons to the same degree as they are coloured in our own day by the commonplaces of the newspaper press.'

But with far more enobling effect, I might add!

So much did the Bible become part and parcel of the individual's life and character, that our literature became steeped in it, personal letters were full of quotations from it, and parliamentary speeches, until less than half a century ago, were punctuated and interwoven with it. The Bible became the very warp and woof of what we, as a nation, said and wrote down. For the sake of those who argue that we never have been a Christian country, let me quote Trevelyan once again in order to show that the Reformation period in England was a time when we came very near to it. He says: 'The conversion of England to Protestantism, which can be traced to origins in the time of Wycliffe, was substantially effected during the long reign of Elizabeth. When she died, *the majority* of the English regarded themselves as ardent Protestants, and *a great number of them* were living religious lives *based on the Bible and Prayer Book.*' (my italics) That speaks for itself.

It should have become quite clear by now, that what we are talking about is the restoration of our original, biblical, Christian foundations. God was undergirding the nation with them all over again. Or to put it another way, God was delivering us from that great period of darkness into which union with Rome, from Whitby onwards, had plunged us, and restoring to us that first stream of Christianity which had begun to flow in Britain at the time of Columba, and which may well have first been deposited here very soon after Pentecost and before the Roman occupation of Britain. That was original New Testament and biblical Christianity.

God even used the time when the printing press – not on this occasion the Roman roads – could aid it forward, and the time when the English language reached its perfection of force and beauty in the mouths of men, in order that this rediscovered, dynamic, New Testament message might be fully expressed.

It was our return to that original stream of Christianity – and our constant desire and determination to ensure that once fully restored, it should so remain – which resulted in our being called 'Protestant'. For Protestantism, in essence, means to take a stand for original biblical Christianity in its purest form, against all other forms which in any way deviate from it.

This is why our country became known, the world over, as a Protestant Christian country. And it is why we were so much hated by King Phillip II of Spain, who, during the reign of Elizabeth I, was the pope's military arm.

The Reformation in England meant that another important landmark had been reached in the history of our island, and in the history of Christianity in Britain. Under Queen Elizabeth I, England became, for the first time, a Protestant Christian country *by law*. That position has been zealously guarded, against all kinds of intrigue, throughout the succeeding centuries, and will, no doubt, need to be so guarded again.

As our British history clearly shows, God has intervened on more than one occasion to ensure that the Protestant Christian position should continue to be maintained. We shall see in Volume 2 that one of his interventions led to the defeat and rout of the Spanish Armada. I say we are a Protestant Christian country because God has made us so.

We should never forget, nor allow anyone else to forget, that our Protestant Christian position is still safeguarded today in that, by our British Constitution, the

Sovereign, and any successor, must be a Protestant.

Here I make bold to say that God may have to intervene yet again in order to keep it that way.

*   *   *   *

The Puritan period was also a time when this country's Christian foundations were being attacked and eroded. They were twice assailed by the royal house of Stuart, and, due to the strong forces working in the realm at that time, were in danger of being replaced by the erroneous teachings and practices of Rome. Yet God moved again, and right through this extremely turbulent period used such Christian luminaries as John Bunyan, Richard Baxter, John Milton, Thomas Goodwin, John Howe and John Owen to keep the true light of the Gospel burning. They, and many of the dissenting bodies, were the chief guardians of the truth at that time, and to remain faithful to it meant their being repeatedly dragged before judges' courts. For many of them it involved terms of imprisonment and being deprived of all their personal possessions. It also meant being forced out of their denominations, and particularly so, at the hand of Archbishop Laud, if they were members of the Church of England.

This period will be remembered, too, as the time when the opposition and persecution levelled against the groups of true believers who had separated themselves from the state church – such as the Baptists, the Presbyterians, and the Independents – were so fierce that many of their number were harried out of the land – some to Amsterdam, others to Leyden, and still more of them across the Atlantic in the *Mayflower* to New England. But there was a divine purpose even in this, for, as is well known, God used the Pilgrim Fathers to be the founders of the present United States of America, and to lay Christian foundations there.

Again, in the midst of all the turbulence at home, God

raised up that great Christian warrior, Oliver Cromwell. During his reign of office, popery and prelacy were prohibited, and Article XXXV of the Protector's Commonwealth Government declared that it was 'The Christian religion, as contained in the Scriptures, which was henceforth to be held forth as the public profession of the nation.' So once more, in an hour of extremity, God had taken steps to see that those original biblical foundations were made secure.

Chapter Six

The Great Awakening

The moral and spiritual tide in England immediately prior to the time of Wesley and Whitefield was at an extremely low ebb. In many ways, the condition of England was very similar to the condition in which we find it today. There are so many parallels, that when one reads the history of that period one gets the impression of reading a present-day account. The explanation is, of course, that history is repeating itself simply because fallen sinful men are still the same.

In the days preceding Wesley and Whitefield, as in the days of some of the Old Testament kings, the rot had set in right from the top. The first two Georges of the royal house of Hanover were unfaithful to their wives and had irregular attachments with other women. To use the blunt, unpolished description of the Bible, they were adulterers. Yet there was no outcry in the land. In fact, more than one historian has observed that one of the saddest comments on the condition of the country was that such disregard of moral sanctions in the royal house could be accepted by most people without question. Neither was there a John the Baptist to take these Sovereigns to task.

When corruption in a nation sets in at the top, it is soon reflected all the way down the line. So Thackeray said of

George II's moral laxity: 'No wonder that the clergy were corrupt and indifferent amidst this indifference and corruption. No wonder sceptics multiplied and morals degenerated.'

The rot had also started to affect the church, and basic Christian doctrines began to be discarded one by one. First, there was a departure from belief in the authority of Scripture. Men would rather build their beliefs on their own reasonings than on the authority of the Word of God. With this vital anchor cut, the nation was inevitably precipitated into an age of drift, and when other vital changes in Christian belief began to be made, these were regarded with comparative unconcern.

The nature and character of God began to be attacked. So-called Christian leaders and theologians began to deprive him of his essential attributes, making him to be a God after their own likeness and according to their own pathetic image.

The person of Jesus Christ came under attack. He was declared to be no more than a man, and therefore no longer to be regarded as God.

When once these three foundational Christian doctrines had been so seriously affected in the circles that mould Christian thought, the next thing that followed was that the supernatural and miraculous were almost entirely removed from Christian belief and outlook, with the result that essential New Testament faith was reduced to nothing more than humanism. Christianity, thus robbed of all that makes it dynamic and powerful, soon became a 'dead' religion. The salt had well and truly lost its savour, and Bishop Butler asserted that Christianity was wearing out of the minds of men. It was everywhere being held up to ridicule, and all that it stood for was being made the object of scorn. This, in turn, inevitably had its effect on the nation. Unbridled immorality, practised quite openly and unabashed, followed hard in the wake of a total disregard for God and of this widespread national ridicule

and scepticism with regard to religion. Men glorified in
their shame, and did so openly. Indeed, so openly defiant
were they of decent moral laws and standards that they
actually wanted to be known as loose and lawless. They
boasted of being so. Had Jeremiah been with us at that
time he would have asked: 'Were they ashamed when
they had committed abomination? Nay, they were not
at all ashamed, neither could they blush' (Jeremiah 6:15).

Stories abound of incredible vices and crimes being
committed in the streets; robberies and brutal murders
were being carried out wholesale. Violence was on every
hand. The whole population seemed to be given over to
one kind of orgy or another, and the very name of
Englishman was made to stink in the nostrils of men of
other nations.

All of this has a very familiar ring today. One can
almost say: 'As then, so now.' In *both* centuries the
various steps in our national decline are seen to be very
much the same. Our literature, art, theatre, and almost all
our culture, were so corrupt that they shocked even the
most hardened of visitors from overseas. And against all
this appalling evil the Christian church, as is also true today,
was a totally powerless and ineffective weapon, either to
fight against it or to stem the tide.

England, therefore, in the early days of the eighteenth
century, had witnessed a decline in religion and public
morality scarcely to be matched in the history of the
nation. We had reached an all-time low. Such appalling
corruption abounded that it seemed to call for nothing
else but an outpouring of divine wrath. *We had become a
nation ripe for judgment.*

Then, just at the point when things were at their worst,
God began to move again in England. In 1735 the Spirit of
God took hold of three men – George Whitefield, Howell
Harris, and Daniel Rowland – in such a way that all were
converted to Jesus Christ in that same year, although
none of them knew this about the others at the time.

We shall see that God's purpose was to use all three, and others in their turn, for an itinerant ministry which was to bring about a great spiritual awakening in England, Scotland and Wales. This awakening is now referred to as the Eighteenth-Century Revival, and by the time that George III came to the throne in 1760, this great Evangelical Revival had swept the land.

So mercy had intervened instead of judgment.

The signs are that Britain is in a 'pre-eighteenth-century revival situation' today, and there are many who are praying for a similar revival. Indeed, Alexander Solzhenitsyn, the Russian author, Professor Arnold Toynbee, the historian, and the recent Archbishop of Canterbury, Dr Coggan, have each said that a revival of Christianity is the only hope for Britain and the western world. Solzhenitsyn has written: 'A moral and religious revival is the only salvation for the East, and also for the West.' But it must be a revival of true Christianity, and it must be brought about by the full power of the Holy Spirit. It may therefore encourage those who are praying and looking for such a revival today, to have a reminder of some of the extraordinary things that happened in the eighteenth century; to see what were some of its most outstanding features and far-reaching effects.

George Whitefield's dynamic new life began as the result of reading a book called *The Life of God in the Soul of Man*. Whilst reading it, he entered into an experience of the new birth and so became a man indwelt by the Holy Spirit of God. As a result of his being repeatedly 'endued with new power from on high', the impact which his life and preaching made on this country and on North America was tremendous.

People often refer to the awakening in England at that time as 'Wesley's Revival', but John Wesley was not then converted to God, neither was he to be for a further three years, and by that time the revival was well and truly under way. No, it was George Whitefield, and not John Wesley, who was used of God to *begin* the revival in

England. And for this reason Whitefield has gone down in history as 'the Great Awakener'.

Yet Whitefield had few indications of the remarkable way in which he was going to be used of God in England when, in 1736, a year after his conversion, he committed himself to go out across the Atlantic as a missionary to Georgia. In fact, just before his ordination as a deacon in the Church of England, he found he was not even able to compose a sermon!

All this was God at work. Like Ezekiel, he had the experience that 'Thou shalt be dumb, but when I speak unto thee, then thou shalt speak.' On the day of his ordination in Gloucester Cathedral he found he was still not able to preach; but the very next morning, some words from the New Testament came with great power to his soul: 'Speak out, Paul'!

Whitefield was not disobedient to this divine commandment. He preached the following Sunday to a crowded audience with as much freedom as if he had been a preacher for years. That sermon meant that the Great Awakening in England had now started, although Whitefield was not to know it at the time.

God then brought him to London although, to Whitefield, this move was only to make preparations for his forthcoming journey overseas. But God had other plans in mind for him and for this country before he could set out. In the providence of God, and due to unforeseen circumstances, Whitefield was to be kept in England for the whole of the following year.

Detained in London, Whitefield preached with great power in Bishopsgate Church and then in the Tower Chapel, which soon became crowded on Sundays as he continued there. So great was the response to his ministry in London that he stayed on for two months, preaching whenever and wherever he had an opportunity.

A new message was now shaking Britain, as it was yet to shake North America: 'You must be born again.' It was a message which was entirely fresh to the majority of people in Britain. They had never heard it before. At least that generation had not. It was entirely new to them because the true, dynamic Christianity of the New Testament which Britain had known in former days had become completely lost. So when people heard it being proclaimed again in the power of the Spirit, it literally startled them.

There was another element also. Each time Whitefield preached this 'new' message he was endued with great power from on high. That power came upon the crowds as they listened, and it brought about a mighty response.

Whitefield returned to his university – Oxford – and there the fire was kindled all over again in his heart.

From Oxford he went to Gloucester, merely, as he thought, to get his bishop's advice about going abroad. But God kept him in Gloucester for three weeks, preaching twice each Sunday, and we read that every time he preached, 'the power of God attended the Word.' There was this 'unction' which was given him from above, and the congregations in Gloucester became very large.

Whitefield went on to Bristol, but merely to take leave of some of his relatives before going overseas to North America. On reaching Bristol and attending a week-day service, as was his custom wherever he went, he was invited to come from his seat and preach.

The sermon startled his hearers. Next day he was invited to preach in another church, and many came to hear him. So great was the reaction to his sermon this time, that on the following Sunday many flocked from the other churches in Bristol to hear him.

All Bristol was now astir, and this widespread reaction to the 'new message' resulted in the mayor inviting Whitefield to preach in the presence of the Bristol Corporation. So Whitefield continued in Bristol for some time after this, preaching on week-days and twice on Sundays, mainly on the doctrines of new birth and of justification by faith.in Jesus Christ alone. Again we read that during all this time 'the mighty power of God attended the Word.'

God now began to use the power of the printed word also, for the people in Bath and Bristol were so stirred by Whitefield's discourses that many asked if he would have his sermons printed, in order that they could both study them for themselves and also distribute them widely in the area. Thus was the fire spread still further.

Whitefield came to London again to make further preparations for going abroad, but God overruled again and circumstances kept him there for three weeks. He preached more frequently than before, and many came to hear him.

Soon he went down to Stonehouse in Gloucestershire, where so many came to listen that neither church nor house could contain the people, and each week the congregations increased. He said of this visit: 'I found uncommon manifestations of the power of God were granted me from above. Sometimes, like St Paul, it was as though I would be taken out of the body.'

Back at Bristol, he found a great hunger for the Word of God. The message seemed so new to them all that multitudes came on foot, with many more in coaches and on horseback. The congregations grew larger and larger. People of all ranks of society and of all denominations came flocking to hear his ministry. And the response was as great in Bath.

Whitefield was in London at the end of August 1737 to prepare to go overseas, but God intervened once more and his departure for America was still further delayed. He preached at St Ann's Cripplegate, Wapping, the Tower, Ludgate and Newgate, and all the time the congregations increased. By September even Fleet Street had begun to take notice and to mention his name in the newspapers. After three whole months of this continuous preaching, the crowds in the churches were so thick that

Whitefield felt he could almost walk on people's heads. In fact, London by now was so stirred that the streets were filled with people going to church long before daybreak. Copies of his printed sermons were being called for, and the awakening was spreading further and further afield. He was a new phenomenon in the Church of England. His message had literally startled the nation. All eyes were upon him.

By anointing his message on 'The Necessity of the New Birth,' and by anointing *him*, God was using Whitefield to restore England's original Christian foundations in the hearts of her people.

At this stage Whitefield had to go aboard the *Whitaker* for Georgia. But God had other plans, and other people, to ensure that the flames now kindled in the west country and in London did not go out while he took Whitefield to light a fire in America.

John Wesley landed in England the day before Whitefield sailed, but as a disillusioned man. He had spent more than two years as a colonial missionary in Georgia, but was now crying out in misery: 'I went to America to convert the Indians, but, Oh! who will convert me?'

Four months later came his spiritual birthday. On 24 May 1738, whilst he sat in an Aldersgate Street meeting-room listening to Luther's *Preface to the Epistle to the Romans* being read, he had a transfiguring experience. To quote his own words: 'At about a quarter before nine, while Luther in his Preface was describing the change which God works in the heart through faith in Christ, I felt my heart strangely warmed. I felt I did trust in Christ, Christ alone, for my salvation; and an assurance was given me that he had taken away my sins, even mine, and saved me from the law of sin and death. I began to pray with all my might . . . I then testified openly to all there, what I now first felt in my heart.'

Like Whitefield, he was born again of the Holy Spirit of

God, and was impregnated with spiritual fire that he, too, might be used to set England ablaze for God. He immediately began to preach that justification was by faith alone, and by so doing was used of God to fan the flames which Whitefield had already lit in 1737.

A second great wave of this mighty revival really began when Whitefield returned to England at the end of 1738. Having been used of God in America to begin a great spiritual awakening there, he returned, as he thought, only in order to be ordained priest at Oxford. But God had other plans.

He landed in Ireland from America in November, having survived a violent Atlantic storm, and his preaching in Limerick and Dublin caused a considerable stir. Arriving in London during December, he was greatly encouraged by the conditions which he found there. He soon perceived that, during his absence in America, God had watered the seed he had sown before his departure, and that as a result of the faithful ministries of John and Charles Wesley, many who had been converted under him a year ago had now grown to be strong men in Christ. A great outpouring of the Spirit followed his initial preaching at St Helen's Bishopsgate and Islington, and nothing short of a miraculous month followed. Despite the devil's activity in causing such resistance from the churches that all but four of them now excluded him from their pulpits, by the end of December Whitefield had preached in Spitalfields and across the river at Southwark, as well as at Bishopsgate and Islington, sometimes no less than nine times in one week, and with as great a power as ever he did in his life. The result was a constant stream of people coming to him for deep personal counselling between his preachings. So much was this the case that he had the firm conviction that it was only the prelude to something far bigger. There was a strong feeling within him that 'God was about to do great things amongst us.' He was not to be disappointed.

New Year's Day dawned. On 1 January 1739, at about three o'clock in the morning, there was a new outpouring of the Holy Spirit. Whilst some of them were in prayer at a 'love feast' being held in Fetter Lane, the power of God came mightily upon them. That outpouring of the Holy Spirit proved to be the precursor of the next wave of this heaven-sent revival. For a most remarkable year followed. One writer says, 'The new outpouring was a glorious preparation for the herculean work on which Whitefield and the Wesleys were about to enter.'

George Whitefield was indeed ordained priest at Oxford on 14 January 1739. In the afternoon he preached to a crowded congregation. 'God enabled me to preach with the demonstration of the Spirit and with power so that I could lift up my voice like a trumpet', he said. And while he preached, gownsmen of all degrees surrounded the church and stood at the windows attentive to every word.

He returned to London from Oxford and preached with great power to thronged congregations throughout the rest of January. At one church not only was the church itself packed, but there were nearly a thousand people in the churchyard. This led him to begin to think about preaching out of doors.

The crowning day of this part of his London ministry came, when on the first Sunday in February 1739, after preaching to vast congregations at Christ Church Spitalfields, St Margaret's Westminster, St Helen's Bishopsgate, and a full meeting-house in Fetter Lane, he wrote in his journal: 'God has owned me before nearly twelve thousand people this day.'

The opposition which arose amongst some church leaders and clergy against the doctrine of the new birth made clear what it was that was opening the eyes of so many people. For after Whitefield and Wesley had talked for a long time with their opponents, Whitefield said that the latter believed only in a Christ who was outside themselves, whereas 'we firmly believe He must be *inwardly* in our hearts.' This is a truth which needs to be rediscovered today.

It was just as this great climax was being reached in London that Whitefield prepared to set out towards the west country to go over the same ground he had covered previously. His arrival in Bristol during the second week in February 1739 was heralded by a letter which he received from one of his opponents. It read: 'Whitefield has set the Town on fire. Now he is gone to kindle a flame in the Country!'

It had been written in mockery, but it proved to be more prophetic than even Whitefield knew. His response to the letter was: 'I trust it is a holy fire that has proceeded from the Holy and Blessed Spirit. Oh that such a fire may not only be kindled, but blow up all England into a flame, and all the world over.' Certainly so far as England was concerned, he was to see his prayer wonderfully answered.

Opposition in Bristol, both from the Chancellor and the Dean of Bristol, caused Whitefield to be driven out into the open air. But in the providence of God this was in order that he might reach the colliers. To preach out in the open was the boldest step any preacher had taken at that time, but it proved to be the beginning of a great revival in the west country. First, two hundred colliers came to hear him at Kingswood; then between two thousand and five thousand people gathered; and within two weeks the crowds at Kingswood reached as many as ten thousand. Whitefield said: 'That man was right. The fire is kindled in the country, and I know all the devils in hell shall not be able to quench it.'

Going over to Hannan Mount and Rose Green Mount in his third week, the combined audiences amounted to no less than eighteen thousand in one day. After addressing fourteen thousand people at Rose Green Mount one Sunday afternoon he said, 'It was worthwhile to come so many miles to see such a sight. The more I am bidden to hold my peace, the more earnestly will I lift up my voice like a trumpet and tell the people what must be done in them, before they can be finally saved by Jesus Christ.'

God also overruled in the matter of his preaching in the Bristol churches, for despite the Chancellor's opposition, when he preached at St Mary Redcliffe it was like opening the sluice gates! Said Whitefield: 'I preached to such a congregation as my eyes never saw. Many went away for want of room.' He then preached to a great multitude inside St Philip's and St Jacob's church next day, but so many thronged to hear him that thousands had to go away because there was no room for them. All Bristol was by now astir.

Whilst this was going on, God was moving mightily in Wales. Howell Harris had been converted in the same year as Whitefield, and God was using him to re-lay the Christian foundations there. Whitefield now went to Wales because, he said, 'I want to catch some of Howell Harris's fire.' Crowds came wherever Whitefield went to preach, and he said he had never seen congregations so melted down. When leaving the Principality on 9 March his comment was: 'I think Wales is excellently well prepared for the Gospel of Christ. I bless God's Holy Name for sending me into this country.'

He went back to Bristol, and the awakening there continued apace. Over fifteen thousand colliers came to hear him preach on the first Sunday of his return; then during the next three weeks the numbers increased until, on Sunday 25 March, he preached in the open to over forty thousand people. The peak of his two months' ministry in that area came on his last Sunday, 1 April 1739, when, in all three places where he preached in the open, the congregations were larger than ever before.

It now became plain that God was bringing about an awakening in other parts of the kingdom. News had reached Whitefield of the wonderful progress which the Gospel was making in Yorkshire through the preaching of a man of God by the name of Ingham. He had seen what God was doing in Wales. Now news came to him of the way the Gospel was flourishing in Oxford. Later, he was told of how the Rev. Ebenezer Erskine had been driven out to preach in the fields in Scotland and had just spoken to fourteen thousand people! Christian foundations were therefore now being relaid everywhere. Whitefield now entrusted the work in Bristol to John Wesley, because the time for him to return to Georgia was fast approaching. He also persuaded Wesley of the necessity of field-preaching as the means most likely to reach the masses. Less than twenty-four hours after Whitefield had left Bristol, Wesley himself embarked on his own open-air preaching course, 'speaking from a little eminence in a ground adjoining the city to about three thousand souls.'

The text for this, the first of his many thousands of such field-sermons, was prophetic of the great things that lay ahead: 'The Spirit of the Lord is upon me, because he hath anointed me to preach the Gospel to the poor; he hath sent me to heal the broken-hearted; to preach deliverance to the captives, and recovering of sight to the blind; to set at liberty them that are bruised, to proclaim the acceptable year of the Lord.'

Whitefield visited Wales again and saw that the awakening there was now spreading everywhere. Then he spent the next fortnight blazing a trail back to London via Chepstow, Gloucester, Cheltenham, Oxford and their surrounding villages, thousands turning out to hear him wherever he stopped to preach. Arriving in London, he was once again driven by circumstances out into the open to preach. Then God worked most remarkably in London in just over a month.

On the first Sunday after his return, the numbers who came to hear him preach exceeded anything he had ever seen before. As many as twenty thousand came to Moorfields on the first Sunday morning, and there were never less than twenty thousand every Sunday morning throughout the whole of May. On Kennington Common there were at least thirty thousand people on that Sunday evening; by the next Sunday evening there were fifty thousand; and, a week later, sixty thousand. London was really being awakened.

At this stage, Whitefield was sometimes preaching for as long as an hour and a half or two hours, and multitudes of people would stand in the pouring rain, and even whilst it was snowing, in order to hear him. Rarely did anyone leave before he had finished. In fact, the people's hunger for spiritual things was so great that Whitefield said on one occasion: 'I felt they would listen all day to the Word of God being preached, if I could preach for that long.'

The climax to all of his London ministry came on the weekend beginning with the glorious first of June 1739. No less than eighty thousand people gathered at Mayfair near Hyde Park to hear him preach on that day, which was a Friday. Then on Sunday, 3 June he preached on Kennington Common to the largest audience he had ever seen in that place. No wonder he said at the end of this London visit: 'I have indeed seen the Kingdom of God come with power in this great city.'

And so Whitefield returned to Georgia. Hundreds, and perhaps thousands, had been converted under his ministry during the last half-year, and together with all that God was doing through Spirit-empowered preachers in other places, the whole of the British Isles was fast becoming ablaze for God.

Chapter Seven
A Changed Society

When Whitefield returned to America, Wesley took up the task and began traversing the land, mightily endued with the Holy Spirit of God. Up and down the country he went, riding on horseback, sometimes proclaiming salvation through Christ to savage Cornish smugglers, and at other times to drunkards and prostitutes in London. He preached to colliers at their pit-heads, to the down-and-outs in the Bristol slums. to the dockers and sailors of Liverpool, and to the 'wild, staring, blasphemers' of Newcastle upon Tyne. Soon this Gospel of salvation was being preached in every town and village in England; and everywhere Wesley's preaching, like Whitefield's, was being accompanied with great spiritual power. He constantly called for repentance and faith – repentance towards God and faith towards our Lord Jesus Christ – and numerous conversions followed.

Wesley was at home on horseback; disregarding rain and tempest, highwaymen and footpads, he journeyed unceasingly all over Britain. In all, he covered some 250,000 miles in the saddle, often over the most appalling of roads, and crossing no less than forty-two times to Ireland. He pursued this ministry for fifty years, and during his lifetime delivered some forty thousand sermons amongst people *where they were* – in the market places, on the commons, anywhere in the open where people would congregate. An ever-enlarging band of evangelists worked with him, and, as his converts mounted, he gathered them into groups – every group, when once it had grown spiritually strong, becoming a centre from which the new life in Christ spread to other lives. Thus through the simple testimony of common people to their new-found faith, longing souls were set alight everywhere. And all the time it was the pungent doctrines of uncompromising biblical Christianity which Wesley, like Whitefield, was consistently setting forth. He was therefore continuing methodically to re-lay Britain's Christian foundations. In fact, Sir C. G. Robertson, in his *Oxford History of England*, has written: 'At a time when Bishop Butler asserted that Christianity was wearing out of the minds of men, Wesley kept the English people Christian.'

Eventually it was not just Wesley who was doing it. Wesley had a vision, and the vision was that every convert should become a soul-winner; every Christian should be a crusader for Christ. This vision was based on the New Testament teaching of 'the priesthood of all believers', and Wesley so put the teaching and the vision into operation that eventually he had an army of no less than 8,600 bringing the impact of the Gospel to bear upon the people of this country. That was one of the secrets of the revival's great spiritual depth, and of why it spread so quickly.

We need to remember that Wesley's Christianity was a Bible-based Christianity. Wherever the revival spread, its first avowed aim was to dispel the appalling spiritual ignorance which was abroad, by an ever-increasing knowledge of the Bible. A Bible religion demanded a thorough knowledge of the Scriptures. Wesley himself taught that one could never be a 'thorough Christian' without extensive reading. This conception set thousands of converts to the task of teaching themselves to read, so that they might search the Scriptures and other books which were designed to strengthen their moral and spiritual lives.

The Bible therefore became central to countless

people's lives. To the individual Christian it was the handbook of moral and spiritual guidance, and because it was, his personal Bible became very much underlined. To the family and the Christian household, the Bible was the medium of family worship. To evangelical Christian society as a whole, the Bible was regarded as both chart and compass in the journey through life.

Wesley and Whitefield's ministry, therefore, together with that of other Spirit-filled preachers, ushered in a period of great spiritual revival and strength, the like of which had never been experienced in this country before. Historians speak of it as 'the great work of grace which transformed England in one of the darkest periods of its history.'

It was a time when 'evangelical Christianity, that is, Bible-based Christianity, laid hold upon multitudes of Englishmen with a firmer grasp and in a greater number of instances than ever before.' With regard to its far-reaching effects, one assessor of this period has said: 'The fires of the Revival had been kindled from heaven, and before the accession of George III the churches had caught the flame. Their ministers were beginning to preach with a new fervour, and their preaching was followed by a new success. The religious life of the people was becoming more intense. A passion for evangelistic work had taken possession of church after church, and by the end of the century the old meeting houses of nonconformity were crowded; many of them had to be enlarged, and new meeting houses had to be erected in town after town, and in village after village, in every part of the country.'

So great, in fact, was the permeating influence of this Evangelical Revival, that Nonconformity, with its primary emphasis on the New Testament and on the Spirit of the Gospel, became again a power in the land and a force to be reckoned with at the very highest levels.

This mighty baptism of fire also revived spiritual vision,

and kindled a great Christian initiative among thousands in the national church; but what is even more important, it reclaimed, for God, multitudes outside the churches who had long been beyond the pale of any immediate spiritual influence. So countless numbers both outside and inside the churches were ultimately affected by the Awakening. Indeed, the revival finally transformed the whole tone of the national life of the country. All areas and departments of life were cleansed, which, as we have seen from the earlier description of England's appalling decline and condition, was the country's direst need. And this is, of course, the most urgent need of our country today.

But it is necessary, in view of a great deal of wrong thinking today, to maintain a clear understanding of exactly how this great national transformation of Wesley's day came about. For Wesley and Whitefield did not believe, as do some in high ecclesiastical and governmental positions today, that it is a man's environment, surroundings and social circumstances which largely determine his character and the way he behaves. Rather they saw that it was the other way about, because they knew that the teaching of the Bible and their own experience of the new birth clearly showed that this was the case. It was not a question of changing society in order to change the behaviour and character of men, but rather a matter of changing *men*, and then *they* would do something about changing their society. Both Whitefield and Wesley saw what the Lord Jesus Christ had clearly taught before them, that the real problem was the human heart. It is out of the heart of a man, out of his innermost being, said Jesus, that all evil things proceed. All these evil things come from within. So the eighteenth-century revival centred Christianity in the individual human heart, not in the state or the environment, and not even in the church. And we need to capture this vision – this basic principle of the Great Revival – again today.

To go even deeper, Wesley and Whitefield saw clearly that men's hearts, because of inbred sin, were estranged and cut off from God; so both of them constantly sought, first and foremost, through the preaching of the cross of Jesus Christ in the power of the Holy Spirit and through its message of atonement, to bring individual souls into an abiding, personal communion with God. This is why their emphasis all the time was on *preaching*. And that is where it needs to be today.

They knew that the central promise of God in the glorious news concerning the new covenant was 'A new heart will I give you, and a new spirit will I put within you', and they knew that for the individual who believed, it was preaching that would bring that promise about. God's method as laid down in the New Testament had always been: 'It pleased God by the foolishness of preaching to save them that believe' (1 Corinthians 1:21), and they realised that this was still God's method.

Their chief and constant concern, therefore, as they preached, was to see the hearts of men changed as a result of individual conversions. For both saw clearly that a man must have the Spirit of the Lord Jesus Christ dwelling within him before he can ever call himself a Christian. They saw that true Christianity was literally the life of God himself being implanted within the innermost soul of a man, and then developing until it brought forth fruit in terms of a new life and Christ-like character. After all, it was seeing this which had led to Whitefield's conversion. Or to put it another way, they saw that the *real* Christian life was the Lord Jesus Christ living out his life from within the heart of a Christian. It was that which made the Christian's life dynamic, and it was that which made it entirely new. And Wesley and Whitefield knew that this new life could only begin with the new birth – with conversion – for they understood that *that* was when the individual, as he believed the message preached, became a partaker of the divine nature (2 Peter 1:4).

Personal conversion, therefore, not social revolution, was Whitefield's and Wesley's primary aim.

As to changes in society, it must be realised that England, before Whitefield's awakening commenced, was almost totally bankrupt of strong moral and spiritual convictions, in much the same way as she is today. Therefore these vital convictions had to be created first, before any of the desperately needed changes and transformations in society could be brought about, or before England could hope to see any turning of the spiritual and moral tide.

Wesley, as much as anybody else, was deeply concerned about the evils and injustices which surrounded him in his day; perhaps even more so, if the truth were known. But he saw clearly that when once men had been brought to the experience of personal conversion to Jesus Christ in sufficient numbers, and, as a result of that conversion, had had their consciences awakened to all the evils and social injustices which were around them, they would automatically and spontaneously begin to do something about changing the evils. 'Give me a hundred men who fear nothing but God and Hell', he said, 'and we will change the world.' So he devoted himself whole-heartedly to travelling his 250,000 miles, preaching his forty thousand sermons in the open, amongst people where they were. Praise God for the changed lives that resulted. The strong moral and spiritual convictions of which England had become so bankrupt were created all over again! Multitudes of people came to a new faith in Jesus Christ, and that new faith gradually created a new conscience as, in all parts of the country, the revival of Christianity changed hearts and gave a new sense of direction and purpose to the lives of great numbers of people. There arose an abiding concern for righteousness within countless souls throughout the land, as newly awakened consciences became more and more aware of the moral evil and social sin which was all around them, and at the same time an overwhelming desire and determination to put things right. And that is what led to change.

That is the order in which things happened then, and that is the order in which, if God gives us the time, we need to see that they happen all over again today.

How did this work out in detail? As is commonly known, a whole series of reforms was ushered in. But it should never be forgotten that these reforms were brought about by changed men. It was through changed men that the abolition of the slave trade came about. William Wilberforce, Zachary Macaulay, Henry Thornton, John Venn, and the other leading champions who fought for the abolition of the British slave trade, were all products of the eighteenth-century revival. Each one in turn had been born again of the Holy Spirit of God under the Spirit-filled preaching of the revival, and it was from a personal Christian faith that all derived their initial inspiration and drive for this courageous venture.

It was through changed men and women that our British prison system became more humanised, and that our British penal code became drastically reformed. The revival of true Christianity had led men to see the spiritual value which man must put on his fellow-man. More than any other religious movement which the English-speaking world has yet known, the Great Awakening emphasised the equal and priceless value in the sight of God of every person, and that the individual is responsible to God for the way his fellow-man is treated. England, at the time of the Awakening, had a particularly ferocious and cruel criminal code. Wilberforce repeatedly joined others in inveighing against it, and thorough-going evangelical Christians worked steadfastly with the robust humanitarian radicals of the day to remove the inhuman and grossly unjust features of our vicious and tyrannical penal system.

John Howard, the champion of prison reform and another evangelical Christian, was a zealous disciple of

John Wesley and a Spirit-filled man. He too was gripped with this burning desire to see that his fellow-men were being properly treated. That is why he travelled thousands of miles to inspect the jails of the entire United Kingdom, and that is why he expended much of his personal fortune in furthering the prisoner's cause and in bringing about reforms.

That is why Elizabeth Fry followed closely in John Howard's wake, spending a great deal of her time reading the Bible to some of the most depraved human beings in prison, and praying with them. She caused true Christianity to have a miraculous effect on the most degraded of prisoners, and particularly in London's Newgate Prison. It was this Christ-like compassion and personal concern for the well-being of others, and particularly for those in distress and who were living in appalling conditions, which inspired the Christian movement towards reforming our prisons and penal code.

It was through changed men that great advances began to be made in the realm of education. Before God sent the great revival, the moral and spiritual decline which was in progress at that time had inevitably caused education to reach an extremely low ebb. Multitudes of adults, let alone children, could not even read. When revival came, and the spiritual awakening spread, there arose – as we have seen – a great longing to read the Bible. This longing generated a persistent craving for popular instruction and teaching, and that craving Wesley was determined to satisfy. He set thousands of his adult converts the task of teaching themselves to read, and made ceaseless use of the printing press in order to supply them with good Christian literature. Tens of thousands must have taught themselves to read from these various publications. Every home which had been deeply affected by the revival had its little collection of much read books, and some of these collections are still in existence today.

Wherever Wesley's teaching penetrated, parents first

desired that their own children should be educated; then they had a similar desire for education to be given to the neglected youngsters around them. The result was a steady increase in schools.

Popular education in England, therefore, grew directly out of the Evangelical Revival itself, and was pioneered by the revival's practical, vital, New Testament Christianity. On all sides, this rebirth of real, dynamic Christianity advanced the efforts for education which Wesley encouraged. The establishment of the Sunday schools movement is an example of this.

This movement first taught reading and writing as well as a knowledge of the Bible; and in the process it grew amazingly. Wesley reported in 1784 that he found these schools springing up everywhere he went, and he lived to visit and examine local Sunday schools with nearly a thousand children in attendance, and with about one tenth of that number of voluntary teachers. George III, a promoter of the revival, gave the movement a further impetus when, in 1805, he made his famous statement: 'It is my wish that every poor child in my dominion shall be taught to read the Bible.'

The movement continued to grow until it became first national and then international; all as a direct product of the revival. When children employed in the factories were eventually set free from child-labour by Lord Shaftesbury's Factory Act in 1847, one of the principles central to that particular piece of reform was 'that children should be freed, and educated nobly to take their place as intelligent, useful, healthy and happy citizens in a Christian State.' Voluntary schools had by this time already come into existence. When the Board School Acts of 1870 were passed, they had as their purpose 'to complete the voluntary system and to fill up the gaps, but not [present parliamentarians and ministers of education please note] to supplant the voluntary system.' Britain therefore owes it to the eighteenth-century revival of Christianity that she ever had a system of popular education.

Then it is to changed men that Britain owes, or owed, its voluntary hospital system. Sir George Newman observed that 'an unprecedented improvement in public health accompanied the progress of the Eighteenth-Century Revival', and it was due to the effect of this revival upon it that 'the splendid, voluntary hospital facilities of modern England came to be more associated with a spiritual rather than with a materialistic concept of life.' And J. W. Bready says: 'The British voluntary hospital system – the only major hospital system in the world which was supported almost exclusively by the free will gifts of an appreciative public – was a product of the Evangelical Revival.'

It was John Wesley who started the first free medical dispensary in England. It was he who established the first centres offering free electrical treatment to the poor. He it was who constantly emphasised the sanctity of the human body as the temple of the living Spirit of God, urging the Christian duty of keeping it healthy and pure.

All these things therefore were introduced into the land by a changed man, and were afterwards developed and expanded by changed men.

Then it was through changed men that we got our modern voluntary social services organisations, welfare systems and facilities. For, as J. W. Bready writes, 'The voluntary hospital system, which is the best known of the voluntary-humanitarian services of Britain, is but symbolic of a unique heritage of modern social service organisations, in the creation of which, nineteenth-century England led the world.'

The same Christian awakening which had inspired and led the abolition of the slave trade, which had humanised the prison system and brought about penal reform and which had laid the foundations of popular education, had also inspired the many modern philanthropic and social service movements of which Dr Barnado's Homes, the

Shaftesbury Society, the National Society for the Prevention of Cruelty to Children, the Salvation Army, and the London City Mission are but a few. All these were brought into being by people who were possessed by the compassionate Spirit of Jesus Christ and who were filled with revival fire. All of them seek to go to the rescue of, or bring relief to, others.

Let it not be forgotten in this modern age of industrial strife, that it was also changed men who, at that time, brought vast improvements to the country's entire industrial system and who caused England's 'industrial slaves' to be set free. The long struggle for the emancipation of the factory workers from unjust and intolerable working conditions was essentially a Christian programme in character, and its Christian standpoint was made the cardinal emphasis throughout.

The crusade was led by Lord Shaftesbury, a thoroughgoing Christian who repeatedly described himself as an evangelical of evangelicals. He profoundly influenced the social welfare, not only of the British people, but of English-speaking peoples everywhere, and became known as 'the Great Emancipator'. But Shaftesbury became an emancipator of his fellow-men because he himself had first been set free by Jesus Christ and in consequence had become a changed man.

How many people today realise that the statue of Eros in London's Piccadilly Circus is a memorial to the monumental work of the great Shaftesbury and all that he did, as a Christian, to obtain the emancipation of his fellow-men from grim working conditions? The statue depicts an arrow of Christian love piercing the world, which is what Shaftesbury's love for his fellow-men sought to do.

Gladstone's tribute to Lord Shaftesbury is to be seen today inscribed round the base of this memorial: 'During a public life of half a century he devoted the influence of his station, the strong sympathies of his heart, and the great power of his mind, to honouring God by serving his fellow-men; an example to his order, a blessing to his people, and a name to be by them ever gratefully remembered.'

Shaftesbury was the inspiring, impelling, and sustaining force behind the Factory Act, the Mines and Colleries Act, the Chimney Sweep's Act, and a score of other important legislative enactments which his ceaseless endeavours on behalf of the working people of this country placed on the Statute Books of Britain.

He was a product of the Evangelical Revival, but so, too, were a good 90 per cent of the colleagues who worked with him in this heroic effort to free the 'industrial slaves'. So the tribute to Shaftesbury, put there in Piccadilly Circus by the freed factory operatives of Britain, stands also, in a very real sense, as an abiding testimony to the eighteenth-century evangelical revival.

We have said that it was changed men who changed conditions in the factories. Their entire campaign was conducted on Christian lines, without violence, either of speech or of action. And – let it please be noted – strikes, lock-outs, mob tactics, intimidation and threats were all regarded as 'out'. A deeply religious and Christian spirit permeated the humblest ranks of the crusade, and when a great national conference of factory operatives was held in London shortly after the passage of the 1847 Factory Act, a great note of thanksgiving to Almighty God was struck. This found its supreme expression in a resolution which was unanimously passed at that conference and which I quote in full because it seems to me that it needs to go on record again today: 'That we are deeply grateful to Almighty God for the success which has hitherto attended our efforts, and now that the object of our labours for the last thirty years is about to be brought to a happy consummation, we pledge ourselves to promote by every means in our power those religious and social blessings which it was the object of the Bill to extend to the factory worker.'

What further testimony is needed to the fact that it was

a Christian spirit which pervaded the whole of this crusade? In this age of industrial strife and unrest it cannot be emphasised enough that Shaftesbury and his colleagues freed the 'industrial slaves' entirely by consti- tutional and Christian means without a protracted strike, without a lock-out, without civil war, and certainly without the loss of a single life. All these ugly things were avoided, and it was because of this that there was left behind no legacy of resentment, and no smouldering hate after the Factory Act had been passed. Rather, there remained a firm foundation, largely of Christian princi- ples, on which succeeding social attainments and changes could be built.

The 1847 Factory Act, and the comprehensive Ten- Hour Programme which was eventually embodied in it, went down in history as 'The Magna Carta of the Industrial Worker's Liberty', and we need to be reminded today of some of the things which it involved. It included the closing-down of factories between the hours of 6 p.m. and 6 a.m., and the keeping of them closed between these hours so as to put a stop to all night-work. It suppressed the guileful practice of 'shifts' and 'relays'. It guaranteed evening leisure; established practical immunity from Sunday labour; enforced a weekly day of rest; and won for British factory workers the Saturday half-holiday, thus providing a prolonged weekly period for recreation and sport long before any other country had even dreamed of such a benefit.

All these things were obtained for the worker by Chris- tian men, and none of these things had been in operation before the Act was passed. In addition, the Act sup- pressed the very vicious practice of the 'free' use of women and children as 'fodder for industry'. And it is a point worthy of particular note by those who are deeply concerned about the breaking-up of family life today, that a principle central to Shaftesbury's radical crusade of social reform was 'that women should be freed from the

tyranny of industry, and be educated to raise home-
making to the standard of a Christian art or skill.'

The Factory Act also initiated the practice of com-
pulsory education, both juvenile and adult, when once it
had freed the children from child-labour. But soon after
all this social and industrial legislation had been put
through Parliament, chiefly under Lord Shaftesbury's
leadership, a whole programme of other social welfare
began to flow from it. Innumerable friendly and benefit
societies, and a hundred self-help and co-operative movements began to come into being, as well as workers
institutes, temperance guilds, literary and debating
societies and, indeed, the sane, self-governing, British
trade union movement.

The great lesson which the eighteenth-century awakening teaches us, therefore, is that the souls of men had had
first to be awakened and created anew before this train of
social reforms could be set in motion. Men were changed
first, when the Christian Gospel was preached amongst
them in the power of the Holy Spirit. Then changed men
began to change their society. *That* is the order in which
things happened.

How many people today appreciate that our British
trade-unionism was a direct product of the Evangelical
Revival, and that it has its very roots in Christianity? We
have already drawn attention to the fact that, under the
impact of Wesley's preaching, Nonconformist chapels all
over the country grew and were multiplied. The British
trade union movement grew directly out of these very
chapels. No doubt there are some union members today
who might find it convenient to forget these origins, but it
is a fact which can neither be disputed nor denied. One of
their leading members has given strong testimony to the
fact.

Jack Lawson, a leading trade unionist who held office
in the first Labour Government of 1924, traced trade-
unionism's origins to the chapels in this way: 'The Evan-

gelical Revival of the Eighteenth Century saturated the industrial masses with a passion for a better life – personal, mental, moral and social. The chapel was their first social centre, where they drew together, found strength in their weakness, and expressed to each other their hidden thoughts and needs. Here men first found the language and art to express their antagonism to grim conditions and injustices. The most powerful force for the mental and moral elevation of the workers during the industrial era has been the chapel' (contemptuously called 'Little Bethel', he said).

So it was in the chapel – in the house of God – that the trade union movement had its beginnings. What is more, the majority of the early leaders were Christians and, as such, were not only members of their local Free Churches but were also either preachers of the Gospel or were doing other active Christian work in their neighbourhood. They had Whitefield, Wesley, and other original founders of what was then the Christ-centred, deeply spiritual, Bible-based Methodist movement as their immediate spiritual ancestors. The entire trade union movement in this country is rooted and grounded in Christianity.

The great Lloyd George also testified to its *Christian* origins. Here is what he said: 'John Wesley inaugurated a movement that gripped the soul of England, that deepened its spiritual instincts, trained them, and uplifted them. That movement which improved the conditions of the working classes, in wages, in hours of labour, and otherwise, found most of its best officers and noncommissioned officers, in men trained in the Christian institutions which were the result of Wesley's Methodism.' Then he added: 'I never realise the effect which Methodism has had upon the national character so much as when I attended international congresses . . . and it is all due to the great religious revival of the eighteenth century.' By 'Methodism' he meant, of course, the

dynamic New Testament Christianity which Wesley and
his Methodist Societies revived and then applied at every
level in the country.

The Christian origins and character of the trade union
movement of England was nowhere made more dramatically conspicuous than when British unionists entered
into international conference with the leaders of organised labour on the Continent. In 1910, for instance, 260
British trade union delegates visited the industrial city of
Lille in the north of France. Like their continental comrades, the British deputation carried the socialist flag and
many trade emblems. But when they appeared in the
streets, the continental labour leaders were dumb-
founded! For the British deputation also carried a banner
which read: 'We represent 500,000 English workmen! We
proclaim the Fatherhood of God and the Brotherhood of
Man! Jesus Christ leads and inspires us.'

That Christian testimony really shook the continentals!
To that extent were British trade union delegates determined to bring Jesus Christ to the fore. Moreover, in
conference, some of the veteran British leaders, quoting
freely from the Bible, declared stoutly that it was their
Christianity which had made them trade unionists, co-
operators, and socialists. That was in 1910, and British
trade-unionism had arisen in England over 90 years before – in the years immediately following 1815. For so
long, therefore, had trade-unionism's Christian origins
and character been preserved. For almost 100 years, the
impact which the Evangelical Revival made upon
Britain's working community had an abiding effect.

So this great spiritual movement continued to cause the
spirit and teaching of our Lord Jesus Christ to penetrate
all departments of life. Having permeated the prisons,
released the slaves, brought better working conditions
into the factories, established hospitals and social welfare
services, it spread the faith, vision and power of vital,
dynamic, New Testament Christianity into the world of

business and of economics, into the realm of politics, and into all national and even international affairs. In all these realms, and in many others, Christian foundations were well and truly laid, or re-laid.

The eighteenth-century revival can claim a whole series of 'firsts' to its credit. In the realm of politics, for instance, the first two men to represent British trade unionists in Parliament were Christians – Alexander Macdonald and Thomas Burt. They were returned after the general election of 1874. So it is correct to say that the first two Labour MPs ever to sit in the House of Commons were Christians; although they were called 'Lib-Labs' at that time, since no independent Labour Party then existed.

When the completely independent Labour Party was formed, the man who inspired and led the movement – Keir Hardie – was a Christian. He then became the first Independent Labour representative to sit in the House of Commons. This was in 1892, when he was elected MP for West Ham.

A year later, in 1893, Hardie became leader of the newly formed Labour Party in the House of Commons. So the first leader of the Labour Party was a Christian. And then Charles Fenwick, a Christian, was the first Labour MP to preside over a House of Commons committee.

Britain's first Labour prime minister, J. Ramsay MacDonald, and three times prime minister of England, was also a Christian. Referring to the effect which the Evangelical Revival had had upon the people of this country, Ramsay MacDonald wrote: 'That Common Baptism into one Free Faith, mediated by those intrepid modern apostles, Wesley and Whitefield, gave men self respect and pride. It did not merely arm them with claims for sharing in this world's goods. The problem . . . will never be solved by rectifying differences in status, or in material possessions. Class conflicts will only mislead us, and give victories which will be barren of results. The generation which loses the spirit of life loses everything worth having.'

These are words which many, surely, need to weigh again today.

But then he issued a warning which needs to be sounded out all over Britain in this so-called progressive age: 'Let us not pride ourselves that we are progressing if we let go the interests and inspiration which brought the Free Churches into being' – by which he meant the very spirit of the revival itself.

Referring to the Christian inspiration behind true democracy, he said: 'Democracy conquered the foothills . . Can it afford now to dispense with that ardour and devotion which only profound religious [Christian] belief and stern ethical principle can provide?' Such strident warnings need to be sounded out to a generation which, once again, has thrown away all its Christian foundations.

The first editor of Labour's daily newspaper, the *Daily Herald* – George Lansbury – was a Christian.

All these men, in one way or another, were products of the continuing baptism of fire which Whitefield and Wesley had originally been used to initiate; and they brought strong Christian influence to bear in other parts of society.

For instance, Alexander Macdonald was for a long time the leader and spokesman of miners all over Scotland. As such, he was elected president of the National Union of Miners, and remained so for eighteen years. As a Christian member of Parliament, he also represented the Scottish miners in Parliament for seven years.

Thomas Burt, that Bible-loving Christian, was for forty-eight years the secretary of the Northumberland Miners' Association. He later became president of the Trades Union Congress. So God was raising these Christian men into positions of leadership and influence in these spheres also.

Keir Hardie, a year after his conversion from atheism to Christianity, was elected secretary of the Ayrshire Miners' Association, so yet another Christian was giving leadership to the miners at that time. In fact, Jack Lawson, the trade unionist already quoted, speaking of the time when Christian socialists and evangelical trade union leaders were most vitally active, and of the time when the Christian influence in the trade union movement of Britain was at its strongest, said: 'The Gospel expressed in social terms has been more of a driving power in northern mining circles, than all the economic teaching put together.'

Such was the strong Christian leadership being given to the miners in those days, and to that extent was the mining industry being permeated by the Spirit of Jesus Christ. Let it please be noted that men like Alexander Macdonald and Thomas Burt loathed class-hatred and classwar. Neither of them would have tolerated the social reforms of the day being carried out along those lines – and most certainly Shaftesbury would not have done so – because to all these men, such class-hatred and classwarfare were foreign to the Spirit of Jesus which was in them.

We have already seen that Ramsay MacDonald was another Christian and product of the Evangelical Revival whom God raised up to a position of influence and leadership. As a young man, he was a pupil-teacher in his local kirk in Scotland, and it is beyond dispute that spiritual and moral forces had been uppermost in shaping all that was most attractive in his life. As a Labour MP, and later as Britain's first Labour prime minister, he found the materialism, economic determinism, class-hatred and atheism of Karl Marx's doctrinaire dogma to be quite repulsive, and was a strong advocate in Parliament for Christian ideals and principles. In fact, when he was prime minister he went so far as to say that he believed that democracy itself – true democracy – had its source in the eighteenth-century revival; that vital Christianity was indeed its very foundation; and that without Christianity, democracy is doomed to perish.

In a foreword to a book on George Whitefield, by Dr Belden, he wrote: 'The Free Churches were one of the pure sources from which free Democracy came. It was by the dynamic of free religion [by which he meant Christianity] that masses were inspired to escape from the quagmire of misery and injustice. The Christian Faith preserved the masses from becoming soul-less things obedient to the convenience and advantage of economic forces.'

That was by no means all from which the Christian faith preserved the masses in Britain. For history shows that when God intervened by sending revival to this country, he saved Britain from being engulfed in the kind of blood-bath that had overtaken France at the time of the French Revolution.

The impact which the Evangelical Revival had upon this country and upon its people, therefore, was incalculable. It was clear to all who were living at that time that there was a mighty power at work in the land, and it is no exaggeration to say that the effect which this great visitation of God made upon the country through the ministries of both Whitefield and Wesley lasted for well over 100 years.

Many testimonies have been written to the force of that impact. Writing of the revival's far-reaching effects, Trevelyan, in his *British History of the Nineteenth Century*, says: 'It was one of the turning points in the history of the world.' Then he said of Britain, after she had abolished the slave trade: 'Her command of the sea, her far-flung Empire, her mounting industrial power, her commercial supremacy, her inventive genius – *above all, her increasing moral stature, and her expanding spiritual vision* – won her a place of unique leadership amongst the nations. More than any other great nation in the middle of the nineteenth century, she was worthy of world power.' (my italics)

In other words, Britain was then in the ascendancy in her position amongst the nations, and her rise to a position of world power can be traced directly to the time of the Evangelical Revival. If she was worthy of world power at that time, it was because God had raised her up into that position. Many other such testimonies have been written. But the greatest testimony I know, and the most inspiring, is the one to be found engraved in marble for all to see just inside the north doors of Westminster Abbey. There on the huge memorial to William Pitt we can read these words: 'During whose administration, and in the reigns of George II and George III, Divine Providence exalted Great Britain to an height of prosperity and glory unknown to any former age.'

I say 'inspiring' because, let it be noted, this was precisely the period in our history which coincided exactly with the Great Awakening which God granted us under the preaching of Whitefield and Wesley. Let every Englishman today dwell deeply on the words and implication of that inscription.

Let us also remember that as a direct result of this revival of Christianity, England became a missionary-hearted country, and so caused the impact of that revival to be felt throughout the world. For whereas at the beginning of the eighteenth century, and for a number of years afterwards, there was not a single Protestant missionary in the entire world (with the exception of a small German group of the Moravian Brethren), by the end of the eighteenth century the Baptist Missionary Society, the London Missionary Society, the Scottish Missionary Society, the Church Missionary Society and the Religious Tract Society had all been founded within the space of twelve years. From these sprang the whole Protestant foreign missionary world movement, and from these various societies, Britain began to send missionaries to the far corners of the world. Thus, from this country, continent after continent began to be penetrated for Jesus Christ. The Evangelical Revival, therefore, did what neither the Reformation in the sixteenth century nor Puritanism in the seventeenth century did. It gave birth to a world-wide missionary zeal.

Moreover, as a result of this revival, the British people themselves became known the world over as 'the people of one Book, and that Book the Bible'; and it was directly due to the revival's influence that it was being said all over the world at that time that 'an Englishman's word is to be trusted; his word is his bond.'

All this had happened because God had mightily intervened in our history to ensure that the Christian foundations which had originally been laid, and which were again in danger of disappearing and of being entirely whittled away, were completely and gloriously restored.

As Queen Victoria put it in a message to two African chiefs: 'England has become great and happy by the knowledge of the true God and Jesus Christ.' Or perhaps she should rather have said: England has become great and happy because she has *rediscovered* the knowledge of the true God and Jesus Christ.

Chapter Eight
The Trumpet Sounds for Britain

Blow ye the trumpet in Zion, and sound an alarm in my holy mountain: let all the inhabitants of the land tremble: for the day of the Lord cometh, for it is nigh at hand. (Joel 2:1) *For a nation is come upon my land, strong, and without number . . . a great people and a strong; there hath not been ever the like, neither shall be any more after it, even to the years of many generations.* (Joel 1:6, 2:2)

The time has come to 'sound the alarm'. It is time to 'sound the trumpet' loud and clear throughout the length and breadth of Britain.

For Britain today is fast heading towards a grievous peril, the like of which she has never experienced before. Like some great ship at sea on a collision course with icebergs, and with both her radio and radar switched off, she has been ignoring all the warnings sent, has already passed all the danger signals, and is moving quickly towards a disaster of truly titanic and world-shattering proportions.

Yet her people 'soldier on', blissfully unaware, it would seem, that they are in any danger at all.

We, in Britain, have become a race of ostriches with heads deeply buried in the sand, quite oblivious of what is going on around us, let alone of the extreme danger which is fast appearing over the horizon. And it is high time to set all the alarm bells ringing.

When I felt the burden of the Lord to issue *A Warning to the Nation* in 1969, I did so because I could see quite clearly that Britain had passed from the position of being a nation which had experienced the hand of Almighty God in *blessing* – all down the years of her history and in remarkable deliverances – to becoming a nation under God's *judgments*, because of the way she had forsaken God and was now deliberately flying in his face.

I also warned at that time that unless Britain repents and returns to the Lord, there is an even worse judgment to come. We need to wake up to the fact that the judgments of God are progressive in character and in severity, and that this is particularly so when gross sin and wickedness are on the increase and continue to remain largely unchecked.

The Bible clearly shows that when one form of judgment fails to bring a people to repentance, God has to visit them with another judgment – of a more severe kind. And often he has to continue with another, and yet another. Each visitation takes a more serious form than the previous one, whilst all the time God is pleading with his people to return to him.

When the leaders and people of a nation, such as our own, stubbornly refuse to heed the warnings which have repeatedly been given and deliberately choose to ignore the many signs which God has been doing amongst them, then God has to resort to far more stringent methods in order to bring such a people to its knees. And if there is still no sign of repentance when he has done that, the Bible clearly teaches that as iniquity in the nation comes to the full, there has to come a day of final reckoning.

Indeed, there has to come the time when, just as in the days of Noah, the storm must finally break; or as in the days of Sodom and Gomorrah, the fire and brimstone must come down from heaven; or as in the days of

Jeremiah, the enemy armies must overrun the land.

To me, that day seems perilously near for Britain.

For the lesson that needs to be understood in this country is that if we will not learn any other way, then we must expect to have to learn the hard way. That means having to experience the very severest type of God's judgments.

And it seems to me, that this is what we are about to see happening to us.

I was really forced to sit up and take notice when I discovered, whilst reading my Bible during the summer of 1976 – the year of the great drought – that the kind of drought which we were then experiencing was, in the days of the prophets Joel and Jeremiah, the precursor of a judgment at the hands of an invading enemy army. The very severe and unusual drought in their day was God switching on the danger lights. It was the harbinger of a far greater evil to follow. It was God's way of setting all the alarm bells ringing – God's way of waking everybody up!

In Jeremiah's case, the judgment at the hands of an invading enemy army followed hard on the heels of judgment by a very serious drought. On the other hand, in Joel's case they practically coincided with each other.

That discovery really worried me then. And it still does, especially when I realise that Britain's great coming day of judgment may only have been delayed temporarily.

Look at what we have done to contribute to our own national landslide, and so to make such a day a terrible possibility. For years we have permitted the whittling away of the nation's Christian foundations until now there is very little of them left. Belief in God has been largely overthrown, together with any belief in the authority of the Bible and of the *whole* of the Bible.

Consequently, our people are no longer being taught that each person will have to give an account to God at the day of judgment for the kind of life he or she has lived;

that there is such a thing as an after life; that there are such places as heaven and hell; and that a man will ultimately spend the whole of eternity in one or the other, depending on whether or not he accepts the Lord Jesus Christ as his own personal Saviour, and as the *only way* of salvation.

The result of all this is that people now live just as they please, with no fear of God before their eyes. All Christian principles and standards have been largely rejected, and have been replaced by loose-living, promiscuity, free-love, dishonesty and deception. The long-accepted standards of truth, virtue, uprightness, nobility, decency and pureness of living have not only been allowed to become outmoded, but to be regarded as things now to be treated with utter derision, to be despised, scorned and mocked at, and finally to be swept utterly away.

With all such restraints and restrictions removed, we have allowed the flood-gates of a great cesspool of iniquity to be thrown wide open, permitting the foul, stinking, sewage-waters of corruption, pornography, immorality, depravity, perversion and decay to surge in and engulf our land. And God is extremely angry on account of this – make no mistake about it. The fire of his fierce wrath has been mightily aroused against us as a nation.

With our moral and spiritual defences down, we have permitted the run-down of the nation's defences to such a degree that Britain is left more vulnerable now than at any time in her long history, whilst all the time the Soviet and Warsaw Pact forces have been building up their military, naval and air strengths alarmingly.

In doing all this, we have been sowing within the nation, and within ourselves, the seeds of our own destruction. And in the process we have created the ideal situation for a Communist take-over, both from within the nation and from without. So let us be quite clear. Were that take-over to happen, it should be interpreted as a judgment of God upon us for all this blatant wickedness.

Britain urgently needs a prophet today. Even secular magazines have frequently expressed this sentiment. More than one of them, in reviewing some aspect or other of our national situation, has said: 'Is there no voice of the prophet to be heard in the land?'

Yes, Britain desperately needs a prophet today. If ever there was a time when our nation needed such a challenging ministry, it is now. And were God to send us such a prophet, I am sure the first thing he would be heard to say is this: 'Britain, you have gone exactly the same way that Israel in the Old Testament went; and because of this, you are suffering the same consequences. *That* is the explanation of all that you see happening to you at the present moment.'

And I am sure he would add: 'Britain, if you still refuse to repent and turn to the Lord your God, despite all that you have been experiencing by way of divine chastisements, you are likely to suffer the same consequences that Israel in the Old Testament eventually suffered, which, I would remind you, was destruction at the hands of an invading enemy.'

Such a prophet might also be heard to say, as Haggai and Amos said in their day: 'Thus saith the Lord concerning Britain, consider your ways. Ye have sown much and bring in little; and he that earneth wages, earneth wages to put it into a bag with holes, and yet ye have not returned unto me', saith the Lord.

'Ye looked for much, and lo, it came to little; and when ye brought it home, I did blow upon it, and yet ye have not returned unto me,' saith the Lord.

'I have smitten your fields with blasting and with mildew, and when the crops of your corn-fields, your vegetable plots and your fruit orchards increased, I sent the aphids, the whitefly and the greenfly to destroy them, and yet ye have not returned unto me, saith the Lord.

'I called for a drought upon the land, and caused the heaven over you to be stayed for dew, and the earth to be stayed from her fruit, and yet ye did not return unto me, saith the Lord.

'I have caused fierce fires to ravage your woodlands, heaths and forests, and yet ye have not returned unto me, saith the Lord.

'I have sent pestilence and disease to your farmsteads, the foot and mouth disease amongst your cattle, the swine-vesicular disease amongst your pigs, the fowl-pest to ravage your chicken and pheasant runs, the wool disease amongst your sheep, and yet ye have not returned unto me, saith the Lord.

'I have withheld success from your factories, causing your national production to fall off, and I called for the curtailing of your oil supplies, and yet ye have not returned unto me, saith the Lord.

'I have even brought you teetering on the brink of financial and economic ruin, so that you did not know which way to turn for financial assistance, and even then ye have not returned unto me, saith the Lord.

'Therefore, thus will I do unto thee, O Britain; and because of what I am about to do unto thee, prepare for what is about to come upon you, O proud and stubborn kingdom situated in the midst of the North Sea.'

The prophet in the Old Testament was also called a seer, because he was endowed by God with a special gift of perception which enabled him to see very clearly what was coming.

I believe that such a prophet would then be heard crying out: 'Blow ye the trumpet in the land, and sound the alarm throughout the length and breadth of Britain; let all the inhabitants of the land *tremble; for, for you, O people of Britain, the day of the Lord cometh;* for it is nigh at hand.'

I believe his message would be strikingly similar to that of the prophet Jeremiah and, like Jeremiah, he would give warning of the danger which he could see approaching: *Blow the trumpet in Tekoa . . . for evil appeareth out of the north, and great destruction.* (Jeremiah 6:1) *The lion (or bear) is come up from the thicket, and the destroyer of the Gentiles is on his way; he is gone forth from his place to make thy land desolate* (Jeremiah 4:7).

And I believe his message would be remarkably like that of the prophet Joel: *Blow ye the trumpet in Zion... sound an alarm...For a nation is come up upon my land, strong, and without number . . . a great people and a strong; there hath not been ever the like, neither shall be any more after it, even to the years of many generations.* (Joel 2:1, 1:6, 2:2)

This is what these two prophets were heard saying in *their* day, and they were proclaiming it in the wake of a very severe and unusual drought. When we consider all the grave warnings that leading military authorities in the West have been issuing about the alarming size of the Soviet build-up in recent years, who can afford to say that judgment such as Jeremiah and Joel were warning their people about, is not a possibility today?

We are told, for instance, that the Soviets have at their disposal 2½ million Warsaw Pact troops; well over 45,000 Soviet tanks; over 10,000 aircraft; 2,000 or more inter-continental ballistic missiles; over 4,000 missile nuclear warheads; 10,000 anti-aircraft missile strategic launchers; and that they have ten times more submarines than Hitler had at the start of the 1939 War, some 80 of which are driven by nuclear power, and some 50 of which are nuclear-powered strategic missile-launching platforms. In addition, they are launching one new nuclear-powered tactical submarine *every month*.

This vast build-up of Soviet military might has been going on for years, despite the fact that our political leaders, who have been drastically reducing our own defence forces, know quite well that Kruschev once said: 'When their guard is down, we will smash them.' And the question which needs increasingly to be asked is: Why?

What is the intention of this phenomenal build-up?

General Sir Walter Walker, formerly NATO Comman-der-in-Chief, Allied Forces, Northern Europe, has written: 'The Kremlin has embarked on a massive arma-ments build-up without parallel in history. This concen-tration of military strength far exceeds any conceivable requirement for the Soviet's own defence, and can only have the most ominous implications for the West. The Warsaw Pact now outnumbers NATO in every con-ceivable category of weapons system on the central front in Europe.'

Dr James Schlesinger, former Defence Secretary of the United States, says that the total picture is of a Soviet force-structure twice NATO's in ground power and essentially twice NATO's in air power. It has in fact been revealed that the Russians have built up an army three times larger than America's, with almost five times as many tanks, six times the artillery, and more than double the number of personnel-carriers. Defence planners in Washington are deeply concerned, if not downright alarmed, by the realisation that the Russians will very soon achieve nuclear parity with them – if they have not done so already.

Again the question inevitably arises in any logically-thinking mind: Why? *Why* are they persistently seeking to overhaul the West in this way?

The then supreme Allied Commander in Europe, General Alexander Haig, said as far back as November 1976: 'A dangerous situation exists in which a blatant crossing of the frontiers in Central Europe is a possibility.'

And General Sir Walter Walker has put it this way: 'This vast Soviet military machine is designed specifically to launch a massive, surprise, *blitzkrieg* attack – without prior concentration of forces, and possibly under the guise of manoeuvres and exercises – aimed at advancing at lightning speed at the rate of 70 miles per day, and at the same time blinding our own forces with their electronic warfare capability.

'They would crunch their way forward, regardless of casualties, at this speed of 70 miles per day, supported in depth by airborne troops, armed helicopters, air attack, amphibious attack on the flanks, and chemical attack. And this rate of advance, so far as Western Europe is concerned, would bring them to the Rhine in less than 48 hours and to the Channel ports in less than a week.

'The speed, devasting power, and velocity of the Soviet onslaught would be such, that NATO would not be able to resort to the use of their tactical nuclear weapons, for the simple reason that there would not be sufficient time for the necessary political decisions to be taken. In any case, the missile sites would already have been overrun. It would be surprising if the Soviet General Staff did not know the number and location of every nuclear bomb site in Western Europe.'

Meanwhile, the Soviet surface and underwater fleet is now so strong and powerful that they are in a position to cut all our main shipping routes at sea almost anywhere in the world.

In late January 1976, Dr Schlesinger issued this grave warning: 'At no point since the 1930s has the western world faced so formidable a threat to its survival.' And General Sir Walter Walker said in the same month: 'Never has the situation in Europe been so grave. The free world stands today in greater peril than at any time since the dark days of the Second World War. And yet from Western Europe, clarion call comes there none.'

Or again, more recently: 'Is there no voice among free men, apart from Solzhenitsyn and Mrs Margaret Thatcher – is there no one else in Western Europe who will sound the alarm as Churchill did before the war?'

So who can possibly afford to bury their heads in the sand? Isn't it time to 'sound the alarm'? I wrote in *A Warning to the Nation*: 'If Sir Winston Churchill had been alive today, he would have raised the alarm long ago.

Britain is more vulnerable now than she was just after Dunkirk.'

But that was in 1969. The situation now is far more serious than it was then. It is even far more serious than it was in 1939 because Britain is in far graver danger.

At that time there were tiny forces at work in this country who were in league with Hitler and his Nazi regime, whereas today there are powerful and treacherous forces in the country at work and in league with Communist Russia, waiting to help effect a take-over when they see the time is ripe to do so.

I am a preacher. And as a preacher, I am deeply concerned with the *spiritual* implications of all this, for the spiritual implications rate far higher in priority than do even the military implications.

When the grave peril, which is without question confronting Britain today, can be interpreted as possibly the next form of judgment with which God will have to visit Britain – then, I say, it is high time to *sound the trumpet and warn the people*.

The trumpet needs to be sounded loud and clear.

It should be sounded out from the roof-tops and from every high hill.

It should be sounded forth in every road and street in Britain.

It should be sounded in all Britain's towns and villages.

It should be sounded in every church, chapel, and meeting-hall in the land.

It should be sounded down the central aisle of every cathedral.

It should be sounded in all our big cities.

It should be sounded in every factory and workshop.

It should be sounded loud and clear, up and down Fleet Street.

Its long resounding notes should be sent reverberating down all the corridors of power within the Palace of Westminster.

It should be sounded outside number 10 Downing Street, in the cabinet room, and in the Treasury.

It should be sounded all down Whitehall and outside Transport House.

It should be sounded loud and clear both outside and inside Buckingham Palace.

It should be sounded to warn the people of a fast approaching day of God in judgment for Britain.

It should be sounded forth to tell them of the urgent need to repent, to turn from their sins, and to get right with God by seeking forgiveness and cleansing in the precious blood of Jesus Christ, lest that day come upon them unawares. For that is why the prophets sounded the trumpet in the days of the Old Testament. They saw clearly what was coming, so they gave out the warning – particularly that men and women should repent and put far from them all their sins, and get right with God.

What we need to see, above all, is that in Jeremiah's and Joel's day God dealt with these wilfully unrepentant people of Israel so severely that he literally brought them, crying out to him in desperation, to their knees. If a people will not learn any *other* way, then they have to learn the hard way, in terms of the very severest forms of the judgments of God.

The coming day of God in Joel's time was so terrible that God commanded his prophet to assemble all the inhabitants of the land into the house of the Lord their God with a long blast of the trumpet, together with their elders and their rulers – every one without exception. It was to be thorough – babes in arms, children, young people just about to get married – everyone!

When he had gathered them all into the house of the Lord, God told Joel that he was to tell the priests and ministers to literally 'cry unto the Lord' – 'to howl', God said, with great tears. And with the enemy streaming across their borders (Joel 2:3-11) and practically on the steps of where they were assembled, they were to cry out: *Spare thy people, O Lord, and give not thine heritage to reproach, that the heathen should rule over them: where-fore should they say among the people, Where is their God?* (Joel 2:17)

In other words, with the enemy already at the gates, the prophet Joel was told by God to call the nation together for an urgent time of repentance and prayer.

Please note that, archbishops and other church leaders in Britain. Days and periods of national prayer and repentance are scriptural! It was God himself who commanded that this one should be called; he did not wait for the leaders of the national church to call one, or for government officials to authorise it, because it would never have happened. No – he used a prophet in the nation to bring it about, and that prophet took complete charge of the national situation.

Even 'the powers that be' had to do what he said, and rally into the house of the Lord! With the enemy rapidly overrunning the land, God said to all those whom he was assembling together: *Therefore also now, saith the Lord, turn ye even to me with all your heart, and with fasting, and with weeping, and with mourning: and rend your heart, and not your garments, and turn unto the Lord your God: for he is gracious and merciful, slow to anger, and of great kindness, and repenteth him of the evil. Who knoweth if he will return and repent, and leave a blessing behind him?* (Joel 2:12-14)

And look what God promised to do as a result of their obedience: *Then will the Lord be jealous for his land, and pity his people. Yea, the Lord will answer . . .* (Joel 2:18-19).

The following verses tell *how* he will answer.

First, he will reverse all the effects of the drought: *Behold, I will send you corn, and wine, and oil, and ye shall be satisfied therewith* (Joel 2:19).

Second, he will drive out the invader: *I will remove far off from you the northern army, and will drive him into a land barren and desolate, with his face towards the east sea*

(Joel 2:20).

Third, he will restore to them their former prosperity: *Fear not, O land; be glad and rejoice: for the Lord will do great things . . .*

And the floors shall be full of wheat, and the vats shall overflow with wine and oil.

And I will restore to you the years that the locust hath eaten, the cankerworm, and the caterpillar, and the palmerworm, my great army which I sent among you.

And ye shall eat in plenty, and be satisfied, and praise the name of the Lord your God, that hath dealt wondrously with you: and my people shall never be ashamed.

And ye shall know that I am in the midst of Israel, and that I am the Lord your God, and none else: and my people shall never be ashamed. (Joel 2:21-7)

Fourth, he will visit them with a great spiritual revival – a Pentecost!

And it shall come to pass afterward, that I will pour out my spirit upon all flesh; and your sons and your daughters shall prophesy, your old men shall dream dreams, your young men shall see visions; and also upon the servants and upon the handmaids in those days will I pour out my spirit. (Joel 2:28,29)

That was the pathway to national restoration and spiritual revival in those days. It is also the pathway to national restoration and spiritual revival today. When will we learn that the way ahead for Britian is *not* by borrowing more millions from the International Monetary Fund; *not* by forming a coalition government; *not* by relying on North Sea oil or by any other man-made solution. It is by crying out to Almighty God for deliverance on our knees in humble repentance.

That was why Joel's trumpet call was sounded; and the trumpet needs to be sounded in just the same way for Britain today. Because Britain has departed from the Lord, and sinned so grievously against him, there is an equally fearful day of judgment coming upon her if she still persists in not repenting and returning to the Lord her

God. And if that judgment comes, I fear it is likely to be extremely severe, and exceedingly terrible.

Chapter Nine
What is Really Wrong with Britain?

The Secular Answer

Now I am well aware that this is a devastatingly strong statement to make. In what sense, then, can it be said to be true? To get at the answer, certain other questions need to be raised: 'What is really wrong with Britain?' and 'Why is she in such a mess?'

It is time we got down to making a thorough and drastic diagnosis of Britain's tragically sick condition in order to discover what is *basically* wrong with this once great nation. In other words, we need to get at the root cause of all our troubles; to see why it is that we have gone to pieces so quickly. If you like, we need to discover what is at the very heart of it all.

Any doctor will tell you that it is no use whatsoever treating the symptoms of a disease – the spots that appear on the skin, or the boils that break out, first in one part of the body and then in another – until he has thoroughly investigated what is causing these symptoms to appear. It is when he has discovered that, and only then, that he can pronounce and begin to apply the cure.

So it is with a nation. Several attempts have been made in recent years to answer our questions, but none of them ever seems to get down deep enough, to get to the heart of the matter. Consequently the findings and conclusions reached tend to be very superficial, even pathetically

112

naive at times.

During the last two years, for instance, a series of articles has been running in one of our leading national newspapers and raising the question: What is wrong with Britain? Some fifteen leading statesmen, scientists, university professors, business magnates and journalists of this and other countries all made contributions to this series.

One of the early contributors said quite rightly: 'Some Gibbon, from a vantage point in the future, will no doubt write of "The Decline and Fall of Great Britain and the British Empire".' He continued: 'In the life-span of some of us still alive, Great Britain has fallen, rung by rung, from a pre-eminent position in both political and industrial fields to second- or even third-rate status.' (And it is very significant indeed that he did not even mention how Britain has fallen from a pre-eminent position in the spiritual and moral realm as well. This dimension of things never seems to come into such people's estimations or calculations. And yet it is *here* that the real answer lies.)

All the contributors reached various conclusions as to what is wrong with our country, but only one of them ever got any deeper than the economic, industrial, political, or social level.

Their conclusions can be summarised in this way: Britain's troubles stem from two world wars; from the destruction of wealth which resulted from these two wars; from the loss of her empire. What is wrong is Britain's *class*-structure. The problem is nothing more than economic – nothing which cannot be cured by mastering inflation, sharply reducing our balance of payments, and becoming self-sufficient in oil. The trouble is due to the Arabs quadrupling the price of oil. It is all due to a faulty system of education; to a failure to train the rising generation for jobs, crafts, and professions where they are most needed. The troubles stem from the desire to consume socially what is not being produced individually; from faulty processes of natural wealth-production and from failure to use the wealth-producing regulator rightly. What is wrong is the intolerable strain which is being imposed on Britain's parliamentary system at the present time. The trouble with Britain is that too much is expected of her! Why should any country continue to be for ever great?

I would suggest that to come to such conclusions is only scratching at the surface. It is merely looking at the symptoms all the time, not at the root cause.

Of all the contributors, Lord Hailsham was the only one who went anywhere near deep enough: 'The cause of our troubles is not economic, nor has it anything to do with world conditions or our loss of Empire, nor with any of the other easy excuses which we are so ready to accept and which our present rulers invent for our comfort. *It is a disease of the spirit* from which there is no one to blame but ourselves.' (my italics)

He warned that in his view the country will only begin to return to sanity by learning the hard way, and this, he said, 'will mean widespread unemployment and financial ruin . . . I do not believe that these catastrophes are far off.'

This was coming much nearer to the truth. But when he began to point to the way out of our malaise, I was not sure whether he meant that we could save the situation by our own self-effort.

Such, then, was the result of the attempt through this series of articles to get at the root of Britain's troubles.

Then the House of Lords conducted a five-and-a half-hour debate about the state of the nation on 14 July 1976. During that debate the same issue was being considered, but in the form of the following question: What has happened in this country in the thirty years since the war, which has caused such a steady decline?

No less than twenty-one peers took part. Lord

Carrington, who opened the debate, categorically stated that nobody could deny that the state of the nation was critical, economically and socially (although, once again, no mention was made, at this stage, of our state *spiritually*). Other speakers said that an overwhelming number of people in this country knew that something was wrong, and that somewhere along the lines over these last twenty-five years or so, the rot in our social fabric has worsened until today we face the question which has faced so many civilisations before. Corruption, and not just bribery and corruption, is there in many areas of our national life for anyone with eyes to see, so that the search for the answer right now as to whether this corruption in our society is curable is more than somewhat urgent.

Yet, despite all this, I was shattered to discover that more than one peer was naive enough to say that there is nothing inherently wrong with our society; that although we have our little malaise periodically – and we are in the midst of a malaise at this moment – there is not really much wrong with us; things are really no different from what they have ever been. And 'I do not believe that the United Kingdom is in any way as bad as some feel that it is.'

True, another did urge obliquely that 'a diagnosis of the state of the nation was necessary.' And yet another said strongly that 'we ought to recognise where we have gone wrong.' But when it came to making that diagnosis, once again the probing did not go anywhere near deep enough.

Some of the speeches made this abundantly clear. They can be summarised in this way: The trouble is due to our present form of Government; to the need for electoral reform; to the fact that power is slipping away from Parliament. One of the many elements in the decline is the malfunction of the constitution. Our problems are due to the fact that many countries in the world have lost faith in Britain. The trouble comes from having tried since the war to do too much and to expect too much from our economic system; from the failure of men and machines to come to terms with themselves. A great deal of the fault lies in industry; the problems facing us now can be seen in economic terms, in terms of greed. What has brought us into the humiliating position in which we find ourselves today is the combination of two clear and different tendencies: one, a greater rate of inflation than elsewhere in the world, and, two, our productivity has been so comparatively low.

A few speakers got nearer to the truth when they said that 'there has been a widespread and continuing decline in organised Christianity in these islands. Having lost that faith . . . we have not found anything comparable to put in its place.' (As if that is possible!) This speaker added: 'We are living in a secular age, and we are reaping the results of that secularity.'

Another speaker commented: 'The biggest and most important change which has vitally concerned everything since the 1930s because of its enormous effect on personal attitudes, is that religion no longer provides the yardstick by which people's behaviour was directly or indirectly influenced. At the same time, the largely accepted, relatively stable order of society which we inherited from the Victorians has passed away. In place of religion, with a belief in an after-life, a humanistic approach has to some extent taken over.'

Lord Home, in an excellent speech, said, 'There is evidence that faith in the essential Christian foundations of our society is faltering. Why do the young not rally to the Christian standard as their forefathers did?'

These speakers lifted the debate on to a higher plane and were probing in the right direction for the root cause of what was wrong. But they were still not going far enough, or digging anywhere near deep enough. For instance, I searched through the whole set of twenty-one speeches in vain for any reference to Almighty God, or to the nation's relationship with him.

The debate was brought to an appalling anti-climax when a closing speaker said: 'The real issue is the economic decline. The pound sterling has been declining for at least fifty years. It has been a continual decline. But the oil which is to be found in the North Sea and in other parts surrounding our coasts, provides us with a real opportunity to put our house in order.' (Would you believe it?)

When I read that, my heart sank into my boots. How pathetic! How blind can a man be? How materialistic can he get? And so the debate closed without ever really getting to the real root of the trouble.

What is needed, therefore, is a far more drastic and radical enquiry into what really is wrong with Britain than was provided by these two investigations, or by any other that I have seen so far.

Chapter Ten
What is Really Wrong with Britain?

The Biblical Answer

What then is the *heart* of the matter? What is really wrong with Britain?

In the first place, the Bible makes it very plain that most of our troubles, both personal and national, are due to the fact that *we, as a people, are living without God*. We do not relate to him in any way. We are not in touch with him. We do not bring matters to him in prayer. This explains why things are going the way that they are; why we, as a nation, and as individuals, are going the way that we are. And I find that this is gradually beginning to dawn on people.

For instance, as I got into an Underground train a short time ago, a Christian man whom I had not seen for a number of years, sat down next to me and said, 'Mr Gardner, my eldest daughter has just taken up teaching in school, and she says it is chaos! – literally chaos! What advice would you give her as to how she can gain some sort of control, when few or no corrective measures are allowed to be introduced today?'

I replied: 'It is not so much the advice I would give *her*, as the advice which all of us need to be given all over again, and that is, that *God* has shown us the principles of bringing up children – whether we are parents, school teachers, youth leaders, Bible class leaders or whatever.

And until we get back to those principles, we shall never get anywhere. God says, 'Train up the child in the way he should go' (Proverbs 22:6). Train him up!

'Training involves discipline, and discipline includes correction. Sometimes it also involves chastisement, and the Bible has a lot to say about chastisement.'

He said, 'Yes, I know. But we are not allowed to do that now.'

I replied: 'It is because we have abandoned these principles which God has given us, that we are reaping the fruits of that abandonment – in terms of chaos in schools, vandalism in public places, riots in the streets, and terrorism and hooliganism on the football terraces. In fact, I believe that the words of the second commandment are terribly applicable today, when God said that the sins of the fathers would be visited upon the children 'unto the third and fourth generation of them that hate me', but that he would show mercy 'unto thousands of them that love me and keep my commandments.' (Exodus 20:5,6) I am obliged to ask: Is a lot of what we see going on in this realm of the nation's children and young people, fulfilment of what God says would happen – 'visiting the iniquity of the fathers upon the children' – for our lack of disciplining them and following the principles of bringing up children which God has outlined in the Bible? The lesson is clear. Abandon these principles and you inevitably suffer the consequences.'

My friend went on to lament the fact that the ten commandments are no longer taught in schools. He said, 'They are not even taught in churches or in the Sunday schools.' And he added, 'Christianity isn't being taught in schools any longer, either. My younger boys are being taught about Buddhism, Hinduism, and Islam – not about Christianity. The result is that they are totally confused. And I brought them up to believe in the Lord Jesus Christ! It seems that we have thrown teaching about God, about Christianity, about Christian standards, about the

Bible, completely overboard – and *what is there left?'*

'Yes', I said. 'So long as we continue to disregard all these things, matters will get worse, not better.'

The Bible says, 'Cursed be he that removeth his neighbour's landmark.' (Deuteronomy 27:17) My fear is that this is what God has caused to be written in large letters over many of our churches, over schools, over our entire educational system, and indeed over Britain's parliament. And I believe that much of what we are experiencing in our nation today is because we have come under that curse. I repeat, we are a nation and a people which is living without God. And that, basically, is *one of the root causes of our troubles*.

*   *   *   *

As if living without God is not serious enough, my reading of the Bible shows me very clearly, in the second place, that *we are defying him openly, and are deliberately going against him.* I believe that to be the next part of the answer as to what is basically wrong with Britain.

During the last ten years or more, we have so reversed our country's laws and changed our moral and spiritual direction, that we have become a nation which has put itself on a direct collision course with God. And because we have, we have been bringing down God's judgments upon us. Now that is a pretty devastating claim to make. How do we establish that it is true, and that this is indeed what is happening?

Surely the answer is that we should examine the position in the light of all that is put to us in the Bible, and apply to our situation what is so clearly revealed to us there. We shall then be left in no doubt whatsoever. And one of the best places in the Bible from which to do that, is Deutronomy chapter 28.

There are at least thirty judgments mentioned in this chapter which can come upon a nation because God is against it, and, in my opinion, Britain has already experienced twenty-seven of them. The remaining three could come upon her at any moment. Indeed, Deuteronomy 28:46 says of these judgments: 'And they shall be upon you for a sign' – for a sign that God is against you. And certainly for a sign that you are going against him.

The deeply disturbing fact is that a whole host of these things has been happening to Britain for some time, giving evidence enough to establish that we are indeed a nation on a collision course with God.

Take, for example, the first few of the judgments mentioned between verses 15 and 20 of Deuteronomy 28.

1) *Cursed shalt thou be in the city.* (v 16) In a modern age, that is the place where the money is made. Or lost! The city – it speaks to us of everything in the realm of finance, or in the realm of the national economy. And look what has been happening to our economy in recent years!

Our entire financial and economic system seems to be under a curse. 'Cursed shalt thou be in the city': it has been happening.

2) *And cursed shalt thou be in the field.* (v 16) The unusually prolonged winter of 1979 was surely a sign of the judgments of God upon us. But for a number of years now we have been experiencing very unusual weather conditions.

For instance, in 1978, early spring crops were held back by the persistently cold, dull weather, and there was so much torrential rain that farmers were reporting whole acres of seed just rotting in the ground. On the other hand, in 1974, soon after much of the seed had been sown in the earlier part of the year, we had an unusually dry spell. The result was that much of the seed just did not germinate. So large areas of farmland had to be re-sown. Then in the beginning of September 1974, all the national newspapers confidently boasted that there was the promise of a bumper harvest. But what happened?

On a number of occasions, the British Isles were

severely shaken and buffeted by unusually severe storms. Strong gales, and winds of hurricane force, swept through the country, wreaking untold havoc and laying much of the corn; added to which the whole of the British Isles were subjected to torrential rains. The wet weather so persisted that it was impossible to lift the sugar beet crop out of the ground, or to take lorries on to the fields to carry it away. Consequently some sugar beet factories had to close down. Then in December 1974 the fields were so wet and sodden that in many areas the potato crop was still in the ground because it was impossible to lift it.

In 1976, there was the prolonged drought which, according to the *Daily Telegraph's* agricultural correspondent, gave the country its worst grain harvest for six years, and also added at least £80 million to the nation's import bill. But the drought also seriously affected the root crops, which shrivelled for lack of moisture. The pea-crop in many areas did not even come up! Milk yields were quite seriously affected, due to the scarcity of grass for the cow-herds.

This kind of thing has been going on for a number of years now. 'Cursed shalt thou be in the field.' And we *have* been.

3) *Cursed shall be thy basket and thy store*. (v 17) That means 'shopping basket' in a modern age, housewives! And it means store-cupboards and larders, anxious mothers – with all the constantly soaring prices in mind, increasing alarmingly almost every week, and with the food supplies in the store-cupboards forever running out. 'Cursed shall be thy basket and thy store.'

4) *Cursed shall be the fruit of thy body*. (v 18) That means your children, people of Britain! I have already referred to this in terms of chaos in our schools, vandalism and terrorism in our streets, and hooliganism on the football terraces. To all that must be added the appalling crime-rate amongst children, even little children, and young people. The national crime statistical reports show that

five-year-olds are now well and truly involved.

What we are seeing is a generation gone wild; a generation almost totally beyond control. 'Cursed shall be the fruit of thy body' – thy children. It is *happening* in the nation. Who cannot say that, somehow, so many of those who have gone wild seem to be under some kind of a curse?

And while we are still dealing with things in the domestic realm, verse 30 says: 'Thou shalt betroth a wife, and another man shall lie with her.' Isn't that happening too, in our homes? Unfaithfulness of husbands and wives on a frightening scale is reflected in the ever-increasing divorce rate; and now there is the appallingly wide-spread practice of husband- and wife-swapping. In terms of such judgments in the domestic realm, family life and homes all over the country seem indeed to be sorely smitten.

5) *Cursed shall be . . . the fruit of thy land.* (v 18) This verse, when linked with such statements as those in verses 30, 39 and 40, obviously includes the fruit of the trees – fruit trees or orchards. For verse 30 says: 'Thou shalt plant a vineyard [or orchard] and shalt not gather the grapes thereof', whilst verse 39 adds 'for the worms [or maggots] shall eat them.' And verse 40: 'Thou shalt have olive trees throughout all thy coasts, but thou shalt not anoint thyself with oil; for thine olive shall cast his fruit [that means drop off].'

This kind of thing has been happening in our English orchards and gardens. We have seen it with heavily laden pear trees. Before the pears had time to grow to their full size, suddenly their stems began to wilt, wither away and decay, and hundreds of the half-formed fruit began falling and littering the ground. The pears, if not the olives, were seen to be casting their fruit. Then just as the remaining fruit was ripening it was discovered that practically every one had a maggot inside! That verse could equally well read: 'Thou shalt plant a fruit orchard and shalt not gather the fruit thereof for the maggots shall eat them.'

We have seen it happen with apples, too; on numerous occasions, thousands of tons of apples have gone to waste, either because they were not fit for marketing, or because there was not the labour available to gather them. 'Thou shalt plant orchards but thou shalt not eat the fruit thereof . . . Cursed shall be the fruit of thy land.'

6) *Cursed shall be . . . the increase of thy kine* [or cattle], *and the flocks of thy sheep.* (v 18) We have already seen in *A Warning to the Nation* what was happening towards the end of 1967. Foot and mouth disease had begun to rage amongst the cattle until it reached the dimensions of a national disaster.

'Thine ox [cattle] shall be slain before thine eyes, and thou shalt not eat thereof' (v 31). Which is exactly what has to happen as a result of foot and mouth disease, isn't it? Our cattle had to be slain before our eyes, and we could not eat them.

Since then, swine vesicular disease began to break out and spread alarmingly, until in a period of four years there had been nearly 400 outbreaks, involving the slaughter of 204,000 pigs. And it cost the taxpayer nearly £8 million in a four-year fight to stamp it out. Then in January 1973, a highly contagious disease amongst sheep suddenly reappeared, seriously affecting the wool-crop.

What has happened since then? In 1975, farmers all over the country were not able to get the necessary feeding stuffs with which to feed their livestock; cows, calves and beef-cattle had to be slaughtered in vast quantities.

In 1976, because of the severe drought, the same thing had to happen. Cattle and livestock had to be slaughtered on a quite frightening scale. 'Your cattle shall be slain before your eyes, and you shall not eat of it.' And it has been happening in Britain ever since 1967. 'Cursed shall be . . . the increase of thy kine, [cattle] and the flocks of thy sheep.'

What we see happening here, is surely not just a *single* judgment of God, but part of a long process of judgments which has been taking place in this country for at least ten years now. God says in Deuteronomy 28:20 that it is 'because of the wickedness of thy doings, whereby thou hast forsaken me.' *That* is the reason. Cannot anybody recognise the signs?

While we are still dealing with agriculture, let me point out that Deutronomy 28:31 also says: 'Thine ass shall be violently taken away from before thy face, and shall not be restored unto thee.' And this has been happening too.

Since *A Warning to the Nation* was first published, the National Farmers Union has had to issue an urgent warning to farmers to brand their cattle, because of a widespread outbreak of night-rustling in cattle-rearing and horse-breeding districts. One report said that many thousands of pounds worth of horses and cattle have been herded away in night raids, and have disappeared without trace. Farmers in Devon, Cornwall, Surrey, Sussex, East Anglia and Yorkshire have reported serious losses. We have only to change the wording of that verse very slightly to read 'Your *horses* and your cattle shall be violently taken away from under your very noses, and shall not be restored to you', and you have a most graphic description of what is actually taking place on many a farm in Britain today. Horses and cattle disappear without trace; not to mention deer in the New Forest.

And in case any farmer should be tempted to say: 'Oh, we are alright. Our farm is 100 per cent mechanised', let me tell him that tractors are now disappearing overnight without trace – not just horses!

7) *The Lord shall send upon thee cursing, vexation [frustration in the RSV] and rebuke, in all that thou settest thine hand unto, for to do, until thou be destroyed, and until thou perish quickly; because of the wickedness of thy doings, whereby thou hast forsaken me.* (v 20) Coupled with that, God says in verse 29, 'And thou shalt not prosper in thy ways'.

The phrase 'in all that thou settest thine hand unto, for

to do', involves pretty well everything that you could mention in any sphere. And it certainly covers everything that has to do with a nation's industry, with its produce-making and wealth-creating processes. Isn't this exactly what has been happening, and is happening, in the nation's industrial realm? No progress is being made anywhere for long.

In that debate on the state of the nation held in the House of Lords, Lord Byers said: 'As compared with our competitors abroad . . . [and he instanced West Germany in particular] the most remarkable thing about the United Kingdom industry over the last twenty-five years has been *the speed of its relative decline.*' (my italics) But nobody ever seems to ask 'Why?'. And Lord Robbins, during the same debate, referred to 'this humiliating position in which we find ourselves today.'

But this has been our position for quite a long time now. It is at least nine years since Prince Philip said, concerning our industry: 'I do not think anyone can claim that Britain's record has been wholly successful during the last twenty years. Many things have gone wrong.'

First came the shattering news that Rolls-Royce had collapsed. That really shook the country. It also shook the United States of America. Indeed it shook the whole world.

Soon after that, we saw the second largest car assurance company go into liquidation. Then came the collapse of Chrysler; followed by Nortons. British Leyland got into serious trouble, and the Government had to 'bale them out'. Next we saw the British postal service beginning to deteriorate, with postal charges rising higher and higher for fewer and less efficient services. Then British Rail got into difficulties and began to be referred to in the Press as 'Bankrupt British Rail'. In the whole realm of British industry we see 'frustration', 'confusion', 'vexation' and 'delays' in all that we, as a nation, 'set our hand unto for to do'. Britain, today, is indeed a frustrated nation. In fact, the Earl of Gowrie said during that same debate in the House of Lords: 'If I had to sum up the national mood in a word, I think I would choose the word "frustration".'

We have been finding the going heavy – *very* heavy – for some time. And very uphill too. But what else can we expect when, as a nation, we have deliberately set ourselves to go directly against Almighty God? Deuteronomy 28:20 says that the Lord will do this; the Lord will bring it about. 'The Lord shall send upon thee cursing, vexation [frustration] and rebuke *in all that thou settest thine hand unto, for to do.*' And the reason? 'Because thou hast forsaken Me.'

And it has happened.

8) *And thou shalt become an astonishment, a proverb, and a byword, among all nations.* (v 37) That has happened, hasn't it?

I need not comment further, surely, except perhaps to say that people overseas speak with astonishment that Britain – *Great* Britain – should have been reduced to her present state in such a short period of time. 'It has all happened in about ten years', they say. The result is that we have become a laughing-stock in the eyes of other, less friendly, countries. 'An astonishment, a proverb, and a byword, among all nations.'

And it has happened.

But then, what about this?

9) *The stranger that is within thee shall get up above thee very high; and thou shalt come down very low. He shall lend to thee, and thou shalt not lend to him: he shall be the head, and thou shalt be the tail.* (vv 43,44)

Is not all *that* happening? I would like to quote here from *A Warning to the Nation:* 'Now I want to be very guarded here. The sojourner (or the stranger) that is within thee (or amongst you) is the person of another nationality, of course. In other words, the immigrant.'

And let me say straight away that I will not hear them referred to as foreigners. 'Our friends from overseas', please. I love them. I enjoy being with them. I like their company. I enjoy spending time with them. I am not a racist in any way. But you notice what this verse says: 'He, the immigrant [or stranger that is within thee], shall get above thee very high; and thou shalt come down very low.'

I wrote in *A Warning to the Nation*, 'I am not saying that this has happened in Britain yet, but it *could* happen. And if it does happen, it needs to be recognised as a judgment from God upon the nation. And according to this statement of Scripture, the process could continue until the "stranger that is within thee", the sojourner, the immigrant, has the upper hand in the nation. "He shall be the head, and you shall be the tail".'

Not a few people have written to me recently, saying we are nearer to that now than we were in 1969. And when the situation reaches the *ultimate* stage, men will say, 'It is the finger of God'. You reach the humiliating position where you are obliged, as the host nation, to borrow from the very people that you should be in a position to assist by lending to them. And it is all part of the judgment of God. 'And', I said, 'we have already received warnings that this could be the position in Britain before very long.'

But it is the position in Britain right now, isn't it? 'He shall lend to thee', for instance, 'and thou shalt not lend to him.' By how much is Britain in debt to the Arabs at the present time? By *billions*, not millions? There is no question about it, we are in debt to them up to the hilt. And more and more of our hotels, country and town houses, business premises, shops and stores, and even factories, are being bought up by them.

An indication of how deeply involved we have now become with the Arabs was given in the summer of 1976 when, after that courageous and daring exploit of the Israelis in rescuing the hostages from Entebbe Airport had been successfully carried out, the government of this country maintained a cool silence about it. When country after country was sending its congratulations to the Israeli Government for this marvellous achievement, the British Government, despite all the pressure which was brought to bear, would not express its admiration in any way. And why? For fear that it would offend the Arab world! I see in this a very ominous sign of something terrible that could happen in the future. For should we ever swing so far pro-Arab that we became completely anti-Israel, we could find ourselves involved in a most terrible judgment of God. For Bible students will know that when the final conflagration against Israel – spoken of in detail in Ezekiel 38 and 39, and in the Book of the Revelation chapter 16 – takes place, those nations which range themselves against Israel will be utterly destroyed by a mighty intervention of God on Israel's behalf. And it will take seven years to collect and burn all the devastated weapons, and seven months to collect and bury the dead (Ezekiel 39:9,14).

That verse 44 in Deuteronomy 28 said: 'He shall lend to thee, and thou shalt not lend to him: he shall be the head, and thou shalt be the tail.' In terms of the Arab world, *he* could become so much the head, and could get up so very high above you, Britain – because of your deep financial involvement with him – that you would be obliged to do just what he dictates. And that could mean involvement with him in the very kind of conflagration which the Scriptures describe. But on the wrong side! Is there not an urgent need, therefore, to 'sound the trumpet'?

Each time I read this twenty-eighth chapter of Deuteronomy, it seems to me that more of it applies to our declining national situation. In these verses, we are told that one of the many punishments which will come upon those who will not listen to God, or obey his voice, is that a stranger, or sojourner in our land, will get above us and will hold monetary power over us.

10) But now there comes a *real* crunch. *The fruit of thy land, and all thy labours, shall a nation which thou*

knowest not eat up; and thou shalt be only oppressed and crushed alway. (v 33)

Is not that exactly what has been happening? For what goes on? First, a butter mountain was created. Then a grain mountain. Then a beef mountain. And even a sugar mountain.

And what has been happening to these things in a number of instances? They have been sold at ridiculously cheap prices to the Soviet Union. That is certainly what happened to the butter mountain a few years ago, and there was a mighty furore! It is also what happened to a massive stock-pile of American grain, if not our own. There was a storm in America about that, and it led to an American dock strike, with dockers refusing to load grain on to ships. It is most certainly what happened to our sugar, here in Britain, just before we experienced an acute sugar shortage.

At that time, it was reported in the Press that when the Russians saw that their own sugar-beet crop was going to fail, they sent a trade mission to this country (in the August of that year) and bought up our sugar (500,000 tons of it, I was told) at a ridiculous price. And housewives will remember when it was that the sugar shortage hit us! The *real* reason for the shortage was largely hushed up at the time; otherwise there would have been very angry scenes outside the Houses of Parliament and 10 Downing Street!

'A nation which you have not known shall eat up the fruit of your ground and of all your labours.' But before we start blaming the Russians too much, let us get it straight that God says there is a *reason* why this kind of thing happens to a people. The Bible says that the Lord brings it about. And why? 'Because you have forsaken *me*, people of Britain! It is *because* you have not listened to the voice of the Lord your God to keep his commandments.'

11) *All thy trees and fruit of thy land shall the locust* [or ravaging insect] *consume.* (v 42) Here is another crunch,

– this time in the realm of nature.

You don't need me to remind you that Dutch elm disease has caused havoc in our woodlands, in the countryside, in our local and national parks and gardens, and all along our roadsides. The evidence can be seen all around you, everywhere you go. You don't have to hunt around looking for it! Hundreds of thousands of elm trees have had to be felled, all over the country. Four years ago 3.2 million were dying or dead in the south of England alone. Then in January 1974, oak trees and silver birch started being attacked by an unidentified tree-blight similar to Dutch elm disease. Two years later there were ominous reports of yet another disease attacking our proud English oaks – a disease called tree-wilt.

A little later, in early January 1976, hurricane-force gales which swept across the country snapped off many thousands more trees as if they were matchsticks, and completely uprooted countless others.

That same year came the drought, and *The Times* reported on 4 September 1976 that the effects of that drought had killed millions of trees, and so had added to the past, present, and future disastrous ravages of Dutch elm disease, whilst there had also been devasting effects due to widespread forest fires.

In addition to all that, in both 1974 and 1975, the gardens, fields, hedge-rows, fruit trees, and other trees in the countryside had been so smothered with greenfly, that leaves turned black with greenfly deposits. And the greenfly were there in such great abundance the next year, 1976, that farmers acknowledged that many of the crops in the fields would have been devastated and utterly destroyed had it not been for massive swarms of ladybirds which descended on the greenfly, wherever they were, and proceeded to eat them up. And then, in 1979, the pine trees were in danger of being destroyed by caterpillars.

'All thy trees shall the ravaging insects eat.' And it is happening, isn't it? On a vast scale. Cannot *anybody* read the signs?

Deuteronomy 28:45 says: *All these curses shall come upon thee, and shall pursue thee, and overtake thee, till thou be destroyed: because thou harkenedst not unto the voice of the Lord thy God to keep his commandments and his statutes which He commanded thee*. Then the next verse says: *And they shall be upon thee for a sign*.

For a sign that you are *going the wrong way*. For a sign that you are going directly *against God*. For a sign that the anger of Almighty God has been aroused against you on account of that fact.

When all the uproar was being created in 1976 over the possibility of a film being made in this country about the sex life of Jesus Christ, I noticed that a certain P. F. Brownsey of the Department of Moral Philosophy, University of Glasgow, said in a letter to *The Times,* 'If it could be shown that, in consequence of Mr Thorsen making the film here in Britain, the country will be visited with plagues and famines, then that would be a compelling reason indeed for stopping him, but there is no reason to think such consequences will ensue.'

How blind can a man be? The country is *already* being visited with such things, and has been for some time. The *signs* abound to show us that this is indeed the case. And it would seem that because, like Mr Brownsey, we as a nation have allowed all these signs to go unheeded, then God Almighty sent the further sign, that very year, in the shape of the summer's prolonged drought.

For does he not say in Deuteronomy 11:16, 17: 'Take heed to yourselves, that your heart be not deceived, and ye turn aside, and serve other gods, and worship them; and then the Lord's wrath be kindled against you, and he shut up the heaven, that there be no rain, and that the land yield not her fruit'? And did that not happen in 1976?

What clearer sign could a nation have? When the news went round the world that summer, that the prime minister was calling an emergency cabinet meeting to consider long-term measures to prevent a recurrence of the water shortage which was threatening disaster to all our crops and vital industries, General Amin of Uganda said: 'The present drought is a judgment of God upon Britain'! They called him the Mad Moslem! I found myself saying at the time: 'Yes, God has to use a modern form of Balaam's ass to tell us! We have refused to listen to everybody else. Can't we see?'

Cannot any, or all of our national leaders see? Cannot our gracious Sovereign see?

Cannot those in authority understand, that to reverse a nation's laws and to change its moral and spiritual direction as we have done, so that the country becomes diametrically opposed to what God Almighty has laid down and commanded, is bound to put the nation on a course which is directly against God? But that is precisely what this nation *has* done, and *is* doing.

Is it any wonder that we, as a nation, are not making any headway, or that we seem to be banging our heads against a brick wall? Is it any wonder that we have been bringing down God's judgments upon us, and have had all these things happening to us?

I tell you: Britain and the British people are not likely to make any headway whatsoever, so long as they are going directly *against* Almighty God. The thing is impossible. Not so long as we continue hell-bent on this collision course. Unless we, as a people and as individuals, turn around pretty quickly and seek forgiveness from, and reconciliation with God Almighty, at the foot of the cross of our Lord Jesus Christ, and unless we do it one by one, in true and heartfelt repentance, a terrible crash is inevitable. It will be a crash with the God and Creator of the universe, in terms of some terrible form of judgment never before experienced in the whole of our history. That is the real crisis which is looming up just ahead of us. Let us have no doubt at all about it.

I say, therefore, with all the force that I can muster:
There is no other way ahead for our nation, and more
particularly for us as individuals, but to turn about – to
repent of our sins, to humble ourselves and get ourselves
right with Almighty God by asking him for cleansing in
the precious blood of the Lord Jesus, one by one, and
then to get back to the old paths and tried ways; back to
the faith of our fathers. For in *that* way, and only in that
way, lies salvation.

All else will be of no avail.

Chapter Eleven

A Nation Ripe for Judgment

So far, we have seen that the *basic* problem with Britain is that we are a nation living without God, that we are defying him openly, and are deliberately going against him.

Now the Bible teaches that if a nation or a people deliberately continues to go in the kind of direction Britain is going, persistently and wilfully refusing to heed the various warnings that God has been giving, then there comes a time when God has to hand them over to various other forms of judgment. It says he has to give them up.

Which brings me to the third part of the answer as to what really is wrong with Britain. *We, as a people, have got so far away from God in our national rebellion against him,* that everything points to the fact that *he has already begun to hand us over* in this kind of way.

The Bible tells us that there are at least five ways in which God can hand over such a people. I included some of them in *Pending Judgment on Britain?*[1] Let me now list all five. He can hand them over to:

1) The gross forms of immorality which are mentioned in Romans chapter 1.
2) Satan for most severe discipline or, as the New Testament puts it, 'unto Satan for the destruction of the flesh' (see 1 Corinthians 5:5; 1 Timothy 1:20).

3) Some great national catastrophe. (Daniel 9:12-14)
4) Enemies within. (Judges 2:13-15)
5) An enemy who is threatening from without. (Deuteronomy 28:47-52)

1) In Romans 1, for instance, we find that because they refused to acknowledge God (*refused* to, notice), '*God also gave them up to uncleanness . . . to dishonour their own bodies between themselves . . . God gave them up unto vile affections: for even their women did change the natural use into that which is against nature; and likewise also the men, leaving the natural use of the woman, burned in their lust one toward another . . . receiving in themselves that recompence of their error which was meet. And even as they did not like to retain God in their knowledge, God gave them over to a reprobate mind, to do those things which are not convenient; being filled with all unrighteousness . . . Who, knowing the judgment of God, that they which commit such things are worthy of death, not only do the same, but have pleasure in them that do them.* (Romans 1:24-32)

Three times over in this passage we read that 'God gave them up': 'God gave them up to uncleanness' (v 24). 'God gave them up unto vile affections' (v 26). 'God gave them over to a reprobate mind' (v 28).

All this is referred to in verse 18 as 'the wrath of God' being 'revealed from heaven against all ungodliness and unrighteousness of men'; which means that 'the handing over' to all these obnoxious and distasteful things that are mentioned in this chapter, is a very definite form of God's judgment. We need to remember that, people of Britain, when we see all these things proliferating around us.

The chapter goes on to say that such people 'receive in their own persons the due penalty for their error.' (v 27, RSV) You do not need me to tell you of the gross immorality with which our country is riddled today. British medical records and reports all show that venereal disease in Britain, even amongst the young, has reached the proportions of a national epidemic: 'receiving in their own persons that recompence of their error which was meet.'

Has God had to hand us over, as a nation, to this, because we refuse to find any place for him in our national life, or because we do not see fit to acknowledge him, and refuse to have anything to do with him *as individuals?* One of the most knowledgeable and highly qualified doctors in this country informed some of us, at a recent meeting of concerned people, that instructions are now being given to hospital staffs, stressing the need to take throat swabs from certain patients to check the possible existence of a particularly abhorrent form of venereal disease in that part of the body. This deeply disturbing report carries its own ghastly implications.

This is the extent to which people are receiving in their own persons the due rewards of their deeds. They are literally destroying themselves as a result of their extremely loose behaviour.

Doesn't *somebody* need to 'sound the trumpet'?

2) The New Testament talks in more than one place of *God having to hand certain individuals over to Satan for severe discipline,* even for the destruction of the flesh, if they still refuse to repent. And this is because of their extreme wilfulness (1 Corinthians 5:5;1 Timothy 1:20).

When I first read this in the Bible I could not bring myself ever to mention it in public. But now I must ask: Does God sometimes have to hand *nations* over to this kind of thing? That question becomes increasingly important in view of the ever-tightening grip which Satanism, spiritism, witchcraft, the black arts, and all other forms of the occult are getting on this country.

The question is relevant, too, in view of the way the people of this country are being constantly bombarded with films about demon-possessed people and exorcism;

about the activities of all the evil powers of darkness, not only in our cinemas but on television; and because of the way these evil practices are discussed on the radio, and even in our schools.

I can never forget how a few years ago, when I was speaking in Oxford along these lines, the rural dean asked me if I would be prepared to talk to a meeting of the clergy in the city. When I asked him why he was so anxious to arrange this, he said it was because he was deeply concerned about the number of people in Oxford who were being initiated into various forms of Satanism and demon-worship every week. He used the word 'initiated', which means going the whole way – committing themselves fully. This, in blunt English, means 'selling themselves, or handing themselves completely over' to the devil. He quoted a figure which, by any count, was extremely alarming. In fact, working out the figure on the way home, the numbers involved were such that I found myself saying, 'If that number of people in Oxford were being converted to faith in Jesus Christ every week, there would be headline news in the national Press telling us that a revival of Christianity had hit one of our major university cities.'

Then this possibility dawned on me: He did not say these people who were being initiated were from the university. He said they were people 'in Oxford'. But they could have included people from the university, and no doubt did. As that alarming figure continued to take hold of my mind I thought: could it possibly be that initiation continues at this rate, we shall find that in ten or twenty years time the occupant of 10 Downing Street is a demon-possessed person? After all, it is the universities which produce most of our future national leaders: our politicians, our professional men, our teachers, our business magnates – in short, most of the influential people of the future.

It happened in Nazi Germany, friends! Those in

authority during the Nazi regime were demon-possessed. Hitler was a demon-possessed person (Rommel, in his papers, describes him as 'the devil-incarnate'). Goebbels was demon-possessed; so was the leader of the SS, many of the SS men, and other of the Nazi leaders. Their very emblem, the swastika, is a symbol of satanical powers.

We should not delude ourselves into believing that it could not possibly happen in this country. Shortly after my Oxford experience, I was in Yorkshire, and learnt on very good authority that a number of witches' covens had just met under a full moon in a forest in Yorkshire, with nearly a thousand people present – and that they had all arrived in Rolls, Daimlers, Jaguars and such like! And in September 1976 a Fleet Street investigation revealed that there are witches who claim that secret covens exist in every big town in the land!

3) *God could visit us with some great national calamity.* In *Pending Judgment on Britain,* I drew attention to the real possibility of one such catastrophe happening. That was the possibility of London being destroyed by a flood.

The British Press has been giving warnings for a number of years, and Lord Bowden, principal of the University of Manchester Institute of Science and Technology, has drawn urgent attention to it when opening a debate in the House of Lords on 'Flood Prevention in the Thames'. He put it in this way.

London has been sinking by a foot every 100 years. The tides have been rising by eighteen inches ever 100 years. Existing flood barriers are sinking under their own weight into the London clay. The barrier confronting the Thames in front of the Houses of Parliament, said Lord Bowden, was two feet lower than 100 years ago. Every so many years there is a tidal surge in the Atlantic which, when the wind is in a certain direction (mainly NW), gets driven round the northern coast of Scotland down into the North

Sea. A big build-up of water occurs. This is accentuated by the Channel, which forms a 'bottle-neck' and prevents the water escaping fast enough into the Atlantic again. The Thames estuary forms a natural gateway through which the excess water rushes. But if this surge coincides with high tides, a full moon, and with the wind in a north-westerly direction – because the wind prevents one high tide in the Thames from ebbing before the next tide is due in – an inevitable high rise in the level of water results all the way up to London, and, having no other means of escape, it must either burst existing banks and river walls, or over-top them. Such a possibility is very real.

Should such a surge occur, an area from Wapping to Richmond, and from the Thames Embankment right across to Kings Cross could be flooded, and in some places to a depth of ten feet or more. This would mean that much of London's Underground system would be put out of action; telecommunication and electrical systems would be seriously affected; damage to property could amount to £1,000 million pounds worth, with a further £1,000 million pounds worth of derivative damage; and there could be very considerable loss of life. London, as a capital city, could be put out of effective action for as long as six to nine months.

At the end of his address Lord Bowden quoted this very significant sentence: 'The angel of death is abroad in the land, and we may almost hear the beating of his wings.' This is the language of judgment.

Lest anyone should be tempted to believe that this danger has now receded, constant warnings have since been issued that the danger is increasing, not diminishing. It could still happen within the next few years, until the flood barrier at Woolwich is completed. London is, in fact, living on borrowed time.[2]

You may ask why I say that, if such a catastrophic event were to happen, it should be seen as a judgment of God upon Britain? In what sense would this be true?

Because of what I find in Daniel chapter 9: *All this calamity (evil, AV) has come upon us, yet we have not prayed unto the Lord our God, turning from our iniquities and giving heed to thy truth. Therefore the Lord has kept ready the calamity and has brought it upon us* (Daniel 9:13-14, RSV).

When Daniel said 'all this calamity', he meant all the *previous* calamity which had come upon his people and upon his nation in recent years. 'All this previous calamity has come upon us', is what he is really saying, 'and yet we have not prayed unto the Lord our God . . . Therefore the Lord has kept ready the calamity [this present one] and has brought it upon us.' That is the full force of his words. So what is their relevance to Britain's situation today?

Daniel lived at a time when the nation was undergoing the judgments of God because it had turned away from him, was rebelling against him, and had ignored his commandments. Because it was a nation under judgment, Daniel had seen it suffer one calamity after another. Its people had sinned and done wickedly (v 5): *that* was the reason.

Yet it still continued along the path of defiance without giving any regard to God whatsoever. Daniel put the full case before the Lord in his prayer; here it is. Notice, as you read it, how much of what he said is relevant to our own situation today.

We have sinned, and have committed iniquity, and have done wickedly, and have rebelled, even by turning aside from thy commandments and from thy ordinances.

Neither have we hearkened unto thy servants the prophets, which spake in thy name to our rulers . . . and to all the people of the land . . . To us, O Lord, belongs confusion of face, and to our rulers . . . because we have sinned against thee. . . . Because we have rebelled . . . and have not obeyed the voice of the Lord our God by following his laws which he set before us.

All Israel [the whole nation, that is] *has transgressed thy law, and turned aside, refusing to obey thy voice.*

And the curse and the oath which are written in the law of Moses the servant of God [Deuteronomy 28 in particular] *have been poured out upon us, because we have sinned against him. He has confirmed his words, which he spoke against us and against our rulers by bringing upon us a great calamity* (Daniel 9:5-12, RSV).

Having put this case before the Lord, Daniel says: 'All this evil is come upon us: yet [*and yet*] made we not our prayer before the Lord our God . ... Therefore the Lord has brought this further calamity upon us which he has been keeping ready' (vv 13, 14). Which is precisely Britain's case. We have suffered God's judgments one after another (each one of those contained in Deuteronomy 28; those which comprise the curse and the oath in the law of Moses the servant of God. We have suffered one national calamity after another, and yet . . . and yet . . . we have persistently and stubbornly refused to pray to the Lord our God as a nation – as a people.

Times without number, urgent appeals have been sent by organisations and individuals, including myself, to the Sovereign, to call the nation to God in prayer as His Majesty King George VI did between 1939 and 1945. Every time the result has been the same. Each successive prime minister (who advises the Sovereign) has replied: 'The situation does not demand it.'

Even the last Archbishop of Canterbury (Dr Donald Coggan), having admitted in print that ever since he took office he had had a steady stream of letters coming in and calling for a Day of Prayer for the Nation (and one of his executives has written that 'One has to record a certain wonder at the sheer volume of pressure for such a Day in the Archbishop's letters') – even the last Archbishop, despite all this weight of demand from so many people, has said, in conjunction with the Archbishop of York: 'A "Call to Prayer" would not be the same as thirty years ago, because the tone of British society since World War II has become less and less traditionally Christian.' Therefore, 'such a call is not likely to be heeded by more than 10 per cent of the nation.' And so that great volume of requests has been rejected on these pathetic grounds. Presumably the advice which has been given to the Sovereign is the same.

I notice that there is no reference whatsoever to the possibility of such a Call to Prayer being heeded *by Almighty God*!

A further appeal was made, by many people, for the nation to be called to God in prayer when the effect of the prolonged drought experienced in Britain throughout the summer of 1976 became extremely acute. Once again the appeal was rejected. The great name of God Almighty, the real controller of the weather, was brought still further into disrepute when it was left to the Sikhs who are living amongst us, out of their deep concern about the drought, to send to the Punjab for their holy men to come and hold a three-day rain-making festival in London in an effort to break it. And God's name was still further mocked when the BBC gleefully announced that the Sikhs were cock-a-hoop because, after but one day of their rain-making festival, London had its first rain in months, and various parts of the country had floods and deluges. 'They had done what nobody else had been able to do.'

Is not this what God himself refers to in the Old Testament as profaning his holy name among the heathen (Ezekiel 36:22)? I would think it is, especially when, only twenty-four hours afterwards, a leading national newspaper carried the headline: 'Archbishop of Canterbury Rejects Call to Prayer'. The stubbornness of the nation's Christian leaders was continuing.

It still continued, even when the Chief Rabbi published a letter in *The Times* saying that the Jewish community had been praying to God in their synagogues for rain.

'All this evil is come upon us', said Daniel, 'yet cried we not unto the Lord our God.' Are we not in exactly the same position as that outlined in Daniel's prayer in chapter 9? Surely there is good reason for saying that were such a catastrophic event to take place as the destruction of our capital by the Thames bursting its banks, it should be seen as a judgment of God upon Britain? 'All these *previous* calamities have come upon us [all those already referred to, including the drought], and yet cried we not unto the Lord our God.' God might well be *keeping ready* such a calamity as this, and could bring it upon us if we *still* refuse to turn from our iniquities and turn to him in humble repentance and prayer.

We are in a 'Daniel chapter 9' situation. But the national calamity need not necessarily take the form of a flood disaster in the Thames. It could take some other form.

a) *The total collapse of our national economy*. For a number of years now our political leaders have been warning us of such a possibility. This is the crash which *they* forsee.

b) *The failure of our entire industrial system*. Sir Maurice Laing has already warned us of the possibility of *that* happening, when he said, 'What we are about to witness is the total collapse of our entire industrial system.'

c) *The total disintegration of the United Kingdom*. The ingredients of that kind of judgment are already there. This theme will be expanded further in Volume 3.

d) *The total loss of our North Sea oil,* on which our leaders have so confidently come to depend, but which is by no means secure – especially when the Soviet Union runs short of oil early in the 1980s!

e) *The total collapse of the whole cultural structure of our society* as we know it. Indeed I see Britain today like a building from which all the cement and mortar are fast being removed. The cement and mortar are the essential Christian foundations and standards which, until recent years, have bonded Britain's structure. Remove the cement and mortar from between the bricks of *any* building and the total collapse of that building is inevitable. Even so with a nation.

Indeed, a recent writer has warned that the whole of western culture is now collapsing. 'Such a collapse', he says, 'is something that we in Britain have never experienced in its totality for centuries, *but we are beginning to see signs of such a critical event.*'[3]

4) The Bible teaches that *God can also hand a people over to enemies within.* The Book of Judges tells us that 'when Israel did evil yet again in the sight of the Lord, he delivered them into the hands of spoilers that spoiled them, and he sold them into the hands of their enemies round about' (Judges 2:14). In the context in which it happened, this meant the enemies within their borders. He delivered them into the hands of enemies who were at work *within the realm* – enemies who were out to disrupt, overthrow, destroy, take over.

We read that Israel was utterly powerless to make any kind of stand against them. Britain is suffering at the hands of such people today. It has happened continuously within British Leyland. But many voices have been raised in warning over a long period of time, including those on the shop-floors of our factories, as well as those of our national leaders.

The 'enemy within' has entered practically every branch of our national life, including MI5 and MI6.[4] Our industry and trade unions have been well and truly infiltrated; so have our universities, schools, and teacher-training colleges. Local and national government, the BBC and the Civil Service have all been penetrated. And since world statesmen, including foreign ministers, say that there has been a very high degree of communist infiltration into most of the world's churches, it is more than likely that our own churches have been affected.

Then there is always a very real possibility of a confrontation between the trade unions and the Government, leading to a take-over of this country by powerful and extreme elements of the Left Wing, who are bent on bringing in communist policies under what would then be their own communist government. That danger has been confronting the country for years, is being orchestrated from Moscow, and could be what all this infiltration is about.

Let us never forget that to bring about the total collapse of a nation's economy, the failure of its entire industrial system, and the total disintegration of a nation itself, is all part of the work of the 'enemies within' in order to bring about their intended aim. As former President Nixon has written in his recently published book *The Real War*, 'Local communist parties and communist-headed unions, by leading strikes, by demanding excessive wage increases, by calling for nationalisation of industries and by sponsoring terrorism amongst businessmen, can damage the investment climate of a country so badly that money will stop flowing in. Their Soviet masters thrive on chaos, confusion and fear. They know that economic depression, revolution and war can destroy the fabric of any society. Therefore they try, by whatever means they can, to exacerbate tensions throughout the world, stir up discontent, foment wars and revolution. The Russians do not want human needs met. They do not want problems solved. They want problems to escalate *in order to seize the nation.*'[5] (my italics)

Britain today is most certainly faced with a very real danger from such enemies – powerful enemies – at work within its borders, some of them just waiting for the right moment to effect a take-over, with or without the assistance of the Soviet Union. We are a prime target for such an attempt.

So I ask: Is this a judgment of God, because, as a nation, we are flying in his face, and openly defying him, after all the good that he has lavished upon us through the centuries of our history?

Judgment could take any or all of these forms. It could even take a form more severe than any of them, or of all of them put together.

5) *For Britain today is also confronted with the very real danger of an enemy from without.* Mrs Margaret Thatcher is by no means the only one who has been raising a voice about the build-up of overwhelming forces in the Soviet Union and Warsaw Pact countries, against which NATO forces form, or should form, the major part of the Western Europe's, and so of Britain's defensive shield. For years now the voices of NATO's most senior officers have been heard, both in and outside Britain, warning all concerned of Russia's intentions and ever-increasing strength: not least those of General Goodpaster, Supreme Commander, NATO forces in Europe; General Alexander Haig; Dr Joseph Luns, Secretary-General of NATO and chairman of the North Atlantic Council; and our own General Sir Walter Walker and Air Chief Marshal Sir Neil Cameron.

More recently, further stringent warnings have been sounded out. Dr Kissinger, for instance, wrote in his recently published memoirs: 'The world stands once again on the brink of military confrontation.' Then he said in Brussels in September 1979: 'The time of greatest peril for Western Europe will be 1982-86, when the Soviet Union's massive defence spending will bear fruit and permit Moscow to jump ahead in military capability.' His sombre words continued: 'The Soviet Union is rapidly achieving superiority over the West in every category of military strength. On present trends, this superiority will be at its most decisive *early in the 1980s*.' (my italics) He then gave this warning: 'In the entire history of the world, no nation has ever achieved such superiority without seeking to translate it into foreign political advantage.'

On 6 October 1979, General Walker sounded the alarm

once more. Speaking in London on 'The Defence of the West against the Soviet Global Threat' – which he illustrated profusely by military wall-charts – he said: 'Never has the world situation been so grave and dangerous since World War II. The Soviet Union's mood is now one of war, as they drive forward to accomplish their objective – which is world domination. We are thus moving into a high-risk period which will be all the more dangerous because of Soviet realisation that their military superiority may be fairly short lived. The temptation to press on will be very great. NATO is now so outnumbered, outgunned and outstripped in every direction that the Soviet Union may well be tempted to flex her muscles.' 'Dr Kissinger', declared General Walker, 'has suggested 1982 as the likely date for this to happen, less than three years off. Other analysists have argued that it may be even sooner than that.'

Then he said: 'The stark reality is that Great Britain and Western Europe over the next three to four years are going to be in supreme danger. We could be facing surrender or defeat by 1982!'

This is to be in a 'Book of Jeremiah' situation. Bible students will know what I mean. General Walker stressed that 'The hour is very late. It may well be too late to prevent the Soviets from striking at England, which could come simultaneously with an attack in the Middle East.'

That was the warning being sounded out last October. But when the news broke at Christmas-time last year that Russian forces had invaded Afghanistan, the alarm bells began to ring all over Europe. They began to ring all over the Middle East as well, because of the Russian threat to Middle East oil wells.

A further clear warning was sounded out as recently as the weekend of 15-16 March 1980. At this time the warning was issued by a very senior *Soviet* general who has sought asylum in the United States. This Russian officer, General Grigorenko, had already been claiming a year ago that Europe would be Russia's next target once the Kremlin had achieved, with Cuban help, its aims in Africa. Now, in the spring of 1980, he issued a warning that the Soviet Union may take military action against Europe before the end of *this* year. He claimed that the Soviet invasion of Afghanistan at the beginning of the year had been a test of the West's capacity for reaction: 'The operation was successful. The western camp is divided.' Then the general said: 'Afghanistan may prove in coming weeks to have been the "detonation" of war with incalculable consequences – a Third World War in fact.' He added, 'I think this will probably happen before the end of the year. Then we will be able to test the theory that Russian troops can cross Germany in three hours.'

These are only some of the warnings given. So who can deny that Britain today is confronted with the very real danger of an enemy from without?

Furthermore, the threat does not only come from overland to the Channel ports and beyond; or from aerial bombardment; or from the 130 or more SS20 medium-range nuclear missiles which the Soviets now have deployed on their extreme western border, each having a range of 2,200 miles and carrying three independently targeted nuclear warheads capable of hitting any target in Western Europe from Gibraltar to the North Cape right up in north Norway – which brings London well within range – and against which there is no western response.

There is the very real threat to all our sea-lines of communication. They could easily be closed by powerful units of the Soviet Navy which are already sitting astride them. For instance, as a result of phenomenal naval expansion and of pushing the naval defence line out beyond Iceland, Russia now has naval forces in position which are capable of closing the sea-passages between the north coast of Scotland and Iceland, including the vital Denmark straits, and of shutting off such sea-routes to and from Britain as the Atlantic approaches, the western approaches, and the Irish Sea. Since Russian electronic intelligence trawlers and submarines operate an almost continuous patrol around the coasts of Britain, and since the Russian backfire bombers are capable of attacking shipping in the Atlantic as far south as the Azores from their bases in Northern Russia, and of returning home without refuelling, there is a very real threat of Britain being blockaded at sea. There is also the possibility of an additional blockade: the threat to the sea-routes leading from the Persian Gulf and round the Cape of South Africa. Were these sea passages to be closed, it would mean that our food and oil supplies would be cut off and all our industry and fighting forces would grind to a stand-still, leaving this country with no alternative but to surrender to domination by a foreign power.

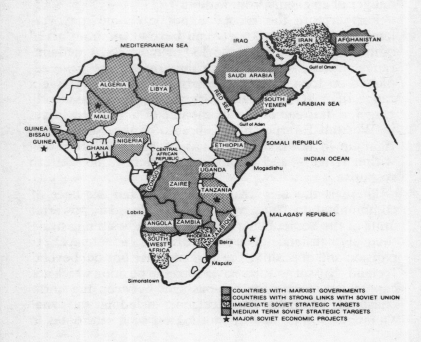

This is the form of national calamity which I fear most of all; and this is why I believe the trumpet should be sounded loud and clear. Were these blockades to happen, it should be seen as very much a judgment of God upon the nation for all our wickedness in forsaking him.

As to exactly what Russia's long and short-term aims with regard to the Cape route are, one of the men in a position to know, probably better than most, is General Sir Walter Walker. He has held two appointments, first as Deputy Chief-of-Staff in charge of plans, operations and intelligence, Allied Forces Central Europe, and then as Commander-in-Chief of Allied Forces Northern Europe. Writing in his bi-monthly paper, *International Summary*, he said: 'I want to state quite categorically and with due solemnity, that Russia intends, by blackmail, revolutionary war by proxy, or by brute force, to absorb the whole of South Africa, deprive the West of vital minerals, and control Europe's life-line round the Cape . . . What is now at stake is not only the whole future of Western Europe, but civilisation itself and the western way of life.'

No less emphatic were the comments of Mr Van Der Byl, a former minister of defence and foreign affairs in what is now Zimbabwe: 'I am firmly convinced, as I believe most thinking people in the world are convinced, that the Soviet tactic is to get hold of the Cape sea-route, and in the process, as much of Africa as possible . . . If they were to take the whole of Southern Africa, which is clearly their intention in one way or another, then of course the position of Western Europe and the NATO countries and the rest would be pretty perilous. Now this is what I believe the whole thing is about. All the indications are there, and nobody denies it.'

Much more recently, no less a person than the Soviet President, Leonid Brezhnev, confirmed this when he said to Somalian President Siad Barre, who was then an ally of the USSR: 'Our aim is to gain control of the two great treasure houses on which the West depends – the energy treasure house of the Persian Gulf, and the mineral treasure house of central and southern Africa.'[6]

So now we know. There is nothing like having it straight from the horse's mouth, or the mouth of the Red Bear for that matter!

As for the threat to the Persian Gulf area and the Middle East oil wells, Richard Nixon says: 'In the near future the Soviet Union may need Persian Gulf oil as their domestic supplies dwindle.

'Never has the region of the Persian Gulf been so vital to the future of the world; never have the nations of the Persian Gulf been so vulnerable to an aggressive power that seeks to impose its will on the world. If the Soviets succeed in taking effective control of the Persian Gulf, Europe and Japan will be at their mercy – and mercy is not one of their most notable virtues.'[7] Furthermore he says, 'The Soviet Union's ultimate target is its chief rival, the United States. Its *intermediate* targets are Western Europe and Japan.'[8]

So the danger to this country of the 'enemy without' is very real, for there is no need to remind the reader that Western Europe includes Britain.

In Daniel's day, the great calamity which the Lord first kept ready, and then brought upon the nation because its people and its leaders persistently refused to return to him, took the form of the overthrow of the capital by a foreign power, followed by total domination. In view of the way *our* nation has departed today, why should *we* expect anything less?

It was a Royal Naval commander who said to me some years ago: 'Something *serious* has got to happen to bring this country to its knees. *Preaching* won't do it any more. Neither will evangelism.' Then, almost in a whisper, he said, 'God may have to use Russia!'

I myself have been warning over the years of the *spiritual* implications of the colossal build-up of Soviet forces and of their threat to Britain and the West, by giving addresses – some of two or three hour's duration – in many different places. And I have backed them up with literature (which has been, and is being, widely distributed) and with tape-recorded messages.

It is about the *spiritual* implications of this build-up that we, as a people, need most to be warned. Deuteronomy 28:47-8 – that same chapter in which all those other curses and judgments are listed – goes on to say: '*Because* thou servedst not the Lord thy God with joyfulness, and with gladness of heart, for the abundance of all things; *therefore* shalt thou serve thine enemies which the Lord shall send against thee.'

'*Because* you do not serve the Lord your God . . . you shall serve your enemies.'

Then we read that 'The *Lord* shall bring a nation against thee from afar, from the end of the earth, as swift as the eagle flieth; a nation whose tongue thou shalt not understand; a nation of a fierce countenance' (Deuteronomy 28:49-50).

'The *Lord* shall', is what it says. For it should be clearly understood that the Bible makes it very plain that God sometimes uses *nations* as his instruments of judgment. For instance, in the early books of the Bible he used the nation of Israel as his instrument of judgment against the notorious Amorites, when the iniquity of the Amorites had come to the full. Then in the later books of the Old Testament, when the iniquity of the nation of Israel itself had reached a very high peak, God raised up nations as his instruments of judgment against *her*. There was Assyria, for instance, and then Nebuchadnezzar and the armies of Babylon.

I believe God does this in a modern age, too. I am prepared to say that God used Britain as an instrument of judgment against Nazi Germany when, under Hitler's influence and leadership, the Third Reich became so indescribably evil, tyrannical and wicked. He certainly used Britain and the combined forces of the Allies as his instrument of *deliverance* when the appointed time had come to deliver the people of the Continent from the hands of a raging maniac.

So we should not be at all surprised if, because of Britain's present departure from God and wilful defiance of him, he is raising up a powerful nation as an instrument of judgment against *her*.

It has happened before in history. In the Book of Judges chapter 3:12 we read: 'And the children of Israel did evil again in the sight of the Lord . . . the Lord strengthened . . . the King of Moab against Israel, because they had done evil in the sight of the Lord.' They had to serve the King of Moab for eighteen years, and that, indeed, could even be the *spiritual* implication behind the colossal Soviet build-up. If so, the verse could read, 'The Lord strengthened the Soviet Union against Britain because they had done evil in the sight of the Lord.'

Notice that the *Lord* did this. 'The *Lord* strengthened . . . ' So my case, in answer to the question 'What *really* is wrong with Britain?', is this:

1) We are a nation living without God, and without any reference to God.
2) We are openly defying him and wilfully flying in his face.
3) We have got so far away from God, as a nation, that we have already become a nation under judgment, and in terms of such judgment have begun to be 'handed over' and to be 'given up' in a number of ways.
4) All the indications are that unless we turn to God and repent, there is a further and more grievous judgment being kept ready for us, and which will be brought upon us. And that judgment could take the form of our being handed over to a foreign power, or of being brought to such a position as to leave us with no alternative but to surrender and to submit to

foreign domination.

My case, furthermore, is that it is no longer a question as to *whether* we have departed from God. That we *have* done so is beyond dispute, and it is now a question of *how far* we have departed. In Volumes 2 and 3 I shall seek to show that.

we have departed from God *historically*,

we have departed from God *spiritually* and *morally*,

we have departed from God *politically* and *legally*, and

we have departed from God *constitutionally*.

NOTES

1. An address delivered by the author at NATO HQ in Rheindahlen, Germany, at the request of its commanding officer, and which has since been available in leaflet form, going into over 100,000 copies.
2. For a graphic account of what *could* happen, read Richard Doyle's novel *Deluge,* Arlington Books, 3 Clifford Street, Mayfair, London W1, 1976.
3. O.R. Johnston, *Christianity in a Collapsing Culture,* Paternoster Press, 3 Mount Radford Crescent, Exeter, 1976.
4. See, for instance, Chapman Pincher's book, *Inside Story,* Sidgwick and Jackson, 1 Tavistock Chambers, Bloomsbury Way, London WC1, 1978, chapters 1, 8 and 9 in particular.
5. Richard Nixon, *The Real War,* Sidgwick and Jackson, London, 1980. Quoted from serialised version published in *Now* magazine, 11-17 April 1980 edition, p23.
6. *Now* magazine, 11-17 April 1980 edition, p19.
7. ibid., p21.
8. ibid., pp18-19.

Acknowledgements

I list with grateful acknowledgements the various publications which I have consulted during the preparation of this book, and from which some of the material has been drawn.

Books

Winston S. Churchill, *History of the English-speaking Peoples,* Volume 1, Cassell, London 1956.

G. M. Trevelyan, *A Shortened History of England,* Pelican, London 1970.

J. Wesley Bready, *England Before and After Wesley,* Hodder and Stoughton, London 1939.

George Whitefield's Journals, The Banner of Truth Trust, Edinburgh 1960.

Richard Doyle, *Deluge* (novel), Arlington Books, London 1976.

O. R. Johnston, *Christianity in a Collapsing Culture,* Paternoster Press, Exeter 1976.

Chapman Pincher, *Inside Story,* Sidgwick and Jackson, London 1978.

Richard Nixon, *The Real War,* Sidgwick and Jackson, London 1980.

The Rommel Papers, ed. B. H. Liddell Hart, Collins, London 1953.

John Poulton, *Dear Archbishop,* Hodder and Stoughton, London 1976.

Leaflets, Magazines and Pamphlets

General Sir Walter Walker, *International Summary.*

Now magazine, 11-17 April 1980.

The Rev. David E. Gardner, *Pending Judgment on Britain,* an address delivered at the NATO Headquarters, Rheindahlen, Germany.

The Rev. David E. Gardner, *A Warning to the Nation,* Christian Foundation Publications, eighth reprint. Available from 45 Appleton Road, Hale, Altrincham, Cheshire.

I would also like to place on record grateful thanks and deep appreciation to all those who have helped with the typing and re-typing of this manuscript and those of Volumes 2 and 3. They include Miss Eileen Devenish, formerly of Twickenham, Middlesex, who undertook the mammoth task of typing a large part of the original manuscript in triplicate; Mrs Margaret Williamsen of Wantage, Oxon, who gallantly took over at a later stage; and more recently Mrs Margaret Greaves of Wandsworth.

I am also greatly indebted to Miss Gwen Saunders for the very valuable help which she has given over a considerable period of time, and to Lance Bidewell for the painstaking and thorough way in which he has scrutinised the text of Volume 1 and given generous help and advice in preparation for its publication.

Also to Rodney Shepherd of Nuprint Services, whose personal Christian commitment led to an interest in the message, resulting in its attractive presentation as the printed word.

Last, but by no means least, I would like to express my grateful appreciation to Dr Brian Taylor of Altrincham, Cheshire, for recognising the extreme urgency and relevance of the message and deciding to go ahead with the utmost possible speed with its publication. Without his generous and courageous help the book may never have seen the light of day.

The
Trumpet Sounds
for Britain

Volume 2
God's Mighty Acts of Deliverance

David E. Gardner

Contents

'Write the vision, and make it plain upon tables, that he may run that readeth it. For the vision is yet for an appointed time, but at the end it shall speak, and not lie: though it tarry, wait for it; because it will surely come, it will not tarry.'

Habakkuk 2:2, 3

Foreword

Group Captain Sir Douglas Bader,
KT, CBE, DSO, DFC, FRA, DL

It is always fascinating to read a book in which the author
has total belief in what he writes. In the case of David
Gardner's book, *The Trumpet Sounds for Britain,* I found
Volume 2 of great interest, because it deals with a period
of history through which I lived. David is a dedicated
Christian. One might suggest that he adjusts historical
events to suit his convictions. This would not be true.

With specific reference to the Battle of Britain, I can say
that at no time did any of us pilots in Fighter Command
believe that the Germans would win. It never crossed our
minds. We had total faith in our senior commanders,
specifically in 'Stuffy' Dowding, the Commander-in-Chief.
The majority of pilots never knew him, but felt that so
long as this father figure was in charge, everything would
be all right. Dowding was a man of faith. Perhaps in some
indefinable way this was transmitted to all of us.

I well recall our surprise that the German offensive
against Britain did not follow after the evacuation of
Dunkirk. This was indeed one of the divine interventions
which David Gardner describes.

I commend this book. It is written with the authority of
the author's personal Christian convictions.

'The Russian Bear'

*By an eighty-nine-year-old lady
written during World War II*

There are many schemes for lasting peace for all who are
    oppressed,
But they are doomed to failure while rulers of East and West
Put their trust in the Russian Bear, who breaks all rules and laws,
And means to hold the world in its Satanic evil claws–
There are many helpless Countries now crushed in its embrace,
Their Heritage of Freedom has been lost, and in its place
Is a state of cruel bondage, and peace is sacrificed
By the Atheistic Hosts of Gog,* the enemies of Christ.

*   *   *   *

Because men's hearts are fearful as dark omens spread abroad,
They put their trust in Foreign Pacts instead of in the Lord,
But they will not be honoured, and never will succeed,
For every single League or Pact will be a broken reed
Until the Prince of Peace is Leader, and His Laws obeyed,
For Peace will never be achieved without His promised aid–
But when the Christian Nations realise their desperate plight,
And they see there is no hope at all without God's Power and
    Might,
Then a great awakening will sweep throughout the land–
And once again God's People will bow to His command . . .
They will recognise His Covenant, and reinstate His Laws,
And a Golden Age of Peace will dawn when there will be no
    Wars.

* See Ezekiel 38:2; 39:1, which many believe refers to Russia.
   The armies 'from the north parts' – see Ezekiel 39:2.

Maud Casson

Introduction

The author has a deep and burning conviction that the root cause of Britain's present predicament is that, as a nation, she has departed from God.

In Volume 1 he began by setting out clearly how the hand of Almighty God has been on the history of this country in blessing, right from its beginnings, especially by giving it *Christian* foundations from the very earliest times; preserving those Christian foundations whenever they have been in danger of being lost or destroyed; bringing about the Reformation; and granting the great spiritual awakening under the preaching of Whitefield and Wesley in the eighteenth century, which resulted in a degree of prosperity and glory unknown to any former age.

The author then raised the question, 'What is wrong with Britain today?', pointing out that, forgetting all these great blessings bestowed upon her in the past, Britain has now become a nation living without God. She makes no reference to him whatsoever. She has tragically departed from him, rejected his laws, jettisoned that Christian faith on which she was founded, and is openly defying him and wilfully flying in his face. Consequently, she has become a nation under judgment. He indicated from the Bible a number of the judgments she has already been going through, and others she is likely to experience.

His firm belief, from a detailed study of the Bible, is

9

that Britain has gone away from God as the nation of Israel did in the Old Testament, which means that she may well suffer the same ultimate consequences. In Israel's case, it was judgment at the hands of an invading enemy army, and the author sees the ingredients of that kind of judgment for Britain in terms of the massive Soviet build-up. This judgment could fall on Britain at any moment: that is why there is an urgent need 'to sound the trumpet'.

He now continues his theme in Volume 2, arguing that it is no longer a question of *whether* we have departed from God, but *how far* we have gone. In order to demonstrate the seriousness of our rebellion, he shows how, in addition to the blessings described in Volume 1, the hand of Almighty God has been on the history of this country, in bringing about *mighty acts of deliverance* whenever she has been in mortal danger.

That hand has also been on her history in giving her Christian and Bible-based laws. Yet, despite all this—and not least the miracles of deliverance during the Second World War—we are now witnessing a tragic moral and spiritual landslide.

Chapter One

The Life and Times
of King Alfred

*The works of The Lord are great, sought out of all them
that have pleasure therein (Psalm 111:2).*

Many times over, when Britain has been in grave danger,
or has been confronted with imminent and almost certain
disaster, God has intervened in a miraculous way and the
calamity has been averted.

On the occasions that this has happened, the course of
our national history has often been altered, and there have
been repercussions on both European and world affairs.
Such interventions have made it clear, too, that 'the most
High ruleth in the kingdom of men'—even over the world's
pagan and heathen kingdoms—and 'giveth it to whomsoever he will' (Daniel 4.25; and see 2 Chronicles 20:6).

Examples of this can be found as early as the days of
King Alfred. A number of my readers and Christian
friends live in Alfred's country, so I cannot resist referring
to this period. The accounts of what happened during
some of Alfred's great battles with the Vikings are just
like reading the stories of great battles in the Bible.

Why? Because the God of the Bible does not change.
He is the same today. Let me sketch in some of the
background.

From about the year AD 789, the incredibly cruel Vikings

11

had been making sudden raids on a number of 'outposts' of this island kingdom. In the north, the wealthy monastry of Lindisfarne, off the Northumbrian coast, had been ravaged and ransacked, and the monastries of Iona and Kildare soon suffered a similar fate. Places in the south of England and the Scottish mainland, as well as the outer isles, were raided and pillaged in turn. But it was not until the year 865 that the great invasion of Northumbria and eastern England began. Then the storm broke in full fury. Using fleets of long boats, sometimes three to four hundred vessels strong, the invaders broke in upon our whole eastern seaboard and, by rowing up the long rivers of England, penetrated and pillaged far inland.

East Anglia fell to Ivar that year; Northumbria in the spring of 866. The Midlands, which were then called Mercia, and which for nearly a hundred years had represented the 'strong-point' of England, were next to succumb, and became tributary to the Danes. It seemed that, before long, the whole of England, which for four centuries had been predominantly in the hands of the Saxons, would have to submit to the devastating inroads which the Vikings were making, and so be obliged to come under their domination.

But this is precisely the point at which God began to intervene. Suddenly, at this critical time in our nation's fortunes when all seemed about to be lost, there appeared on the scene one of the great figures of our national history. There is no doubt that he was a man raised up by God, and it soon became apparent that here was a man through whom the tide of our fortunes was to be turned.

Alfred was not yet king. He was at this time second in command to his elder brother Ethelred, king of Wessex, who commanded the West Saxon armies. Alfred, like his brother, was a devout and godly man; a man of vision and great faith. He was also a man of prayer. It is obvious, too, from the way in which, later on, he treated his Viking foes, and from the way in which he began to fashion our laws, that he had so inbibed the Lord's teaching in the

Sermon on the Mount, that it had become part of himself and therefore found ready and spontaneous expression.

It is also obvious that he derived much inspiration from his knowledge of past history, and that he looked to some of the outstanding figures of those earlier days as his example, for he once wrote to the then Bishop of Worcester in the following terms:

'I would have you informed that it has often come into my remembrance what wise men there formerly were among the English race, both of the sacred orders and the secular; and what happy times those were throughout the English race, and how the kings who had the government of the folk in those days *obeyed God* and His ministers; and they, on the one hand, maintained their peace and morality and their authority within their borders, while at the same time they enlarged their territory abroad; it has often come into my remembrance *how they prospered* both in war and in wisdom... and how foreigners came to this land for wisdom and instruction' (my italics).

He then lamented 'how clean was it [now] fallen away in the English race', and endeavoured by all means within his power to bring about a restoration. Would that the things which had come into Alfred's remembrance from his study of past history, were to be remembered by our ruling authorities today! I think they would derive much inspiration therefrom, and maybe learn a lesson or two!

It was such a man, then, that God raised up for this hour. We can surely liken him to one of the deliverers whom God provided for another nation which was in similar straits during the time of the book of Judges.

God not only provided a man; he was at work to meet this hour of danger in another way as well. For generations it had been the aim of West Saxon policy to bring about a union of the two kingdoms of Kent and Wessex. Now, at the time when Wessex had become the leading English kingdom, God saw to it that that union was achieved so as to create a solid southern bloc just in time to encounter the Viking invasion which was about to fall upon it from the north. Here was one of those instances of God over-ruling in the affairs of nations so as to further his purposes in history.

Divine providence had also arranged that Wessex was strategically strong geographically, with sharp ridges facing north, and with none of those long, slow rivers up which the Danes had been able to steer their longboats into the heart of the now vassal kingdom of Mercia.

When Alfred first appeared on the scene, the north of England, the Midlands and the East had all gone down under the Viking fury. Wessex was the one remaining Saxon kingdom yet to be assaulted. Would it be able to withstand the onslaught?

Its people had not long to wait for the answer, for by this time the Viking army had penetrated southwards and was now fortifying itself in Reading. In January 871 the invaders moved forward from their encampment and met King Ethelred's and Alfred's West Saxon forces on the Berkshire downs. The famous Battle of Ashdown was about to begin.

In battle, King Ethelred and his younger brother Alfred formed a perfect spiritual team. Ethelred held strongly to the view that it was primarily by faith and prayer that the invader's army would be overcome, so he went to pray and spent a long time at his devotions.

Alfred, as we have seen, was also a man of prayer, but as second in command of the army he had obviously agreed to stand by his arms whilst his elder brother prayed.

Bishop Asser tells us what happened next.

The Vikings began slowly approaching the West Saxon forces, clashing their shields and raising their war-cries. Missiles began to fly. King Ethelred, who was still at his prayers, was warned that the battle must soon be joined. 'God comes first', he declared, and continued to pray.

With his brother thus calling upon God to help, Alfred, trusting in God no less, decided to launch the attack. 'And so', to quote Bishop Asser, 'relying on God's counsel and trusting to his help, he closed the shield-wall in due order, and thereupon moved his standard against the enemy.'

King Ethelred soon joined him. Despite the fact that the Vikings had seized the higher ground and put the West Saxon forces at a disadvantage, the Christians advanced uphill and met the opposing forces in deadly conflict. The fight was long and hard, but at last the Danes gave way and fled back to Reading, hotly pursued and leaving the whole length of the Berkshire hills strewn with their dead—one of the Viking kings and five of his earls lying amongst them.

God had certainly answered prayer. This was the first time the invading Vikings had been beaten on the field. It was also Alfred's first battle. Under his courageous leadership, the last of the Saxon kingdoms to be thus attacked had withstood the assault upon it.

True, the results of this victory did not break the power of the Danish army, for they were back in the field within a fortnight. But it is the view of historians that the Battle of Ashdown still ranks high amongst historic encounters because of the greatness of what followed from it.

If Wessex had succumbed to the Viking assault, all would have been lost. For it is an indisputable fact of history that had King Ethelred, Alfred, and their West Saxon forces been beaten on Ashdown, the whole of England would have been overrun by this great heathen Viking army and they would have dragged the country back into anarchy and darkness once more. God did not allow that to happen: he brought about a gracious deliverance.

What is more, by giving the West Saxon forces the victory, God had opened up the way for Alfred, when once the Vikings had been sufficiently subdued, to lay those Christian foundations upon which this country, by divine decree, was to become established.

Furthermore, it is clear from what followed during the next seven years that God firmly intended to keep that way open, although Alfred had to go through at least three periods of grave crisis before God's ultimate purpose for his life could be fulfilled. Yet out of each of these crises, God was to deliver him by means of a miracle.

The *first* of these critical periods came about in this way.

King Ethelred fell sick and died, and Alfred became king at the age of twenty-four. He had inherited a desperate situation, for the Vikings had already returned to the attack and were once again engaged in deadly combat with his West Saxon armies. To and fro the battles were swaying, first one side prevailing and then the other. With seven or eight battles fought, Alfred's numbers were being worn down, whilst the Vikings were receiving strong reinforcements from overseas in the form of their 'summer armies', who were coming over in great numbers, eager to join in the fight. About a month after he had assumed the crown, Alfred suffered a terrible defeat in the heart of his own country. As one of these battles was in progress, the Vikings suddenly used one of their favourite ruses of feigning a retreat. The West Saxons gave chase, and then the fleeing Vikings suddenly turned on their pursuers and Alfred's forces suffered such heavy losses that he thought it best to come to terms while he still had an army.

Nobody knows the exact conditions into which he entered. What we do know is that he somehow managed to 'buy off' the Danes in order to secure five years in which to consolidate his forces. There is no doubt that a heavy price had to be paid in gold.

Despite this dreadful setback, God continued to work with him, overruling events to further his own purposes. For at the very time when Alfred was undergoing this gruelling experience, and whilst this dearly bought period of truce was in operation, an amazing miracle happened. A profound change began to come over the Viking army. Nearly half of these barbarous and heathen sea pirates began to settle down on the land and till the soil. It was literally a case of thousands of them 'beating their swords into ploughshares, and their spears into pruning-hooks.' They forgot the sea, they forgot the army, and they became cultivators of the land. This began to happen on a considerable scale in those parts of the country which they had already won with the sword, namely Northumbria and East Anglia. A new wind was therefore blowing amongst them, and who can deny that it was the wind of the Spirit of God?

When Winston Churchill, in his *History of the English-speaking Peoples,* said of this amazing development, 'It remained only for conversion to Christianity to mingle these races inextricably in the soul and body of the nation', he was but stating what God was intending to do. It was all part of his unfolding plan in the history of our nation.

The *second* period of crisis came after the five-year period of truce was over.

Ivar had departed, and a new Viking war leader named Guthrum stepped on to the scene. He had formulated a large design for the complete and final subjugation of obstinate Wessex. His plan was to attack it by sea and land. So he marched his land army to Wareham, near Portland Bill, where he was joined by his sea army in Poole harbour. The two armies fortified themselves in this region of Dorset, and then proceeded to attack Alfred's kingdom from every quarter. Alfred, it seems, hemmed in the Viking land army and pinned it down near Wareham. Then he offered gold and sued for peace on condition that the Danes would go away. They took the gold and 'swore upon the Holy Ring' that they would depart and remain at peace. But, with a sudden fierce act of treachery, they made a dash for Exeter and seized it. Alfred, with mounted infantry, followed hard in pursuit but arrived too late. The enemy were in the fortress and could not be confronted.

Again something happened which, at the time, was believed to be a direct intervention of God.

A frightful storm hit Guthrum's sea army as they sought to join their comrades at Exeter. A hundred and twenty of their ships were dashed against the cliffs near Swanage and sunk. Upwards of five thousand of these treacherous treaty-breakers perished. Thus by a storm of great fury, and not by force of arms, Guthrum's carefully laid plan, to destroy Wessex and then to overrun the rest of England, was shattered in pieces. Alfred, in the summer of 877, found his enemies ready for a new period of peace. God was therefore continuing to work miracles to ensure that it was not the Vikings who gained the upper hand in England. Alfred's Wessex had once again been saved by a mighty deliverance of God.

Yet the year was scarcely out when the *third* grave period of crisis struck. It was the crisis of King Alfred's life.

He had set up his headquarters and royal court at Chippenham. Early in January 878, whilst his army was keeping the Christian festival of Twelfth Night, he met with the most surprising and harrowing reversal of his fortunes. The enemy suddenly swept down upon his camp, taking it completely off guard. Alfred's entire army was thrown into confusion and disarray. The soldiers scattered—some to their homes, whilst others even fled overseas. Alfred himself, with a few officers and personal aides, managed to escape to the marshes and thence to the forests of Somerset. Thus began the blackest period of this saintly warrior-king's life. It was during this period that he was allegedly seen disguised as a minstrel playing his harp in the Danish camps. It was during this time, too, that the story arose of how he burnt the cakes! With their king now a fugitive and in hiding, it seemed to the people of Wessex that all was over.

Then came an unexpected turning-point. News reached King Alfred of a victory which had been achieved by some of his forces in Devon.

Toward the end of Lent in that year, a strong force of Vikings, who had been ravaging Wales, sailed in twenty-three ships to Devon and marched to attack one of Alfred's strongholds on Exmoor. They thought that because this fortress had no supply of water, Alfred's thanes would be obliged to give way very quickly.

The Anglo-Saxon chronicler says that Alfred's men, on the contrary, 'by the inspiration of heaven, judged it to be better either to suffer death or to gain the victory before they endured any such distress.' So, 'at daybreak they suddenly rushed forth against the heathen. In the first attack they laid low most of the enemy, including their king. Eight hundred Danes were killed in the attack. Only a few, by fleeing, escaped to their ships.'

Alfred was greatly encouraged on hearing this news, and decided that the time had come for him to rally his forces and take to the field again. Word was sent out giving the appointed place of rendezvous. When the troops heard that their king was still alive, there was a great response, and the forces of Somerset, Wiltshire and Hampshire rallied to him, concentrating near Selwood at a point where those three shires met. It is said that when the assembled army saw the king, they welcomed him as though he had come back from the dead.

The Danes were still encamped at Chippenham. Alfred advanced with his army to Ethandon and there, on the downs, the largest and culminating battle of Alfred's wars was fought. The shield-walls were formed, and the two armies clashed against each other, fighting for hours with sword and axe.

Eventually the Danes turned and fled, with Alfred's thanes in full pursuit. However, this time the enemy did not turn. As with his first battle, so with this: God had once again given the victory to Alfred. Guthrum, king of the entire Viking army, found himself penned in his camp and entirely at King Alfred's mercy.

The chronicler says that by this time the Danes were so terrified by hunger, cold and fear, and so full of despair, that they begged for peace, even offering to give Alfred as many hostages as he cared to pick. With Guthrum and his army now completely in his power, Alfred could have starved them into surrender and slaughtered them to a man. Instead, he invited Guthrum and thirty of his prominent chieftains into his camp, where he entertained them for twelve days.

Here a different kind of miracle was wrought—a miracle

of grace. No doubt it was due to the effect which King Alfred's remarkable Christian life and character had upon his guests.

We do not know precisely what happened during those crucial twelve days, but we believe that Alfred treated Guthrum and his warriors as brothers. He shewed them Christian love; he presented them with costly gifts; and they dined with him at his table. In fact, his whole attitude towards Guthrum was an outstanding example of a well-known Scripture being put into practice: 'If thine enemy hunger, feed him; if he thirst, give him drink: for in so doing thou shalt heap coals of fire on his head. Be not overcome of evil, but overcome evil with good' (Romans 12:20, 21).

Alfred was certainly fulfilling the Lord's command literally: 'Love your enemies, bless them that curse you, do good to them that hate you, and pray for them which despitefully use you, and persecute you; That ye may be the children of your father which is in heaven' (Matthew 5:44, 45a).

And he did it for twelve days!

I do not think it is unreasonable to suppose that Alfred talked to Guthrum about trust in God and faith in Jesus Christ. Indeed, I would suggest that everything points to the fact that he did. For either as a result of his generous treatment, or of his sharing his faith, or of both these things, the miracle occurred.

When the twelve days were over, Guthrum emerged from King Alfred's camp a baptised Christian. Furthermore, according to the historians, Alfred now looked upon him as his son, which is full of significance if 'son in the Lord' is what is meant.

There is no doubt that the Spirit of God had been working with the saintly Alfred whilst he entertained his guest. It had always been King Alfred's long-term spiritual aim to bring about the conversion to Christ of these savage foes, and history shows that this is what God himself intended to do. So Alfred was in line with God's will. In the conversion of the Viking king, a tremendous prize had been won. A whole series of Viking conversions followed.

Winston Churchill was so impressed by this outcome that he wrote: 'We must still wonder how the hearts of these hard-bitten swordsmen and pirates could be changed in a single day.' Then he reflected: 'The workings of the spirit are mysterious.'

But it happened—and it did not stop there!

Such conversions continued until they became quite widespread. In fact, the impact of King Alfred's Christian influence upon these barbaric hordes of Vikings was so great that hundreds, indeed thousands, of them were converted to faith in Christ. No wonder the historian G. M. Trevelyan describes King Alfred in *A Shortened History of England* as 'the champion of Christ against the heathen.'

Nor can anybody say that the majority of these conversions were not genuine. How else could the lives and characters of such notoriously cruel men have been so completely transformed?

Only the saving gospel of Jesus Christ, when it is ministered in the power of the Holy Spirit, can change the heart of a man. Praise God, it did that in terms of thousands of these cruel barbarians, and they now began to settle down in the land as Christian families.

Furthermore, the fact that they abandoned the worship of Woden for Christ is a further sign of the genuineness of many of these conversions. They would not have done that had their conversion not been real.

Such then, was the power of the Wessex king's Christian influence over these invaders. But over and above all that, we can say that the Spirit of God must have been moving in the land in a mighty way throughout the whole of this period. God was overruling all events, and bringing about these miracles of conversion in order to fulfil his long-term purposes in our history. Of that there is no shadow of doubt.

With the conversion of Guthrum, the tide of events so

flowed with King Alfred that he was now able to put into effect those things which were very near to his heart. He was able to encourage the restoration of the Christian religion. He brought about a return to Christian education and learning. He even founded the first of our 'public schools'. Above all else, he set about shaping and fashioning our laws in such a way as to base them on Christian principles and upon the law of Moses as set out in the Ten Commandments. It was upon these laws of Alfred, amplified and developed by his various successors, that English common law was founded.

All this stemmed from the fact that God had overruled and brought about mighty deliverances from the Danes. It would never have been possible otherwise. As G. M. Trevelyan says, 'The course of history would have been very different had not the royal family of Wessex provided a long succession of able warriors and statesmen, including Alfred the Great.' But it was *God* who was doing this. Churchill says of this period that 'We are watching the birth of a nation. The result of Alfred's work was the future mingling of Saxon and Dane in a common Christian England.'

God continued to preserve the royal house of Wessex so that through Alfred's son Edward, and later through his grandson, all the territory in Northumbria and East Anglia was reconquered from the Danes and brought under the rulership of one king. Thus was made possible the further development of Christian laws, education and learning, and the establishment, throughout the land, of the Christian religion which King Alfred had done so much to set on foot.

None of this would have been possible had events gone in the other direction, with the whole land being overrun by the Vikings. In such a way, then, can the hand of God be traced at this very early and formative stage of our history.

Chapter Two

Creating Our Legal System

In a book called *Under God and the Law,* Richard O'Sullivan, KC traces in detail the moral origins of English common law, and in doing so takes us back as far as Roman times, showing that it was then that English law began to take some of its Christian roots.

He points out that there were three great systems of law which have moulded western civilisation as a whole: Roman canon law, Roman civil law and English common law. He is speaking as a lawyer, and not as a theologian, when he says: 'Like the three languages of Latin, Greek and Hebrew which Pilate used in the words of the inscription placed over the head of the Lord Jesus on the Cross, all three of these systems of law, in turn, paid homage to the Lord Jesus Christ.'

O'Sullivan begins to explain what he means when he adds: 'The Roman canon law, for instance, takes as its first principle the existence of God and the divinity of Jesus Christ.' In other words, it takes God into account first and foremost, and also regards Jesus Christ himself as God.

O'Sullivan then goes on to show how Roman canon law developed and what effect it began to have: 'The expansion of the living church and the growth of the canon law led in due course to the abolition of the heathen laws of barbarian people and to the remodelling of their savage customs on more human lines.'

We need to appreciate what he is saying. He is talking of the period when the early Christian church was growing, and when Roman canon law was developing alongside it. He is describing the dynamic effect that the growth of these two influences made upon barbarous people and upon their savage heathen laws and customs.

So powerful was the effect of the New Testament faith, expressed through a living Christian church under the influence of the Holy Spirit, that existing barbaric laws and customs in the various Roman provinces were being changed into something far more noble, and far more Christian. A process of transformation was in progress. A wind of change was blowing throughout the Roman Empire.

All this should cause us in present-day Britain to stop and think.

During the last ten years, have we not seen the gradual removal of Christian laws and the introduction of some that, if not exactly *heathen,* are far from Christian?

Have we not seen the behaviour, if not yet the customs, of many of Britain's people becoming more savage and more violent?

How do we react to the 'muggings' in our towns and cities; the thefts and break-ins; the persecution and molesting of the elderly? What about the violent scenes on football terraces; the trail of wanton destruction, injury and carnage left on railway stations, underground trains and platforms in the wake of football supporters, and in the streets of whatever town or city their team and its rivals happen to be playing? What of the damage done on main-line trains which is now costing British Rail over a million pounds a year?

Hooliganism and vandalism in public parks, in seaside and other resorts, according to the Home Office, now costs the community tens of millions of pounds a year. And there is the violence and indiscipline so rampant in our schools, which reports say is on the increase. A deeply disturbing report, released recently, revealed that most of

London's boys have committed some violence; that 10 per cent of these boys literally *enjoy* violence for its own sake; that the London crime statistics alone, during 1980, showed that robberies and other violent thefts had increased by 20 per cent, and that of those that were arrested for robbery, 60 per cent were under 21.The crime rate throughout the country is still rising alarmingly and is a very real cause for concern.[1]

Then what about the damage done by vandalism to the building industry, now running into millions of pounds annually, and which, for the small builder, could easily result in his being put out of business? Then we have the intimidation that takes place during industrial strikes, with the violent disruption of the picket lines. All this is to say nothing of such crimes as murder and rape, which we see reported almost daily in our newspapers.

I feel obliged to ask: Are all these disturbing developments ominous signs that Britain is now heading back along the road that leads to the barbarism from which she once turned?

Is all this the result of putting back the clock of our own history? As I want to point out later, I think that it might be. In any case, these disturbing developments within our nation would seem to indicate that in recent years a proportion of the British population—and not only the young—has become more savage.

Now we must return to Richard O'Sullivan as he continues to trace how, from the earliest times, Christian influences affected our English system of law: 'This expansion of the living church in those early days and the growth of the Roman canon law led also to the reform of the Roman civil law, of which the rigour and harshness were tempered by Christian conceptions of justice and equity.'

He then sums up his account of what happened in the days of the Roman Empire, and shows the high peak which was reached: 'By the time Emperor Justinian (AD 527–65) drew up the great body of civil law called the "Corpus

Juris Civilis", almost everything in that body of civil law which was new—as compared with the law which had been elaborated by Roman jurists—is the consequence of Christian moral principles.'

There are few rulers in Europe whose work is still so widely remembered as Justinian's, and his final systematisation of Roman law exercised an immediate and continuous influence throughout the then Roman Empire, and later throughout the western world as a whole.

So we can see what had been happening.

From Bethlehem onwards, the life, teaching and example of our Lord Jesus Christ—followed, after his crucifixion, resurrection and ascension by the dynamic message of early Christianity—had an ever-increasing and marked effect upon the Roman Empire. Countless lives were transformed under the power of the Holy Spirit until, eventually, those in authority were affected. Then these people in authority began to remould and refashion the two existing systems of Roman law. In consequence the people in the provinces—many of whom were barbarians—and their laws were brought more and more into line with the revealed will of Almighty God.

It is significant, too, that Christianity had brought about such a change in the Roman Empire by the time of Emperor Justinian, that when he published the great works which make up the 'Corpus Juris Civilis', he issued each one of them 'in the name of our Lord Jesus Christ', and, by so doing, testified to the world concerning the influence which Christianity had had upon his own life and times, and of his deep devotion, as emperor, to doing the will of God.

All that is established historically. Interestingly enough, O'Sullivan then takes us on a few years to a point in English history just beyond the year 597, which is nearly three hundred years before King Alfred. Here he traces another stage in the developing process of law. And it is English law to which he refers this time: 'The law of England, even in its first recorded utterances, reveals the influence of the

Christian faith.' That takes us back as far as English written legal records go.

'This fact', he says, 'is revealed and established in a decree issued as far back as Ethelbert of Kent and which is said to have been issued in the lifetime of Augustine.'

I find that very significant indeed. For when Augustine landed in Kent in 597, King Ethelbert of Kent was a worshipper of the heathen gods, Thor and Woden. As king of Kent, he held sway over great areas of terrain; so much so, that he also bore the title 'Overlord of England'.

Shortly after Augustine arrived, Ethelbert, under the influence of Augustine's monks, was converted to Christianity. It was the result of his conversion to Jesus Christ from the worship of these heathen gods, that Ethelbert fashioned one of the earliest recorded English laws so as to give it Christian influence. We have the evidence in the decree to which O'Sullivan refers. The historian H. A. L. Fisher tells us in *A History of Europe* that 'the stream which was eventually to broaden out into a great river of the English common law, began under Ethelbert of Kent, at a time when Roman jurisprudence was speaking its valediction in the Institutes of Justinian, and receiving substantial additions to its volume under the kings of Wessex.' The stream of English common law began then, with the conversion of Ethelbert of Kent. And any conversion, if it is a true one, is an act of God. In such ways, therefore, have our nation's laws been given Christian influence from the earliest traceable beginnings. It was all connected with this continuing movement of the Holy Spirit of God, as Christianity began to spread westwards from its original cradle in the Holy Land.

Notice again that it is Britain's legal authorities and historians, not the theologians, who have readily given such testimony. It is they who have provided the evidence which establishes, beyond any shadow of doubt, that there was this powerful process of Christian impact and influence operating on these three great systems of law which moulded the whole of western civilisation.

Why go into all this? Because everything which took place in those very early days has much to do with what developed later in our English history.

If we move on another two hundred and fifty years after King Alfred, to the days of Henry II, the Plantagenet (1154–89), we reach that other significant landmark in the Christian history of England and English law.

If King Alfred the Great was England's first lawgiver, then Henry Plantagenet was her second. Of him, Winston Churchill wrote that 'No man has left a deeper mark upon our laws and institutions than he.... Henry II possessed an instinct for the problems and government of law.... His fame will live with the English Constitution, and the English common law.'

When Henry arrived in England from the Continent to become king, something tantamount to a miracle happened in relation to the continuing Christian influence upon this country's laws and institutions. For there were two systems of law which he could have chosen. One was the Roman system, which still dominated the Continent and other parts of the world. The other was the English common law.

Since Henry Plantagenet was by birth and upbringing a Continental, and since he was fully acquainted with the Roman system, it would have been quite natural, and indeed to be expected, if he had chosen to adopt it in England. The remarkable thing is that he did not do so. Under the determined influence of his kingship, it was English common law which prevailed—one of those almost inexplicable 'twists' in our history. Or was it more than that? Since God had seen to it that our country's laws had already come under Christian influence, I think that he was overruling once again in order to ensure that this foundation remained.

However that may be, Winston Churchill declared of Henry Plantagenet: 'The measure of this great king's achievements was that he had laid the foundations of the English common law upon which succeeding generations

would build.... It was this system of English common law',
says Churchill, 'this system of English criminal and civil
procedure, which, having prevailed over all other systems
under Henry II, and which, by the time Edward I, his
grandson, had died in 1303, had settled into a mould and a
tradition which governed the English people, and which
in the mass, still governs the English-speaking peoples
today. Its main outlines were not to be altered.'

Thus boasted Churchill with considerable pride. In
effect, he was saying that the *Christian* system of law had
prevailed, and in doing so had determined the way in
which the English people would be governed in the future.

'Its main outlines were not to be altered', proclaimed
Churchill! And he could add: 'England became finally and
for all time one coherent kingdom based on Christianity'.

Ever since the days of Henry Plantagenet, lawyers and
historians who have traced the moral and spiritual origins
of the common law of England have reached the same
conclusion. Hear what just a few of the outstanding legal
authorities have said.

Blackstone wrote in his commentaries: 'All the great
lawyers from Henry Bracton, Judge of Assize in AD 1250
to Lord Mansfield of more recent times—all these great
lawyers proclaimed that ethics had their first principle in
God, and jurisprudence was a part of ethics.' (Henry
Bracton, as Judge of Assize in the reign of Henry II,
produced his famous 900-page book entitled *A Tract on
the Laws and Customs of England*.)

Ginsberg, writing on *Justice in Society*, said: 'The ultimate justice of law is that it serves moral ends. On this
conviction, endorsed by Christians, our legal system, and
indeed the whole of western civilization has been built.'

When George Polson, QC, Recorder of Exeter, was
delivering an address on the subject of 'The Christian
Content of the Rule of Law and its Contribution to Human
Rights' on 19 February 1969, he summed it all up by
declaring: 'The true basis of English common law is
Christianity, which itself was founded on older principles

which are enshrined in Judaism.' By 'enshrined in Judaism' he meant, of course, the principles which are laid down in the Old Testament.

'So', Polson concluded, 'to speak of the Christian content of the Rule of Law is to speak of the Christian content of English Law as a whole.'

There is thus an abundance of historical and legal evidence to establish that the laws of this country, which have long stood the test of time, are Christian in origin, and owe much of their influence to the Bible.

Some of this evidence is in stone, and anybody travelling up the Strand towards Fleet Street can see it for himself. For when the new Law Courts were built in the Strand in the year 1873, a full-size figure of the Lord Jesus Christ was placed high above the main entrance. It is said to be the only statue of its kind in the United Kingdom.

George Polson draws attention to this, and says: 'That was not put there just as an architect's foible. It was put there because of a belief that the administration of the law in this country is founded on the Christian ethic.'

It was these laws, whose history we have traced, which eventually became embodied in the British Constitution, and which, by Act of Parliament, are embodied in the Coronation Oath. When the Sovereign is crowned, he or she is required to place one hand on the open Bible, and is then required to take a solemn oath before Almighty God 'to uphold to the utmost of my power, the Laws of God within the Realm, and the true profession of the Christian Gospel.'

Parliament, through its peers, pledges itself to support the sovereign in this. This is the British position constitutionally.

Anyone who pauses to reflect on these amazing developments down the centuries of British history, must surely find it impossible to reach any other conclusion than that the hand of God has been on that history to ensure that this country was based on Christian laws.

Note
1. From the Report of the Commissioner of Police of the Metropolis, 1980, HMSO.

Chapter Three

Defeat for the Spanish Armada

The defeat of the Spanish Armada is one of the instances in English history when God intervened in order to ensure that the Protestant Christian position in England should continue to be maintained.

The historical background to this momentous event was, of course the Reformation and, as we saw in Volume 1, this movement of the Holy Spirit of God had been spreading increasingly across Europe. Spain, as head of Roman Catholic Europe, was strongly resisting it, whilst England, on the other hand, had become Protestant. Because of this same work of the Holy Spirit, the religious outlook of her people had changed. There was a Puritan and Protestant influence abroad in the land, and London, for instance, was Protestant to the core. Throughout the country, the English church was rapidly settling on its new foundations of a Reformed Christian faith. In southern Scotland, largely under the influence of people like John Knox, the Reformation had been made secure, and therefore the first essential steps had been taken towards the union of the two countries. Furthermore, Queen Elizabeth the First of England was, by early training and upbringing, strongly Protestant, and, on ascending the throne, she was determined to continue as such. Matters were clinched when, in the very early years of her reign, England became for the first time a Protestant country by *law*.

Philip the Second of Spain, head of the Spanish Empire, was greatly incensed by these developments. He was a devout and dutiful Roman Catholic ruler, who considered it to be his principle mission in life to uproot 'heresy' from his own dominions and to support the Roman Catholic faith throughout the world. In the process, he would not countenance any opposition.

England, by going Protestant, had become a real thorn in his flesh, for she now stood as a major challenge to the Roman faith and to Philip's dreams of its expansion.

On the Continent he was set, for instance, on reconquering the Netherlands and extending Spain's Roman Catholic influence there, and he saw that England threatened to stand in the way of his doing so. He also had dreams of world domination.

The Spanish Empire had already extended its dominions to the West Indies and the western coast of the South American continent as far as Mexico and Peru, but the Elizabethan 'mariners of England' were making repeated attacks with their men-of-war on his Spanish galleons, thus making Philip's empire increasingly insecure.

For a long time he had been doing his utmost to rid himself of the embarrassment which this 'Island Bastion for Truth' caused him by threatening constantly to stand in his way.

There was the further inconvenience of England's independence from Rome. On account of this, Pope Pius V had excommunicated Elizabeth in 1570 and had decreed that she should be deposed. Philip would not tolerate an England permanently severed from the Holy See, and increasingly assumed the role of the authority called to execute the Pope's decree of deposition.

Plot after plot had been laid in England to overthrow her Protestant Queen and to reintroduce the Roman Catholic faith in the realm, and all these attempts had been encouraged by Philip himself, by the Pope, and by English Roman Catholic exiles operating against England from the Continent.

What is more, all such plotting and intrigue had been greatly assisted by a new and formidable type of missionary who had begun to slip into the country, namely, the Jesuit heralds of the Counter-Reformation, whose lives were dedicated not only to re-establishing Roman Catholicism in England, but throughout the whole of Christendom as well. However, at this particular time, it was England which had been singled out as the main target of the attack.

Churchill describes the situation in this way: 'The whole force of the Counter-Reformation was unloosed against the one, united Protestant country in Europe. It seemed that if England were destroyed, then Protestantism could be stamped out in every other land.'

Such were the issues, and all this provides the historical background to the story of the Armada.

Suddenly events were brought to a head. It was discovered that the Roman Catholic Mary Queen of Scots had connived in a plot to destroy Elizabeth and assume the English throne herself. There was a great outcry from Elizabeth's subjects all over the land, for if Mary were to become Queen, the work of the Reformation would be undone. The alternative was civil war, with consequences too dreadful even to be contemplated. Parliament, people and ministers therefore prevailed on Elizabeth for Mary's execution, and eventually obtained it on grounds of treason. In Philip's eyes this was England's final act of defiance towards her enemies. With the execution of Mary, war with England was inevitable.

Philip had already commissioned his subjects in 1580 to prepare for the conquest of England. His plans to invade these islands were now set in train. The objects were to depose Elizabeth, set up the Infanta of Spain in her place, and restore the Roman Catholic faith by bringing this country once again under the dominion and power of Rome. The Spanish Armada was thus conceived in the spirit of a religious crusade, and England's Protestant position was at stake.

The base from which the invasion was to be launched was the Netherlands. An army, 16,000 strong, had been mustered in the vicinity of Dunkirk and, in order to ensure the success of the landing operation, the Duke of Parma, who was regarded as the most accomplished soldier and diplomatist in the whole of the Spanish Empire and the greatest general of the century, was put in charge of it.

In order to guarantee that army a safe passage across the English Channel, the plan was for a Spanish fleet of some 130 ships to sail from Spanish ports, proceed across the Bay of Biscay and up the English Channel to Dunkirk and Nieuport, and there rendezvous with the Duke of Parma. When he had embarked his army on transport vessels, the Spanish fleet was to escort it across the Channel to England where the landing was to take place. The army would then proceed to invade the south of England, overthrow Elizabeth, and set up the Infanta.

But like so many carefully laid plans—military or otherwise—it did not take into account the existence of an Almighty God.

At least three great miracles happened.

In the *first* place, no sooner had the Armada left the Tagus on 20 May 1588 and nosed out to sea, than this great fleet of Spanish warships was battered by a southern gale. They found the very elements against them, and so much damage was done to the ships that the whole fleet had to put into Corunna to refit.

This major set-back meant that the whole operation was delayed for two months—which leads me to the firm belief that Almighty God is a great strategist! For this delay gave England two months' breathing-space in which to make the final preparations for meeting the invasion.

Furthermore, as we shall see, the delay also resulted in the Spaniards' calculation of the tides being completely upset.

Meanwhile, an English army of 20,000 men was

assembled at Tilbury; others mustered in adjacent counties, ready to meet Parma's army when it crossed over from the Flemish shore. Warning beacons were prepared. All England was alerted. The main English fleet gathered in the port of Plymouth, ready to intercept the enemy fleet when it began to approach the western entrance to the Channel. At the eastern end of the Channel, a small squadron of the Queen's ships was concentrated in order to keep watch on Parma and his movements. All this was possible because of the breathing-space which had been granted.

This respite also gave the English admirals plenty of time to consider their strategy. The same storms which had repulsed the Spaniards had driven Lord Howard of Effingham, the commander of the English fleet, and the famous Drake, back into Plymouth when they had already been at sea intent on attacking the Spanish coast. So they were now ready to meet the Armada when it did arrive. I venture to suggest that this also can be regarded as a providential overruling.

On 12 July 1588, the Armada set sail the second time. It was a formidable fleet by any standards, carrying 2,500 guns and more than 30,000 men, two-thirds of whom were soldiers. It was considered to be invincible.

News that it was approaching the Lizard reached Plymouth harbour on the evening of 19 July. A broad crescent formation of its galleons, armed merchantmen, Mediterranean galleys and transport craft was sweeping past Plymouth into the English Channel.

Howard and Drake put to sea against light but adverse winds, with about 130 ships. By tacking skilfully they got to windward of the Spaniards the next day and, whilst carefully keeping out of range themselves, proceeded to engage with their heavier long-range guns.

There was a four-hour gun battle, followed by a nine-day running fight up Channel. That Channel passage proved to be torture for the Spaniards, whose soldiers stood in ranks on deck with their musketeers in front of their pikemen, waiting in vain for the English ships to draw near enough to board. Instead, the English remained out of range and raked the Spaniards' decks with their superior guns, killing their crews and demoralising the soldiers, whilst suffering hardly any losses themselves.

In the agony of it all, the Spanish sailors exclaimed: 'God has deserted us.'

When the Armada had reached the eastern end of the Channel, it made the fatal mistake of anchoring in Calais Roads. The squadron of the Queen's ships which had been stationed there, now joined the main fleet in the Straits, which meant that the whole of the English sea power was combined against the Spaniards.

As the Armada lay at anchor, a council of war was held on the English flagship during the evening of 28 July, and the decision was taken that Drake should send his fire-ships amongst the crowded Spanish galleons. When this was done, the Spaniards cut their cables and stood out to the open sea in panic, losing some of their ships in collision. One of the largest of their galleons, the *San Lorenzo,* lost its rudder in the midst of all this confusion and drifted aground in Calais harbour where its crew was interned.

Despite the demoralising effect of all this, the rest of the Spanish fleet, still intent on fulfilling their mission to rendezvous with Parma and his armies, and finding a south-south-west wind behind them, made eastwards towards Gravelines and Dunkirk.

Then came another extraordinary and unexpected turn of events: the *second* miracle. The Duke of Medina-Sidonia, who was in command of the Armada, had sent messengers on ahead to the awaiting Duke of Parma at Dunkirk, announcing his arrival off shore. Therefore, when his galleons reached Gravelines Sandbanks, he fully expected to find Parma's troop-laden transport vessels coming out to meet him in order to be convoyed to England.

Not a sail was in sight.

There were two conditions required to sail out of

Dunkirk harbour. First, there had to be a favourable wind; and, secondly, it was only possible to sail out on a high tide.

Neither of these conditions prevailed. Furthermore, not only was it low water in Dunkirk harbour, but the tides were at the neap, which means that the phase of the moon was such that the difference between high and low water was far less than it would have been at any other period of the month. In fact, there was very little water in the harbour at all!

So just at that point when these galleons, which had battled their way up the whole length of the Channel, were approaching to meet him, Parma, the greatest and most acomplished soldier in the whole of the Spanish Empire, found himself and his armies well and truly locked in harbour by adverse winds and tides.

Who had arranged it? Not only would I say that God Almighty is a great strategist, but I would also suggest that he is a past master at delaying tactics! For the state of the tide at Dunkirk might well have been different had the Armada been able to arrive off Gravelines towards the end of the first week in June as had originally been planned, and had it not been delayed and damaged by those fierce storms in May.

I submit that there could not be any clearer example of England being delivered by a direct intervention of God.

With no army to escort across the Channel, the awaiting Armada turned to face its pursuers. A desperate gun battle raged at close quarters for about eight hours; three of the Spanish ships were sunk; others were mauled and ruined; and four or five more were driven on the sandbanks and wrecked. But still the bulk of the Spanish vessels remained.

Suddenly, at this crucial moment, when it seemed that hardly a Spanish ship would be able to get away, both sides ran out of ammunition. The English also found that they were short of food, so some of them had to break off the action and put back into harbour.

The work of destruction had been left to a mightier foe than either Howard or Drake, and this is where the *third* miracle took place.

As the tormented Armada headed northwards out of the fight—not once turning on the now silent English ships which followed them—it was caught by a fierce gale and driven, in mountainous seas, by strong winds and racing tides round the north of Scotland, whilst some of its ships were driven even further north, where they were wrecked on the coast of Norway.

When the remainder of the galleons had rounded Scotland, the wind suddenly shifted to the north-east, compelling them, as they were heading southwards for home, to make for the west coast of Ireland, where seventeen were driven ashore on the rocky coast and perished. No less than 5,000 lives were lost.

The English fleet, on the other hand, had not lost a single ship, and scarcely a hundred men.

To the English people, the defeat of the Spanish Armada was a stupendous miracle. There was no question whatsoever that it had been due to a mighty intervention of God.

As for the English sailors who took part, history tells us that the Elizabethan mariners believed in an overruling Providence who governed the waves and the winds, and that in his hands rested the fate of men and of nations.

True, the Armada had been outmanoeuvred, outsailed, and outgunned in the Channel by its nimbler English opponents; true, the Spaniards had been badly bruised and beaten in the great sea battle off Gravelines; but even then a great number of their vessels had remained intact.

Yet at the time, it was not to Howard and Drake, nor to the navigational skill of our great Elizabethan captains, nor to the accuracy and fire-power of our guns and gunners, and not even to Drake's fire-ships at Calais that the defeat of the Armada was attributed.

Queen Elizabeth the First understood, and made sure that it was recorded for all generations to see. The words which she ordered to be engraved on the monument overlooking Plymouth Sound can still be seen today: 'He blew with his winds and they were scattered.'

Elizabeth also left a permanent record concerning the main issue involved, and the real reason why God had intervened. For, to commemorate this great deliverance, she ordered gold and silver medals to be struck. On one side of the silver medal we have the name 'Jehovah' inscribed in Hebrew, together with the words 'He blew... and they were scattered.' On the other side we find the engraving of a church founded upon a rock; and, underneath, the Latin inscription, 'I am assailed, but not injured.'

Winston Churchill, in more recent times, made his assessment in this way: 'The Armada had completed the process which persecution under Mary had begun, that of making England a Protestant Christian country.'

Thus the course of English history had been set for many centuries to come. But what of Europe?

The victory over the Spanish fleet had been so decisive that the shadow of Spanish power—which for thirty years had darkened the political scene—had now been removed.

G. M. Trevelyan comments: 'The mighty power that seemed on the eve of universal lordship over the white man and all his new dominions had put out its full strength and failed. All Europe at once recognised that by this single event, *a turning point in history had been reached* [my italics]. The fate of the Armada demonstrated to all the world that the rule of the seas had passed from the Mediterranean peoples to the Northern folk. This meant not only the survival of the Reformation in Northern Europe to a degree not fully determined, but the world leadership of the Northerners in the new oceanic era.' England itself emerged from the Armada year as a first class sea power.

Let us never forget that it was Almighty God who had changed the course of history. All this was due entirely to these mighty interventions which had brought about such an utter defeat of the Spaniards.

As to the effect of this defeat on the Spanish nation

itself, it is interesting to discover that at least one historian records that the country was later brought to believe that, in the defeat of its Armada, Spain had been punished by an act of judgment because the nation had deserted God.

It is of deep significance to learn that, in the view of the Spanish priests of the time, the first essential step towards the revival and recovery of the Spanish nation was not to refashion or rebuild its sorely stricken navy, or even to attempt to restore the nation's economy. It was rather to seek to propitiate an angry and jealous God—a lesson which Britain surely needs to learn today.

Furthermore, history confirms that it was God's intention that the Protestant position in England should remain. Another Armada was gathered in the ports of western Spain in 1597 and was defeated entirely by the weather. In the summer of that year, when it became obvious that another 'enterprise against England' was about to sail, the Earl of Essex was given command of an expedition to intercept it. The English ships sailed as far as the Azores, but saw no sign of this great fleet whose passage they were sent to bar and decided to remain in that area. The Armada put out into the Bay of Biscay with the seas clear of defending ships, since the English expedition was now behind them. Once again the winds of heaven intervened, and England was saved from the approaching danger. The badly manned Spanish galleons tottered into a northerly gale which caused some of them to be sunk and the remainder to be scattered.

King Philip was kneeling in his chapel in the Escorial, praying for his ships, when the disorganised fleet crept back into its ports. Before the news of their return could reach him, he was seized with a paralytic stroke, and the tale of their failure was brought to him on his death-bed. So his second expedition against England had been thwarted by an overruling of God—which simply shows that, if what a man (even the ruler of an empire) plans to do is directly against the will of God, no matter how much or how earnestly he prays, his prayers will avail nothing.

Chapter Four

The Year 1918

My father, who was in action on the Somme during the First World War, used to talk to me as a boy, and to many of his friends, about the 'Angels of Mons', but it was only two or three years ago that I came across an authentic account of what happened.

In the Spring of 1918, the Germans had broken through the Allied line. Heavy casualties were sustained, reserves were practically exhausted, and the situation was becoming quite desperate for the Allied armies. What happened next was described in an article which appeared in the winter 1942 journal of the Brigade of Guards.

As the break-through continued, 'the Germans concentrated high explosive and machine-gun fire at Béthune, in Belgium, the focal point of their advance, preparatory to a bayonet attack in mass formation. Suddenly the enemy shell fire lifted and concentrated on a slight rise beyond the town. The ground here was absolutely bare—yet enemy machine-guns and shells raked it from end to end with a hail of lead. As suddenly as it started, the enemy's fire ceased. The dense line of German troops, which had started to move forward to victory in mass formation, halted dead. And as the British watched, they saw that line break! The Germans threw down everything they had—and fled in frantic panic.'

What was the explanation? Why this sudden dramatic turn of events?

It was a senior German officer, a member of the Prussian Guard who was taken prisoner immediately afterwards, who gave the explanation.

'The order was given to advance in mass formation, and our troops were marching behind us singing their way to victory when Fritz, my lieutenant here, said: "Herr Kapitan, just look at that open ground behind Béthune. There is a Brigade of Cavalry coming up through the smoke drifting across it. They must be mad, these English to advance against such a force as ours in the open. I suppose they must be cavalry or one of their colonial forces, for, see, they are all in white uniform and are mounted on white horses."

'"Strange", I said; "I have never heard of the English having any white-uniformed cavalry, whether colonial or not. They have all been fighting on foot for several years past, and anyway they are in khaki, not white."

'"Well, they are plain enough", he replied. "See, our guns have got their range now; they will be blown to pieces in no time."

'We saw the shells bursting among the horses and their riders, all of whom came forward at a quiet walk-trot, in parade-ground formation, each man and horse in his exact place.

'Shortly afterwards our machine-guns opened a heavy fire, raking the advancing cavalry with a hail of lead; but on they came, and not a single man or horse fell.

'Steadily they advanced, clear in the shining sunlight, and a few paces in front of them rode their leader, a fine figure of a man, whose hair, like spun gold, shone in an aura around his head. By his side was a great sword, but his hands lay quietly holding the reins, as his huge white charger bore him proudly forward.

'In spite of heavy shell and concentrated machine-gun fire the White Cavalry advanced, remorsely as fate, like the incoming tide surging over a sandy beach....

'Then a great fear fell on me, and I turned to flee; yes, I, an officer of the Prussian Guard, fled, panic stricken, and around me were hundreds of terrified men, whimpering like children, throwing away their arms and accoutrements in order not to have their movements impeded...all running. Their one desire was to get away from that advancing White Cavalry; above all, from their awe-inspiring leader whose hair shone like a golden aureole.

'That is all I have to tell you. We are beaten. The German Army is broken. There may be fighting, but we have lost the war; we are beaten—by the White Cavalry ...I cannot understand...I cannot understand.'

This is taken from the account of the staff captain, 1st Corps Intelligence, 1st British Army Headquarters, 1916-18, who was present himself and took the statement from the German officer. The article continues:

'Many German prisoners were examined during the days that followed, and their accounts tallied in substance with the one given here.'

Thus during two days' fierce fighting around Mons, the German advance was halted long enough to allow the British Expeditionary Force to withdraw to safer positions, and begin to prepare a counter-attack.

Much has been written on the subject of the 'Angels of Mons' and there have been many versions of the phenomenon; but it is not inconsistent to believe that they were all substantially true, though they differed in certain aspects. A number of accounts are gathered together and examined by Harold Begbie in his book *On the Side of the Angels*.

It is plain that those who were there, both German and British, were well aware that something by way of a divine intervention had taken place to halt the German advance and to turn the tide in favour of the Allies at this very critical time, and they talked about it for years afterwards.

*   *   *   *

There was another, and even more significant turning-point.

When the Germans had launched their offensive in March 1918, they had broken through that part of the Allied line which was held by the Fifth Army, with the result that British arms were brought close to disaster. Heavy casualties were sustained; reserves were practically exhausted; our line was driven back a long way; and the connection between the British and French armies was stretched almost to breaking point. As the news broke back home in Britain, it became very apparent that the British army in France had suffered a serious reverse and that we were on the very brink of losing the war. A period of depression set in throughout the country during the months immediately following this disaster, and the morale of the people of Britain sank to its lowest ebb.

Apparently this alarming turn of events caused a number of people to think. British forces had been close to defeat on a number of occasions during almost four years of war, and yet disaster had not quite overwhelmed us. Lieutenant-General Sir William Dobbie, making this observation in his book *A Very Present Help*, adds that it is equally true to say that, at other times in the same period, we had been within an ace of sweeping success, and yet complete success had not been achieved. In his view, it seemed as though God was witholding success from us, although keeping us from disaster.

Another point which General Dobbie makes is that, on the Western Front, it was generally true to say that the weather had been unfavourable to our own operations, whilst it favoured those of the enemy.

These things, he says, gave many people food for thought. There were also those who noticed that these phenomena coincided with a complete absence of national prayer to God. For whilst it was true to say that many individuals and organisations had urged the people of Britain to seek God in prayer during this period, there was no move from the Government, or from anybody in authority.

Suddenly there was a change. A proclamation went out

that it was proposed to hold a National Day of Prayer on 4 August 1918—the fourth anniversary of Britain's declaration of war against Germany.

This was an unprecedented act.

It was to be led by His Majesty King George V in the form of a service in St Margaret's, Westminster, and designed to be truly representative of the nation and empire, with the ministers of the Crown present, supported by both Houses of Parliament. The King was to lead the people in turning to God in prayer on a great state occasion, just like some of the godly kings of the Old Testament had done.

Had somebody in high places, in this critical hour of the nation's history, heard God saying: 'Call upon me in the day of trouble. I will deliver thee, and thou shalt glorify me'? And had they decided to do something about it?

Whatever the case, General Dobbie tells us that the decision to issue the call for this National Day of Prayer was taken by the Government round about the first of July.

'Immediately that decision was taken', records General Dobbie, 'a remarkable change came over the situation. On 18 July, Marshal Foch gained a signal victory over the Germans between the Aisne and the Marne, and caused them to effect a hasty and costly withdrawal.'

It was a clear case of 'before they call I will answer, and while they are yet speaking I will hear' (Isa. 65:24).

On 4 August, the National Day of Prayer was duly observed, and it had the most amazing results. Just four days later an Allied attack on the Western Front began, during the opening stages of which the tide was so turned in the Allies' favour that an advance commenced, which never ceased until the Armistice was signed on 11 November 1918. It really was miraculous.

General Dobbie says: 'On August 8 began the Battle of Amiens—the first of a series of brilliant victories in the British sector, which, in a hundred days, brought about the complete downfall of the German army, and brought to an end the power of the German nation to continue the war.'

Those 'brilliant victories' were victories in which God was seen to be at work in many wonderful ways.

We are fortunate in having both 'inside' and 'outside' accounts of the events of those momentous one hundred days. For instance, just two days after the attack was launched, *The Times* declared on 10 August: 'The new offensive initiated under the command of Sir Douglas Haig is one of the greatest and most gratifying surprises of the war. Even the weather favoured the Allies, for the assault was launched under cover of a thick mist. No offensive in which the British army has participated has ever made so much progress on the opening day.'

Some days later, a jubilant *Times* leader reported: 'During the last day or two, the pace of the German retreat on the Western Front has been accelerated. This is a good sign. Armies claiming to retire by their own choice do not hurry back as the Germans have been doing.'

This same newspaper's special correspondent had reason to record at the end of the year: 'The great advance fully launched in a flowing tide on August 8 swept all before it, until the armies heard the call "Cease Fire!" on Armistice Day. Surely it was more than mere coincidence that depression was turned into triumph *immediately following the National Day of Prayer. Victory was in the air from that day forward*' (my italics).

That is what Fleet Street had to say when viewing events, as it were, from the 'outside'.

But the story as seen from the 'inside' is even more remarkable. General Sir William Dobbie, who became Governor of Malta at a critical stage in World War Two, was on the staff of the Commander-in-Chief, Sir Douglas Haig, in the Operations Section of General Staff Head-quarters in France. He provides further insight as to how God was working on behalf of the Allies, particularly with regard to the weather.

'The weather, which hitherto had mostly been unfavourable to us, now was just what we needed.

'It was decided that our first attack should take place in

front of Amiens. It was obviously most necessary to keep the enemy in ignorance of this decision, and elaborate precautions were taken to make him think that the attack would be launched elsewhere.

'To launch an offensive on the scale intended, involved the collection of a vast force of all arms. The component parts of this force were mostly moved by night, and hidden, so far as was possible, by day. But the day came when all the available cover around and behind Amiens was full to saturation-point. Many units had to be disposed in the open, and, eventually, for the two final days before the opening of the assault, the number of such units was so great that concealment was impossible, and any hostile aircraft coming over would be bound to see them. If that had happened, there was only one inference which the Germans could have drawn, and surprise would have been impossible. But during those two days, the weather was such that flying was almost impossible. In any event, no German aircraft came over; the surprise was complete, and our attack overwhelmingly successful.'

'This', says General Dobbie, 'coupled as it was with the first official day of National Prayer, and the unexpectedly complete successes which followed, caused many people to think seriously. Many of those in high places thought that it was a clear example of cause and effect when we gained striking success after asking God for his help.'

German sources also added their testimony to the significant part which the weather had played in this surprising and remarkable change in fortunes.

'The Allies were favoured by a thick fog', they complained!

So there was plenty of evidence available that God had worked to turn the tide on the Western Front from that momentous July 1918 decision onwards. He moved to deliver in response to the nation's prayers, which is proof positive that Almighty God not only answers the prayers of individuals. He also answers the prayers of nations.

Chapter Five

Dunkirk, 1940

May 1940 was a time of grave crisis for the British Empire and for the whole civilised world.

On 10 May Hitler had launched his blitzkrieg against the Low Countries and France. By the end of the second week in May the French defences had been broken. German panzer forces, led by Rommel and his 7th Panzer Division, burst through, and with lightning speed began a rapid advance across France and Belgium. Very soon Rommel's armoured pincer movement was threatening the British army with encirclement, and our forces were being obliged to withdraw.

Back at home Mr Churchill feared that it would be his hard lot to announce the greatest military disaster in our long history, whilst on 27 May the German High Command went so far as to boast that 'The British army is encircled and our troops are proceeding to its annihilation.'

With the entire front collapsing rapidly, the decision was reached at home to evacuate our forces from the Continent. But the only port from which to evacuate the British Expeditionary Force was Dunkirk, and that was already being seriously threatened by the Germans. Taking stock of the predicament, Churchill said in *The Second World War*: 'I thought—and some good judges agreed with me—that perhaps 20,000 or 30,000 men might be re-embarked.... The whole root and core and brain of the British army...seemed about to perish upon the field, or to be led into ignominious and starving captivity.' All therefore seemed about to be lost.

But Britain had a godly Sovereign. Seeing this situation developing, His Majesty King George VI requested that Sunday, 26 May should be observed as a National Day of Prayer. In a stirring broadcast, he called the people of Britain and of the Empire to commit their cause to God. Together with members of the Cabinet, the King attended Westminster Abbey, whilst millions of his subjects in all parts of the Commonwealth and Empire flocked to the churches to join in prayer. Britain was given inspiring leadership in those days, and her people responded immediately when this kind of initiative was taken. The whole nation was at prayer on that Sunday. The scene outside Westminster Abbey was remarkable—photographs show long queues of people who could not even get in, the Abbey was so crowded! So much so, that the following morning the *Daily Sketch* exclaimed, 'Nothing like it has ever happened before.'

In its hour of deep distress a heart-cry from both monarch and people alike was going up to God in prayer. And that cry did not go unanswered. For very soon, at least three miracles were seen to happen.

The first was that for some reason—which has never yet been fully explained—Hitler overruled his generals and halted the advance of his armoured columns at the very point when they could have proceeded to the British army's annihilation. They were now only ten miles away! Later, Mr Churchill asserted in his memoirs that this was because Hitler undoubtedly believed 'that his air superiority would be sufficient to prevent a large-scale evacuation by sea.'

That is very significant in terms of the second miracle.

A storm of unprecedented fury broke over Flanders on Tuesday, 28 May, grounding the German Luftwaffe squadrons and enabling the British army formations, now eight to twelve miles from Dunkirk, to move up on foot to the coast in the darkness of the storm and the violence of the rain, with scarcely any interruption from aircraft, which were unable to operate in such turbulent conditions.

The Fuehrer had obviously not taken the weather into his reckoning, nor the One who controls the weather!

And the third miracle? Despite the storm in Flanders, a great calm—such as has rarely been experienced—settled over the English Channel during the days which followed, and its waters became as still as a mill pond.

It was this quite extraordinary calm which enabled a vast armada of little ships, big ships, warships, privately owned motor-cruisers from British rivers and estuaries—in fact, almost anything that would float—to ply back and forth in a desperate bid to rescue as many of our men as possible. There were so many ships involved in the evacuation that this is the way in which Douglas Bader, the legless Spitfire fighter ace, who sped over with his squadrons from the fighter base at Martlesham, near Ipswich, to help cover the operation, described the scene in *Fight for the Sky*: 'The sea from Dunkirk to Dover during these days of the evacuation looked like any coastal road in England on a bank holiday. It was solid with shipping. One felt one could walk across without getting one's feet wet, or that's what it looked like from the air. There were naval escort vessels, sailing dinghies, rowing boats, paddle-steamers, indeed every floating device known in this country. They were all taking British soldiers from Dunkirk back home. You could identify Dunkirk from the Thames estuary by the huge pall of black smoke rising straight up into a windless sky from the oil tanks which were ablaze just inside the harbour.'

Yet still, to a very large extent, the German air squadrons were unable to intervene. Certainly not in force, nor in the way Hitler had anticipated, for so many of these squadrons still remained grounded. So much so that General Halder, Chief of the German General Staff, three days after the High Command had so proudly boasted that the British Army was about to be annihilated, was obliged to record in his diary on 30 May that 'Bad weather has grounded the Luftwaffe, and now we must stand by and watch countless thousands of the enemy getting away to England right under our noses.'

Even though some squadrons did get through, it seems that yet another miracle happened. Many of the troops on the beaches were favoured with a strange immunity. When about 400 men were being machine-gunned and bombed, systematically, by about sixty enemy aircraft, one man who flung himself down with the rest reported that, after the strafing was over, he was amazed to find that there was not a single casualty.

Another man, a chaplain, was likewise machine-gunned and bombed as he lay on the beach. After what seemed an eternity, he realized he had not been hit, and rose to his feet to find that the sand all around where he had been lying was pitted with bullet holes, and that his figure was outlined on the ground.

Truly, amazing things were happening. There were signs on every hand that an intervening Power was at work. Officers and men alike had seen the hand of God, powerful to save, delivering them from the hands of a mighty foe who, humanly speaking, had them at its mercy.

And they were not slow to say so. Even Fleet Street has placed it on record that two miracles had made possible what had seemed impossible.

So grateful was the nation for this mighty deliverance that Sunday, 9 June 1940 was appointed as a Day of National Thanksgiving. On the eve of that day, C. B. Mortlock stated in an article in *The Daily Telegraph* that 'the prayers of the nation were answered', and that 'the God of hosts himself had supported the valiant men of the British Expeditionary Force.'

'Two great wonders stand forth', he said. 'On them have turned the fortune of our troops.

'I have talked to officers and men who have got safely back to England, and all of them tell of these two phenomena. The first was the great storm which broke over Flanders on Tuesday, 28 May. The second was the great calm which settled on the English Channel during the days following.

'Officers of high rank do not hesitate to put down the deliverance of the British Expeditionary Force to the fact of the nation being at prayer on Sunday, 26 May, two days before that great storm in Flanders and the calm that came over the Channel.'

The word 'miracle' was soon being heard on all sides, and a consciousness of a miraculous deliverance pervaded the camps in which the troops were being housed back in England.

Mr Churchill, when he chose 4 June as the occasion for making a statement to the House of Commons, spoke with a voice charged with emotion when he reported that, rather than 20,000 or 30,000 men being re-embarked, '335,000 men had been carried out of the jaws of death and shame to their native land.'

He referred to what had happened as 'a miracle of deliverance'.

When the services of national thanksgiving were held in all churches on the following Sunday, 9 June, it was with great feeling that many a choir and congregation sang the words of Psalm 124, for they were seen to apply to that situation through which the nation had just passed:

'If the Lord himself had not been on our side, now may Israel say: if the Lord himself had not been on our side, when men rose up against us; They would have swallowed us up quick: when they were so wrathfully displeased at us. Yea, the waters had drowned us: and the stream had gone over our soul. The deep waters of the proud would have gone over our soul.... But praised be the Lord: Who has not given us over for a prey unto their teeth. Our soul is escaped even as a bird out of the snare of the fowler: the snare is broken, and we are delivered. Our help standeth in the name of the Lord: who hath made heaven and earth' (*The Book of Common Prayer*).

No other passage of Scripture could have more aptly described the nation's experience on that day. The words seem to have been especially written for the occasion.

Chapter Six

The Battle of Britain

By 5 June 1940, the Germans had launched their final offensive against the French army. This led to an armistice between France and Germany which had come into effect by 25 June.

Britain therefore stood alone. The whole Continent had been overrun by the Nazi war machine, and the German panzer divisions were standing on the French coast opposite the Straits of Dover. Kent and Sussex had been brought within reach of German fighter cover. Nothing seemed to lie between Britain and disaster but the twenty-five miles of Channel water. With the fall and occupation of France, the threat of a German invasion of the British Isles had become a grave possibility.

Hitler, in his first heady days as Chancellor of the Third Reich, had boasted to an astonished Rauschning: 'I will succeed where Napoleon failed. I will land on the shores of Britain.'

He seemed within an ace of doing it. There are those today who belittle this danger as if it was never really there. By way of refuting such nonsense, I would remind these people that Mr Churchill states in his history of World War II that it was 'soon after war broke out on September 3rd, 1939, that the German Admiralty, as we have learned from their captured archives, began their staff study of the invasion of Britain.'

So invasion was 'on the cards' even then. It is now known that, only five days after the fall of France, General Alfred Jodl, Hitler's personal adviser on military operations, had prepared a memorandum on 'The Continuation of the War against England', and that he wrote it with invasion in mind. Having advocated that 'air attacks should be made on the RAF and on the British aircraft industry, and that these should be supplemented by a sea blockade of Britain's vital imports', he went on to state that 'a landing operation should only be attempted after air supremacy had been achieved.'

It is true that, in his heart, Jodl was hoping all along that Britain would come to terms with Germany and so make these military operations against her unnecessary. But despite this, Hitler himself now came into the picture and authorised that concrete planning for invasion was to begin. On 2 July 1940, an order went out to the three German armed services that Hitler had decided that an invasion of Britain might be undertaken—given that Germany achieved air superiority. The landing project which Hitler had in mind was, at this stage, given the code name 'Lion'. So there is no question that the danger of invasion was there. All that I have said, provides the historical background against which a series of miracles took place.

As to Britain's extreme vulnerability at that time, it is acknowledged that if the Germans could have got a size-able landing-force ashore as early as June or July 1940, it is as certain as anything can be, in historical speculation, that they would have been able to penetrate the British defences and defeat the British army with little more difficulty than brushing away cobwebs. There are also some military minds who are of the opinion that the Germans could probably have captured London at the end of May or the beginning of June simply by using their parachute and airborne divisions in no greater strength than they did against Crete in the following year. In any event, military authorities as a whole find it hard to resist the conclusion that had the Germans been able to launch their onslaught against the United Kingdom in July, Britain would have fallen.

The very *first* miracle that happened, therefore, was that Hitler did not follow through across the Channel almost immediately after Dunkirk, when so much was within his grasp. Who was holding him back?

The *second* miracle can be seen in Hitler's continued hesitation. When he looked across the Channel from Cap Griz Nez in the early days of June 1940, as Napoleon had done before him, he must have had in his mind Britain's present plight—that of a nation still in possession of an army, but of an army without any weapons. It was in this kind of context that Admiral Raeder, the Commander-in-Chief of the German navy, twice spoke to his Fuehrer about the German Admiralty's plans for invasion, and yet Hitler hesitated.

He had hoped that the war would end after the armistice with France, and that the British Government could be expected to change its policy and put out feelers for peace. But Britain was made of tougher stuff in those days. She realised that if she were to go under, the whole of western civilisation would follow. That was the issue at stake. Britain, therefore, was determined to resist at all costs.

Hitler then began to realise that the British were never going to bargain with a dictator like himself. By July, he had concluded that, in order to wind up the war, Britain must finally be crushed.

On 10 July, in accordance with part of Jodl's memorandum, the Luftwaffe began its initial bid for air superiority over the Channel. It did this by launching heavy attacks against shipping and upon coastal towns, with the double object in mind of drawing the Spitfires and Hurricanes into battle with a view to depleting them, whilst at the same time damaging the towns and cities which were marked as objectives for the coming invasion. The attack on Channel shipping was also part of the sea blockade. It was to be the prelude to a greater onslaught against the

United Kingdom. Invasion now appeared inevitable.

Therefore, on 14 July, a watchful Mr Churchill alerted the nation to the pending threat. In a stirring broadcast, he said:

'Now it has come to us to stand alone in the breach and face the worst that the tyrant's might and enmity can do.

'Bearing ourselves humbly before God, but conscious that we serve an unfolding purpose, we are ready to defend our native land against the invasion by which it is threatened.

'We are fighting by ourselves alone; but we are not fighting for ourselves alone.

'Here in this strong City of Refuge which enshrines the title-deeds of human progress and is of deep consequence to Christian civilisation; here, girt about by the seas and oceans where the Navy reigns; shielded from above by the prowess and devotion of our airmen—we await undismayed the impending assault.

'Perhaps it will come tonight.

'Perhaps it will come next week.

'Perhaps it will never come.'

Just two days later, on 16 July, Hitler issued his famous Directive Number 16, which began: 'As England, in spite of her hopeless military situation, still shows no sign of willingness to come to terms, I have decided to prepare, and if necessary to carry out, a landing operation against her. The aim of this operation is to eliminate the English Motherland as a base from which the war against Germany can be continued, and, if necessary, to occupy the country completely.'

To show how definite and specific his intentions were, I would add that this directive then laid down that the landing operation should take the form of a surprise crossing on a broad front stretching from Ramsgate to an area west of the Isle of Wight.

The code name which it had originally been given was then changed from 'Operation Lion' to 'Operation Sea Lion'. Furthermore, General von Brauschitsch, the

Commander-in-Chief of the German army, reckoned that the whole operation would be relatively easy and could be concluded in a month. From this point onwards 'Operation Sea Lion' was in business.

Now I come to what I see to be a *third* miracle.

Admiral Raeder had laid down, at a very early stage, the two prime requirements for the invasion of Britain: 1) that the invasion fleet should have full protection from the German navy, and 2) that Germany should have complete air superiority. Later on—in the opening days of Germany's Norwegian campaign—the German navy had lost nearly three-quarters of its surface strength. So this hoped-for protection from the navy was entirely ruled out, and it was no longer possible to fulfil the first of these two prime requirements.

We might well ask, 'Who had taken care of that?'

However, Field Marshal Herman Goering, head of the German Luftwaffe, and Hitler's supreme adviser, did promise Hitler that he would have his much needed air superiority! A vain boast indeed, in the light of what was to take place.

Yet Hitler must still have been hesitating, for three days after he had issued his Directive Number 16, he made a final offer of 'peace' to the United Kingdom in a speech to the Reichstag which was conveyed by radio to the British people.

Churchill promptly rejected it with contempt the same day.

It finally clinched matters for Hitler. On 21 July he summoned his Chiefs of Staff and told them that he regarded the execution of 'Operation Sea Lion' as 'the most effective method of bringing about a rapid conclusion of the war.' He also insisted that the main operation must be completed by 15 September, because of the possibility of unreliable weather in the Channel after that.

At the same time he warned them that the invasion was 'an exceptionally bold and daring undertaking.' 'It is not just a river crossing', he declared, 'but a crossing of a sea which is dominated by the enemy.' 'Therefore', he emphasised, 'the chief prerequisite is that we have complete mastery of the air.'

Back at home, Premier Churchill had put this direct question to the Chiefs of Staff at a War Cabinet: 'Could Britain survive, should the enemy succeed in establishing a force firmly ashore, and with her own army so devoid of weapons and equipment?'

He was told that if the Germans did succeed in establishing a force ashore, the army in its present condition lacked the offensive power to drive it out. The Chiefs of Staff then said that 'the crux of the matter is air superiority.'

So on both sides of the Channel the armed forces were in agreement. A great air battle must inevitably ensue. On the one hand, the Luftwaffe held the only key which could open the defences of the British Isles for the German forces waiting to invade. On the other hand, the fate of Britain hinged on the ability of British Fighter Command to deny the Germans air superiority over the coast. It was to be a case of fighting for the possession of the sky.

That is what the Battle of Britain was all about. And the scene was fast being set for it, which brings me to what I consider was a *fourth* miracle in this developing chain of events.

In the aftermath of Dunkirk, had the fight for air supremacy been joined immediately after the fall of France, Britain's Fighter Command could only have mustered 331 Spitfires and Hurricanes against the full might of the German air force. This would have made the odds against the Royal Air Force exceedingly cruel indeed, and had caused the Chief of the British Air Staff to ask a point-blank question of Air Chief Marshal Sir Hugh Dowding, the Commander-in-Chief of Fighter Command: 'What are your plans for defeating an overwhelming number of the German Luftwaffe?'

To which Dowding had characteristically replied: 'I believe in God. And then there is radar.'

By now there was evidence that his faith was being

honoured. Hitler's hesitation, causing nearly two months' delay over his invasion plans, had provided Britain with a precious breathing-space, and in that breathing-space an opportunity to build up her strength in fighter aircraft.

I believe that we can again see evidence that the over-ruling hand of God was at work.

At last, Hitler came to the point in July where he ceased to hesitate. He made himself supreme commander of the invasion of Britain, gave 'Operation Sea Lion' the highest priority, and ordered Admiral Raeder to intensify all efforts to mobilise the shipping of Western Europe.

Meanwhile, Field Marshal Goering, with his eyes on the white cliffs of Dover, told his air commanders that the way ahead for launching the invasion was to annihilate the Royal Air Force. So confident was he, that he proudly boasted that Germany could counter the strategic advantage of Britain's island position by the full exercise of her air power. And he began to use that power in full strength, for on 8 August the first important phase of the Battle of Britain began, which meant that the heaviest fighting experienced during it was now to commence.

The battle was to develop in three phases.

First, the attack launched on 10 July against Channel shipping and south and south-east coastal towns was to be considerably stepped up. This was in order to lure our fighters increasingly into battle with a view to destroying them.

The second phase was against inland airfields, fighter stations and radar installations. The third phase was aimed at London.

And so to the Battle of Britain itself, and to the miracle which happened in the middle of it. We need to recapture the main course of events in order to appreciate the magnitude of this miracle. Douglas Bader and others have provided us with much of the detail.

The first phase of the battle went largely in favour of the RAF. Hundreds of German bombers, escorted by fighters, suddenly began launching fiendish attacks both on shipping and on seaports along the 200-mile coastline between the North Foreland in Kent and Portland Bill in Dorset.

The intensity of the attack was such that, in the Channel, one convoy alone was attacked on one day by as many as 160 aircraft, whilst, on the same afternoon, another convoy off Bournemouth was attacked by more than 130 of the enemy.

As to the ports, Dover was attacked three days later by no less than eleven waves of hostile aircraft, with eighteen or more in each wave. On the same day, 150 enemy aircraft headed west to attack Portsmouth and the Isle of Wight area. A few days later, the enemy pressed home this attack against Portsmouth by using between two and three hundred aircraft.

So far, despite the intensity of all the attacks, thanks to radar and to the exceedingly great efficiency of Fighter Command's control and communication system in guiding our fighter squadrons to intercept the attackers, the battle was remaining consistently in Britain's favour. The enemy's carefully laid plan to destroy Fighter Command was just not succeeding. Rather, it was the German losses which were mounting. In fact, these losses were so high by 15 August that the enemy decided to turn the full venom of his attack on the fighter airfields all over the south and south-east of England, with the object of putting them out of action and rendering Fighter Command inoperative. But it was still the enemy who suffered most. They found that they lost about 180 aircraft whilst attacking ten of Fighter Command's airfields several times in one day; and that they were still getting the worst of it the next day when repeating their attacks against nine fighter aerodromes, despite the fact that they threw in five to six hundred aircraft and used as many as three fighters to escort every bomber. The toll which was being inflicted on their aircraft proved to be more than the Germans could stand. After eleven days of intensive fighting, Goering decided he must withdraw the attack to rest his pilots and count his losses.

He had lost 367 aircraft since this phase of the battle had been opened eleven days previously, against fighter Command's 183 planes lost in the air, plus a further thirty destroyed on the ground.

The first round, therefore, had definitely gone to the RAF! On 24 August, the second main phase of the air battle commenced when Goering renewed the air attacks. For the Germans it was very nearly the decisive phase. The Luftwaffe switched their major attack against Fighter Command itself, and began to concentrate on its more inland airfields, on the aircraft factories, and, in particular, on the very hub around which the fighter control system revolved, namely the various sector stations, in addition to continuing to pound many key coastal towns and cities from Southampton to the Thames Estuary. So such stations as North Weald, Stanmore, Hornchurch and Biggin Hill began to receive special attention.

Some thirty-five major attacks were launched on sector stations during the opening days of this new phase. No fewer than 800 enemy aircraft darkened the skies of southern England on 30 August as they flew in to hammer and attempt to neutralise nine of these key airfields.

Very soon things began to go badly for British Fighter Command. Right into the first week in September, the Luftwaffe pressed home its onslaughts on the sector stations and inland airfields, striking relentlessly at the very nerve centre of our air defences. By 6 September, Fighter Command was in serious trouble. The sector stations were damaged to the extent that their efficiency was becoming more and more impaired. Losses to the RAF during this last fortnight had been 295 fighters totally destroyed, and 171 seriously damaged, which meant that losses were now far in excess of replacements. Even more seriously, the British had lost as many as 300 pilots at a time when there were only 260 inexperienced pilots being turned out from the flying schools to replace them.

An extremely critical situation was therefore developing, and Dowding knew that if the battle continued like this, he faced inevitable defeat. With air superiority at last in German hands, the way would be open for invasion.

It was then that the really big miracle happened. At the very moment when they were right on the edge of final victory in the air, and when the German plans for invasion were complete, Hitler suddenly ordered the Luftwaffe to switch its attack to London! It saved Fighter Command.

The German leadership had committed the most catastrophic blunder, and in so doing had saved the day!

The sector stations and airfields found, to their amazement, that they were being left alone.

We might well ask whether it was not a far stronger Power than Hitler who had suddenly brought about this strange turn of events. Was it the result of some people's prayers? Anyway, it was not very long before the miraculous effect of this German switch of attack began to be seen in their tables of losses.

In compliance with Hitler's order to concentrate everything on the capital, Goering, on 7 September, sent over the largest force he could muster in an enormous effort to reach London and the docks.

More than one thousand bombers and fighters came in at intervals of twenty minutes, and in two or three distinct waves. There were twenty to forty bombers in each wave, heavily escorted by fighters. High above them, at altitudes of between 26,000 and 30,000 feet, large groups of additional fighters provided extra protection. Group Captain Douglas Bader tells us how one fighter pilot reported that there were so many German fighters layered up to 30,000 feet, that it was 'just like looking up the escalator at Piccadilly Circus!'

Unbeknown to Goering, big-wing fighter formations, consisting of three squadrons of thirty-six aircraft in all, had been formed and based on Duxford, only about forty miles from London. The object was that all three squadrons would operate together as one wing, and Douglas Bader led them into action for the first time on that September day. Though they had the disadvantage of not being able to gain height in time, and were badly shot about, they accounted for eleven of the enemy destroyed. Meanwhile, other squadrons were intercepting the enemy south of London, and dog-fights developed all over the Kent skies.

The result of this brilliant aerial counter-attack was that once again the balance of losses swung against the Germans. In consequence, the prize of air superiority, which the Luftwaffe had so nearly won before the major switch of attack to London, now slipped out of its hands. And the mammoth attack with which it had opened this third major phase of the Battle of Britain had completely failed into the bargain. The German formations had been broken up and driven away as the RAF gained the mastery of our skies. Furthermore, during the respite now being enjoyed by the sector stations and airfields, Fighter Command was once again able to build up its strength. It really was a miracle of the first magnitude.

Dowding said later: 'By mid to late September we were all right for aircraft. I think it was because we had faith.'

Meanwhile, on the other side of the Channel, things had by no means been at a standstill. Preparations for 'Sea Lion' had been surging ahead, and Hitler had authorised Admiral Raeder to requisition 'anything that would float' from every German lake and river. Furthermore, on 30 August, General von Brauschitsch, as Commander-in-Chief of the German army, had signed the instructions for 'the mighty landing in England'.

Churchill tells us what happened after that.

'By the beginning of September the German naval staff were able to report that the following had been requisitioned: 168 transports of 700,000 tons; 1,910 barges; 419 tugs and trawlers; 1,600 motor boats.'

'All this Armada', continued Mr Churchill, 'had to be manned, and brought to the assembly ports by sea and canal. On September 1st the great southward flow of invasion shipping began, and it was watched, reported, and violently assailed by the Royal Air Force along the whole front from Antwerp to Havre.'

The crisis mounted still further on 4 September, when, on this side of the Channel, the Chief of Naval Staff gave a warning that if the Germans could get possession of the Dover defile and capture its gun defences from us, then, by holding the points on both sides of the Straits, they would be in a position largely to deny those waters to our naval forces and thereby bring a serious land attack to bear on this country.

Once again the situation was becoming tense.

It became increasingly so on 7 September, the day when the Luftwaffe began to concentrate its attacks on London, and this was reflected by the fact that two urgent meetings of the Chiefs of Staff were called on that day, with Churchill, as Minister of Defence, presiding over the second one held in the late afternoon.

The reason for this sudden hive of VIP activity very soon became apparent.

Against the noise of the mounting air battle in the skies above London, the Director of Military Intelligence presented a report in which he stated that 8–10 September was the period between which it was considered that the best and most favourable conditions would prevail for the Germans to launch their invasion across the Channel. The conditions were believed to be those which would ensure a dark passage for their crossing, give half-light on arrival, and a tide that was rising.

He also reported that the enemy now had a concentration of barges in ports from Ostend to Le Havre sufficient to lift 50,000 men and much of their equipment, and that, in view of these two factors, he must warn the Chiefs of Staff that a German invasion was imminent.

Whereupon it was decided that all defences should stand by on immediate alert, and the code word 'Cromwell' was promptly sent out.

Suddenly, in the midst of this rising tension, it began to dawn on some people that another miracle was taking place—one as great as that which had just saved Fighter

Command. Something was happening to the weather!

Those who were keeping a watch out to sea, became aware that conditions in the Channel—which, at this time of the year, can usually be reckoned upon to be quiet— were now becoming far from favourable. In fact, they were completely opposite to the calm conditions which had prevailed at the time of Dunkirk. And this unexpected change in the weather was presenting real difficulties to the Germans, as the following extract, taken from *Hitler's Strategy,* by Hinsley, shows very clearly:

'Great numbers of ships had to be moved to the embarkation area: and bad weather added to the difficulties. By September 6th the movement of barges was already behind schedule: minesweeping had not yet been possible on account of bad weather, and on account of interference by British aircraft. On September 10th it was still the case that the weather, which for the time of the year was completely abnormal and unstable, greatly impaired transport movements and minesweeping.'

The same God, who had calmed the Channel at the time of Dunkirk and made it the means of our own army's salvation, was now using it as an effective barrier to hold back the Germans as they prepared to make the crossing. In consequence, as is now known, Hitler was obliged to rule out 8 and 10 September and postpone the proposed date of sailing until 14 September.

Despite the postponement, Hitler continued to press on with preparations for the impending invasion. After a brief spell in which to recover and regroup from the heavy losses sustained on 7 September, the Luftwaffe resumed its concentrated daylight raids on London on 10 September, and continued them throughout the next three crucial days. As the gallant 'Few' weaved in and out to break up their heavy formations, one of the most decisive battles of the world was being fought in the skies above the English Channel, and over the fields and towns of southern England.

Whilst this battle was raging, it had become clear to the

British War Cabinet that if the invasion was going to be undertaken at all, it could not now be long delayed. On 11 September, Mr Churchill broadcast this stirring call to the nation:

'We must regard the next week or so as a very important period in our history.

'It ranks with the days when the Spanish Armada was approaching the Channel, and Drake was finishing his game of bowls; or when Nelson stood between us and Napoleon's Grand Army at Boulogne. We have read about this in the history books; but what is happening now is on a far greater scale and of far more consequence to the life and future of the world and its civilisation than these brave old days of the past.

'Every man and woman will therefore prepare himself to do his duty whatever it may be, with special pride and care.... It is with devout but sure confidence that I say— "Let God defend the right."'

We now know that, three days later, the final deployment for the embarkation of the German troops began. On that same day also, Saturday, 14 September, the German army issued its final plan to force a landing between Folkestone and Worthing. Across the Channel, all was set for launching the invasion.

Apart from one crucial factor! The vast armada, which had continued to be assembled against these adverse weather conditions, was still without the necessary mastery of the air to enable it to sail. The RAF had not been destroyed. The crucial air battle upon which everything would hinge had yet to take place.

On the Sunday prior to this all-decisive week-end, the nation had been at prayer.

His Majesty King George VI, as if gifted with some prescience or foreknowledge, had, some time before all the momentous events of Saturday, 7 September, expressed the desire that the following day, Sunday, 8 September, should be fixed as a National Day of Prayer.

Once again there had been a tremendous response, and

it is significant that, at a crowded service held in West-minster Abbey, the final prayer began: 'Remember, O God, for good, these watchmen; who by day and by night climb into the air. Let thy hand lead them, we beseech thee, and thy right hand hold them.'

It was a prayer that was mightily answered. For the following Sunday saw the crisis of the Battle of Britain. Douglas Bader puts it this way: '15th September 1940 was the day that the Battle was won. It was a Sunday.'

He recalls how the day had dawned a little misty in the south-east of England, but had cleared by 8 a.m. Visibility was good on the whole, and remained so, with light cumulus cloud at 2,000 to 3,000 feet against a blue sky—almost ideal conditions for our waiting fighters.

God had given a fine day! And a still one.

The first enemy arrived soon after 9 a.m. They were coming in from a number of directions—over the Straits of Dover, over the Thames Estuary, off Harwich, and between Lympne and Dungeness. Wave after wave after wave of them came droning over the south coast and on over Kent and Sussex in an attempt to saturate the defences. It was as if the enemy was about to deliver a knock-out blow. Goering had sent across the strongest escort ever provided for his bombers—no less than five fighters for every bomber in his formations. And the common destination of all these formations was London.

No less than twenty-six fighter squadrons took off to engage the enemy that morning: a total of 312 Hurricanes and Spitfires.

Battle commenced, and raged for about three-quarters of an hour. Dog-fights erupted all over the sky. The air over south-east England became one colossal battle-field, from the Thames Estuary to Dover, from London to the coast.

About a hundred bombers managed to reach the eastern and southern quarters of the capital, and were over central London by about midday. Fourteen squadrons of Hurri-canes and three squadrons of Spitfires took up this challenge, making 204 attacking fighters in all. There followed an engagement extending all the way from London to the coast and beyond.

Suddenly, at this stage of the struggle, it began to dawn on the British fighter pilots that the tide was beginning to turn. The enemy bomber crews were not pressing on. As soon as our fighter pilots went in to the attack, and even before then, they were jettisoning their bombs, breaking formation, and heading for home. By the time Sunday worshippers were leaving their churches, and others were getting ready to sit down to lunch, the routed air armada was in full flight back to its bases in northern France. By 12.30 p.m. the first phase of this day's great battle was over, and with comparatively few bombs having been dropped on the capital. Rather than the RAF being knocked out, it was the enemy who had been sent reeling!

Shortly after 2 p.m., following a lull in the conflict of about an hour and a half, fresh forces returned in about the same strength as before. Enemy aircraft crossed the coast near Dover in two great waves. This time, twenty-one squadrons of Spitfires and Hurricanes, comprising 252 fighters in all, went up to attack them. The blue sky became full of the criss-crosses of condensation trails, as, in ideal conditions, our fighters weaved in and out to the attack. This time also, the big-wing formations had had ample time to gain height, and now they too dived down upon the approaching German formations out of the sun. At the height of the Battle, Winston Churchill, who had spent the day in 11 Group's Operations Room, and who was now fully absorbed in the map in front of him, turned to Air Vice-Marshal Keith Park, the Air Officer Commanding 11 Group, with cigar still unlit, and asked what fighter reserves were available.

Park replied: 'There are none.'

All that we had, had been thrown into the battle. Ten minutes after that dramatic reply, the action ended. The Germans had cracked. The miracle had happened. And the long wailing note of the 'all-clear' sounded out—level and reassuring. By tea-time on Sunday, 15 September, the tide of the enemy offensive had been turned. As Bader puts it: 'The fact remains that the Germans quit before we did and so they lost. It is as simple as that.'

In many a church that Sunday evening the words, 'O sing unto the Lord a new song: for he hath done marvellous things, With his own right hand, and with his holy arm: hath he gotten himself the victory', were sung with profound fervour. But it was by no means church worshippers alone who felt that this sudden turn in Britain's fortunes was God's wonderful answer to all the earnest prayer that had gone up the Sunday before.

As for all those German amphibious and airborne forces waiting to cross over from the other side of the Channel, it is now known that Hitler had again postponed the date of the invasion from the fourteenth to the seventeenth of September, presumably to await the outcome of the great air battles of this crucial week-end.

After this Sunday, the nerve required to unleash the storm on Britain was lacking. Instead of launching 'Operation Sea Lion' across the Channel on 17 September, a tele-type message clacked out from the German Supreme Command. It read: 'Postponed until further notice.'

This explains why it was that the reconnaissance planes, which had continually reported the build-up of invasion barges in the ports of northern France and Belgium, noted after 15 September that they were being dispersed.

The incredible thing was that, had they not been dispersed, and had Hitler waited a few more days, the weather in the Channel following 21 September would have been calm!

So for at least the fourth time in her long history, Britain had been saved from invasion by a miracle—by a whole series of miracles—and in answer to a Sovereign's, and a nation's, prayer.

This element of the miraculous is borne out very forcibly by someone who saw everything from the inside as it happened, and who was in a position to speak with greater authority than anybody else. That man was Air Chief

Marshal Sir Hugh Dowding. He had been Commander-in-Chief of Fighter Command ever since it was founded in July 1936, and therefore knew all the facts that there were to be known. Furthermore, it was he who had seen to it that Britain, *humanly speaking,* had in her possession the keys to survival, namely, the fast single-seater fighters, the radar chain, and the communications network. But he has left on record how conscious he was that there was another element at work on Britain's behalf to ensure her survival over and above all these. Listen to what he says in a speech reported in the *Daily Sketch* on 15 September 1943: 'Even during the Battle, one realised from day to day how much external support was coming in. At the end of the Battle one had the feeling that there had been some special Divine Intervention to alter some sequence of events which would otherwise have occurred. I see that this Intervention was no last minute happening...it was all part of the Mighty Plan.'

Again, on one of the anniversaries of the Battle of Britain, he spoke of the part that national prayer had played in the battle, and of the divine interventions resulting from them. 'Britain was not too proud to recognise National Days of Prayer', he said, 'and should therefore not be too proud to acknowledge the results of those prayers.

'I pay homage to those gallant boys who gave their all that our nation might live. I pay tribute to their leaders and commanders. But I say with absolute conviction that I can trace the Intervention of God, not only in the Battle itself, but in the events which led up to it; and that if it had not been for this Intervention, the battle would have been joined in conditions which, humanly speaking, would have rendered victory impossible' (*Birmingham Daily Post,* 8 June 1942). Very convincing words, when they come with such conviction from the mouth of no less a person than the Commander-in-Chief.

It is believed that, when he spoke of the intervention of God in the events which had led up to the battle, he had two things particularly in mind.

One was the Air Staff's decision, long before the war, to go ahead with the Hurricane and Spitfire—fighters which then possessed far greater hitting power, speed, and manoeuverability than any foreign aircraft.

The other was a demonstration held in February 1935, when a primitive form of radar equipment had picked up an aircraft at a range of eight miles. With a quickness of appreciation and a foresight seldom encountered when a service ministry is offered a revolutionary idea, the Air Council had seen its potential immediately, and had given Robert Watson-Watt the support he needed to develop his discoveries of using radio waves to detect and plot approaching enemy aircraft, with the Treasury readily providing the money for research. It is thought that Dowding saw in these quick and ready decisions more than the human element at work. For it was the development of Robert Watson-Watt's discovery which provided the basis of the system which gave long-range warning of the approach of enemy aircraft, and enabled their movements to be accurately plotted and then successfully countered. Looking back down those years, it is easy to see now that, without those precious Spitfire and Hurricane squadrons, and without the use of radar in operation to assist them, the Battle of Britain would indeed have been joined, as Dowding had put it, 'in conditions which, humanly speaking, would have rendered victory impossible.' Therefore, even in the remarkable way Britain had been provided with them, Dowding could trace the intervening hand of God.

Mr Churchill wrote later, that 'September 15th was the crux of the Battle of Britain.' And Douglas Bader described it as 'the day when the Hurricane and Spitfire had outfought the Luftwaffe to change the course of history.'

Completing the story, Churchill provides further insight into what happened after the German air formations had turned for home. 'That same night', he says, 'our Bomber

Command attacked in strength the shipping in the ports from Boulogne to Antwerp. At Antwerp particularly heavy losses were inflicted. On September 17th, as we now know, the Fuehrer decided to postpone "Sea Lion" indefinitely. It was not till October 12th that the invasion was called off until the following Spring. In July 1941 it was postponed again by Hitler till the Spring of 1942. On February 13th, 1942, Admiral Raeder had his final interview on "Sea Lion" and got Hitler to agree to a complete stand-down. Thus perished operation "Sea Lion". And September 15th may stand as the date of its demise.'

Thus records Winston Churchill, and in so doing makes it plain that Britain's deliverance from invasion was complete.

There is no doubt at all that what we have in these events of the high summer of 1940 is an outstanding example in modern history of the great works of the Lord which he has done for Britain.

The question has often been asked: Why did Hitler abandon 'Sea Lion'? Both historians and military authorities say the question still defies an answer. In fact, one such authority has said: 'The development and fate of "Operation Sea Lion" remains one of the great imponderables of the Second World War.'

When we stand back, and view events as one complete whole, there is no question at all that it was due to the hand of Almighty God on our history.

It was a *miracle* that Hitler did not invade this country in June or July 1940, immediately after the fall of France.

It was a *miracle* that he continued to hesitate, and so gave Britain a breathing-space in which to build up her fighting strength.

It was a *miracle* that Germany was deprived of so much of her naval strength at the very time when it was needed to cover such a massive sea-borne operation.

It was certainly a *miracle* that Hitler suddenly decided to switch his air attacks to London just at the point when the Luftwaffe had the air superiority within its grasp.

And it was definitely a *miracle* that bad weather in the Channel delayed his operation during that very week when the conditions were expected to be favourable.

All this is to say nothing of the way the Germans suddenly cracked and made for home on 15 September, or of the way the High Command lost its nerve to launch 'Sea Lion' across the Channel soon after that.

There was still *one more* miracle in store, had the Germans, in fact, been able to achieve air superiority. British naval authorities have always argued very strongly that even had the Luftwaffe been able to gain complete mastery of the air, the whole enterprise might have been ruined by a spell of bad weather. And that possibility is borne out by the Germans, for their navy has since admitted that the strings of river barges to which Hitler was prepared to entrust his crack divisions were grossly unsuited for a Channel crossing. They say they were only seaworthy in winds up to force 2, which meant that it would only require one sharp squall to swamp them and send them to the bottom. Admiral Rüge has even said: 'They could stand nothing more than a slight breeze!'

Had they sailed, even having achieved complete mastery of the skies, we might well have seen a repetition of what happened to the Spanish Armada, and at the hands of the same sovereign Protector. After all, there is evidence enough to show that the same God, who worked to prevent an invasion in 1588, was working mightily to save Britain from suffering a similar fate during the summer of 1940.

Chapter Seven

Malta under Siege

From about the time of Dunkirk onwards, the course of the war in the Mediterranean also began to be punctuated with instances of divine overruling.

For instance, there was the outstanding example of the siege of Malta, lying in the path of Italy's vital supply lines to North Africa, and on the holding of which so much was to depend.

General Sir William Dobbie, who was sent at short notice to take up the post of governor of the fortress in April 1940, has left it on record in *A Very Present Help* that 'the story of the siege of Malta from 1940–1942 is rich in illustrations of God's help and of his interventions.'

When France fell, and the continent of Europe was overrun by Nazi forces, Italy entered the war against the Allies on the side of Germany, and immediately Malta was left in a state of extreme isolation. With Sicily, Sardinia and the Italian mainland all dangerously close, and with the nearby African coast of Tripoli and Libya dominated by the enemy, Malta suddenly found herself hemmed in by hostile territory. The nearest friendly neighbourhood was now almost a thousand miles away. Those responsible for Malta's defence were also fully aware that the Italians had long boasted that they intended to occupy her as soon as war was declared. What is more, they had said they

expected to capture the fortress within a day or two! So
Malta found herself faced with the immediate threat of a
full-scale invasion by sea and air.

The authorities on the island also knew that no
immediate reinforcements could be expected, and that
there was no prospect whatsoever of getting any in the
foreseeable future, because every unit of the British Army
was needed to meet the threat of an invasion of the home
country. Malta would have to depend for its defence on
such resources as it happened to have on hand—and these
were extremely meagre. The entire garrison consisted of
no more than 5,000 officers and men, and that was taking
into account all three Services.

To meet the imminent threat of aerial bombardment,
Malta had only sixteen anti-aircraft guns, and most of
these were obsolete. As for fighter aircraft, four Fleet Air
Arm Gloster Gladiator fighters were found in crates in
the naval dockyard stores. They were slow, out-of-date
machines, but they were all that Malta had, and it was
with these that they started the air war against the strong
Italian Regia Aeronautica! With more than thirty miles of
beaches to watch and defend, plus the various places
inland where airborne landings might be attempted, there
were only four battalions of the Regular Army and one
Maltese Territorial battalion.

Yet Malta had to be held at all costs. For if it were to be
lost, there could be no stopping the flow of supplies from
Italy reaching the armies of Mussolini in North Africa, or
of preventing them from being reinforced.

Furthermore, there would be no landing-base for aircraft flying between Great Britain and Egypt to reinforce
our air forces in the Middle East. And when Rommel
came on the scene early in 1941, there would have been no
way of stopping supplies reaching his Afrika Korps across
the Mediterranean from Italy, which in turn meant that
there could be no stopping Rommel. If Malta were to fall
at any time, we might not have been able to hold Egypt,
and the consequences of that—both for the Allies and for

the rest of the world—did not bear contemplating.

Egypt would be Rommel's, and with it Suez. Then the Persian Gulf would be taken, with its vital oil supplies. That would open up to the Axis forces the routes to India on the one hand—which would enable Rommel to link up with the Japanese armies—and on the other, would enable him to push through to the Caucasus, with the object of joining forces with those German armies which were heading through Russia in the direction of the Black Sea and the Caspian. If all of this were to be achieved, it would result in the complete encirclement of the Allied forces and bring a world victory for Nazism.

Malta, therefore, was the kingpin to the whole Mediterranean and Middle-East situation.

But how was Malta to be held? And even if held, how was the garrison and the extremely dense population to continue to be fed when nearly all the food that was needed, and everything that was required for its defence, had to be brought by sea?

These were the problems which confronted General Dobbie when, less than two months after his arrival as governor, Malta was plunged into this predicament as a result of Italy suddenly stepping into the war and tipping the balance of power in the Mediterranean in favour of the Axis.

Well, I believe that in the appointment of General Dobbie we can see *yet another* of those great works of the Lord which he had done for Britain.

For Dobbie knew wherein the secret lay. God had been preparing him down the years: now, in his infinite mercy, he had seen to it that his man was brought to a position of great responsibility for such a time as this.

The way in which he was appointed was a miracle, and the hand of God can be seen clearly in it. I am sure it was a modern example of the Lord raising up a governor or leader who was to deliver the people out of the hands of those who oppressed them, as was the case in Judges 2:16. For the inspiring leadership which Dobbie gave, forms a major part of the story of how God, during the entire siege, delivered Malta from the hands of Hitler and Mussolini.

General Dobbie had returned home from an army command in Malaya in August 1939, and had been obliged to retire from the army soon afterwards, owing to some new age rules which had been brought in. When war broke out, he had offered his services to the War Office in any capacity in which he might be of use, but for a long time nothing was forthcoming. Then, early in 1940, he learnt of two possible appointments for which he might be considered, but nothing had come of either of these. Being a firm believer in divine guidance, he felt that these two doors had been shut because God had something better for him.

On 18 or 19 April 1940—he could not quite remember which—he had just finished lunch in his London club, when he was told that the Chief of the Imperial General Staff, General Sir Edmund Ironside, who was also lunching there, wanted to speak to him. Dobbie went up to Ironside's table, and the CIG said, 'Will you go to Malta?' 'Certainly', Dobbie replied. 'In what capacity?' 'As Governor', said Ironside.

This was something General Dobbie had never dreamed of in his wildest flights of imagination. 'But', he said afterwards, 'I knew that that was what God had in mind for me.'

The man, then, who took over the great responsibility for Malta, was a man of God—a man of faith. He had also proved the power of prayer.

He was a man who believed that, in fighting Nazism, Britain was involved in a righteous cause; and for that reason, he believed that God was on our side. Since it was obvious to him that the human resources on Malta were woefully inadequate, he says he was constrained to 'turn his eyes to the hills, from whence came his help', and to encourage others to do the same. He saw clearly where the secret of Malta's defence lay—in a quiet reliance upon God.

The Bible had always been a great stand-by to him, and, as he confronted the task, he recalled many instances in the Old Testament of how God had helped his people when they had been faced with similar situations. So he believed that the Lord would do so now.

In particular, he remembered Elisha at Dothan, and how the young man, seeing that the city, where he and his master were staying, was compassed about with enemy armies which had come to capture them, had said to Elisha, 'Alas my master, how shall we do?'—and how Elisha had replied, 'Fear not: for they that be with us are more than they that be with them' (2 Kings 6:16). He felt the same could be said with regard to himself and the people of Malta.

He remembered King Asa, who, finding himself being invaded by an enemy army of over a million strong, when his own army was less than half that number, had cried to the Lord his God for help, saying, 'Lord, it is nothing with thee to help, whether with many, or with them that have no power: help us, O Lord our God; for we rest on thee, and in thy name we go against this multitude. O Lord, thou art our God; let not man prevail against thee' (2 Chronicles 14:11). He remembered how man did *not* prevail—not even a million men—because, as the record goes on to say: 'The *Lord* smote...them'—and so they were overthrown (vv. 12, 13).

Inspired by a similar confidence that the same God would help them now, General Dobbie decided in the early days of the siege to issue to the garrison, weak as it was, a special Order of the Day, defining the policy which was to govern the defence of the fortress. It read as follows:

'The decision of His Majesty's Government to fight on until our enemies are defeated, will have been heard with the greatest satisfaction by all ranks of the garrison of Malta. It may be that hard times lie ahead of us, but however hard they may be, I know that the courage and determination of all ranks will not falter, and that *with*

God's help we will maintain the security of this fortress.

'I therefore call upon all officers and other ranks, humbly to seek God's help, and then, *in reliance upon him,* to do their duty unflinchingly.' (The words in italics stress what the governing policy of the island's defence was going to be.)

At the same time, he issued another special Order of the Day, worded similarly but addressed to the people of Malta, and aimed at turning their minds away from their difficulties and fears to the great God who alone could deliver. He said that by no other means could they be sure of holding this vital outpost of empire, and so they were turning to God who alone is the giver of victory.

Such, then, was the inspiring lead which this man of God gave to Malta, as the island prepared to face its fiery ordeal.

He was greatly encouraged by a telegram he received from General Sir Edmund Ironside (later Lord Ironside). It was addressed to him personally, and contained the reference: 'Deuteronomy chapter 3, verse 22.'

He looked up the reference and read: 'Ye shall not fear them: for the Lord your God he shall fight for you.' It showed him that others in high places at home were thinking along the same lines as they were in Malta. To General Dobbie the reference was a timely reminder of a great and well-proved truth, and he said, 'Coming as it did from a person in his position, and being addressed to one in mine, it meant much to us, in view of the special circumstances of the time.'

With all this taking place, it was no wonder that Dobbie wrote later: 'When the siege of Malta began, behind all the human factors was God.'

The story of the next two years was the story of that belief being worked out in quite remarkable ways. Many miracles happened which proved beyond a shadow of doubt that God was at work on their behalf. The help which he gave was, to the garrison and people of Malta, very obvious and very real. General Dobbie said that they soon became aware that it was the same help which was seen at the time of the withdrawal from Dunkirk and during the Battle of Britain.

The *first* miracle which they experienced, for instance, was that Italy made no attempt whatsoever to invade them, although at that time everything was in her favour. Commenting on this, General Dobbie writes: 'It is truly remarkable that Italy did not attempt the invasion, immediately after she had declared war, when the advantages were all in her favour, nor at any other time.

'We are justified in asking, Why?

'By the same token we are justified in asking another question: Why did not the Germans invade Great Britain immediately after Dunkirk?

'It is difficult to find satisfactory answers to either of these questions on the human level. It seems that our two enemies each made a colossal blunder when they did not seize the opportunities given them of gaining a decisive success.'

'What caused them to make these blunders?', asked General Dobbie. 'The only reason which I can find', he said, 'and which seems to cover the facts, is that in each case, God's restraining hand kept them from attacking us at a time when we were very ill-prepared to meet such attacks. If this is so, and I firmly believe it is, it was not the first time that God has acted in this way. Scripture has many instances of just this thing, instances which are recorded for our comfort and hope.'

If invasion did not take place immediately after Italy entered the war, the aerial bombardment, aimed at crushing all resistance on Malta, did. And here, perhaps, is the *second* great miracle. For the story of that bombardment is the story, not so much of how God delivered them from this prolonged attack, but of how he sustained, enabled, and protected them throughout it.

Italian bombers came over Malta in the early morning of 11 June 1940, dropping their loads and causing much devastation and many casualties, especially amongst the civilian population.

The attack was repeated many times that day, and on many subsequent days, until these visitations became commonplace experiences in the everyday life of the people. By the time General Dobbie left the island two years later, the fortress had been subjected to over two thousand bombing attacks. But God's protecting hand was so much in evidence during those two years that people were noticing it and remarking on it.

On a number of occasions, says General Dobbie, officers came up to him and remarked quite spontaneously, 'Do you know, sir, I think someone up there (pointing upwards) has been helping us today.' To which he replied, 'Yes, I think so too. You may remember that we asked him to help us, and today we have been watching him doing it.'

If he thought it remarkable that Italy did not attempt to invade Malta in the summer of 1940 when everything was so much in her favour, the governor must have thought it even more remarkable that, when Rommel arrived in the Western Desert in 1941, the Germans did not attempt an invasion of the island. He said later that he believed that this also was due to the same restraining hand of God. Little did he realize how true it was. Information now available makes it even more clear that this was indeed the case. We owe it to Brigadier Desmond Young for disclosing to us some quite extraordinary things which were happening on the German side at that time; things which reveal that the story of the siege of Malta was even more miraculous than it had first appeared to be.

It will no doubt be recalled that the reason why General Rommel was sent to the Western Desert in the first place, was because General Wavell, the then British Commander-in-Chief, Middle East, had launched a brilliant and daring offensive against Marshal Graziani's Italian forces in Cyrenaica at the end of 1940, had resoundingly defeated them, and had driven them back from the Egyptian frontier as far as Benghazi. To prevent the Italians from losing the whole of North Africa, Hitler had reacted immediately by despatching German troops. General Rommel was sent out in February 1941 to command them.

This famous German general soon made it clear that he had other things in mind than 'merely to help or "stiffen" the Italians and to prevent a British advance to Tripoli.' Early in April 1941, in a lightning thrust—which took not only the British, but even his own Chiefs of Staff back home in Germany, by surprise—he had completely reconquered the whole of Cyrenaica (with the exception of Tobruk) in less than a month, and had reached the frontier of Egypt. This immediately brought the strategic position of Malta to the forefront again. For Rommel's problem now became one of supplies. If he was to continue his advance into Egypt, which is what he intended to do, he must have reinforcements, and the only way the German authorities could get these to him was across the Mediterranean from Italy. But they were in danger of being sunk on the way by the surface warships, aircraft, and submarines operating from Malta. Therefore it was imperative to Rommel's continued success that action be taken against the island base.

The extraordinary thing is that the German High Command ruled at this time that since nothing could be done about Rommel's supplies without an operation against Malta, Rommel must restrict himself to planning the capture of Tobruk and, even if that fell, he was not to advance into Egypt. In other words, they intended to make no move whatsoever to take the fortress.

'Rommel', says Desmond Young in his book of the same name, 'saw all along what the German and Italian General Staffs were strangely blind in not seeing, until it was too late, that the key to all supply problems, and indeed, the key to the control of the Mediterranean, was the capture of Malta.' His superiors were 'strangely blind' to this—note the words which Young uses. He goes on to record that 'Rommel continually told his staff, and later his family, that he could not understand what on earth the High

Command was about, not to take Malta. This, he thought, could easily have been done during the summer of 1941 with airborne troops and with the use of smoke screens.'

It seems to me that some explanation is needed for these two diametrically opposite views.

Was not this another clear case of the restraining hand of God at work? We have examples in the Bible of God blinding people's eyes.

Since General Dobbie had been reminded more than once of the story of Elisha at Dothan, and of the way God had smitten the encircling Syrian army with blindness in answer to Elisha's prayer—and since the General had been encouraging the garrison and the people of Malta to look to God for help—could it not have been that the same God had made Hitler and the members of the German and Italian High Commands blind to the situation in the Mediterranean?

Had those who had spent so much time in prayer on Malta realised what was happening in the German High Command at that time, I think that they would have come to that conclusion.

Yet this incredible stupor and lack of initiative which seems to have hung over Hitler and his Chiefs of Staff is only one of the ways in which God was at work to save Malta when Rommel appeared on the scene in the Middle East.

Despite the frustrations caused by his High Command, Rommel was still intent on pressing on into Egypt. He successfully defeated the counter-offensives which General Wavell had launched against him in May and June 1941. On 27 July 1941, although Tobruk still stood in his path, threatening to cut his supply lines should he make any attempt to advance, he sought permission from the German High Command to launch an offensive, with the Suez canal as its objective. In order to allow time to build up his forces, he set February 1942 as its target date.

In fact, his ideas went far further than that, as General von Ravenstein, who was with him in the Western Desert at that time, later disclosed.

This advance was to be only the prelude to a further move right through to Basra in Iraq on the Persian Gulf, with the object of stopping the flow of American supplies to Russia through the Gulf. And that was not all. General Halder, Chief of the German General Staff, says that Rommel spoke to him in 1942 of taking East Africa also, after Suez.

In any event, both sides in the Western Desert were desperately trying to build up their forces during the summer of 1941 with the next round of the combat very much in mind.

Rommel soon found that he was at a disadvantage. For, throughout this period and until the spring of 1942, out of a total supply requirement of 60,000 tons, only 18,000 tons reached the German army on African soil.

The thorn in Rommel's side was still Malta. The damage being inflicted by the forces operating from there was such that 35 per cent of his supplies and reinforcements were sunk in August 1941 and 63 per cent in October, with the percentage continuing to rise.

Yet it was not until the end of 1941, when sinkings had risen to something like 75 per cent, that Hitler and the High Command at last woke up to the importance of Malta for the command of the Mediterranean. Even then, they did not act decisively.

They reinforced the Luftwaffe in Sicily, it is true; and from there launched incessant air attacks against the island. They also sent U-boats and light surface craft to operate in the area. The result was that, by early 1942, the Germans virtually controlled the central Mediterranean and succeeded in effectively neutralising Malta. The remarkable thing was that, even having gone as far as achieving this, they still made no move whatsoever to capture the island.

These facts are really quite extraordinary when we find that Rommel states in his official papers that 'it had actually been intended that Malta should be taken by Italian and

German parachute and landing forces early in 1942', before he started his intended offensive against Alexandria, Suez and Egypt. 'But', he says, 'for some unaccountable reason our High Command abandoned the scheme.' He states that he even made a request to have 'this attractive little job' entrusted to his own army, 'but unfortunately', he says, his request 'had been turned down in the Spring.'

Have we not, in this further incredible attitude of the German High Command, abundant evidence to show the great extent to which God, in answer to their many prayers, was at work on behalf of the people of Malta throughout this very critical time?

Are we not justified in believing that these repeated decisions not to take decisive action against Malta, when it would have been comparatively easy to do so, were a sure sign of how much the restraining hand of God was resting on the German High Command?

If we believe that *God* was speaking to General Dobbie through the Deuteronomy reference in General Ironside's telegram—'Ye shall not fear them: for the Lord your God he shall fight for you'—then it is my conviction that we are justified in thinking in this way.

It is also my belief that, had Rommel been gifted with spiritual perception, and had he reflected on the 'unaccountable reason' which had caused the High Command to abandon the plan to take Malta before he launched his Spring offensive, he might have come to that conclusion too.

As for the people of Malta, General Dobbie has recorded for us that he was encouraged on more than one occasion by the words with which King Hezekiah had inspired faith in his people at the time when the king of Assyria came and encamped against their cities. We also have reason to believe that on more than one occasion Dobbie passed these words on to others: 'Be strong and courageous, be not afraid nor dismayed for the king of Assyria, nor for all the multitude that is with him: for there be more with us than with him: With him is an arm of flesh; but with us is the Lord our God to help us, and to fight our battles' (2 Chronicles 32:7, 8). Had they known what was going on at Hitler's Staff Headquarters, it would have been proof positive to them that this passage from the Bible was a very definite 'Word from the Lord'. As we look back with all this information to hand, we realise with amazement that no other Word from the Lord could have been more true or fitting for those days.

During these same critical months, a major crisis developed on the British side. As a result of the Germans taking action to neutralise Malta, enemy aircraft and submarines had now closed the central Mediterranean to the convoys on which the little fortress depended so much. The most crucial time of the entire siege had therefore begun.

Such heavy losses had been inflicted on our naval forces, that Admiral Cunningham was left with only three cruisers and a few destroyers, and his flagship was on the bottom of the harbour in Alexandria. Escort vessels were therefore at a minimum.

During December 1941 and early January 1942, Rommel had been driven right back from the Egyptian frontier to Agheila in Tripolitania by an offensive launched against him by the newly-appointed British Commander-in-Chief, Middle East, General Auchinleck. Although this made Rommel's intended Spring offensive far less likely, he was very quickly back, due largely to the fact that he did not lose a single ton of his supplies that January, and in February a convoy carrying a large number of tanks destined for his Afrika Korps had got through to Tripoli. To make matters worse, this happened just when some of Auchinleck's key forces had been transferred from the Western Desert to other vital theatres of war. So, with amazing resilience, Rommel had counter-attacked on 21 January, had caught the weakened Eighth Army off balance, and by 7 February, with surprising speed, was two-thirds of the way back to the Egyptian frontier. The vital airfields in Western Cyrenaica, so necessary for the protection of any convoys making for Malta, were once again in Rommel's hands. It seemed certain to the British War Cabinet that, with no convoys getting through to her, Malta must fall, unless we could regain possession of these airfields and so give cover to the convoys which were seeking to fight their way through the blockade to relieve her.

Churchill and his Cabinet considered the situation to have become so desperate that, in order to regain possession of the airfields and save Malta, they were insisting that General Auchinleck should stage an offensive against Rommel at the earliest possible moment.

Auchinleck, on the other hand, protested strongly that he could not launch such an offensive until his strength in both tanks and aircraft was such that it would guarantee him some chance of success. His fear was that, in launching a premature attempt to save Malta without the necessary military strength at his command, he would lose Egypt to Rommel and the whole of the Middle East as well. In his opinion, the earliest he could attack was in June, and he continued to build up his forces with that in mind.

In the event, Rommel attacked first, on 27 May, and so began that spectacular assault which, in a month, carried him over and past Tobruk, past the Egyptian frontier, past Mersa Matruh, Bagush and El Daba, to El Alamein and the very gates of Alexandria.

The airfields of Western Cyrenaica were not recaptured from him. Yet Malta did not fall, which was indeed a miracle! Desmond Young says that this was thanks to Hitler's folly in postponing the airborne assault on it. I think we need to look a little deeper than that, because I believe that Hitler's folly was due in turn to the fact that once again the influence of God was at work restraining him.

That conviction is greatly strengthened when we see how this strange overruling continued right through to the end of the siege. For Brigadier Young also discloses that at the end of April 1942, under pressure from Admiral Raeder, Hitler actually gave permission for a surprise attack on the island to take place at the beginning of June, using German and Italian troops. It was given the code name 'Operation Hercules'.

It was twice put off, which in itself is extraordinary, because had it been launched at the beginning of June, it would have coincided with Rommel's spectacular advance, and his supplies would have been guaranteed, thus strengthening the possibility of a successful dash to Cairo.

Desmond Young goes on to say that at the beginning of July, the last minute of the eleventh hour, Hitler postponed 'Operation Hercules' until after the conquest of Egypt! That, of course, never happened.

So Malta was saved from the hands of Hitler and Mussolini—the danger was past. General Dobbie reminds us that the threat of invasion had hung over them for two full years.

'Thus God's restraining hand continued to be strong for us for a long period. It was not just one instantaneous act of deliverance', he says. 'It was a long drawn-out process. We were very conscious of God's protecting hand, constantly evident in many ways. We saw it when he restrained the enemy from invading us at a time when we were ill-prepared to resist. We saw it in the results achieved by our pitiably weak air defences. We saw it in the steadfastness and courage of the people. We saw it in the achievements of the Royal Navy and Merchant Navy in bringing supplies to Malta, sometimes in seemingly impossible conditions. We saw it in many details, some big and some small, throughout the long, drawn-out period of siege. And as we now look back from the vantage point of a little distance, and see things, perhaps, in a truer perspective—the very fact that, in spite of all her disadvantages, Malta had remained in British hands, and, by the offensive action based on Malta, had made a definite contribution toward our ultimate sweeping success in the Mediterranean—that, surely, is a miracle which cannot be gainsaid. It is God who works such miracles.'

Chapter Eight

At the Gates of Cairo

Tobruk had fallen to Rommel in June 1942. With nothing now to prevent his onward advance, and with General Ritchie, commander of the Eighth Army, finding it too late to stand on the Egyptian frontier at Sollum, Rommel had the Eighth Army on the run.

We had had superiority in men, munitions, tanks and aircraft, and our hopes had been high for an early and complete victory in the Middle East, but instead came this humiliation and defeat.

Winston Churchill declared in the House of Commons that 'we were defeated under conditions which gave every reasonable expectancy of success. We had in the desert', he said, '100,000 men, whereas the Axis had 90,000, including 50,000 Germans. Our superiority in numbers of tanks were 7–5; in guns nearly 8–5, including several regiments of the latest howitzers and certain secret weapons. We had air superiority too, and Rommel's dive-bombers were neither a decisive nor a massive factor in the battle.' Yet our front had collapsed.

As Rommel said in his *Papers*: 'It was obvious to me that the fall of Tobruk, and the collapse of the Eighth Army, was one moment in the African war when the road lay open to Alexandria, with only a few British troops to defend it. I and my colleagues would have been fools if we had not done everything to exploit this one and only chance.

'Ahead of us were territories containing an enormous wealth of raw materials—Africa, for example, and the Middle East—which could have freed us from all our anxieties about oil.'

Surely, he must have thought, with the glittering prize of Egypt and the Suez Canal almost within his grasp, both the German and the Italian High Command must now realise what was at stake and give him the extra supplies and support he needed to take them.

A young Swedish reporter who was in Berlin during those days wrote later: 'A miracle happened in the desert—Rommel began his forward sweep and the fall of Tobruk gave the Germans greater stimulus than any event since the fall of France.' Absolute intoxication gripped official Berlin, with people saying to the reporter, 'Perhaps Rommel will win the war for us yet', and a Wilhelmstrasse spokesman remarking to him one day that 'We are going to strangle the Middle East with two great fists. Soon there will be a great drive against India to link up with Japan, and our parachutists will be in Afghanistan.'

Yet General Bayerlein, Chief of Staff of the Afrika Korps, and later Chief of Staff to Rommel himself, had to say: 'No one would have guessed that Hitler, with his famous intuition, and Keitel, Jodl and Halder with their trained staff minds, would not even see the opportunity that lay before them.'

Of course Rommel must go on!

Go on he did—and at speed. During the evening of 24 June, just four days after the fall of Tobruk, Rommel was up to Sidi Barrani. Next day his columns were within forty miles of Mersa Matruh, and the situation was desperate. That evening General Auchinleck personally took over command of the Eighth Army. As a precautionary measure the El Alamein position was occupied, but somehow Rommel had to be stopped before he reached there, if possible in the area between Mersa Matruh and

El Alamein.

There was no stopping him. By the evening of 26 June, the German tanks had broken through the defensive mine-fields, and the next day they succeeded in cutting the road twenty miles east of Mersa Matruh. There was nothing for it, therefore, but to withdraw all our forces behind the El Alamein position, which General Auchinleck had long before prepared, and to make a last ditch stand.

The retreating and frustrated Eighth Army reached this Alamein line of defence on Monday 29 June. Rommel came up to it the next day. Alexandria was only sixty-five miles away, and since German bombers were already over the naval base there, the British fleet left discreetly. On Wednesday, 1 July, the German radio proudly boasted that General Rommel and the Afrika Korps would be sleeping in Alexandria on Saturday night. Meanwhile, Mussolini had hurried to Africa in order to head victory parades in Alexandria and Cairo! On the British side, official documents and papers were burnt in Alexandria, which led to that particular day being referred to later as 'Ash Wednesday'!

On the same day Rommel launched an attack on El Alamein itself, because, as he said in his *Papers*: 'I wanted to reach the open desert beyond this line, in front of Alexandria, where I could exploit the absolute operational superiority we enjoyed in open desert battles.'

Had this happened, undoubtedly the Eighth Army would have had its lines of communication cut and been practically annihilated.

How near Rommel came to actually achieving this break-through to Alexandria, can be seen from the following report: 'It certainly seemed that Rommel would keep the Saturday night appointment in Alexandria, for, on Friday night, July 3rd [the night before he was due to sleep there] the German armour, having breached the Alamein Line, went into leaguer a bare 40 miles from the city. A moment had come when all Islam and Christendom held its breath.'

Suddenly the advance stopped and, a little later, Rommel began to withdraw!

By the third week in July his panzer divisions had begun rolling back westwards. He had broken off the battle. We had been saved by the merest hair's breadth.

This sudden receding of the tide still remains one of the unexplained mysteries of history. What was it that caused Rommel to halt at the very moment when he was practically knocking at the gates of Cairo? His own exasperation is obvious, for in his *Papers* he records that 'Our strength failed in front of El Alamein.'

When we view with hindsight the course of the war as a whole, and consider all that was at stake for the Free World, it would seem that it was at this point that the God in whose hands rests the destiny of men and of nations, had said: 'So far shalt thou go and no further. Here shall thy proud waves be stayed.'

Is there anything which justifies my making such a claim? I have tried to unravel and get to the bottom of this mystery for a long time, and I believe there is evidence available.

If we examine the records, it is obvious that a victory for Rommel should have been assured. To quote his *Papers* again: 'Given six or seven German motorised divisions, we could, in the summer of 1942, have so thoroughly mauled the British that the threat from the south would have been eliminated for a long time. The reinforcement of my army by a few German motorised divisions would have been sufficient to bring about the complete defeat of the entire British forces in the Near East.... If success had depended, as it did in olden days, on the stronger will of the soldiers and their leader, then we would have overrun Alamein.'

What then prevented such an outcome?

It had 'so happened' that, some time previously, 1 July 1942 had been appointed as the seventy-fifth anniversary of the Dominion of Canada, and on that day our King and Queen, together with the Archbishop of Canterbury, several members of the War Cabinet, other ministers and ambassadors, were present in Westminster Abbey in their official capacity.

At that Service *a special prayer was offered for those fighting in Egypt and the Mediterranean.*

The Press reported the following day that it really was a *special* prayer from the hearts of this representative body of our war-time leaders. It was not just a cold formality: it was prayed with real feeling.

Surely it was not coincidence that from 1 July 1942, Rommel's advance was first checked and then repelled, and we never looked back in North Africa. Surely God was at work with us. We now know that Hitler and the German High Command still did not see the opportunity that lay open before them. That strange blindness persisted. Could this have been due to that prayer?

Rommel's repeated demands to be reinforced by additional formations were never granted. In fact, as far back as 27 July 1941, when he first sought permission to launch this offensive with the Suez Canal as its objective and February 1942 as its target date, the German Army Command had jibbed at providing the additional three German and three Italian divisions which he had asked for. General Halder, or one of his staff, had even written rude comments on the margin of the plan of campaign which Rommel had submitted to the High Command!

Such an attitude requires more than human explanation, especially when the information now available shows that if these extra divisions had been granted, Rommel's victory would have been assured.

As events turned out, the beginning of 1942 was the very time when Malta had been effectively neutralised, so Rommel could easily have been given the little help that he needed to take Cairo, because all the troops and supplies would have reached him in safety. There was nothing to stop them.

When Rommel's spectacular advance did begin at the end of May 1942, the Italian High Command made no move whatsoever to exploit and use the harbours which Rommel captured as he moved rapidly forward, so as to keep him continuously fed with the necessary reinforcements. At the same time, Hitler, as we have already seen, decided to postpone the taking of Malta rather than go ahead immediately and capture it so as to make sure there would be no sinkings to interrupt the flow of Rommel's supplies. To add to Rommel's frustration, the German and Italian High Commands together failed to give him the extra supplies and support just when he most required them. That was at a time when the petrol which he sorely needed was reported to be lying about in Southern Italy in profusion, and only had to be shipped or flown across.

It is no wonder, therefore, that Rommel exclaims with such despair: 'Our sources of supply dried up in front of Alamein.'

I believe it was all directly related to that special prayer in Westminster Abbey on 1 July, and to the prayers of others elsewhere. *God* was at work.

There was another remarkable event which serves to substantiate this conviction. Major Peter Rainer, who was responsible for supplying the Eighth Army with water, tells the story of a remarkable and possibly decisive incident in the battle for Alexandria. He had been appointed by the British General Staff to supervise the construction of a pipe-line from the Nile Delta out into the desert, so that water for the British forces might be pumped to the battle line.

In his book *Pipe Line to Battle*[1], he relates: 'July 4th was the critical day' [the day, significantly enough, when Rommel was due to sleep in Alexandria!].

'To counter the German thrust, General Auchinleck had massed the battle-scarred remnant of his tank forces, together with what he had been able to collect from repair shops back at base.

'Between Rommel's men and Alexandria, therefore, were the remnants of a British army—fifty tanks, a few score field guns, and about 5,000 soldiers. The sides were equally matched, with the Germans holding the advantage because of their superior 88mm guns. Both armies were near exhaustion, dead tired from heat, dust and lack of water.

'The armoured forces met, supported by infantry . . . the battle was grim. The sun was almost overhead, and our men were fast reaching the end of their endurance. There was nothing brilliant about the fight. The side that could longest sustain an uninspired pounding would win.

'The Afrika Korps gave first. Suddenly, the Nazis broke. Ten minutes more, and it might have been us. After a couple of hours of fumbling, Rommel's forces began to withdraw. Slowly, sullenly, the German Mark IV tanks lumbered back from their battle smoke. The high tide of invasion had been stemmed. Never again would the invaders reach so near their goal of the Egyptian Delta.

'Our men were too weary to drive their advantage home.

'And then an incredible thing happened. As the battle broke off, more than 1,100 men of the 90th Light Panzer Division, the élite of the Afrika Korps, came stumbling across the barren sand to our line with their hands in the air.

'Cracked and black with coagulated blood, their swollen tongues were protruding from their mouths. Crazily they tore water bottles from the necks of our men and poured life-giving swallows between their parched lips. Thirst had done it. For thirty-six hours they had had no fresh water to drink. When they over-ran the British defences they found a 6-inch water pipe, shot holes in it, and drank deeply. Only when they had taken great gulps did they realise that it was sea water. The sea water in it had increased their thirst almost to the point of delirium.'

In an article in *Reader's Digest,* entitled 'A Drink that made History', Major Rainer comments: 'For 1,100 of them to surrender when escape lay open—that was nothing short of a miracle!'

He continues: 'Why was that pipe-line full of salt water?

'As the officer responsible for supplying the Eighth

Army with water through all its desert campaigns, I can give you the answer.

'The pipe-line was a new one. It had only just been laid, and I never wasted precious fresh water in testing a line; I always used salt water.

'If the Panzers had punched through Alamein the day before, that pipe-line would have been empty. Two days later it would have been full of fresh water. As it happened, the Nazis got salt water, and they didn't detect the salt at once because their sense of taste had already been anaesthetised by the brackish water they had been used to, and by thirst.

'The balance of the crucial desert battle was so even that I believe the enemy, without that salted torture, might have outlasted us. And then defenceless Alexandria would have fallen into their hands. The surrender of those 1,100 crack soldiers, therefore, may have been the deciding incident in the battle for Alexandria.

'On so small a turn of fate is history written!'

It cannot be disputed that there is a God who overrules history, and he does so, particularly, in answer to heartfelt, believing prayer. Was that not the way the Press described the special prayer which was offered by our King and Queen and the representative body of war-time leaders in Westminster Abbey on 1 July? The constant refrain of Psalm 107 is: 'Then they cried unto the Lord in their trouble, and he delivered them out of their distresses.' He most certainly did—near Alexandria.

*   *   *   *

The gates of Cairo remained barred against Rommel. The unseen hand still continued to hold him back.

This was demonstrated when he made one last bid to get there.

There was a full moon due at the end of August, and, from the British side, General Auchinleck judged correctly that a counter-attack must be expected then.

Rommel, knowing that this full moon presented him with his last chance of taking the offensive before the British launched their own, had given the order for the attack to be carried out on the night of 30–31 August.

Everything had been prepared several days before that date, but since success rested on adequate supplies of petrol, a meeting was held, three days before the battle was due to commence, between General Count Cavallero, the Chief of the Italian General Staff, Field Marshal Kesselring, Rommel's immediate German superior, and Rommel himself. At that meeting, the first two gentlemen guaranteed Rommel 6,000 tons of petrol, and Kesselring even promised to fly over 500 tons a day, in case of need, to the vicinity of the front.

'That is my condition', said Rommel. 'The whole battle depends on it.'

'You can go on with the battle', replied General Cavallero; 'it is on its way.'

In consequence, Rommel launched his attack on the night he had planned, but his offensive failed. He was routed during the battle of Alam-El-Halfa, and was forced to withdraw.

He records one of the reasons in his *Papers*: 'The urgently needed supplies of ammunition which had been promised by the Supreme Command still had not arrived by the end of August, and the petrol, which was a necessary condition of the carrying out of our plans, did not arrive either. Kesselring too, had unfortunately not been able to fulfil his promise.' This was possibly due to the timely arrival of Spitfires on Malta endangering his air fleets! But Brigadier Young also reveals that Rommel was so ill during this attack, that he could not even get out of his truck, which may have been yet another reason why his offensive failed.

So there were several mysterious circumstances continuing to hold him back, when he was himself seeking to surge forward to Suez.

Note

1. As quoted in the magazine of the Merchant Service Officers' Christian Association, April 1944.

Chapter Nine

Alamein and the 'Hinge of Fate'

While General Montgomery was making preparations to launch the British offensive against Rommel and his Afrika Korps, so important did His Majesty King George VI consider the outcome of the forthcoming battle to be, that he declared his desire that it should be preceded by a National Day of Prayer.

September 3, 1942—the third anniversary of the outbreak of the war against Hitler's Germany—was his specially chosen date, and, in taking this action, he was following in the footsteps which his father, King George V, took in August 1918.

For the first time, a National Day of Prayer was held on a week-day, and for this reason it seemed to many that it was observed far more sincerely than any of its predecessors.

Once again, people flocked to the churches and Westminster Abbey was crowded to capacity, with the King and Queen, other members of the royal family, and Members of Parliament present.

God answered that time of prayer in a marvellous way. A whole series of miracles followed in its wake.

The Lord had already seen to it that two dedicated Christian men, Field Marshal Alexander and General Montgomery, were appointed to the most responsible positions in the Middle East at this very crucial time. Field

Marshal Alexander took up his post as the new Commander-in-Chief, Middle East on 15 August 1942, and, on the same day, General Montgomery assumed command of the Eighth Army.

It soon became apparent that, as a result, a new wind had begun to blow in the Western Desert. Immediately Montgomery arrived to take over command, he declared: 'The soldiers must have faith in God.' And just before the Battle of Alamein was opened at 9.40 p.m. on 23 October, Montgomery issued to the Eighth Army this inspiring Order of the Day: 'Let us pray that the Lord, mighty in battle, will give us the victory.'

How did the Lord, mighty in battle, answer?

First, when the attack was opened with the devastating roar of nearly a thousand guns, it found Rommel absent in Germany! He had been compelled to report sick at the end of September for the first time in his life, and had flown to Germany for treatment.

The Afrika Korps had therefore been 'caught on the hop' without their famous leader, and that at the most critical and decisive moment of their history. Rommel had appointed General Stümme as commander during his absence.

Secondly, just twenty-four hours after Montgomery's bombardment opened, General Stümme died from a heart attack, which left the German command structure in a hopeless state of confusion.

Thirdly, to add to this confusion, and incredible as it may seem, the start of the battle found Rommel's Chief of Staff, General Bayerlein, away on leave!

Fourthly, due to faulty intelligence, the Afrika Korps was taken completely off its guard when the bombardment began.

So firmly convinced had the German Intelligence Service been that the British could not possibly attack during October, that the German Army Command Headquarters had sent an officer over to the Western Desert at the beginning of the month to say so. Some forces, therefore, were stood down, whilst others relaxed their guard. Over the whole of the Afrika Korps desert front there was a general easing of vigilance.

Fifthly, the extraordinary fact was that Montgomery's vast pre-offensive build-up had remained completely hidden from the Germans, despite the fact that it included the movement of literally hundreds of guns and 900 tanks, and the preparation of dumps containing 7,500 tons of petrol. It was a similar miracle to the one which had happened after King George V had called that National Day of Prayer in August 1918. The same Lord, mighty in battle, was now working on behalf of the Eighth Army.

And *lastly*, when, at Hitler's personal request, Rommel arrived at his Desert Headquarters from a hospital bed to take command of the situation two days after Montgomery's barrage had been laid down, he found to his anger that there had been a complete and catastrophic failure of supplies. He discovered that General von Rintelen, the German Military Attaché in Rome who was responsible for ensuring that supplies of petrol reached the Afrika Korps, had been on leave and had thus been unable to give sufficient attention to the problem!

Consequently, by the time Rommel arrived at his head-quarters in North Africa at 8 p.m. on 25 October, the battle was already lost. As his General Cramer said, 'Alamein was lost before it was fought. We had not the petrol.' In fact, Rommel's *Papers* reveal that throughout the battle of the next few days his tank forces were frequently standing immobilised on the battle-field for sheer lack of petrol.

None of these things could have been due to coincidence. The fact that so many key people were absent when they were most needed, that the whole of the Afrika Korp was completely caught off its guard, and that there were no supplies of petrol available, were surely all signs of how much God was answering the prayers of the nation.

In the early hours of 2 November, Montgomery struck with his famous 'Operation Supercharge' at the point

where the German and Italian lines met. It was the decisive
blow. Our infantry broke through on a 4,000-yard front
and opened the road for the British armoured tanks to
pass. Soon they were pouring through the gaps and out
into the open desert beyond.

It was the beginning of the end.

That night Rommel decided to withdraw. He conducted
the retreat with great skill, but he had only eighty German
tanks left against nearly six hundred British. In the pursuit
that followed, the Eighth Army covered the seven hundred
miles from El Alamein to Benghazi in fifteen days. And
this time, Rommel was not allowed to stand at El Agheila!

'The Lord, mighty in battle', had most certainly given
the Eighth Army the victory, and as a result caused the
tide of the war to be completely turned.

Said Churchill afterwards, concerning the Battle of
Alamein: 'It marked the turning of the Hinge of Fate. It
may also be said: Before Alamein we never had a victory.
After Alamein we never had a defeat.'

Chapter Ten

A Continent Redeemed

Rommel had retreated right back into Tripolitania. In order to drive his forces out of Africa completely, it was necessary to open up a second front by landing other Allied armies behind him in North-West Africa. A giant pincer movement would thus be formed. With Montgomery and the Eighth Army driving on through Tripoli, and with these new forces advancing on Rommel's rear through Tunisia, the Axis forces would be caught in between.

A vast armada of troopships and supply ships, sailing in convoy both from Britain and from the United States, was needed to land these new armies, and the route across the Atlantic at that time was infested with packs of marauding U-boats. Furthermore, even if the ships did get safely across, it still needed favourable weather to make a landing on the beaches of Casablanca, and the Allied General Staff had been warned by weather experts that after 1 October the Atlantic swell off the coast of Morocco would probably be too high for landing operations. It was now November.

Yet there was soon convincing evidence that the God who had wrought such miracles at Alamein was at work to overcome these difficulties also.

The initial sign was a demonstration of divine protection all the time that vast armada was at sea. There were no less than 650 ships involved in this massive operation, code-named 'Torch'. The first of the convoys left the Clyde on 22 October, the day before Montgomery's Alamein barrage was laid down, whilst the other convoys sailed direct from the United States. This vast concourse of Allied shipping traversed the Bay of Biscay from Britain on the one hand, and the Atlantic Ocean from the United States on the other, completely unseen and undetected, either by U-boats or by the German Luftwaffe. To those anxiously watching, it seemed quite unbelievable.

Lieutenant-General Sir Frederick Morgan, the head of the British and American Planning Staff in General Eisenhower's Rear Headquarters in London, has this remarkable story to tell. He was watching the charts which showed those convoys making their tortuous progress in the direction of North Africa both from Britain and from the United States. The location and movement of every enemy submarine was also being plotted.

'There was one breath-taking moment', he said, 'when a U-boat caught sight of the tail ship of one convoy and only thought it worth making a mere routine report! The rest of the ships were being *obscured in a squall that seemed to be travelling with our ships*' (my italics).[1] When I read that, it seemed to me just like the pillar of cloud which stood behind the children of Israel and obscured them from Pharoah and the oncoming Egyptians as they prepared to cross the Red Sea in Moses' day, and which travelled with them later through the wilderness (see Exodus 14:19, 20). And why not? The God of the Bible is the same God today. We should therefore expect to see him working in similar ways in times like these, and especially in answer to prayer.

Admiral Sir Andrew Cunningham, the Commander-in-Chief, Mediterranean at the time, later recorded his own amazement about the crossing in *A Sailor's Odyssey*: 'It was the almost incredible fact that that procession of large convoys was not attacked, and sustained no casualties.'

The next amazing thing about the crossing was that

when the leading ships, which were bound for Algeria, began to enter the Mediterranean through the comparatively narrow Straits of Gibraltar on the night of 5–6 November, they still remained undetected and sailed through unmolested.

Yet another miracle happened. General Marshall has said that 'It had been found, when planning "Operation Torch", that all the British and American Air Forces, except for a few long-range bombers and the small number of carrier-based planes, had to be funnelled through the single restricted airfield at Gibraltar, which could have been put out of action in less than an hour.'

According to the *New York Times*, this added one more to the famous 'ifs' of history. It asked, 'What effect would it have had on the course of the war if German bombers had put that airfield out of action and thus made these Algerian and Tunisian campaigns impossible?'

Then a fourth intervention occurred. As all those troopships were nearing their destination off the Moroccan coast on 6 November, they found the Atlantic swell so high and the weather so bad that landings were impossible. This was in line with the weather forecasts. The surf was fifteen feet high!

Just as it seemed inevitable that General Patton must call off the whole affair, the wind suddenly changed from on-shore to off-shore. The sea went down, and let the small craft in!

The Bible says: 'They that go down to the sea in ships, that do business in great waters; These see the works of the Lord, and his wonders in the deep...He maketh the storm a calm, so that the waves thereof are still. Then are they glad because they be quiet; so he bringeth them unto their desired haven' (Psalm 107:23–30).

All on board the troopships and their escorts had certainly seen one of those mighty works of the Lord.

As G. Ward Price wrote in the *Daily Mail* on 14 November 1942: 'Only the thoughtless can fail to realise how great a part Providence has played in the swift and successful transformation of the war situation. Those who have heard something of the inside story of the dramatic events of this historic week are reminded of that dispensation that smoothed the waters of Dunkirk.

'In that remarkable change in the weather, off Morocco, sceptics may see no more than a fortunate "coincidence", but it is not the only feature of a great undertaking that will suggest to others the need for expressing their gratitude to God, when the victory bells begin their cheering chimes.'

The landings of these new armies in North Africa on 8 November, and their eventual convergence with Montgomery's Eighth Army at the beginning of the following May, led to the total capitulation of the remaining Axis Forces in North Africa—just six months after the Battle of Alamein had been joined.

'The Lord, mighty in battle' had answered the prayers of a godly King, of the people at home, and of Montgomery and others in the Western Desert, by giving us a complete and resounding victory.

It was therefore due to a whole chain of miracles in the Middle East War that Churchill, whilst on a visit to the United States at this time, was able to declare to Congress: 'We have arrived at a significant milestone in this war. We can say, "One Continent Redeemed".'

Note

1. From an article in the *Daily Telegraph*, 7 April 1947, by Lt-Gen. Sir Frederick Morgan.

Chapter Eleven

The Shape of Things to Come

With the continent of Africa set free, all attention was focused on the liberation of Europe.

A strike at its underbelly through Italy was envisaged as a prelude to the invasion of France and Germany, but to reach Italy, the Allied armies had first to take possession of Sicily, now held by strong German forces. Plans were therefore laid to assemble what one Royal Naval commander described as 'The Greatest Armada in History'.

This new phase of the war was to begin on 10 July 1943. It entailed long months of careful preparation, and a great company of ships was to be involved. Yet the planning did not go ahead without prayer. Indeed the whole enterprise was impregnated with faith in God.

On board the headquarters ship on the day before the attack, a Canadian forces Press correspondent, Ross Monro, witnessed a meeting of the officers, held in the lounge and addressed by the colonel. 'We are on the eve of a never-to-be-forgotten night in the history of the world', he declared. 'We will remember this night, and our children will.'[1] He invited them to bow their heads in prayer. Everyone repeated the Lord's Prayer, and they then joined hands.

On board a destroyer, the captain mustered all hands on deck to explain the part the ship would play in the invasion. Having done that, he proclaimed: 'I have every faith in God, and in you.' Then he led his ship's company in prayer, using the words which Nelson uttered on the eve of Trafalgar:

> May the Great God whom I worship grant to my country and for the benefit of Europe in general, a great and glorious victory, and may no misconduct in anyone tarnish it.
>
> May humanity, after victory, be the predominant feature in the British Fleet.
>
> For myself, individually, I commit my life to him who made me, and may his blessing alight on my endeavours for serving my country faithfully.
>
> To him I resign myself, and the just cause which is entrusted to me to defend.

These are but two examples of the prayerful spirit which prevailed. All the evidence shows that this time it was prayer going up from the various units on the spot which were involved in the vast operation, rather than in terms of a National Day of Prayer back home. God answered prayer and honoured faith, so that it was obvious that he was still working with us.

Commander Anthony Kimmins bears testimony to this in an article published in *The Listener* on 22 July 1943.

'As we rendezvoused at sea, our own force looked almost big enough to do the job by itself: escorting warships, big troopships with their assault-craft hanging on the davits, and literally hundreds of other landing-craft steaming under their own power.

'And yet we knew we were only a tiny part of the whole.

'Beyond the horizon there were other forces, some even larger than our own, approaching Sicily to arrive with us dead on zero hour.

'But although we could not see them, we knew that there was one thing which was worrying them just as much as us—the weather.

'By all the rules, one expects fine weather and a calm sea in the Mediterranean at this time of the year.

'But now it suddenly started to blow, a real blow, force 6, half a gale, from the north-west. This meant that it would be blowing down the coast and that many of the beaches would have little lee. The surf would be terrific, and it would be almost impossible for our landing craft to force their way through and land their precious cargoes intact. We hoped and prayed that with sunset the wind would drop, but as the sun dipped over the horizon the wind if anything seemed to grow stronger.

'It was a strange, and to me anyhow, a terrifying feeling.

'In spite of everything that man's ingenuity could do to produce the most modern and up-to-date ships and landing craft; in spite of all the elaborate preparations: here we were, in the long run, at the mercy of the elements.

'The memory of how a gale had sealed the fate of the Spanish Armada sent a nasty chill down one's spine.

'Foul weather: the eternal enemy of the sailor. But there was nothing to be done about it, and the ships ploughed on with many of the smaller craft taking it over green as they wallowed in the high seas.

'But there was no turning back now, and as the darkness closed down and the ships ploughed on, I couldn't help thinking of some of the miracles of weather which had already favoured us in this war:

'Dunkirk; North Africa.

'Perhaps three times was too much to expect.

'Perhaps... and then it happened.

'With barely an hour and a half to go before zero hour the wind suddenly dropped, the white horses disappeared, and the swell went down quicker than I have ever seen it do before.

'It was so sudden it was almost unbelievable, and as people stared into the darkness it seemed miraculous, as if... well, put it this way, many a silent prayer of thanks was offered up.'

Admiral Sir Andrew Cunningham, in command of the Allied Naval Forces, takes up the story. He shows us how miraculous this unfavourable weather had been.

'At many places along the Sicilian coast, the enemy garrisons had been on the alert for weeks. One expected that the Italians might even maintain off-shore patrols.

'But the garrisons, lulled into a sense of security by the wild weather, and believing that no one would attempt a landing in such conditions, allowed their vigilance to relax.

'Syracuse and Augusta were quite close: but the Italian sailors apparently confined their small craft to harbour and themselves to bed.'

Behind this entire story there stands the calm and confident faith of one particular man, the man on whose shoulders rested the crushing weight of the main responsibility—General Eisenhower. The secret of this weather miracle may lie in a sentence he uttered from a hill-top as he watched that great armada setting forth, and the scene is well described by W. H. Elliott.[2]

'The man was standing, silhouetted sharp and clear in the moonlight, on the crest of a little hill, looking out to sea.

'In front of him glittered a wide expanse of waters.

'Near him on that hilltop was a group of other men, watching what he watched, and without a word.

'They were watching a great company of ships, a most wonderful sight indeed, big ships and little ships, hundreds of them, thousands of them, grey monsters on the sky line, quick darting destroyers, troopships, tankers, freighters, almost down to tugs and boats, all full of men.

'A great moment, tense, historic, a moment of silence, too, were it not for all the planes, hundreds of them, buzzing, zooming, circling overhead and over those ships.

'But a man can be silent anywhere—within himself.

'Suddenly, said an eye-witness, the man drew himself stiffly to attention.

'He lifted his hand to salute, and so for some minutes he remained.

'Then he dropped his hand and bent his head, once again motionless, quiet.

'He was praying.

'Well he might, with that great Armada setting out for

Sicily and he commanded them.

'Thank Heaven he was one of that sort.

'Presently he turned to the group beside him—to one of his aides. "There comes a time", he said, "when you have done all that you can possibly do; when you have used your brains, your training, your technical skill, and the die is cast, and events are in the hands of God—and there you have to put them."'

God always honours faith. What he did to that weather was a perfect example. The successful campaign in Sicily was soon followed by the invasion of the mainland of Italy and Mussolini's dramatic downfall. It marked, as President Roosevelt declared, 'The beginning of the end'.

Notes

1. From *We Have a Guardian*, compiled by W. B. Grant, Covenant Publishing Company, London 1958.
2. The Rev. W. H. Elliott, 'The Faith of a General', *Sunday Graphic*, 28 May 1944.

Chapter Twelve

A Welsh Prayer Meeting

In the battle for Italy, the danger spot was Salerno, where our troops landed in September 1943 to capture some strategic heights and open the way for the invading forces from the south to reach Rome.

While that landing was taking place, a very strange thing happened. Hundreds of miles away, back in the United Kingdom, the usual evening prayer meeting was taking place in the conference hall at the Bible College of Wales in Swansea. Soon after 9.45 p.m., the director of that college, Rees Howells, began to announce with a trembling voice that the Lord had given him a heavy burden for the invasion of Salerno.

'I believe our men are in great difficulties', he said, 'and the Lord has told me that unless we can pray through, they are in danger of losing their hold.' As is recounted in *Rees Howells: Intercessor,* by Norman Grubb, the awe of God settled upon everybody at the meeting, for this news came as a complete surprise. There had been no official news on the radio to the effect that something was wrong. Rather to the contrary, those at the prayer meeting had recently been rejoicing that Italy was at last on the point of being delivered from the Fascist and Nazi yoke.

Before long, all were on their knees crying to God for him to intervene. As they were doing so, they had the experience of the Holy Spirit taking hold of them and causing them to break right through to victory in their prayers. They found themselves praising and rejoicing, fully believing that God had not only heard, but had also answered their prayers. So much so, that they just could not go on praying any longer, but rose to their feet and began to sing praises. The Holy Spirit was witnessing in their hearts that God had wrought some miraculous intervention in Italy. This break-through into victory in prayer was so outstanding that somebody present felt obliged to look at the clock as they started to sing, to see at what time the victory through prayer had taken place.

It was on the stroke of 11 p.m.

The midnight news confirmed the fact that our troops were in real trouble, and were in grave danger of losing the beach-head before morning. Those who were at the prayer meeting were confident, however, that something had happened out there.

On the Thursday morning of that week, one of the daily newspapers displayed a front-page headline, 'The Miracle of Salerno'. A reporter, who was at the front, recounted it thus: 'I was with our advanced troops in the invasion of Salerno on Monday. The enemy artillery was advancing rapidly and with ceaseless firing. The noise was terrible, and it was obvious that, unless a miracle happened, our troops could never hold up the advance long enough for the beach-head to be established. Suddenly, for no accountable reason, the firing ceased and the Nazi artillery stopped its advance. A deathly stillness settled on the scene. We waited in breathless anticipation, but nothing happened. I looked at my watch—*it was eleven o'clock at night*. Still we waited, but still nothing happened; and nothing happened all that night, but those hours made all the difference to the invasion. By the morning the beach-head was established' (the italics are mine).

It was another amazing example of how God was working with us in those momentous days. Even to the extent of giving a heavy burden of prayer to believing people,

hundreds of miles away, who could not possibly have
known what was happening on the scene of battle, and of
enabling them to pray through to victory.

Chapter Thirteen

Bumper Harvest

Throughout the crucial year of 1942 and the months immediately following it, the entire nation was provided with evidence that God was at work in *the fields of Britain*.

During this critical year, the shipping which normally brings food to these shores from overseas, was urgently required for carrying men and munitions. Yet the people in beleagured Britain had to be fed. There was need, therefore, for a bumper harvest.

To that end, a supreme effort was made by British agriculture, and a degree of co-operation and united labour was achieved as never before in our history. Added to this were the prayers of innumerable people that God would bless these efforts.

The yields in the fields that year far exceeded all expectations. It had obviously become very apparent to R. S. Hudson, the minister of Agriculture, that God had been with us, for in a postscript to the BBC nine o'clock news on Old Michaelmas Night 1942, he said: 'But this also I would say to you, in humility and seriousness. Much hard work and technical skill have played their part in these mighty yields, amongst the richest of all time. But I believe that we have a higher Power to thank as well, and from the depths of our hearts.

'Some Power has wrought a miracle in the English

harvest fields this summer, for in this, our year of greatest need, the land has given us bread in greater abundance than we have ever known before. The prayer, "Give us this day our daily bread" has in these times a very direct meaning for us all.'

God had indeed 'crowned the year with his goodness', and granted us the much needed special harvest.

Divine blessing continued during the following months, a fact which Fleet Street brought to the nation's notice. In an article in the *News Chronicle* dated 6 May 1943, L. F. Easterbrook described the first part of 1943 as 'this wonderful year', and said:

'Mr Hudson was not ashamed to acknowledge last year the divine power that gave us a record harvest just when we most needed it. Can anyone doubt that the Power has been at work again?

'It has brought us through what might have been a very difficult winter with an unerring hand.

'For that, we can be thankful for having sufficient fuel and sufficient milk, for wheat in the fields that never looked better, for grass in the meadows that has enabled winter feeding stuffs to be conserved, so that the small poultry keeper is now to get more food for his hens, and the housewife to get more milk for the family.

'We are still only half-way to harvest, and disaster can still happen. But nothing should take away our thankfulness for a season that has warmed and fed our bodies and cheered our hearts more generously than any dared hope.'

There was another acknowledgement that God was visiting the earth—*Britain's* earth—and blessing it. He was preparing the corn, watering the furrows, making the fields soft with showers of rain and blessing the increase, so as to ensure that once again the valleys should 'stand so thick with corn' that they would 'laugh and sing' (see Psalm 65:10, 11, 14, *The Book of Common Prayer*).

All Britain therefore was made aware that God's hand was upon our history throughout those important years of 1942 and 1943, not least by providing enough food.

Chapter Fourteen

Preparation for Victory

At the close of 1943, the invasion of France was the major task for the year ahead, and the nation prepared for the greatest military adventure ever undertaken in its long history.

Forty years later, many people seem to have forgotten that the whole of the continent of Europe had fallen under the domination of a tyrant—Adolf Hitler.

France, Belgium, Holland, Norway, Denmark, Czechoslovakia, Poland—all had been overrun by his Nazi armies. The continent of Europe was a subjugated people. It was looking westwards, pinning its hopes on Britain and America for its liberation.

Deliverance! That was what they all longed for, and no doubt it was that for which, in their anguish, many of them were praying. But the task was so mammoth that, to achieve it, God needed a massive instrument.

One was being fashioned, and its four components form an integral part of the next chapter of world history: godly leaders; a clear vision of the purpose set before them; a dedicated force; and a miracle.

Chief amongst the leaders whom God had been preparing down the years were King George VI, with his simple but deep awareness that he reigned through the grace of God; General Montgomery; Admiral Cunningham;

Admiral Tovey; General Sir Miles Dempsey, Commander of the British Second Army in the invasion of Europe; and General Eisenhower, the Supreme Commander. All these had a testimony of his faith in Almighty God to declare.

Was it not remarkable that at this vital time in our history the most responsible tasks of leadership should fall to God-fearing, God-honouring, God-trusting men such as these, just as in the case of the Battle of Britain, God had prepared Air Chief Marshal Sir Hugh Dowding?

As at so many other critical points in the war, this chapter of our history was opened with a solemn call to prayer and dedication.

On the eve of D-Day, King George VI broadcast again to the nation and to the world:

'Four years ago our nation and empire stood alone against an overwhelming enemy, with our backs to the wall. Tested as never before in our history, in God's providence we survived that test.

'The spirit of the people, resolute, dedicated, burned like a bright flame, lit surely from those unseen fires which nothing can quench.

'Now once more a supreme test has to be faced.

'This time the challenge is not to fight to survive but to fight to win the final victory for the good cause....

'That we may be worthily matched with this new summons of destiny, I desire solemnly to call my people to prayer and to dedication.

'We are not unmindful of our shortcomings, past and present.

'We shall ask not that God may do our will, but that we may be enabled to do the will of God.

'And we dare to believe that God has used our nation and empire as an instrument for fulfilling his high purpose. Surely not one of us is too busy to play our part in a nation-wide, perchance a world-wide, vigil of prayer as the great crusade sets forth.'

So we come to the vision which God gave.

General Montgomery, by the way he ordered his

soldiers to be spiritually prepared, and in a great speech which he delivered at the Mansion House on 24 March 1944, revealed that he saw this vision very clearly.

'Only from an inspired nation can go forth, under these conditions, an inspired army', he declared. 'When our men go forth to battle on this great endeavour—that is the time when there must swell up in the nation every noble thought, every high ideal, every great purpose which has waited through the weary years.

'And then, as the sap rises in the nation, the men will feel themselves to be the instrument of a new-born national vigour.

'The special glory of the whole endeavour must be a surge of the whole people's finest qualities worthy to be the prayer: "Let God arise and let His enemies be scattered".'

Talking of the sacrifice likely to be involved, General Montgomery continued:

'A special gallantry is required of our soldiers.

'If necessary, we have got to hazard all, and give our lives, that others may enjoy it.

'From a consecrated nation such men will abundantly come, and "the Lord, mighty in battle" will go forth with our armies and His special providence will assist our battle.'

So the need for consecration was stressed, and the sense of being launched out on a great mission was also there.

For General Montgomery went on to say:

'The substance of the tide which has to turn and flow is quite clear.

'It is not a personal fad or a one-man doctrine.

'It is the tide which has borne the nation through its history.

'It is found in the Coronation Service of our King and Queen.

'The nation's Church handed to our King from the altar of Westminster Abbey the Sword of State: "With this sword do justice, stop the growth of iniquity".

'The task now in hand is the use of His Majesty's

consecrated sword in the reawakened spirit of that day.'

General Montgomery then reminded his listeners at the Mansion House that, just prior to the Battle of El Alamein, he had sent his eve-of-battle message to all ranks: 'Let us pray that the Lord, mighty in battle, will give us the victory.'

As a result, the Eighth Army soon became known as 'the victorious Desert Army'.

Nor did Montgomery ever forget to return thanks to God for the victories. In his 1943 Christmas message to the forces under his command, he quoted his former words and added: 'He has done so, and I know that you will agree with me when I say that we must not forget to thank him for his mercy.'

There was also the preparation of the forces about to be involved in the coming invasion. General Montgomery's chief padre, in a broadcast made shortly after the Normandy landings, showed how the forces invading France had one clear objective set before them. He spoke of them as 'going on this liberating enterprise', but went further in saying, 'They were freely and fully convinced that the business in hand was liberation according to the will of God.'

That involved spiritual preparation.

The Deputy Chaplain-General, Canon Llewellyn Hughes, has indicated how thorough and painstaking had been the task given to the chaplains to prepare the fighting forces spiritually.

'The consecration of our armies had not been a last minute effort', he declared. 'It has been a long and laborious process. We aimed at a permanent attitude of mind, at giving to soldiers such a vision of God's will as would make the doing of it their main purpose.'

After the landings had taken place, he said, 'As you read incident after incident, comradeship, self-sacrifice, and humour, will you weigh my evidence, as General Montgomery's chief padre, that many many thousands of them went forth for righteousness' sake, and for no other reason.'

What was involved in that long, laborious but happy

process? What was instilled into their minds? The chief padre tells us.

'Let an army and a people learn what God stands for, and then they will know when they are for, or against, his purpose.

'They will then support or oppose with confidence as His Commissioned Servants.

'It is not enough for an army or a nation to have a vague faith in God.

'It is not enough for us to rest content that our commanders are godly, and that God's flag is publicly flown.

'Faith in God is useless until it governs action.

'What does God want done?

'We believe in God—as what?

'As a nonentity, content to be recognised, and then ignored?

'As a vague power, meaningless, purposeless, inarticulate, and therefore unfit to command a platoon, let alone a world?

'No.

'We believe in God who wants, and means to have done, all that Christ embodied, taught, and lived out.'

Then he added: 'The leaders of the invasion force wished most of all that God should impart His own life and desires to the men, and they were certain that then the army would have a sound and honest heart, would hate evil and love good, and go upon this liberating enterprise with a free and genuine enthusiasm.

'We were asked, and strongly asked, to make our men as Christian as we could, to preach the Word of Christ faithfully because it is true; to bring men to God that he might make them good.

'Most of the men are not regular church-going men but they are God-going men, and they have their picture of the King of kings in the sanctuary of their hearts.

'And when General Eisenhower and General Montgomery in their final Orders of the Day asked us all to pray that God would prosper us, that prayer went up, and went up from honest hearts, freely and fully convinced that the business in hand was a liberation according to the will of God.'

So, while the physical preparations for invasion proceeded, the chaplains set about their task of preparing the fighting forces spiritually.

The culmination of this long and painstaking task took the form of services of dedication held on the eve of D-Day, and General Montgomery's chief padre could report soon after the landings: 'There have been crowded pre-battle services everywhere.'

A plaque in Christ Church, Portsdown, bears the following inscription concerning just one of them: 'On June 4th, 1944, forty-eight hours before the invasion of Normandy, Headquarters Second Army held a service of dedication for battle in this church. To commemorate that service and the great events which followed, these two windows were dedicated on June 6th, 1948.'

Further evidence was supplied when General Sir Miles Dempsey, Commander of the British Second Army, broke the secret four years after one of the most historic and dramatic religious services that has ever been held.

As reported in the *Sunday Express* of 28 March 1948, he explained that this 70-year-old parish church overlooks the road down which the Allied forces trooped twenty-four hours later to the invasion ships. The idea of a knight's vigil, as on battle eve in olden days, came from the Rev. J. W. J. Steele, the Assistant Chaplain-General of the Second Army. The vigil lasted an hour, and the church was filled by 400 officers and men of Second Army Headquarters Staff.

'It was one of the most moving experiences of my life', said General Dempsey. 'With military police guarding the doors, and the Allied armies poised in sealed camps in the surrounding woods, the Chaplain recited the famous prayer Drake offered before Cadiz in 1587:

O Lord God, when Thou givest to Thy servants to endeavour any great matter, grant us also to know that it is not the beginning, but the continuing of the same, until it be thoroughly finished, which yieldeth the true glory; through Him that for the finishing of Thy work laid down His life, our Redeemer, Jesus Christ.

'Then came this challenge read out by the Assistant Chaplain-General: "To the Second Army there has been given a glorious part in a great task. To relieve the oppressed, to restore freedom in Europe, and to bring peace to the world. As we stand upon the threshold of the greatest adventure in our history, let us now offer to Almighty God all our powers of body, mind, and spirit, so that our great endeavour may be thoroughly finished. To this end, will you undertake the heavy responsibility that such a task places upon each of you, and with God's help carry it through, giving of the best, until Victory is won and Peace assured?"

'Four hundred voices responded, "I will, the Lord being my helper".'

Eve-of-battle services were taking place at the same time on ships, on landing-craft, on airfields—everywhere. They were deeply religious acts of dedication and consecration, and so the whole of the coming endeavour was committed into the hands of God.

Chapter Fifteen

D-Day, 1944

Testimony to what took place during the next forty-eight hours was not left only to the rank and file to declare, though they had many an amazing story to tell. What happened was witnessed by those in the best positions to see all the details.

The head of the British and American Planning Staff preparing for the invasion, Lt-Gen. Sir Frederick Morgan, was one of these. He gave his account of D-Day in an article in the *Daily Telegraph* of 7 April 1947.

'There comes a point in so many of our affairs at which, when we have done everything of which we are capable, there remains no more but to leave it all . . .

'We hope so often for a miracle. And miracles happen still.

'How many of them have we not seen enacted before our very eyes in these past years?'

'The history of them is now in the writing, and when we come to read it I sometimes wonder how the attribution of success will be worked out.'

He then recounted three of them. 'Dunkirk, and its flat calm sea. Who planned that?', he asked . . . . 'The landings in North Africa, and the passage of the convoys from Britain and the United States undetected and unmolested.'

'Then, but a day before General Patton was due to land

on the Casablanca beaches, open to the full Atlantic swell, just as it seemed inevitable that his whole affair must be called off, the wind changed from on-shore to off-shore and let the small craft in. There was surely more than planning here, too.'

'The history of our other theatres of war will inevitably tell of many similar happenings', he continued, 'but I doubt if any will be such as to compare with the miracle of D-Day in 1944, when our troops from Britain set foot once more in France and opened the last campaign against Germany.

'Every hazard that could be eliminated had been eliminated. Every foreseeable risk had been covered, and then came that weather!

'All culminated at a terrific moment when General Eisenhower, the Supreme Commander, gave his fateful decision that the attack be launched across the Channel, which at that moment looked as forbidding as only our Channel can look.

'Seldom can one man have been faced with the making of a decision so critical!'

The Times (11 September 1944) commented in its editorial: 'The whole meteorological episode had provided interesting reading for those who spent their days tapping barometers in a fever of anxiety and looking out of the window every five minutes to see whether the wind was treating the trees less boisterously and the clouds were giving a less impressive imitation of November storms.

'It seemed that those normally placid and sunlit days when May and June mingle, were, this summer, malignantly possessed.

'Yet all the time, had we but known it, the clouds we so much dreaded were big with opportunities which Supreme Headquarters was quick to grasp.

'The weather, indeed, while we were able to probe its secrets, bluffed the enemy completely, for, in the words of the report: "The German commanders were advised by their meteorological service that there could be no invasion in the period including June 6 because of continuous stormy weather. That is why D-Day forces, landing during a brief break in the windiest month in Normandy for at least 20 years, found so many German troops without officers, and why other enemy coastal units were having exercises at the time of the landings."'

How close a thing it was, can be judged by the official story of the invasion weather forecast being studied by experts on this side of the Channel. This was reported in *The Times* on 2 September 1944.

'For months the meteorological section at Supreme Headquarters had been studying the relative advantages of May, June and July for weather. Using statistics, they found that the chances were about 50 to 1 against weather, tide and moon being favourable for all services: land, sea and air.

'When the Commanders' final series of meetings began on Thursday, June 1, the first indication was given that conditions in the Channel on the Monday were unlikely to meet even the minimum requirements.

'In the early hours of Sunday morning the Supreme Commander postponed the biggest military operation in history on a day to day basis. Late in the evening of Sunday there was fairly strong evidence that after a stormy Monday there would be a temporary improvement overnight, and for the greater part of Tuesday. By now the weather in the Atlantic was more like mid-winter than early June. Any improvement on Tuesday would be short-lived.

'The assault could not take place on the Wednesday because some of the naval forces from the more distant embarkation ports had set out in advance of the final decision and would need to return to port if the assault was deferred beyond Tuesday.'

Then late on Sunday evening came this historic weather report: 'An interval of fair conditions will spread throughout the Channel area on Monday and last until at least dawn on Tuesday, June 6th. Winds will fall to force 3 or 4 on the Normandy coasts, and cloud will be well broken with a base height of about 3,000 feet.

'After that interval it will become cloudy or overcast again during Tuesday afternoon. Then, following a brief fair interval on Tuesday night or early Wednesday, conditions will continue variable with indeterminate periods of overcast skies and fresh winds until Friday.'

Shortly afterwards, the Supreme Commander said that he had provisionally decided that the invasion should go forward on Tuesday morning. He, his Commander-in-Chief, and their Chiefs of Staff met again at 4 a.m. on Monday for 'the final and irrevocable decision'. Messages went to all the vast forces concerned: the invasion of France would start on the morning of the next day.

General Eisenhower gave testimony to the effect that this had on him, when he was speaking in Abilene, Kansas, his home town, on 4 June 1952 (*Time* magazine, 16 June 1952).

'This day, eight years ago, I made the most agonising decision of my life.

'I had to decide to postpone by at least twenty-four hours the most formidable array of fighting ships and of fighting men that was ever launched across the sea against a hostile shore.

'The consequences of that decision at that moment could not have been foreseen by anyone.

'If there was nothing else in my life to prove the existence of an Almighty and Merciful God, the events of the next twenty-four hours did it. The greatest break in a terrible outlay of weather occurred the next day and allowed that great invasion to proceed, with losses far below those we had anticipated.'

The Times editorial of 11 September 1944 indicated what some of those consequences were. 'On the morning of the assault the wind had moderated, and the cloud was not only well broken, but its base was at least 4,000 feet high, ideally suited for the large-scale airborne operations.

'In the hour preceding the landings, when perfect conditions for pin-point bombing were so essential, there were large areas of temporarily clear sky, and throughout the critical time medium and light bombers were unhampered.'

Furthermore, the *Daily Telegraph* reported that this was the only night the U-boats did not patrol the Channel. The way our forces went over to Normandy was beyond imagination—4,000 ships and 11,000 planes—and they never met a single enemy ship or plane! There could hardly be anything in our history to compare with the night we invaded Normandy.

Rear-Admiral William Tennant, who directed the construction off the Normandy beaches of the prefabricated Mulberry harbours, adds his testimony to the fact that this was an amazing example of God's perfect timing. He said in an article which appeared in *The Times* on 27 October 1944:

'It has perhaps never been fully appreciated how near the invasion forces came to a disaster comparable with the fate of the Spanish Armada....

'D-Day had already been postponed for 24 hours on account of bad weather....Had it been put off for a day more, the expedition would probably have been delayed until June 18th, the earliest day of propitious tides.'

Admiral Tennant reminded us that Sunday, 18 June was a perfect summer evening on the Channel. The forecast was good. His staff had taken advantage of fair weather to sail twenty-three tows of pier equipment across for the harbours. Yet only one of those tows survived. At four o'clock the next morning the gale began and became steadily worse for twenty-four hours before it moderated and died away after two and a half days.

'Had the invasion fleet come in on that Sunday', declared Rear-Admiral Tennant, 'as could easily have happened, the whole expedition might have been wrecked.'

Said Lt-Gen. Sir Frederick Morgan: 'There was something more than ordinary, surely, in that decision of General Eisenhower's to attack.'

All the evidence bears testimony that it was made under the overruling hand of God.

General Morgan then gave testimony to the assurance held by all, that this vast mission would succeed:

'At the Supreme Commander's word there set out a combined American and British Navy and Army and Air Force in which every individual, or so it seemed, had no thought in his mind but success.

'Somehow it all seemed inevitable to everyone. None took counsel of their fears, for, in truth, the contemplation of failure would have been more than could be borne.

'So fears were set aside and off went the ships and the aircraft and their men, into the unknown, certain of victory.

'There was something more than ordinary also, surely, in that spirit of success that permeated the ranks.'

There were abundant indications that God was with them. But who would have thought they would also be given signs in the sky?

We have it on record that as the combined British and United States Army of Liberation landed on the beaches of Normandy, a magnificent rainbow was arched over the battle area. On 24 June 1944 it was reported in *The Sphere* in this manner:

'Lately there has been talk in some parts of the country about signs in the sky. The one depicted by our artist in this drawing was witnessed over the invasion area at dawn on D-Day. The rainbow spread right across the combat zone in brilliant colours, only fading from sight after thousands of our men had seen it and been heartened by its appearance at the outset of the Great Adventure.

'One aeroplane crew reported that they had flown through the middle of it whilst carrying out a bombing mission over the beaches. "It stood out as plain as it could be. I watched it for quite a while", said the aircraft's turret gunner.

'Below him at that moment was the whole panorama of the invasion, with vessels crowding in on the beaches, gun-flashes and bomb-bursts all along the coast, and fleets of aircraft flying over to cover the ground forces. Coming at the precise moment when it did, the Rainbow of Invasion Morn might rank with the Angels of Mons of the last war.'

This sign in the heavens, at such a time, was surely a

confirmation of the Almighty's blessing resting upon this just cause of setting so many captives free, and was a guarantee of ultimate victory.

There followed the triumphant advance through France, so unexpectedly rapid (after some initial setbacks had been overcome) that General Montgomery said in a message sent to his armies, 'Such an historic march of events can seldom have taken place in such a short space of time...Let us say to each other, "This was the Lord's doing, and it is marvellous in our eyes".' Victory was now within sight.

My argument, therefore, is that the entire period of the war is full of the great works of the Lord. Soldiers, statesmen, our own monarch, and the events themselves, all bear testimony to this fact. The hand of God was clearly on our history. I contend that it is an indisputable fact that the whole story of the 1939–45 War is a story of one mighty deliverance or intervention of God after another. God was with us.

No wonder Churchill had said, when addressing three thousand mine owners and mineworkers' delegates eight days after the opening of the Battle of Alamein: 'I sometimes have a feeling of interference. I want to stress that. I have a feeling sometimes that some Guiding Hand has interfered.

'I have a feeling that we have a Guardian, because we have a great Cause, and we shall have that Guardian so long as we serve that Cause faithfully. And what a cause it is.'

O that those words had been engraved around his memorial plaque in Westminster Abbey under the inscription, 'Remember Winston Churchill'.

In view of the tragic landslide which has happened since, the British people, whom he once led and inspired, now need desperately to be reminded not only of what he said about that Guardian, but of the condition he laid down for keeping that Guardian: 'We shall have that Guardian so long as we serve that cause faithfully.'

We might well ask: 'Are we still doing that?'

Chapter Sixteen

Saved for a Purpose

On 8 May 1945, victory in Europe was joyfully proclaimed. The Allied forces had accomplished their mission. The whole continent of Western Europe had been liberated. Mr Churchill, in a world broadcast that day, proclaimed:

'Yesterday morning at 2.41 a.m. at Headquarters, General Jodl, the representative of the German High Command, and Grand Admiral Doenitz, the designated head of the German State, signed the act of unconditional surrender of all German land, sea, and air forces in Europe to the Allied Expeditionary Force...'

'Hostilities will end officially at one minute after midnight tonight (Tuesday 8 May), but in the interests of saving lives the "Cease Fire" began yesterday to be sounded all along the front.'

A longer speech followed, in which he made the details known to all the world.

He read the same statement to the House of Commons a few minutes later, and after expressing his deep gratitude to Parliament for all the help and co-operation given throughout the long years of the war, said:

'I recollect well at the end of the last war, more than a quarter of a century ago, that the House when it heard the long list of surrender terms, the armistice terms, which had been imposed upon the Germans, did not feel inclined

131

for debate or business, but desired to offer thanks to Almighty God, to the Great Power which seems to shape and design the fortunes of nations and the destiny of man; and I therefore beg, sir, with your permission to move "That this House do now attend at the Church of St Margaret, Westminster, to give humble and reverent thanks to Almighty God for our deliverance from the threat of German domination".'

This was identical to the motion which was moved in 1918.

I well remember 'VE-Day'. London was rejoicing. The royal family, the Prime Minister, the Service chiefs, and members of the Cabinet, all appeared on the balcony of Buckingham Palace before a joyful and tumultous throng.

It was a proud moment in our history. The Service chiefs came to the microphone in turn, made short speeches, and paid tribute to the part which their respective arm of the Services had played in bringing about this great victory. The Prime Minister spoke—the one who had always been conscious of that overruling providence, that guiding, guardian hand. He must have come straight from the Thanksgiving Service in St Margaret's, Westminster. His Majesty King George VI then stepped quietly to the microphone. I can still hear his voice today, as he said with great emphasis: 'We give thanks to Almighty God for the victory he has granted us in Europe'.

It brought things to the right crescendo.

The godly Sovereign who, by his inspiring leadership, had caused Britain and the Commonwealth to turn to God for help at each of the critical points during the war, and who, in consequence, had been largely responsible for causing Britain to spend no less than twenty-six days and two whole weeks in urgent prayer, was now publicly proclaiming before the entire world where the honour was rightly due. He did so quietly, humbly, but yet firmly.

There were voices in the nation who were striking an additional note. Some of those in high positions believed that we had been saved for a purpose, and they began saying so.

Certain of my critics refuse to believe this, but here is some of the evidence.

William Temple, Archbishop of Canterbury, during a sermon in St Paul's Cathedral on 'Battle of Britain' Sunday, 26 September 1943, said: 'We may, and we must believe, that he who has preserved our land in a manner so marvellous, has a purpose for us to serve.'

The Bishop of Chelmsford, in an article published in the *Sunday Chronicle* in April 1945 wrote: 'If ever a great nation was on the point of supreme and final disaster, and yet was saved and reinstated, it was ourselves. We have been saved for a purpose. We have a mission to discharge in the world.'

Mr L. D. Gammans, MP, when broadcasting in March 1942 on the miracles of Dunkirk and the way we were saved from invasion asked: 'But why were we saved then? It was not that we could go back to our football matches, our dog tracks, our winter sports in Switzerland, our industrial squabbles and our party bickerings. I believe that we were saved then, because, in spite of the past twenty years, there was still something worth saving, still a task we had to do.'

Air Chief Marshal Sir Hugh Dowding, a deeply spiritual and most discerning man, on the occasion when he was sharing his conviction that he could trace the intervention of God all through the Battle of Britain to alter the sequence of events in that battle and in the period which led up to it, asserted: 'That intervention of God was no last-minute happening. It was a part of the mighty plan.'

Others went even further than that. They said that not only had we been saved for a purpose, but that we ought to find out what that purpose was.

Sir Archibald Sinclair, the Air Minister, was one of them. He put it this way: 'God has delivered us and brought us to our present position for some great purpose and now we must seek humbly to discover what that purpose is and then to be faithful to it.'

Sir Hugh Dowding was, perhaps, the man who came very near to discovering the purpose when he said it had to do with 'the part that our dear country is to take in the regeneration of the world.'

In other words, he saw that it was of a *spiritual* nature. But apart from his insight, the evidence suggests that no one in Britain really did discover what it was.

Yet there is a clue, which I came across in the course of a different search, and which may serve as a pointer to that supreme purpose. I believe, too, that the Lord led me to make this discovery. I was looking for further information as to why it was that Rommel suddenly stopped at the gates of Cairo in 1942. So I went to Hatchards in Piccadilly to find out what books they had on the Middle East War, and there spotted a book with the one word *Rommel* in large white letters on the spine. I took it out and knew instinctively that this was what I needed.

I was staying at a friend's house on Mersea Island at the time, and when I got back there, it was such a lovely sunny afternoon that I took the book out into the garden to read. Whilst searching for information about the campaign in North Africa, I suddenly came across something else. And when I did so, I was so arrested by it, that I found myself pacing up and down for hours. It seemed to me that here was the missing piece of a puzzle at which I had been looking for years. Here was the clue which threw some light on what may have been the purpose for which we had been saved.

What I discovered was that when Field Marshal Rommel returned to Germany from North Africa in March 1943, he began to see for himself the evil of the Hitler regime.

For the first time, he began to learn from German officers what atrocities the dreaded Gestapo and SS had been carrying out in Poland and Russia, and what they were still doing in the occupied countries of Western Europe. He learnt of the gas chambers, the mass extermination of Jews, the persecution of the churches, the concentration camps, the slave labour, the battle of the

Warsaw ghetto, and all manner of other things. He was appalled. Going straight to Hitler with these discoveries, he said, 'If such things are allowed to go on, we shall lose the War', and asked that they should cease forthwith. Hitler left no doubt in Rommel's mind that he had not the slightest intention of changing his methods.

Rommel brooded over these matters throughout that summer, realising that Hitler—whom he described privately as 'the Devil incarnate'—was leading Germany to ruin. With such evils being perpetrated, he saw that Germany could do nothing else but perish.

Then he found that there were those in responsible positions in Germany who were equally concerned and troubled, and that, furthermore, they were looking to him for the solution. They regarded him as the soul of honour, as Germany's greatest general, as a man who already had the confidence of the German people, and as someone who had the courage to act.

During an interview, which lasted between five and six hours, the situation was put to him. For some time Rommel thought over what had been discussed, and then said: 'I believe it is my duty to come to the rescue of Germany.'

Now comes the revelation which so arrested me that it caused me to pace up and down for so long! Rommel's will to act was fortified by a secretly prepared Draft Peace Treaty which, soon after, was put into his hands. It was a Peace Treaty (and I quote) 'founded on the idea of uniting Europe *on the basis of Christianity*' (the italics are mine).

This draft Treaty proposed (and again I quote) 'the abolition of frontiers and bringing about the return of the masses to the Christian faith.'

I was staggered when I read this. I could hardly believe my eyes. Surely this was where we went wrong! That treaty's proposal was not to bring about a Common Market—nothing so materialistic!

It was to bring the people of Europe to a common faith in Jesus Christ. The vision was of an United Europe founded on the basis of Christianity, just as this country was once brought to that point in her history when she became 'one coherent kingdom based on Christianity'. The Draft Treaty added: 'Only thus could the threat of Bolshevism be defeated.'

It is recorded that Rommel found this idea both moving and convincing and was anxious that the Draft Peace Treaty should be published when the opportunity presented itself. It was now for him to create that opportunity, for he saw that it could be the salvation of Europe. Please note those words.[1]

From then on he sought to do two things together. As a soldier he was already entrusted with the task of defeating the Allied invasion on the beaches, and he devoted himself to that task with all the powers he could muster, even though he knew within himself that the invasion could not, in fact, be defeated.

At the same time he was secretly committed to making an approach to the Allies and proposing an armistice to Generals Eisenhower and Montgomery—both known to him as Christian soldiers. Had he been able to make the approach, undoubtedly he would have discussed this vision of the new Europe with them.

Unfortunately for all of us, he was severely wounded before he could complete his plan of action, and whilst he was still recovering from these wounds, the dreaded Nazi secret police called on him and forced him to take poison. So he perished before he could put the vision into operation.

However, he did share the whole idea with his son Manfred, who was fifteen years old at the time. In order to complete this part of the record, I would add that I have since been in correspondence with Manfred Rommel, who is now Mayor of Stuttgart, and in a letter received on Christmas Day 1974 he said: 'I still have the vision of a united Europe based on Christianity.'

His father's vision has become his own.

Maybe it is still not too late to see that vision implemented.

Rommel perished at the enemy's hand—his and ours—so it was left to this country, and to its leadership, to discover the great purpose for which we had been saved.

Note

1. Desmond Young, *Rommel*, Collins, London 1950, p.225.

Chapter Seventeen

The Tragic Landslide

The tragedy is that we did not discover that purpose. Somehow we seemed to have 'missed the boat'.

Despite all these mighty acts of deliverance, and all the great works which God had done for Britain, we turned our back upon him.

We, the British people, tore ourselves away from our original Christian foundations, and proceeded to throw all our past history overboard. We did exactly what Israel did in Judges 2:12. We forsook the Lord God of our fathers and proceeded to fly in his face.

A month or so after the war in Europe had been brought to a conclusion, *Towards the Conversion of England* was published. This aroused such interest and caused such excitement in Christian circles that, within four months, it had been reprinted four times.

But it all came to nothing. Rather than put the plan into operation, it was 'shunted into a siding', where it has remained ever since. Far less important things than the proclamation of the gospel were put 'on the main line', and reunion with the Church of Rome seemed to become *the* major priority.

Britain first ignored, and then rejected that plan completely. She then turned a blind eye to the Christian part of our Constitution, which had for so long been committed to us as a sacred trust, did a U-turn, and deliberately proceeded to put our country's laws into reverse.

By doing so she put back the clock of national history by a good number of years, and sparked off a catastrophic landslide similar to the one into which Israel plunged in Judges 2:10b–15. As in the case of Israel, there arose in Britain another generation which did not know the Lord or the works which he had done for Britain. They forsook the Lord, the god of their fathers... they went after other gods... the people of Britain did what was evil in the sight of the Lord... they provoked the Lord to anger... So the anger of the Lord was kindled against Britain.

Is it any wonder that God is angry with us as a people, and that we now find that he is working against the British nation, just as he was working against the nation of Israel in those days? In Israel's case, we read that, as the result of their landslide, 'God gave them over to plunderers (or spoilers) who plundered them; and he sold them into the power of their enemies round about, so that they could no longer withstand their enemies....Whenever they marched out, the hand of the Lord was against them, for evil, as the Lord had warned, and as the Lord had sworn to them. And they were in sore straits' (Judges 2:14, 15 RSV).

Britain is in sore straits too, and I see a parallel here. Is it surprising that we find God working against us in the same way? For we began to reverse our legislation by placing laws on our Statute Book which legalise things which the Bible specifically states are an abomination in the sight of the Lord.

I would suggest that that is to depart from God legally.

For instance, we have legalised *homosexuality*, which was one of the sins rife in Sodom and Gomorrah, and on account of which God's wrath and indignation was so aroused, that he rained down fire and brimstone to destroy those cities. His fiery indignation and wrath is no less aroused against us, as a nation, today.

This sin took its name from Sodom, which is why the Bible calls it sodomy. Our modern age has given it a respectable name, but the Bible does exactly the opposite. It describes it as 'indulging in un-natural lust' (Jude 7 RSV); it shows it to be ugly and repulsive. So much so, in fact, that God describes it as 'evil in the sight of the Lord', or as 'an abomination in God's sight'.

Parliament, knowing this only too well, has made such a sin legal at a certain age; and ever since it did so, the media have made it more and more respectable. Now the pendulum has swung so far that sodomy has become more and more acceptable within the church. Indeed, many people were horrified to learn of the formation in 1976 of the Gay Christian Movement, with its objective of gaining acceptance for homosexuality amongst church-going people. This movement has escalated considerably since then.

Nationally, we now find that demonstrations to promote the activities of the Gay Liberation Front are being held in public places in some of Britain's towns and cities, much to the consternation of many citizens.

There is no doubt that God is angry, and I believe that, because of such things, we are inviting some of the most terrible forms of his judgments upon us as a nation.

But not only that: Parliament has legalised easy *divorce* by placing the Divorce Reform Act on our Statute Book. As a result of that Act, we have even made 'divorce by post' possible, and so have escalated the divorce rate still further. This has been done in spite of the fact that God says, 'I *hate* divorce and putting away' (Malachi 2:16 RSV), and 'Let none be faithless or treacherous to the wife of his youth' (v. 15 RSV).

The Bill, which has provided what amounts to 'divorce on demand', making husbands and wives 'disposable people', has led to such widespread practice of it, that it is having a disastrous effect upon the young. Many of them have imbibed such a superficial and shallow attitude towards marriage that, in discussion, it is by no means uncommon to hear them say, 'Well if our marriage does not work, we can easily get a divorce.'

Even more alarming is the fact that the number of divorces, and consequently of broken homes—with all the tragedy and human suffering, not least to children—had risen from 27,000 to 110,000 in the ten years between 1961 and 1971. Now the increase is so great, that statistics show that one in three of all marriages in Britain ends in divorce. It was a Government statistician who reported that 'the steep increase reflects the Divorce Reform Act coming into effect in England and Wales.'

The nation needs to be reminded all over again that it was our Lord Jesus Christ who said, 'What therefore God hath joined together, let not man put asunder' (Matthew 19:6).

I repeat, God hates divorce. Our Lord Jesus showed it up in its true light when he said, 'I say unto you, Whosoever shall put away his wife, except it be for fornication, and shall marry another, committeth adultery: and whoso marrieth her which is put away doth commit adultery' (Matthew 19:9).

When divorce, aided and abetted by Parliament, is happening in the country on such an alarming scale, surely this is another reason why God's fiery indignation is being aroused against us as a people, and why a severe form of divine judgment is likely to be brought down upon us.

In addition to providing easy divorce, we have legalised *abortion* as a result of Parliament passing the United Kingdom Abortion Act on to the Statute book in 1967. And that is something even more serious, for it has involved the nation in blood-guiltiness, which is a very grievous thing in the sight of a Holy God.

The passing of this dastardly Act has fostered the idea in people's minds that abortion is obtainable at any time, and the British public now largely accept this particular piece of legislation as giving them the *right* to 'abortion on demand', irrespective of whether they are married or single, and particularly if they have the means of paying for it.

Furthermore, the introduction of this legislation in

Britain has resulted in the slaughter of no less than 300,000 living human creatures per year—a truly horrifying figure—and that is what involves us in blood-guiltiness.

Let us make no mistake about it, these are living human beings which are involved. That is a fact which can be established both biblically and medically. For the Bible teaches very clearly, in the *first* place, that it is God alone who gives life. We need to understand, therefore, that whether a child is conceived legitimately or illegitimately—and a high percentage of these conceptions are illegitimate—it is still God who has given life. And to God Almighty, all human life is sacred. It is impossible to emphasise that strongly enough. So sacred is human life, that God has safeguarded it with the commandment 'Thou shalt not kill'—or, as in other translations, 'Thou shalt not murder'—and has imposed the extreme penalty of death upon those who do kill or murder. Once he has given that life, he, the life-giver, reserves to himself the right to take it away, or to *authorise* that it should be taken away.

Yet, in terms of abortions, literally hundreds of thousands of living, pulsating, and often whimpering and crying human creatures are now being consigned to the hospital incinerators every year.

On account of this alone, we have become a blood-guilty nation. And I say that God is exceedingly angry.

Secondly, the Bible teaches that these little ones are stamped with the image and likeness of their Creator God: 'God created man in his own image' (Genesis 1:27). Thus the wholesale termination of so many lives is not only a sin against humanity: it is also a hideous and barbaric crime against Almighty God himself. We need to see the enormity of it.

Thirdly, man is not just a mere body of flesh and blood. He has a soul; and he has a spirit, which is God-given. This is what makes him a being of the highest order in the whole of creation—next to the angels, in fact.

Not only does the Bible tell us that it is God who gives to every man his spirit; it also says that no one knows exactly when or how it is that his spirit comes into him.

Of the one, we read in Ecclesiastes 12:7: 'Then shall the dust return to the earth as it was; and the spirit shall return unto God who gave it.' Of the other, Ecclesiastes 11:5 (RSV) says: 'As you do not know how the spirit comes to the bones in the womb of a woman with child, so you do not know the work of God who makes everything.'

There is therefore an element of mystery surrounding the nature of every human life before birth. Whereas medical science and technology have established that the heart beats seventeen days after a baby has been conceived in the womb; that its mouth begins to open after twenty-one days; that its arms and legs are taking shape within twenty-eight days; that it has a brain of unmistakeable proportions which produce a measurable impulse at five weeks, and has eyes, ears, mouth, kidneys, and liver by that time; and that by sixty-three days it will grasp an object placed in its palm and can make a fist; yet the wisest of man's wisdom has not been able to unravel the ultimate mystery as to exactly when the spirit enters into this life and so causes it to become a living soul.

So what a dastardly crime it is against Almighty God to despatch that spirit once he has placed it there. Yet that is precisely what abortion does.

In the *fourth* place, the Bible teaches us that Almighty God has a personal and intimate relationship with the unborn child from the very moment of its conception, right through the nine-month period that it is in the womb. There are several very clear statements in Psalm 139 which show this, for here the individual's prenatal development is set out before him: '*Thou* didst knit me together in my mother's womb' (Psalm 139:13, RSV).

God was intimately involved in the process, in the whole of the process, and in the very earliest stages of that process.

So every individual can say, concerning the way in which he was formed into a human being in the womb, before ever he saw the light of day, that the hand of

Almighty God was at work, forming him. But this psalm moves on to something even more intimate and intricate, and goes back further when it says, 'My substance was not hid from thee, when I was made in secret' (Psalm 139:15). That, in medical terms, surely means the foetus. Indeed, it could mean a stage of development much earlier than the foetus—the point at which conception takes place.

My 'substance' is not hid from God, even at this very early stage! How sacred, therefore, to Almighty God, must be the process involved in every human birth, when he is so personally and actively involved in it.

How dare a surgeon, with instruments poised for destruction, interfere with that process, or proceed to destroy the life now being formed?

How dare a national parliament authorise him to do it?

Again, the psalm says, 'Thine eyes did see my substance, yet being unperfect; and in thy book all my members were written, which in continuance [day by day] were fashioned, when as yet there was none of them' (Psalm 139:16). 'All my members'—that means, presumably, all my external members such as hands, fingers, legs, feet, arms, nose, ears.

God was involved—intimately and closely—watching over, shaping, moulding, and even recording in a 'book', the coming into being of each one of my members, from the very earliest stages and right on through the various processes, until the whole was complete.

The psalm says yet again, 'Thou didst form my inward parts' (Psalm 139:13 RSV). My 'inward' parts—meaning my internal organs, surely—my heart, lungs, kidneys etc. God did the forming and the fashioning. You could not have more clear statements of painstaking oversight and watchful care. That is the nature of the process we are talking about. Here, in Psalm 139, is set before us how God sees every human life developing from its inception.

I notice that the *Living Bible* puts Psalm 139 in this way: 'You were there, while I was being formed in utter seclusion' (v. 15). 'You saw me before I was born' (v. 16).

'You made all the delicate, inner parts of my body, and knit them together in my mother's womb' (v. 13). 'Thank you for making me so wonderfully complex. Your workmanship is marvellous, and how well I know it' (v. 14).

This is nothing less than an inspiration to worship. When Almighty God is seen to be so intimately involved in fashioning a human life long before it finally emerges into the world, what an outrageous and heinous crime it is against him, to terminate suddenly the very process of creation which he himself is caught up in.

The effrontery of it all! It is like snatching a tiny infant out of the very hands of God and dashing its head against the rocks in front of him. Surely this is enough to arouse his wrath and fiery indignation.

In view of the teaching of Psalm 139, I find it intensely interesting to read what an eminent professor of medicine has said: 'Medically speaking, the first thirty-eight weeks spent *in utero* are more eventful and important than the next thirty-eight years. But of these', he says, 'the first twelve weeks are even more important still.'

So this abominable practice of abortion is condemned on medical grounds also.

Fifthly, there are several biblical examples to show how God sometimes appoints to the unborn child his life's work, even before he is born.

This was true of Jeremiah, for instance. When God called the young Jeremiah to commence his work, he said to him: 'Before I formed thee in the belly I knew thee; and before thou camest forth out of the womb I sanctified thee, and I ordained thee a prophet unto the nations' (Jeremiah 1:5). Not only did God say that he had formed Jeremiah in the belly, but that he knew him even before that. Even before he came out of the womb God had sanctified him and ordained him a prophet to the nations.

Another example, and perhaps the most vivid one in the Old Testament, is that of Samson. For the angel of the Lord appeared to Samson's mother prior to his conception, and said: 'Thou shalt conceive, and bear a son; and no razor shall come on his head: for the child shall be a Nazarite unto God from the womb: and he shall begin to deliver Israel out of the hand of the Philistines' (Judges 13:5).

God had therefore appointed his life's work to Samson even before he had been conceived. So important to God was Samson, and so important was that life's work in God's eyes, that he even gave special instructions to his mother with regard to the prenatal diet which God required her strictly to adhere to, throughout the time of her coming pregnancy (Judges 13).

In the New Testament we have the example of the apostle Paul. He says, in Galatians 1:15 and 16, that 'it pleased God, who separated me from my mother's womb, and called me by his grace to reveal his Son in me, that I might preach him among the heathen.' He was conscious, therefore, that God had appointed to him his life's work from birth, and even before that.

Then there is the well-known example of John the Baptist. Before ever he was conceived, the angel of the Lord said to Zacharias: 'Thy wife Elisabeth shall bear thee a son, and thou shalt call his name John . . . he shall be great in the sight of the Lord . . . he shall be filled with the Holy Ghost, even from his mother's womb. . . . And he shall go before [the Lord] in the spirit and power of Elias, to turn the hearts of the fathers to the children, and the disobedient to the wisdom of the just; to make ready a people prepared for the Lord' (Luke 1:13, 15, 17).

Now no one would argue that the life's work of the forerunner of our blessed Lord was not predetermined by God, long before he was born. So were his personality and character, the kind of person he was going to be. Zacharias even knew what the sex of this infant was going to be, before he was conceived: 'Thy wife Elisabeth shall bear thee a son, and thou shalt call his name John.'

Neither was there any argument at all as to whether it was a living human being who was in his mother's womb after conception, for it is recorded that, when Mary the mother of Jesus came to see Elisabeth six months after Elisabeth's baby had been conceived, 'the babe leaped in her womb for joy' (Luke 1:41 RSV). It could respond to influences and circumstances, therefore, and even gave vent to emotions. What an appalling thing it would have been if someone had taken steps to bring that life to an untimely end!

In all these examples, it is clear that the divine call to a life's work began no later than the conception of the individual, sometimes before conception, and never after the individual was born.

God therefore had a purpose for bringing these individuals into being, and into the world. He still has a purpose today, and it is certainly not that individuals should be thrown into hospital incinerators by the thousand, as if they were worthless scraps of garbage. Rather, God is creating individuals to fulfil a divinely intended destiny.

This means that if just one life, which God has created, is suddenly brought to an abrupt end before birth by abortion, the purpose for which God has created that life will inevitably be foiled and frustrated. One is obliged to ask: Suppose it had happened to Paul, to Samson or to Jeremiah? Suppose it had happened to Churchill, or to Nelson? Multiply that one life by the thousands, indeed the hundreds of thousands, which are being destroyed in Britain, and the enormity of the sin, as it appears in God's sight, can surely be clearly seen.

The force of all this was brought home to me recently at a conference where more than three hundred evangelical Christian ministers and pastors were present. The subjects of abortion and birth control were under discussion. I was appalled to hear a leading evangelical minister state that, in his opinion, a rigid form of birth control, together with widespread abortion, should have been introduced into this country at least fifty years ago. Looking around the room at all these ministers, I found myself wondering what percentage of *them* would have been present on that day—and more importantly, ministering in their various churches—if those measures had been introduced! But that represents only one category of valuable citizens of which this country could have been deprived, not to mention other professions and vocations which are related to the eternal purposes of God.

Sixthly, there are passages in the Bible which even refer to a person existing while 'he was yet in the loins of his father' (Hebrews 7:10). The previous verse goes so far as to say that when Abraham, who was Levi's great grandfather, paid tithes, Levi, in Abraham, paid tithes also, although he did not actually come into the world for a further three generations. And this is to say nothing of that other, and even more profound, realm of biblical teaching, which speaks of God having chosen believing people, in Christ, 'before the foundation of the world' (Ephesians 1:4), and having foreordained the good works that they should walk in (Ephesians 2:10).

We therefore just do not know what we are doing when we interfere with this profound mystery of human birth. For individuals, let alone a Government, to terminate the process of a human life, is to lay themselves open to the danger of foiling and frustrating the very purposes of Almighty God.

In the light of that salutary realisation, the entire emphasis of Governments should be placed on preserving life that has been conceived—not on destroying it. That is where Holy Scripture places the emphasis, and that is where, until recent years, the entire medical profession placed it.

So it should be clear that abortion is not primarily a medical matter, but is fundamentally a moral and ethical issue, because it raises the basic question of the orgin, nature, sanctity, purpose and destiny of human life. Highly qualified consultant surgeons in the medical profession will readily testify to that fact. In other words, it is primarily a theological matter, because God Almighty is involved. So it is what God says about it that counts in the long run.

What is so alarming, when looked at in that light, is the fact that it is largely being done for money, and also to cover up sin by getting rid of its consequences. On the one hand, vast sums of money are being made out of it, and profiteering is flourishing as never before; and on the other hand, the statistical figures show that a high percentage of the living creatures which were aborted, have been conceived outside the married state and were therefore the result of adultery and fornication. And God calls that sin. To our shame, a considerable number of those having abortions are girls in their early teens.

As to the wholesale termination of human life before birth—remember that in Britain this amounts to something like 300,000 babies per year—I call it 'the mass slaughter of the holy innocents'. That is how I believe God sees it too. Britain has murdered no less than one million, unique, distinct, irreplaceable human beings since 1967, according to the latest reliable figures, and I say, without any hesitation whatsoever, that God is going to require it of us in terms of terrible judgment. It is what the Bible calls 'shedding innocent blood'. When Israel did something similar in the later stages of her Old Testament history, God said, 'Behold, I am bringing such evil upon Jerusalem and Judah [because you have done these abominations] that whosoever heareth of it, both his ears shall tingle' (2 Kings 21:11, 12). And the evil which God said he was about to bring on the nation of Israel was judgment at the hands of an invading enemy. 'Shedding innocent blood' was amongst the abominations listed as his reason for doing that (see 2 Kings 21:16 and vv. 10–12).

I fear Britain is likely to undergo a similar severe form of judgment to that which Israel underwent when she was guilty of this kind of thing. My reasons for saying this will be made quite plain in Volume 3.

*   *   *   *

We have also legally abolished capital punishment.

Now I am well aware that this is a very controversial subject at the present time, but not, I would suggest, according to the teaching of Scripture. The Bible again tells us what God says, and it is what God says about issues like this—not what man thinks—that counts.

Because there seems to be a great deal of confusion over this, even in Christian circles, and because the question of what God says about it is rarely, if ever, raised, there is need to state it very clearly.

We need to begin with the commandments. In the sixth commandment God has said, 'Thou shalt not kill' (Exodus 20:13). Jesus, when quoting some of the commandments to the rich young ruler, reinforced this: 'Thou shalt do no murder' (Matthew 19:18).

Secondly, we need to realise that God has said there is a penalty to be paid for committing murder: 'At the hand of every man's brother will I require the life of man. Whoso sheddeth man's blood, by man shall his blood be shed: for in the image of God made he man' (Genesis 9:5, 6).

That is what God requires. And I can find no evidence in Scripture to suggest that that requirement has ever been withdrawn.

Put in its simplest form, it means that if I take another man's life in an act of violence, or in deliberate, cold-blooded murder, then God requires my life to be forfeit.

So when questions were being raised in Parliament on 28 November 1975, about the brutal gunning-down of Ross McWhirter on his own doorstep, Margaret Thatcher could not have been on stronger ground when she said to the Home Secretary, 'I believe that those who have committed this terrible crime against humanity have forfeited their right to live.' She added that 'this was her personal belief.' It is also precisely what God says.

Thirdly, God has laid down how such brutal killers should forfeit their right to live. 'At the hand of every man's brother will I require the life of man' (Genesis 9:5).

This means that their lives should be forfeited by the hand of their brother man. God requires that: he does not expect it to be left to him. It reveals how utterly wrong were the archbishops and bishops when, the day before a debate on the restoration of capital punishment was due to take place in the House of Commons, they published a letter in *The Times* (10 December 1975) saying that this matter of administering capital punishment was a matter which they, as Christians, considered should be 'left to God'. They were quite wrong when they said that 'there comes a point...where weak and fallible humans must say: "This is where we give place to divine judgment and mercy".' They were quite wrong when they backed up their argument in the letter by quoting, quite out of its context, part of Romans 12:19—'Avenge not yourselves, but rather give place unto wrath: for it is written, Vengeance is mine; I will repay, saith the Lord.' This verse, when read in context, deals with another matter entirely.

The archbishops and bishops were quite wrong because, in adopting this attitude and in following this weak line of argument, they were absolving themselves and others of the responsibility which God has placed well and truly in human hands. They were totally misleading the public, to say nothing of those who were about to take part in the debate. No: God has not only laid it down that the lives of the guilty should be forfeited by the hand of their brother man, but he has appointed and ordained human agencies and ordinances for the purpose of executing justice in respect of such persons. In the New Testament, these human agencies are referred to as 'rulers', 'governors', 'kings', 'judges' and 'magistrates' (1 Peter 2:14). All of these are referred to in Romans 13:1 as 'the powers that be' and as the 'higher powers', which even goes on to say that they 'are ordained of God', and twice describes them as 'ministers of God'.

For what are they ordained? What is their function as ministers?

1 Peter 2:14 tells us that they are sent by God 'for the punishment of evil doers, and for the praise of them that do well.' Indeed, Romans 13:4 says that those who do evil

need to be afraid, for the minister of God, 'beareth not the sword in vain'. As the minister of God, he is 'a revenger to execute wrath upon him that doeth evil.'

We need to understand, therefore, that these God-ordained agencies are authorised by God to administer punishment on God's behalf, and that that includes extreme punishment, however much we may dislike the word 'punishment' in this modern permissive age.

The Bible clearly teaches that magistrates, judges, governors, monarchs, and other heads of state, are all part of the system of ordinances which God has introduced into the world to keep sin in check and to prevent the spreading of evil. It also teaches that when they administer punishment upon the guilty, they do it as ministers of God and therefore are acting on God's behalf. They are his divinely appointed means of carrying out his requirements. Indeed, I would go further and say that when God says, 'Whoso sheddeth man's blood, by man shall his blood be shed', he requires it of judges, magistrates and heads of state to ensure that this is done.

Romans 13 is talking about this when it says of the power which has been ordained of God: 'He is the minister of God, a revenger to execute wrath upon him that doeth evil.'

This whole biblical idea of the function of these 'higher powers' was so much part of our British way of life and national outlook, until recent years, that we find words to that effect incorporated into the Coronation Service. I will quote the relevant part of that Service as it was used at the coronation of Her Majesty Queen Elizabeth II.

After the Sovereign had been anointed with oil, a sword—representing the sword of state—was delivered to the officiating archbishop, which he laid upon the altar.

The archbishop next offered this prayer: 'Hear our prayers, O Lord, we beseech thee, and so direct and support thy servant Queen Elizabeth, that she may not bear the sword in vain; but may use it as the minister of God for the terror and punishment of evildoers, and for the protection and encouragement of those that do well, through Jesus Christ our Lord. Amen.'

Then the archbishop took the sword off the altar and delivered it into the Sovereign's hands, saying, 'Receive this kingly sword, brought now from the altar of God... With this sword do justice, stop the growth of iniquity, protect the holy church of God, help and defend the widows and orphans, restore the things that are gone to decay, maintain the things that are restored, punish and reform what is amiss, and confirm what is in good order: that doing these things you may be glorious in all virtue: and so faithfully serve our Lord Jesus Christ in this life, that you may reign for ever with him in the life which is to come. Amen.'

All this was done to show that, as a nation, we adhered to the biblical position with regard to recognising 'the powers that be' and their divinely appointed function, particularly as far as our own Sovereign was concerned.

So scriptural, in fact, is the prayer during that part of the Service, that the Sovereign, as Head of State, is referred to not just as *a* minister of God, but as *the* minister of God in respect of bearing that sword of justice. It is precisely the wording of Romans 13:4, 'He is the minister of God to thee for good. But if thou do that which is evil, be afraid; for he beareth not the sword in vain: for he is the minister of God, a revenger to execute wrath upon him that doeth evil.' 'The minister' means one who is God's representative, and so is one who acts on God's behalf.

The wording found throughout this part of the Service consists of almost direct quotations of Scripture, and the symbolic use of the sword of state upholds the scriptural position with regard to the administration of justice.

When we compare that wording with the present outlook of the nation concerning the administration of justice and punishment, it should serve to remind us of how far we have departed, even since that Service was used, from the biblical position which we used to hold.

Fourthly, it has to be said that there is a great deal of

evidence in the Bible to show that if a nation does not fulfil its responsibilities, through these divinely appointed 'higher powers', in seeing to it that what God requires is carried out, then God is going to require the blood of the murdered victims at the hands of that nation. This means some terrible, and perhaps catastrophic, judgment on the nation. God has said 'For blood it defileth the land: and the land cannot be cleansed of the blood that is shed therein but by the blood of him that shed it. Defile not therefore the land which ye shall inhabit, wherein I dwell' (Numbers 35:33–34).

We need to notice that God does not just say that the blood defiles the hands of the violent person who has shed it. He says it defiles the land.

But he goes on to say that 'the land cannot be cleansed of the blood that is shed therein, but by the blood of him that shed it.' What happens then, if the land is *not* cleansed, because the blood of him who shed it is not taken?

I fear the answer is that God will require it of the people. For this again raises the whole question of blood-guiltiness, because a nation which has not fulfilled God's requirements in this way, has become a blood-guilty nation. It has the blood of all the murdered people on its hands. As a result of a thorough study of the Bible, I have been brought to the strong conviction that there is far more to this matter of blood-guiltiness than ever we realise; which ought to make us far more concerned about what God says and requires with regard to an issue like capital punishment, than about what man thinks.

I believe the Lord Jesus Christ gives us a clue to what happens if a land is not cleansed because the blood of the one who shed another person's blood is not taken. In confronting the scribes and Pharisees, and the crowds in Jerusalem shortly before his arrest and crucifixion, things had come to such a pass in the Jewish nation that Jesus was obliged to say: 'Upon you may come all the righteous blood shed upon the earth, from the blood of righteous Abel [which is going back a long way!], unto the blood of

Zacharias son of Barachias whom ye slew between the temple and the altar. Verily I say unto you, All these things shall come on this generation' (Matthew 23:35, 36).

Here was a pronouncement of judgment on blood-guiltiness. Almighty God was going to require all that blood of which Jesus spoke. He was warning the Jewish people that judgment was now imminent.

It fell in AD 70, just thirty-seven years or so after that utterance was made, when Jerusalem was overthrown at the hands of Titus and his Roman armies.

That is a fact of history, and it was a terrible judgment, in which there was literally not left in Jerusalem one stone upon another, just as our Lord had predicted.

Blood-guiltiness is therefore by no means regarded lightly by Almighty God. The Bible clearly shows that if his just requirements are not met in one way, he will ensure that they are met in another. The events which happened to the Jewish nation are an illustration of this. The blood which had been shed all down the years of its history was eventually required of the land—of the nation.

The theme is one which also runs right through the book of Revelation. There, innocent blood is not only required by God of a city or a land. This book teaches that the innocent blood which has been shed all down the ages in every nation will be required by God of the entire world (see, for example Revelation 17–19).

As for those who argue about whether it is right or wrong to 'inflict' upon society such an ordinance as capital punishment for brutal murder, I would merely remind them of what the repentant thief said to the unrepentant thief as the latter abused Jesus at the scene of the crucifixion. 'Dost not thou fear God, seeing thou art in the same condemnation? And we indeed justly; for we receive the due reward of our deeds: but this man hath done nothing amiss' (Luke 23:40, 41). He did not complain that his punishment was unjust: quite the reverse. His utterance was a recognition, surely—and even by a criminal—that he considered the death penalty was justly deserved.

*   *   *   *

As if it is not grievous enough to have reversed the country's laws in all of the ways so far mentioned, this terrible and deeply disturbing trend to legalise sheer wickedness continues. For a long time now, there has been a strong move afoot, both behind the scenes and within the Palace of Westminster, to get Parliament to legalise *euthanasia*.

Such is the word for the deliberate 'putting down' of the elderly and the so-called 'incurables', thus depriving them of their right to go on living. This move is eventually meant to include the liquidation, by subtle means, of the deformed, the disabled, the mentally handicapped, the mutilated, the infirm, and even the unwanted. People's minds are already being conditioned by the mass-media to accept it. Ways and means are even being sought, by the strong humanist lobby which is behind all this, of changing the law so as to make it possible to bring these things about *without reference to Parliament*. 'Legislation by the back door method' is another name for it.

The same lobby's declared policy also includes legalised *drug-taking*—cannabis, marijuana, and other forms of dangerous drugs—on the grounds, if you please, that so many people are taking drugs now, that the taking of them should be made legal!

Why not legalise shop-lifting, on the basis that so many people are doing it now? Or rioting on the football terraces? Or any evil-doing? For that is the logical conclusion!

This same group of materialistic atheists—for that is what they really are—is also making a frontal attack on Christianity itself.

They are seeking to have removed by statute, such things as prayers each day in Parliament; all forms of Christian worship and religious ceremonies connected with state and local government occasions; Christian assemblies for worship in schools; and even Christian education itself.

This is their declared policy, and they have been stren-
uously pursuing it for some time. Their express intention
is deliberately to create a totally atheistic society in Britain,
and to do it by so-called legal and 'constitutional' means—
hence their efforts to rid the country of every vestige of
Christianity.

For what purpose? Well, the answer should be obvious.
It is to pave the way for a take-over by the extreme Left.

Meanwhile, the trend to legalise wickedness goes on.
As examples, we have attempts being made to bring down
the age of consent for girls, and the age of 'permissible'
homosexuality, to as low as 14.

Is it not fair to say that everything we have looked at in
this chapter proves us guilty of departing from God legally
and morally? By changing our laws, we have made sin *legal*.

I believe that God is angry, and that he is going to
require all this of us. He has already been visiting us with
judgments, as we saw in Volume 1. I believe that he will
visit us with yet more, and of a much more severe kind.

And no wonder! Said David in Psalm 119:126, 'It is time
for thee, Lord, to work, for they have made void thy law.'

Acknowledgements

I list with grateful acknowledgements the various publications which I have consulted during the preparation of this volume, and from which some of the material has been drawn.

Books

Winston S. Churchill, *History of the English-speaking Peoples;* Volume 1, Cassell, London 1956.

G. M. Trevelyan, *A Shortened History of England*, Pelican, London 1970.

Richard O'Sullivan, KC, *Under God and the Law*, Blackwell, Oxford 1950.

H. A. L. Fisher, *A History of Europe,* Volume 1, 'From the Earliest Times to 1713', Collins, The Fontana Library, London 1969.

Harold Begbie, *On the Side of the Angels,* Hodder and Stoughton, London 1918.

Winston S. Churchill, *The Second World War*, Volumes 2 and 4, 'Their Finest Hour' and 'The Hinge of Fate', The Reprint Society, London, by arrangement with Cassell, London 1951.

Sir William Dobbie, *A Very Present Help*, Marshall Morgan and Scott, London 1945.

Douglas Bader, *Fight for the Sky,* Sidgwick Jackson, London 1940.

F. H. Hinsley, *Hitler's Strategy,* Cambridge University Press, Cambridge 1951.

Brigadier Desmond Young, *Rommel,* Collins, London 1950.

Edited B. H. Liddell Hart, *The Rommel Papers,* Collins, London 1953.

Major Peter W. Rainier, *Pipeline to Battle,* Hamilton, London 1955.

Admiral of the Fleet Viscount Cunningham of Hyndhope, *A Sailor's Odyssey,* Hutchinson, London 1951.

Norman Grubb, *Rees Howells: Intercessor,* Lutterworth Press, Guildford and London 1973.

Sir Winston Churchill, KG, OM, CH, MP, *Great War Speeches,* Corgi Books, Transworld Publishers, London 1957.

Leaflets, Magazines and Pamphlets

Household Brigade Magazine, Winter Number 1942.

Magazine of the Merchant Service Officers Christian Association, April 1944.

The Coronation of Her Majesty Queen Elizabeth II, approved souvenir programme, Odham's Press, London 1953.

We have a Guardian, compiled by W. B. Grant, Covenant Publishing Co., London 1958 (with W. B. Grant's full permission to quote).

The Christian Content of the Rule of Law and its Contribution to Human Rights, an Address by George Polson QC, the then Recorder of Exeter, delivered at Christian Business Man's Lunch-Hour Meeting in Leicester, 19 February 1969 (with his permission to quote).

Report of Commissioner of Police of the Metropolis 1980, HMSO.

I would also like to place on record grateful thanks and deep appreciation to all those who have helped with the typing and re-typing of this manuscript and those of Volumes 1 and 3. They include Miss Eileen Devenish, formerly of Twickenham, Middlesex, who undertook the mammoth task of typing a large part of the original manuscript in triplicate; Mrs Margaret Williamsen of Wantage, Oxon, who gallantly took over at a later stage; Mrs Phyllis Goodchild of Liphook, Hants; and more recently Mrs Margaret Greaves of Wandsworth.

I am also greatly indebted to Miss Gwen Saunders for the very valuable help which she has given over a considerable period of time, and to Lance Bidewell for the painstaking and thorough way in which he has scrutinised the text of Volume 2, giving generous help and advice in preparation for its publication.

I am grateful to Mr and Mrs Fred Wright of Prentices Lane, Woodbridge, Suffolk, for kindly placing their bungalow entirely at my disposal for a week whilst writing a large section of the manuscript, and to Mr and Mrs Winston Rees of West Mersea for the use of their Beach Lodge over a three-month period whilst writing much of the last part. Without the quietness enjoyed in these places such writing would have been impossible.

Also to Rodney Shepherd of Nuprint Services, whose personal Christian commitment led to an interest in the message, resulting in its attractive presentation as the printed word.

Last, but by no means least, I would like to express my grateful appreciation to Dr Brian Taylor of Altrincham, Cheshire, for recognising the extreme urgency and relevance of the message and deciding to go ahead with the utmost possible speed with its publication. Without his generous and courageous help the book may never have seen the light of day.

The
Trumpet Sounds
for Britain

Volume 3

The Alarming Apostasy and It's
Inevitable Consequences

David E. Gardner

Contents

'*Write the vision, and make it plain upon tables, that he may run that readeth it. For the vision is yet for an appointed time, but at the end it shall speak, and not lie: though it tarry, wait for it; because it will surely come, it will not tarry.*'

Habakkuk 2:2, 3

Forewords

General Sir Walter Walker, KCB, CBE, DSO, (former Commander-in-Chief, Allied Forces Northern Europe).

My friend the padre, the Rev David Gardner, has once again sounded a stern tocsin for the Christian West.

Through the prophet Ezekiel, we are admonished that he who 'seeth the sword come upon the land, [if] he blow the trumpet, and warn the people', he is free from blood-guiltiness (Ezekiel 33:3–5). In this book the padre has sounded an alarm with all the resonance of a resounding trumpet blast.

Dr T. R. V. Gurney, MB, ChB, (former medical missionary and army surgeon, now ministering in the United Kingdom).

When *A Warning to the Nation*, by my friend the Rev David Gardner, was first published in 1967, I was tremendously impressed and saw it as a very important and timely book-let. Some years later, Mr Gardner told me about *The Trumpet Sounds for Britain*, which was soon to be published. I felt strongly then the urgent need to get this book into the hands of the people of Britain. Volumes I and II were subsequently published, and continue to be much in demand. Now Volume III has come. I agree wholeheartedly with the entire message of the book, and pray earnestly that Christians who are alarmed at the state of Britain today will not only read it and heed the message, but will make it as widely known as possible.

All who take the Bible seriously should be shaken out of any apathy or complacency as they read this book. May God grant that they and countless others who for one reason or another read it, may find food for serious thought, leading them to seek the Lord while there is time. The author has so clearly shown the direction in which our nation is going, while all the sins of Manasseh are committed and tolerated in this once Christian country.

God is not mocked, and the judgment he meted out to the nation of Judah in her apostasy is surely coming to us unless a true, deep, national turning back to God takes place very quickly.

Let us pray that, even at this late hour the living God, who has so miraculously delivered us from defeat time and time again, may lead the nation to return to himself. Let us pray, too, for a return to the Bible and obedience to the laws of God which for so long have been the very foundation of our national life, but which have now been largely replaced by laws to suit man's convenience.

I believe very much that Christians have a duty to read this book and to refuse to put it on one side or forget its message. Rather, we must do everything in our power to make it widely known, read and acted upon. I fear we are under God's judgment *now*, and that Britain is in serious danger. If we *have* passed the point of no return in our downward slide away from God, we must be heading, as did the nation of Judah under Manasseh in the Old Testament, for a much more serious form of judgment. To Christians comes the 'trumpet call' to watch and pray while there is time.

May God's rich blessing be on this book as it goes out, and may he grant the Holy Spirit revival so sorely needed, and for which the author and many others long and pray.

12

Introduction

The author is gripped with the burning and overwhelming
conviction that Britain is fast heading towards an extremely
severe judgment of *God*, the like of which she has never
before experienced in any period of her long history. He
therefore feels convinced that there is an urgent need, like
the prophets of old, to 'sound the trumpet and warn the
people'.

   In the previous two volumes he set out to explain how
Britain got herself into such a state:

1. she has forsaken *God;*
2. she is now living without him;
3. she has reversed *God's* laws and is flying in the face of
    them;
4. she has become a blood-guilty nation.

   He was at great pains to point out that it is neither a
heathen nor a pagan nation which is guilty of all this. That is
the appalling thing. On the contrary, it is a nation which has
had a long and rich Christian heritage; a nation which was
once known throughout the world as a godly nation—
Bible-loving, missionary-hearted and God-fearing.

13

To establish this, the author indicated clearly in volumes 1 and 2 how the hand of Almighty God has been on the history of this country *in blessing*, right from its very earliest beginnings, and how God has been at work on her behalf throughout all that time in many marvellous ways, raising her up until, at various points in her history, she had become a great nation.

He pointed out, for instance, that it was due to a mighty act of God, way back in the dim, distant past, that she became an island, or a group of islands.

He then traced how God caused the pure, New Testament form of Christianity to come to these islands at an extremely early time—long before Augustine—thus ensuring that they were established on strong, true, Christian foundations, and how, once those foundations were secured, God continued to preserve or restore them whenever they were in danger of being lost, weakened or destroyed.

The author showed how God did this through Patrick, then at the Reformation, and yet again at the time of the Great Awakening under the preaching of Whitefield and Wesley when, as it is recorded in Westminster Abbey, 'Divine Providence exalted Great Britain to an height of prosperity and glory unknown to any former age.'

He also made clear that it was through the working of Almighty God that these islands became based on Christian and Bible-based *laws*, even before the reign of King Alfred.

He quoted Winston Churchill as showing in his *History of the English-speaking Peoples*, how we, as a nation, were brought by Divine Providence to three great landmarks in our history:

1. When 'there was no kingdom in the realm in which heathen religions and practices now prevailed. The whole Island was now Christian.'
2. How, during the twelfth century, 'After...years of being the encampment and battleground of an invading army,

14

England became finally and for all time one coherent kingdom *based on Christianity'*. That is what Churchill wrote in 1956, for so he then thought (italics mine).

3. How God moved by his Holy Spirit through the Reformation, to cause the nation to become so Protestant in its *faith*, that England, under Queen Elizabeth I, became Protestant *by law*. Thereafter, the Christian faith (and it needs to be stressed that it was the Protestant, New Testament-based, Christian faith) became Britain's *constitutional* position to such an extent that it was embodied by Act of Parliament in the Coronation Oath—which commits every British Sovereign, pledged with the full support of Parliament, 'to uphold to the utmost of our power the Laws of God in the realm and the True Profession of the Christian Gospel.' This *Christian* constitutional position was also embodied in the Act of Settlement of 1701, which requires that only a *Protestant* Christian may ascend and occupy the British throne.

He then made plain in volume 2 how the hand of Almighty God can be traced all down the years of our nation's history, bringing about mighty acts of deliverance whenever this country has been in mortal danger. He recounted the amazing interventions of God from as far back as the time of King Alfred, and at the time of the Spanish Armada, and wrote about two extraordinary interventions which brought us through to victory in 1918. Then he went on to relate in detail at least twelve of the amazing miracles which took place between 1939 and 1945, seven of which came as direct answers to National Days of Prayer called by King George VI, or in answer to times of *special* prayer—showing that God was indisputably with us in those days.

Prime Minister Winston Churchill was full of thanksgiving to God for all this when, after announcing victory in Europe to a crowded House of Commons on 8 May 1945, he turned towards the Speaker and said: 'I therefore beg, sir, with your permission, to move 'That this House do now attend at the Church of St Margaret Westminster, to give humble and reverent thanks to Almighty God for our deliverance from the threat of German domination.'

As the author said, 'God was clearly *with* us then: he was also *working* with us, and on our behalf during all these long years of war'. Our national leaders recognised this, and many of them proclaimed at that time, 'We have been saved for a purpose. God has delivered us and brought us to our present position for some great purpose and now we must seek humbly to discover what that purpose is and then to be faithful to it.'

'But', the author lamented, 'Britain has forgotten all that.' She has completely forgotten and even put out of her mind all these great blessings which God has so richly bestowed upon her in the past. Despite the fact that her history has been steeped in God's miracles of deliverance and acts of divine mercy, Britain has rejected all her rich Christian heritage. And in contrast to all these experiences of divine activity on her behalf, she has now become a nation which has no time for God. She has shut her ears to him, and is therefore living without him. Indeed, she is openly defying him, and is deliberately and wilfully flying in his face.

Furthermore, her Parliament—the so-called Mother of Parliaments—has even gone against the nation's own Constitution by placing on her Statute Books, laws which make legal things which the Bible expressly declares are an abomination in the sight of the Lord and which provoke him to anger. Britain's Parliament, by doing this, has therefore legalized *sin*, and by deliberately changing our moral and spiritual direction as a nation, Britain has become a nation which has put itself on a direct collision course with God.

Due to the iniquitous United Kingdom Abortion Act, the nation now has the blood of no less than two million legally murdered living creatures on its hands, plus all the unrequited blood which has been shed since the abolition of capital punishment. Britain has, in consequence, become a blood-guilty nation, and God is angry. The author clearly sees that the Bible makes it plain that God is going to require all that blood at the hands of the nation and its people.

He asked in desperation in volume 1, 'Can't we see? Cannot any, or all of our national leaders see? Cannot our gracious Sovereign see?' Cannot our Prime Minister see? Cannot our Church Leaders see? Cannot Parliament and all those in authority understand that to reverse a nation's laws and to change its moral and spiritual direction as we have done, so that the country becomes diametrically opposed to what God Almighty has commanded, is bound to put the nation on a course which is directly against God? And *that* means that God is now *against* us? Whereas he was once working with us. But that is precisely what this nation *has* done and *is* doing, even to the extent of going directly against the written and Christian part of its Constitution.

The author firmly believes that unless we, as a people, and as individuals, truly repent of having done all this, take steps to put it all right, and turn back to God very quickly, a terrible crash is inevitable. It will be a meeting with God Almighty, the Creator, Supreme Ruler and Judge of the universe, in terms of some terrible and grievous form of judgment never before experienced in our history. For as the Holy Spirit said through David in Psalm 119:126: 'It is time for thee, Lord, to work, for they have made void thy law.'

Again, in volume 1, he pointed out that the nation has already been visited by a number of God's judgments. He identified several of these from a study of Deuteronomy, chapter 28 and some of the Old Testament prophets.

He also showed how, because of our continued national rebellion against him, God has also been handing us over to other forms of judgment, such as the gross forms of

17

immorality and perversion which are mentioned in the epistle to the Romans, chapter one.

Then he drew attention to certain forms of divine judgment which could *yet* be visited upon us, such as the total collapse of our national economy; a great national calamity like our capital being destroyed by a flood or earthquake; or the nation being handed over to 'enemies within', in terms of a take-over by extreme left-wing elements with the connivance and co-operation of Moscow, in order to overthrow the existing democratically elected government.

At the end of volume 2 the author saw the situation as even worse. In viewing the tragic landslide which has taken place in the nation since 1945, and the reversing of the nation's laws, he feared that in our rebellion and departure from God we have gone so far away from him, and have sinned against him so grievously, *especially in our bloodguiltiness*, that we are inviting on our land and on our people a judgment of a most devastating kind.

As a nation, we have gone as far away from God as the nation of Israel did in the later stages of her Old Testament history—if not, indeed, further—and therefore we are likely to suffer the same kind of judgment. That, in Israel's case, was judgment at the hands of an invading enemy army. In this present volume the author fulfils the promise he made in Volume 2 to make quite plain his reasons for reaching that solemn conclusion.

It is no longer a question of *whether* we have departed from God. That we *have* done so is quite beyond dispute. It is now a question of showing *how far* we have departed.

In direct contrast to the tremendous blessings which God has bestowed upon the nation all down the centuries, and the high spiritual peaks which, in consequence, God has caused it to reach, the author clearly shows the awful depths to which we, as a nation, have now sunk. This he does in order to face us with the enormity and heinousness of our sin in so seriously departing from the God who has mightily delivered us on so many occasions.

It is when we have seen how loathsome that sin is, that we must surely conclude that it is inevitable that a terrible judgment of God will be visited upon the nation unless there is a speedy turning to God in deep and heartfelt repentance.

That is why the author considers it to be desperately urgent to sound the trumpet and call the nation back to God before it is too late. It is the purpose of all three of these volumes to do just that.

Chapter One

Making Sin Legal

And the children of Israel did evil again in the sight of the Lord: and the Lord strengthened... the king of Moab against Israel, because they had done evil in the sight of the Lord. And he gathered unto him the children of Ammon and Amalek, and went and smote Israel.... So the children of Israel served... the king of Moab eighteen years. But when the children of Israel cried unto the Lord, the Lord raised them up a deliverer (Judges 3:12–15).

On the day after Alexander Solzhenitsyn's 'Warning to the West' had been issued by means of the BBC's 'Panorama' programme, I had been invited to see Dr Coggan, the former Archbishop of Canterbury, at Lambeth Palace.

The 'Warning' was headline news that day on the front pages of our leading national newspapers. So, as Dr Coggan welcomed me into his study, I said, 'I don't think it is mere coincidence that I have been invited to see the highest spiritual authority in the realm on the very day that Solzhenitsyn's "Warning to the West" has hit the headlines.'

We discussed the 'Panorama' programme and Solzhenitsyn's warning for a while, and then the Archbishop looked directly at me and said, 'What do *you* think of the state of the nation?'

I said, '*You*, Sir, have been saying in your "Call to the Nation" that we are a nation which has got away from its foundations, that we are like a ship cut adrift from her moorings and that many people feel that we are "drifting towards chaos", and I quite agree with all you say. But I think the situation is far more serious than that. I believe that the *root* of our trouble is that we are, today, a nation that has got away from God. In fact, I believe that we have got so far away from God that we have become a nation under judgment... the indications are that we have got so far away from God that, in terms of his judgments, he has already begun to hand us over...'

The Archbishop interjected here, and said: 'You mean to the kind of things which are listed in Romans 1?' (I knew, by that, that he had been reading *A Warning to The Nation*!')

I said, 'Yes—and to things like "the enemy within", which *you*, Sir, have been warning the country about when you said, in your "Call to the Nation", "There are enemies within the gates."'

The Archbishop nodded assent.

I added, 'Yes—but the Bible also teaches that it is terribly possible for a nation to go so far away from God that he has to hand them over to an enemy from without, in terms of his judgments. And *that*, your Grace, is what Solzhenitsyn is warning us about.'

A long conversation followed, in the course of which I put it to the Archbishop that it was quite clear to me from the way things had been going, and from my knowledge of the Bible, that in our departure from God, we have gone precisely the way that the nation of Israel went in the days of the Old Testament, and that *because* we have, we are likely to suffer the same consequences.

I said, 'Israel, for instance, in *her* departure from God, went so far away from him that, despite his persistent warnings through prophet after prophet, and despite his many attempts through these prophets to call her back and

to bring her to repentance by *other* forms of judgment—
when all this went unheeded, God eventually had to bring
extreme measures of chastisement and judgment to bear,
by using the instrument of a forgeign power and its armies
against her.'

The Archbishop responded 'You mean such as the armies
of Assyria, and the armies of Nebuchadnezzar and of
Babylon, and of Cyrus, my servant?'

I replied, 'Yes, and the ingredients of *that* kind of judgment are already very much there as far as *this* country is
concerned, in terms of the Soviet military build-up about
which Mrs Margaret Thatcher has been raising her voice,
and for which she earned herself the title of the "Iron
Lady". I said, 'It could happen to *us*. This is what General
Sir Walter Walker, the former Commander-in-Chief, Allied
Forces in Northern Europe, has been warning this country
about for goodness knows how many years now. He was
doing that from Norway, while he still held that responsible
position.'

I then said, as I have said so often, and in so many places
around the country, as I have been sounding out this warning, and as I have said to General Sir Walter Walker
himself, 'Sir, we are *in an Ezekiel Chapter 33* situation, and
what we need is a watchman to sound the trumpet and warn
the people. I have been trying to do that as best I can in
different parts of the country, but my biggest problem is
how to get the message out on a large enough scale—how to
reach our 56 million or more people with this message, and
with the message of salvation which needs to accompany it,
when 90 per cent of our people no longer go to church or to
any Christian place of worship, and when most of the
nation's main channels of communication today are denied
to a forthright, clear-cut, Bible-based Christian message
and declaration. The people urgently need to be warned
and to be called back to God.'

The Archbishop allowed all this to register, and in no
sense pooh-poohed or disagreed with what I had been

saying. He asked me how I was getting the message out now.

I said, 'At public meetings which are being arranged for me during the week in town halls and the like.' And then I added that I was committing it all to print. He got very excited about the prospect of a book and asked when it was going to be published.

Then he said, 'The answer to your question, "How to get the message out on a large enough scale?" is by the way you *are* doing it—by the *spoken* word, and by the *written* word.' And then he repeated, several times over , 'I think you should go on television.' He said this again as he shook me by the hand at the door.

What exactly did I mean when I put it to Dr Coggan that as I compared what has happened in Britain during recent years with what happened in the Bible, I could see quite clearly that we, as a nation, have gone as far away—if not further—from God as the nation of Israel went in the days of the Old Testament, and that *because* we have, we are likely to suffer the same consequence, which was judgment at the hands of invading enemy armies?

This is a devastatingly strong statement to make. How can it be justified?

Well, if we continue to analyse our national situation from what is revealed to us in the Bible, and particularly during the period I have mentioned, it should become abundantly clear to us that we have gone as far as:

1. committing the sin of Jeroboam the son of Nebat;
2. committing the sin of Solomon;
3. committing the sin of the notoriously wicked Manasseh.

Students of the Bible will realize that these were the three fatal steps which led to the decline and fall of the Hebrew kingdom.

It is in *that* sense that we have gone precisely the same

way as Israel went in the days of the Old Testament, and we are therefore likely to suffer the same consequences.

Let me elaborate.

In the first place, Jeroboam the son of Nebat went down in history as 'the man who made Israel to sin'.

This constant refrain about him runs throughout the books of Kings and Chronicles (see, for instance, 1 Kings 15:29–30, 34; there are many other such references too). The particular reference refers to 'the sins of Jeroboam which he sinned, and which he made Israel to sin' as 'his provocation wherewith he provoked the Lord God of Israel to anger.'

When a nation, through its Parliament, legalizes sin, that is what it does. It both sins itself, and makes its people to sin—which is exactly how Jeroboam is described in 1 Kings 16:26. And *that* provokes God to anger.'

Oh, I know that it is human nature for people to sin, because sin is *within* them. They are born with sin in them. Everybody is. And because sin is within them, they are sinners in the sight of God. They need to turn to God, and seek his forgiveness, and come to the Lord Jesus Christ in faith, when they will receive that forgiveness on the basis of the atonement which he made for their sin on the cross. Furthermore, the Holy Spirit will come upon them and *into* them when they do that. They will be born again of the Holy Spirit of God, and become new creatures in Christ Jesus.

That is the glory of the Christian Gospel!

That is why it is Good News!

The power of the Gospel can change the heart of a man; it can change his very nature. It makes a sinner into a saint. Oh yes, it is of the nature of man to commit sin.

But when *Parliament* legalises sin, that Parliament—the Government, if you like—is *causing the people to sin*. The British Parliament, the mother of Parliaments, in placing on our Statute Book laws which make legal things which the Bible specifically states are an abomination in the sight of the Lord, and things which God hates, has made it legal for the British people to commit *gross wickedness*.

The Bible calls all these things *wicked*. For Parliament legislates on behalf of the entire nation—on behalf of Britain's 56 million people—the rising generations included. So I contend that, by legislating *in favour of evil*, Parliament has become guilty of causing the nation to *sin*, and to sin most grievously. I say that, in doing this, Parliament has gone as far as committing the sin of Jeroboam the son of Nebat.

Not only has Parliament done *that*, but it has obtained the Royal Assent for the British people to do what God says is *wicked*. Just imagine! The laws could not otherwise have got on to the Statute Book.

Exactly *how* Parliament managed to obtain the Royal Assent remains a mystery to me. I just do not understand how it could happen. But the fact remains that it did, and by so doing I believe Parliament betrayed a sacred trust. For I contend that in gaining the Royal Assent to pass evil laws on to the Statute Book, Parliament caused the Royal Oath to be broken and the *Christian* part of the British Constitution to be violated.

The Royal oath is a sacred undertaking made before God by the Sovereign, during the Coronation Service, to 'uphold to the utmost of our power the *Laws of God* in the realm, and the True Profession of the Christian Gospel', and that undertaking is embodied in the Oath *by Act of Parliament*. And Parliament, through its senior peer, at the Coronation Service, pledges itself to support that Oath.

How can it happen, therefore, that Parliament is able to obtain the Royal Assent for something which is directly against what it is pledged to support, and which the Sovereign has solemnly undertaken before GOD to uphold 'to the utmost of our power'? But it did. And because it did, I maintain that Parliament acted *against the British Constitution*.

So far, therefore, has Parliament taken us, as a nation,

away from God. Not only have we departed from God historically, spiritually, morally and legally, but we have departed from God *constitutionally* and politically as well. As a result, I dread to think how we shall be answerable to God.

I am well aware of the argument which is put forward that no Prime Minister today will ever advise the Sovereign to withold the Royal Assent. It is because I have been deeply disturbed by what has occurred that I have engaged in some correspondence with the appropriate Government department, and they say that it has only happened once in British history, during the reign of George III.

Why did *he* withold the Royal Assent? I'll tell you. It was because George III was a Christian! And as a Christian he could not, and *would* not, go against his own conscience.

To him the Oath he had taken at his coronation was sacred. On the occasion in question, he asked, 'Where is the power on earth to absolve me from the due observance of every sentence of the Coronation Oath?'

George III also told Lord North in 1771 that 'It is the duty of ministers as much as possible *to prevent any altera-tions in so essential a part of the Constitution as everything that relates to religion*' (my italics).

There you have his position with relation to the *religious* part of the Constitution. That is where he stood.

King George III was a Christian.

He had a very strong belief in God.

In his letters he constantly referred to his 'trust in Divine Providence', and this was no mere form of words. It was the expression of his living faith.

For instance, he read his Bible every morning and even-ing, recommended others to do the same, and began and ended each day with prayer. When the Royal Family was at Windsor or in London, divine service was held in the King's private chapel every morning at eight o'clock. Sunday was always kept as a special day, and when the King and Queen were in London on Sundays they attended morning service

27

at the Chapel Royal. If they were at Windsor they attended the Service at St George's Chapel—the services in those eighteenth-century days always lasted about two hours. The King took a keen interest, too, in the sermons, and became an expert judge of a good one. Then the Queen would read another sermon to her children later on in the day.

Further evidence that George III was a Christian is provided by his firm belief in the truth about the cross. He said in a letter that 'God's goodness had been so unbounded as to have sent his only Son to suffer death on the cross for the redemption of man.' 'This', he wrote, 'was a consideration which must warm the heart of everyone who possesses the smallest spark of gratitude, and be the cause of the strongest resolutions to obey his laws.'

Such was the man. Such was the strength of his Christian position and conviction. As to the particular question of his refusing to give the Royal Assent, this is the background.

It should be remembered that George III was a member of the Royal House of Hanover, and that the House of Hanover—as in the case of William of Orange less than thirty years before—had been summoned to Great Britain by Act of Parliament *to preserve the Protestant establishment*, a fact which the authorities seem to keep quiet about these days, or deftly to sweep under the carpet!

George III, when he eventually came to the throne, took a solemn oath at his Coronation to maintain the rights and privileges of the Church of England and all else that was entailed in maintaining Britain's Protestant Christian position, just as our Sovereign does today. And to King George III an oath was sacred. On the occasion in question, the King was being asked by his ministers to do something which was *contrary to the first principles of the Constitution*. He refused to do it, and showed that he was determined to stick by everything that he had undertaken in the Oath. It was *then* that he asked, 'Where is the power on earth to absolve me from the due observance of every sentence of the Coronation Oath?'

Would to God that a similar stand had been made today! And I am a strong and loyal supporter of the monarchy when I say this.

When Lord Dundas tried to argue with the King that the Oath was binding only in his executive, and not in his legislative capacity (as some may argue today), the King retorted, 'None of your Scottish metaphysics'!

His biographer says that he may not have had a head for fine distinctions, but he knew right from wrong. He refused to budge. Therefore he declined to give the Royal Assent on that occasion.

We are told that the King reached his conclusion after consulting the highest authorities in church and state, but his biographer also says: 'from what we know of his character we can be sure that he had prayed earnestly about it.'

This, according to the authorities, is the only occasion in our history when the Sovereign has refused to give the Royal Assent. It could not be more clear that it was because he was a Christian, and one who *feared God*, that King George III made this bold stand.

I believe, therefore, that on the grounds of Christianity, and in order 'to uphold to the utmost of our power the laws of God in the realm', a British Prime Minister *can* in fact, and indeed *must*, advise any Sovereign to withold the Royal Assent from any Bill which is contrary to the laws of God and the teachings of the Bible, and which is contrary to the Christian part of the British Constitution embodied by Act of Parliament in the Coronation Oath. I believe God would *honour* such a move, for he says, 'Him that honours me, I will honour'. Furthermore, I am convinced that both the Prime Minister and the Sovereign would have the whole-hearted and welcome support of the British people in making such a courageous stand.

Would to God such a position had been taken when Parliament and its ministers were seeking to pass evil and abominable laws on to our Statute Book—especially when

King George III had created this precedent. That would have stopped the rot!

I sometimes wonder if it has been recorded in the archives of heaven, of the British Parliament which was sitting during the 1960s and early '70s: 'The Parliament which made Britain and the British people to sin.'

I rather think that it might have been. At any rate, we are told that books are kept in heaven, and the Bible says that one day the books will be opened (Revelation 20:12).

Then, no doubt, there will be Prime Ministers, Home Secretaries, ministers of the Crown and many a parliamentarian, who will be held responsible and answerable to the bar of heaven for allowing themselves, as 'the Powers that be who are ordained of God', to actually take part in legalising *evil*.

There will certainly be a great deal for which a number of these 'higher powers' will be answerable. I maintain that when they caused the Royal oath to be broken or to be set aside, and when they caused the *Christian* part of our British Constitution to be breached so as to make it possible for offensive laws to be passed on to the Statute Book, they not only made sin and wickedness legal. They made a major contribution towards setting off the great moral and spiritual landslide that we have seen taking place in the country, and which has been going on, unarrested, for so many years now.

Indeed, I believe that they accelerated it. I believe that when Parliament went as far as to make *sinning* legal, the fury and indignation of Almighty God was aroused against this nation. He has already handed us over to many of the things already mentioned in these volumes. And I believe that unless we, as a people, repent of what has happened, and rise up with one voice to call upon Parliament to repeal all these offending and offensive laws so as to completely reverse the present position, terrible judgment is bound to overtake us. Because, 'for all this his anger is not turned away, but his hand is stretched out still' (Isaiah 5:25).

It is in *that* sense—in the sense that we have made sin legal, and have therefore made the British people to sin—that we, as a nation, have gone as far as *committing the sin of Jeroboam the Son of Nebat*. But this is only *part* of what we have done.

Note

1. David E. Gardner, *A Warning to the Nation*, Christian Foundation Publications, eighth reprint.

Chapter Two

A Mountain of Faiths

Britain has also gone as far as, if not further than, *committing the sin of Solomon*.

And what was that?

We read all about it in 1 Kings 11, where we find that, for all his wisdom, Solomon was guilty of putting back the clock of his country's history, literally by generations.

He brought back into the land the *heathen* gods and forms of worship which Almighty God had long since driven out. And in doing so, he undid what God had done, all down the centuries in the history of his country, to ensure that the nation became worshippers of the one true God alone.

God was exceedingly angry, for by bringing back these heathen religions, Solomon caused his country to change its outlook and attitude towards religion entirely.

As to *how* this came about, Solomon did it when he created a multi-racial society.

Now I am fully aware that immediately I say this, I am touching on an area which is extremely controversial today. Yet it is something which needs to be said.

This was a terribly retrograde step which Solomon took, and dreadful consequences followed. Such a move was bound to cause an escalation of trouble, for the creation of a multi-racial society inevitably leads to a multi-religious society. You cannot escape it. And this brings in its wake further and more serious consequences, as we shall see.

It was what this step *led to* which really constituted the sin of Solomon. And there is no getting away from the fact that God called it *sin*.

The Bible states quite specifically that it was *evil* in the sight of the Lord (1 Kings 11:6), and that is what determines whether an act is right or wrong. It is how it appears *in the sight of the Lord* that matters, not—how it seems to man. But what did Solomon actually *do*?

In answer to that question, let me trace the course of events which developed from that initial retrograde step of his.

His creation of a multi-racial society stemmed, we are told, from the fact that he 'loved many strange [foreign] women'. They were princesses, in fact—daughters of at least seven foreign ruling powers or potentates. They were princesses of Egypt, Moab, Amon, Edom and Sidon, and of the powerful Hittites.

Solomon wanted to have all these princesses around him, so he invited them into his country and set up residences for them. He did this on quite a considerable scale, for we are told that there were no less than seven hundred of these foreign royal personages involved, plus three hundred concubines. So they took some housing! And they came from this wide variety of countries and cultures.

Now it happens that you cannot bring princesses from foreign lands and invite them to take up permanent residence in your country without their also bringing retinues. This is what happened in Solomon's case, so the influx of migratory people into the country at his invitation would have been very considerable. When they arrived, Solomon proceeded to concentrate many of them in houses in and around his capital. We have archaeological evidence to testify to this.

The number of these foreign princesses was so great, that in due course Solomon found that he was obliged to disperse many of them to other towns and cities in different parts of his country. Of course, immediately he had spread them all over the country, he had taken a major step towards creating a multi-racial society. That this happened, is a fact of Old Testament history. I am quoting it in order to show the consequences which must inevitably follow. There is no escaping from them—not in *any* age.

When these foreign nationals came into Solomon's country, they brought with them all their foreign religions. It was not likely that they would leave any of them behind. Therefore a whole variety of false religions and practices were introduced into the land, with their gods and images. Solomon, with all his wisdom, should have had the foresight to see that this would happen. But *when* it happened, he was obliged to provide the facilities and buildings which the practice of these false religions and their various customs required. So he proceeded to erect heathen temples, heathen altars and shrines, and heathen places of worship throughout his country. He did this 'on every high hill', and in other open places.'

The record in the Bible puts it this way: 'Then did Solomon build an high place for Chemosh, the abomination of Moab, in the hill that is before Jerusalem, and for Molech, the abomination of the children of Amon. And likewise did he for all his strange wives, which burnt incense and sacrificed unto their Gods' (1 Kings 11:7, 8). And we need to notice that God called these heathen altars, temples, shrines and places of worship 'abominations' (See 1 Kings 11:5, 7).

Furthermore, God has left it on record that in doing all this, 'Solomon did *evil* in the sight of the Lord' (1 Kings 11:6).

But what was there about it that was so evil?

Let me explain it in the following way. God had given a specific commandment concerning all these other nations, that the children of Israel should not fraternise with them, and he had given his reason for issuing such a commandment: 'For surely *they will turn away your heart after their gods.*'

That was the danger.

That is precisely what happened, and it happened in a two-fold way.

In the first place we read that Solomon's wives 'turned away *his* heart after other gods...For Solomon went after Ashtoreth the Goddess of the Zidonians, and after Milcom the abomination of the Ammonites: and he went not fully after the Lord' (1 Kings 11:4, 5, 6). That happened, despite the fact that God had commanded him that 'he should *not* go after other gods' (1 Kings 11:10).

It is on account of this that we read: 'And the Lord was angry with Solomon, because his heart was turned from the Lord God of Israel, which had appeared to him twice' (1 Kings 11:9). But it didn't stop there.

For in the second place, what he did had the same effect upon his people. We find that he turned their hearts, and they began to go after other gods also' (1 Kings 11:33).

That was what was so evil, because it was apostasy. And God was exceedingly angry.

It followed, too, of course, that when Solomon deliberately disobeyed God's commandment and brought in all these foreign people, it led also to a direct violation of God's first and second commandments, which Solomon knew very well: 'Thou shalt have *no other* gods before *me*'—'Thou shalt not make unto thee *any* graven image,...thou shalt not bow down thyself to them, nor serve them'. Yet by going after these other gods, both he and his people were doing that.

God had driven out all these foreign religions, and the foul practices that went with them, way back in the time of Joshua, in order that the children of Israel might become worshippers of the one, true, living God. Now, by bringing them all back in their midst, the nation of Israel had put the clock of their country's history back hundreds of years, to where it was before God had taken action. In God's sight this was extremely serious—so serious did God consider this sin to be, that he said: 'Behold, I will *rend the kingdom out of the hand of Solomon, and hand it over to others*', 'Because that they have forsaken me, and have worshipped Ashtoreth the goddess of the Zidonians, Chemosh the god of the Moabites, and Milcom the god of the children of Ammon, and have not walked in *my* ways, to do that which is right in mine eyes, and to keep my statutes and judgments', (see 1 Kings 11:31, 33). It was a terrible pronouncement of judgement.

In other words, so *evil* did God consider Solomon's retrograde step to be, that God said neither he, nor his nation, were worthy to continue any longer under their present form of government. On account of what they had done, the government and rulership of their country would be taken from them and given to other people. This happened in the space of a very few years.

Yet Britain has been repeating Israel's history in almost exact detail by going precisely the same way. So we need to ask ourselves: If God regarded Solomon's retrograde step as 'evil in the sight of the Lord', does he view such a step any differently today?

For Parliament, during the past few years, and for some reason or another, has decided to create a multi-racial society.

In King Solomon's case, the motive was love of foreign women. In Britain's case, I rather suspect that one of the reasons was the need for cheap labour! If this was so, I am not at all convinced that it was the *only* reason. In any case, since it was done without consulting the British people, I am not aware that they have ever been given the reason.

Whatever the case, the effect was bound to be the same as in Solomon's day, whether or not the authorities in Parliament and Whitehall exercised sufficient foresight to realize it. A multi-racial society inevitably leads to a multi-*religious*

37

society. It is impossible to avoid it. And in saying that, I am not being racist in any sense. I am merely stating a fact.

A multi-*religious* society has to be provided for. So Buddhist pagodas, Moslem mosques and Hindu shrines must be erected. Not only in and around the capital, but in towns and cities all over the United Kingdom as well. All this has been done throughout Britain despite the fact that, as Churchill so proudly recorded, God had brought us to that point in our history when 'there was no kingdom in the realm where heathen religions and practices now prevailed. The whole Island was now Christian.'[1] Is it not correct to say, therefore, that in *that* sense, Britain has put back the nation's history literally by generations, just as Israel did in the days of Solomon?

And is not that to be guilty of departing from God *historically*? For it must be true to say of Britain in these 1980s that there is no county in the United Kingdom now, where heathen religions are *not* practised!. So far have we put back the clock of our nation's history!

In May 1983 the Islamic Foundation in Leicester stated in their literature that there are now no less than 1,000 Muslim mosques dotted about all over Britain, and that there are approximately a million Muslims in our midst. It is estimated, too, that there are at least eight Buddhist temples in the United Kingdom and roughly 250,000 Buddhist followers. According to the 1983 Buddhist directory (a Buddhist Society publication) there are no less than 107 Buddhist societies, centres, communities, fellowships, associations, groups and foundations in England, Scotland and Wales, with a heavy concentration in and around London and the south, and to a slightly lesser degree in Birmingham, Wolverhampton, the West Country, Manchester and Liverpool. These include Buddhist monastries, meditation centres and temples. And London now has a huge Buddhist pagoda in Battersea Park! In addition, Buddhist societies exist in a number of Britain's universities and polytechnics. Many groups also meet in private homes.

Then there are goodness knows how many Hindu shrines.

To cap it all, a huge Muslim mosque has been built in Regent's Park, London, which dominates the skyline of that side of London with its golden dome, just as the Mosque of Omar dominates the skyline in Jerusalem. To add insult to injury, it has been erected in Hanover Terrace—named after the Royal House of Hanover, from which King George 1 was sent to preserve the Protestant succession to the English throne!

Since then, one of the Free churches in Fulham has been taken over for use as a Muslim mosque, and another mosque has now been built in Kensington within sight of Harrods's! And so the encroachment goes on.

In addition to all this, heathen gods and images are being worshipped in the open—in the parks and public squares of Britain. As the next few pages will show, this can only happen in Britain with the full approval and authorisation of the Government.

Whether or not the majority of British people are aware of all this, the fact remains that it has all been happening in Britain—and it has been happening for quite a number of years.

For the benefit of any who are not aware of what has been going on, let me trace just a few of the steps which have been taken in this multi-religious direction in recent years. It should serve to show the way in which things are going and where the trend-setters intend that it should ultimately lead.

For instance, the first step towards setting off a Solomon-like landslide was taken in the autumn of 1972, when it was announced that the British Council of Churches had reached the decision that redundant church buildings could now be taken over by devotees of other faiths and used for the practice of their religions. At the same time it was also announced that the then Archbishop of Canterbury had given his approval to the decision.

What we are talking about, of course, are church buildings which had been consecrated to the service of Almighty God and dedicated for the purpose of specifically *Christian* worship. These were buildings which had been erected and then set apart for the worship and service of our Lord Jesus Christ. I say that to hand them over to *other faiths* is sheer sacrilege.

Indeed, our English dictionaries use a biblical term to describe what sacrilege means. They say it means 'to profane', which I consider is very significant, for when used in the biblical sense, it means 'to profane the house of the Lord'. This is what takes place when a Christian church, which has been dedicated and set apart for the worship of Jesus Christ, is taken over and used to promote a heathen religion. It is 'to profane the house of the Lord'. To say the least, it is certainly an affront to the Lord Jesus Christ himself.

Furthermore, the decision to hand over redundant church buildings was certainly a retrograde step. For it meant that the door was now wide open for what must inevitably follow. We are now seeing an increasing number of Christian places of worship of various denominations all over the country being used as centres for the practice and propagation of all kinds of heathen religions and false faiths. Other church buildings, alas, are being used as factories, warehouses, workshops, Masonic halls, and even as Bingo halls! And what is all that, if it is not to desecrate and profane the house of the Lord?

Within a year of this atrocious decision, the first visit *ever* of a group of Buddhist priests (or lamas) from Tibet had been made to a fashionable London church, and Buddhist priests had been invited to introduce their tantric chants within the church. In fact, they performed Buddhist religious ceremonies within that church as well. A BBC reporter described what happened very cynically as 'a variation on Matins'!

Then Westminster Abbey, of all places, was used on a later ocasion for a Special Service, the object of which was to bring *all* the world faiths and religions together as one body.

Of course, this is another trend which has been set in motion. Its ultimate aim is the amalgamation of all the world religions into a 'One World Faith'. I will have more to say about this later. But this, indeed, is where all these other various steps are meant ultimately to lead—and so the escalation continues.

It should be quite clear that it is not simply a case of heathen faiths and practices being reintroduced into *the country* as such. It is a case of their being introduced into *Christian church buildings* as well. And I stress all over again that these are buildings which, in the context of a divine service, have been dedicated and set apart for the worship of Almighty God and of his Son, the Lord Jesus Christ. They have been consecrated for that purpose, and so, in that sense, have been pronounced *holy*. 'What difference is there', I ask, 'between *this*, and the wicked kings of Israel bringing all those heathen gods and abominable heathen practices into *their* holy places?'

Does it not amount to exactly the same thing? To do it, is surely to be guilty of desecrating the house of the Lord. It is to be guilty of profaning the holy places of the Christian faith all over the land. In the sight of Almighty God, it can be nothing short of outrageous. It is an affront to his most holy name.

For if this was so when the nations of Israel and Judah were guilty of doing such things, surely it must still be so today. And has it not had the same effect on the people of Britain today as it did on the people of Israel and Judah, namely, to change their outlook and attitude towards religion entirely, and towards Christianity in particular?

Is it not true to say that everywhere one goes now, one hears even some Christians saying, 'We need to have a multi-faith outlook on religion. All the religions are the same, aren't they?' It is even being preached in some churches that the religions of the world are like one great mountain, the summit of which (God) is shrouded in mist so that we cannot see him. We are all on that mountain in different places, but it all leads to God in the end, and each person finds himself in the way that is most appropriate to his circumstances!

A few weeks before Easter 1984, all the 'evangelical' churches in the area where I live came together in a local Free church, and a lecturer from a local theological college came to speak. In the course of his address, he stated very strongly, 'Jesus Christ is the *only* way of salvation'. He said, 'Jesus himself made that quite plain when he said, "I am the way, the truth and the life. No man cometh unto the Father but by me."'

There was uproar during question time! The dust has not settled yet! Voices everywhere were heard saying in protest, 'But what about all these other religions? All of them are ways to God, aren't they?'

And I stress, these were *evangelical* congregations, so called! There certainly would not have been *that* uproar fifty years ago!

The creation of a multi-religious society in Britain, for whatever reason, has had precisely the same effect on the people of Britain, as a multi-religious society had on the people of Israel and Judah in Solomon's day. It has changed their whole outlook and attitude towards religion entirely. And Almighty God must be just as angry as he was then. But this is not all that has been happening in recent years.

Note

1. See *The Trumpet Sounds for Britain*, Volume 1, p.32.

Chapter Three

Trafalgar Square

In addition to Christian churches and chapels in different parts of the country being taken over by people of other faiths, the heart of Britain's capital—Trafalgar Square—has been used for the propagation of false religions on numerous occasions. What is more, this has happened with the full authorisation and protection of the British Government. And because of this, I believe that Almighty God has been outraged to an even greater degree.

Yet to a large extent, the British people remain blissfully unaware of what has been taking place, although they should be warned about what is going on, and where it is all leading. Christian and church-going people, in particular, need to be informed. So I intend to place it on record. I want to make it plain that what I am relating is not hearsay; neither is it something I have read about. Rather, it is something which I have seen for myself. In fact, I would go further, and say that I believe it is something which God brought me to see for myself; and I believe that, for *this* reason, he wants me to make it known.

On the first occasion that I witnessed these disturbing events—during the week-end of 16 July 1972—I had been invited by a Christian friend to attend his wedding in Yorkshire. This meant that had I gone to the North, I would have been away from London throughout the whole of that week-end. Somehow I could get no peace about going, although I did not know why at the time. So I reluctantly declined the invitation and sent my apologies. I was now free of any commitments on the Sunday, so I decided that for evening worship I would go to a church in Central London. But then again, for no reason that I could have explained at that time, I set out far earlier than was necessary, and travelled by Underground as far as the Strand. It was a newsvendor in the Strand who, with considerable disgust, said, 'Have you seen what they are up to, over on the Square, gov'nor?' I went over to Trafalgar Square to investigate and there, to my horror, I saw that a huge shrine, mounted on wheels, had been brought to the Square, and had been drawn up alongside Nelson's Column on the right hand side of the main plinth, to face in the direction of the National Gallery. This shrine was draped with brilliant red and gold drapings, and, in height, almost reached the level of the roof gutterings of the nearby buildings. Therefore it could easily be seen towering above the heads of the Sunday afternoon crowds who were gathered on the Square. In addition, smaller shrines had been set up near the lions, and three large, carved, highly-coloured, but most fearsome-looking images, had been set up along the base of the main plinth below the Column. The most grotesque and frightening-looking of these was referred to in a glossy magazine, which was being offered for sale on the Square, as 'The Deity Incarnation of The Lord'. The sheer ugliness of the image proclaimed that this was blasphemy in itself. Then, during the afternoon, a robed figure could be seen at intervals squatting on his haunches inside the large shrine.

It was obvious that a most colourful and elaborate set of heathen religious ceremonies was in progress. But what horrified and sickened me more than anything else, was to see a number of people, draped in orange robes, prostrating themselves down to the ground with their heads touching the paving stones, as they did obeisance to the solemn figure squatting in the shrine, in full view of the gathered crowds. It was appalling.

The entire scene recalled immediately to my mind the story in the book of Daniel of the crowds bowing down to the golden image which Nebuchadnezzar had set up in the Plains of Dura. The story had made a vivid impression on my mind in my Sunday-school days, but never did I imagine that I would ever see anything even approaching the same kind of thing happening here—in my own native Christian England. At that time, such a thing was not considered to be even remotely possible. Certainly, Members of Parliament and the highest in the land would have brushed the whole idea on one side as totally impossible.

Yet here was something very similar happening now, right in front of my eyes. Not on the plains of Dura, nor even on an English cinema screen in the form of a religious epic, but in Trafalgar Square, of all places.

Neither was I the only one to be appalled. One Englishman in the crowd was so indignant over what he saw taking place, that he exclaimed: 'Have we, who once took pride in calling ourselves a *Christian* country, sunk to the level of all this?' and senior police officers on the Square had *their* feelings of disgust written all over their faces.

Furthermore, it was happening on a Sunday—*the Lord's day*—of all days! This was the day set apart for specifically *Christian* worship. If this was not desecration of the Lord's Day, I thought, then what is?

Winston Churchill once said at Blackpool, 'It is the policy of the Conservative Party to defend the Christian religion in the United Kingdom.' Yet all this was happening with the full authorisation of a *Conservative* government!

As the early evening drew on, I heard a speaker, on the main plinth, give an invitation to all the people on the Square to stay behind after the religious rites and ceremonies were over in order 'to partake of certain foods after

45

they had been offered up in worship to Krishna and the deities'—a practice which Christians and Bible students will know is strongly condemned in the New Testament, and which is described as 'partaking of foods offered up to idols' or 'foods offered to *demons*, not to God' (1 Corinthians 10:20 RSV). It can even lead to demon-possession.

I was severely shaken. Here I was, on my way to a commemoration of the Lord's Supper—a service at which, as any believer will know, that particular passage from 1 Corinthians is read very frequently. When I finally arrived, I was so abhorred and shaken by what I had just witnessed that the Lord's Supper was completely ruined for me. The scene kept returning with horror to my mind.

I would hasten to add that, having witnessed all this, I did not just stand idly by. It weighed upon my mind so heavily that I wrote to the Home Secretary that night, asking him how all this could possibly be allowed to happen, and making the strongest possible protest. For it seemed to me that, in addition to desecrating the Lord's Day, all that I had witnessed in terms of the images, shrines and doing public obeisance to false deities, was a flagrant violation of our British Constitution. It was certainly in breach of that part of the Constitution which the sovereign is required by Parliament, *on oath* before Almighty God, 'to uphold to the utmost of our power', and which Parliament is pledged to support: to maintain 'the *laws* of *God* in the realm,' *and* 'the True Profession of the *Christian* Gospel.'

Maintaining the 'Laws of *God* in the realm, surely includes upholding the first two commandments: 'Thou shalt have *no other* gods before me', and 'Thou shalt not *bow down* thyself to them, nor serve them.' Indeed it includes upholding the third: 'Thou shalt not take the name of the Lord thy God in vain; for the Lord *will not hold him guiltless* that taketh his name in vain' (Exodus 20:3–7).

And that is not to mention the fourth: 'Remember the sabbath day, to keep it holy'!

I remembered how I had stood on the Square that afternoon watching what was going on and thinking that this solemn undertaking, as contained in the Coronation Oath, has now most seriously gone by default. So I also wrote to Her Majesty the Queen, to ask if *she* was aware of what was happening at the heart of her capital on a Sunday afternoon.

It would appear that this second letter caused an inquiry to be sparked off amongst the Government departments concerned. For in addition to an acknowledgement from Buckingham Palace, letters which I subsequently received from Whitehall revealed that, not only had what had taken place on that Sunday afternoon been authorised by a Government department—the Ministry for the Environment—but that it had actually been authorised by *the Minister of State* for that department, a fact which I found very disturbing indeed.

It follows, of course, that immediately such an authorisation has been given, the police are informed, in order that they can provide the necessary surveillance and be present to preserve law and order. In any case, I had seen them there, with very senior officers amongst them, doing just that, and with looks of distaste on their faces. So I am fully justified in saying that it is *with the full authorisation and protection of the British Government* that Trafalgar Square was, and is, being used for the purpose of propagating heathen religions and practices. My inquiries had at least established *that* fact.

Furthermore, almost immediately after the letters had been sent, a learned QC, with whom I discussed this whole matter in the House of Commons, told me that he could see a very real inconsistency between what was undertaken in the Coronation Oath and what had later been authorised by a Minister of State and a Government Department, and he considered I should continue to speak out about it. When I said that I wanted to be quite sure of my ground before doing so, for fear of harming the monarchy, he said that, by speaking out, I would strengthen, rather than harm, the monarchy. So I became greatly assured that I was

THE TRUMPET SOUNDS FOR BRITAIN

pursuing matters along the right lines.

But the thing which, more than anything else, caused me to become deeply exercised about all that I have related, was the strange way in which I had been brought to the scene of these highly disturbing activities. I said earlier that I believe it was *God* who brought me there to see them, and I will now explain what I mean.

The Bible says in several places that God orders our goings, and directs our steps (see Proverbs 16:9; Psalm 37:23). And he had most certainly done this. There was the strange way in which I could get no peace about going to Yorkshire. There was the extraordinary way in which the timing of my journey into Central London was overruled so that I arrived there at the right time. There was the news-vendor's question, drawing my attention to all that was happening in the Square.

The Bible talks about 'the sons of God' being 'led by the Spirit of God' (Romans 8:14). And I have good reason to believe that this was one of those occasions. In any event, I have often had the experience of God guiding my steps so that I should arrive at a certain place, at a certain time, in order to fulfil a certain purpose which he had in mind. And here it was happening all over again.

As I contemplated it, my mind was taken to Ezekiel. I recalled how, at a time when his nation had become guilty of changing God's laws into wickedness, as our own nation has done, the Spirit of God brought Ezekiel into his capital city (Jerusalem) in a strange way, to show him what was happening (Ezekiel 5–6 and 8–9 AV).

We read that God did so to show him all the idolatry which was being practised in the city: first, out in the open, in full view of the people (Ezekiel 8: 3–5); then within the temple itself (Ezekiel 8:16), and again 'in the dark', behind closed doors, where there were wicked and abominable things 'portrayed upon the wall', and where the 'ancients of the house of Israel' were doing evil things, 'every man in the chambers of his imagery' (Ezekiel 8:8–12).

We read that Ezekiel was taken and shown a certain group of men standing within the inner precincts of the house of the Lord (the temple), between the porch and the altar, with their backs deliberately turned on the Lord and his temple, and their faces towards the east to engage in idolatrous sun-worship (Ezekiel 8:16).

The Lord showed Ezekiel all these things in turn, and on each occasion he said to him, 'But turn thee yet again, and thou shalt see greater abominations [than these]' (vv. 6, 13, 15).

I referred to this chapter later that night and read how the Spirit of God asked Ezekiel whether he saw what they were doing, whether he saw the great abominations that they were committing in order *to drive God from his own sanctuary*?

That was a spine-chilling question indeed, especially when I realised that, in *their* day, the consequences of what these people were doing was that God would not only be driven from his sanctuary, but also driven to *forsake their nation*.

It was spine-chilling, too, because it was clear that there was much in these Ezekiel passages which was relevant to the wickedness going on in London today, openly in the streets, and behind closed doors. So I became more and more convinced that it was God who had brought me into the centre of London that afternoon.

He could also be driven to forsake *our* nation.

Now I had hoped that, as a result of the strong protests I had made to the Home Secretary, and the enquiries which my letter to the Queen seemed to have sparked off, these heathen ceremonies would have been stopped immediately. But not a bit of it.

One Sunday in July of the following year, 1973, I was again brought into Central London as a result of extraordinary circumstances. And there I saw it all happening again—on a far more elaborate scale than before. For this time, the *whole* of Trafalgar Square, and not just the area round the main plinth, was being devoted to these heathen ceremonies. It seemed a deliberate act of defiance, in the face of the protests which had been made the year before.

The proceedings and chantings continued so far into the evening, and were so loud, that the noise penetrated into the nearby church of St Martin-in-the-Fields and actually disturbed the Christian service which was being held there, interrupting the sermon. The 'partaking of foods after they had been offered to the deities' had been greatly increased. This time, huge gold-coloured awnings had been put up high over the Square between the famous fountains, and the foods were being served on plates and offered to members of the general public from long tables placed under these awnings. In addition, people all over the Square were being accosted and vigorously encouraged to eat some of the food from the plates which were being offered to them. At the same time, robed figures could again be seen prostrating themselves to the ground in front of the shrine, and in front of two purple thrones, adorned with peacock feathers, which were placed against the main plinth.

A study of the Bible had made it abundantly clear that Almighty God by no means views lightly such idolatrous practices. He did not do so in King Solomon's day. Nor did he do so in Ezekiel's time. Is there any reason to suppose that he feels differently today? Can we, in Britain, afford to regard such things lightly?

So I considered it my duty, before God, to continue raising strong protests with the 'powers that be', but now with some desperation.

I engaged in further correspondence with the then Home Secretary and the Government department concerned, and with the then Lord Chancellor. I even sent further letters to the Queen to enquire about the present position of the Constitution in relation to these things. Then I requested an interview with the Home Secretary, in an attempt to get him to clarify the present position of Parliament in relation to the constitution and the Coronation Oath. But this

request for an interview was never taken up. Since then I
have tried on many occasions to discover from other leading
Parliamentarians what has happened to the Christian part
of our British Constitution, but they have either side-
stepped or evaded the issue. Finally, after a long chain of
correspondence with the Department and the Home
Secretary, I received a very weak letter from the Home
Office, saying, 'This is a matter about which the Home
Secretary is not prepared to intervene.'

So these disturbing heathen ceremonies and practices
have been occurring annually since 1973. And each year,
right up to July 1978, there were these extraordinary overrulings of God, causing me to be brought into Central
London and to the Square to witness them. The overrulings
even happened when, unbeknown to me, the now established date in July for holding such 'ceremonies' was
switched to another Sunday. The ceremonies have continued right up to 1985. God had brought me there each
year to witness them for some purpose. To me, what has
been happening on the Square each year is a clear case of
Britain having departed from God *constitutionally*.

I tell you, that if Britain continues to travel down the
path which she has deliberately and wilfully decided to take
during these many years, there *is* going to be an intervention, sooner or later. And that intervention is going to be an
intervention of God!

All Home Secretaries, please note!

Britain needs to be reminded that, in Ezekiel's day, the
time came when God summoned the six angels who had
charge over the city to draw near, 'even every man with his
destroying weapon in his hand' (Ezekiel 9:1). For God's
indignation and wrath had been so aroused against these
heathen religions and their abominable practices, that he
was about to bring a terrible judgment upon both the
capital and the country. So strong is the language which
God used to describe his indignation that he even said,
'Therefore will I also deal *in fury*' (Ezekiel 8:18).

But God, in his infinite mercy, granted a short breathing-space. This was in order to provide for the salvation of those who were vexed by all the wickedness which they saw going on. For we read that during that short space, God commanded the six destroying angels to withold the judgment until another angel, clothed with linen, had gone through the city to 'set a mark upon the foreheads of the men that sigh and that cry for all the abominations that be done in the midst [of the city]' (Ezekiel 9:1–11). This was to seal them for salvation.

When this had been done, and these people had been made secure, the angel clothed in linen reported, 'I have done as thou hast commanded me.' Then God's judgment did indeed fall, for he said to the other angels, in Ezekiel's hearing, 'Go ye after him through the city, and smite: let not your eye spare, neither have ye pity. Slay utterly... but come not near any man upon whom is the mark; *and begin at my sanctuary*' (Ezekiel 9:5, 6).

So they went, and we read that 'they began at the ancient men which were before the house.' And by 'ancient men', it means the *rulers*, ecclesiastical and otherwise—all in authority in Church and State today, please notice.

I believe that the signs show that we in Britain are very much in an Ezekiel, chapters 5–9 situation. If indeed we are, we have no right to take it for granted that *we* will be allowed a similar respite. That would be sheer presumption.

On the other hand, if the time that we are passing through at the moment *is* such a breathing-space, then be sure of this, it has been granted to provide some with an opportunity of salvation. Pray God they may take full advantage of it. Yet the granting of a brief respite in Ezekiel's day did not prevent the judgment from eventually falling. That is a fact which we cannot possibly afford to ignore.

Chapter Four

A Matter of Convenience

It should be abundantly clear that Britain has indeed gone as far as committing the sin of Solomon. Because the creation of a multi-racial society in Britain—for whatever reason—has led to the creation of a multi-religious society, in that it has brought into the country a whole variety of foreign religions and practices. And that, in turn, has necessitated the erection of numerous temples and shrines, and has caused heathen rites and ceremonies to be practised even in public places. So the same kind of escalation has taken place in this country as occurred in Solomon's day.

We have seen that it was what Solomon's retrograde step *led* to, which constituted the real evil in God's sight. For the bringing-in of all these other religions had the effect of turning his heart, and the hearts of his people, after these other gods. In our own day, it is what *Britain's* retrograde step is leading to, which constitutes the real evil, for the creation of a multi-religious society in Britain is already resulting in 'turning the hearts of British people after some of these other faiths.'

Take, for example, the influence which Islam is now having on the British people. Certain Christian speakers from the Middle East have been warning us that it is the agreed policy of the Muslims to turn Britain into an Islamic country *within the next ten years*, and that they aim to make London the Islamic capital of Europe in that time.

One of our bishops has said that immigration has increased the number of Muslims in this country to nearly a million. According to a Muslim newspaper published in Mecca, 'there can be no doubt that many English people have been influenced by their Muslim immigrants.' It goes on: 'A lot of native English people have accepted Islam, and practise it as the *Way of Life*, even though it does not go with their culture. They come from all walks of life. They include university professors, students, business men, writers, professional people, men and women, boys and girls.' And that same article says they are turning away from the churches to embrace Islam.

Islam is certainly on the march in this country. Muslim missionaries are even engaged in door-to-door visitation with a view to winning people over to their faith. Furthermore, a former Muslim, who now believes in Christ, says that Muslims are asking more of their people to come to Britain as missionaries, to convert British people to Islam. He adds: 'It was through an Englishman that I heard the Gospel, so it is incredible to me to see how many English people are becoming Muslims.'

In addition to all this, there is a strong move afoot to get the Government to introduce Muslim laws into this country.

Yes, whilst more and more churches are closing down, and whilst Christianity in Britain increasingly adopts a defeatist attitude, Islam is on the march and is turning the hearts of many British people to its faith.

The same can be said of Buddhism, of Krishna worship, and of a number of the eastern mystic religions. They are all fast winning converts. Indeed it is true to say that many British people, having rejected Christianity and turned away from the Lord, are now going after the religions of the East, with their transcendental-type meditations and their various forms of drug culture.

So in that sense, too, Britain has committed the sin of Solomon.

But I would contend that Britain has gone still further than Solomon went, for, in a modern age, to create a multi-racial and multi-religious society leads to the introduction of multi-religious education in schools. This is precisely what has happened in Britain and, furthermore, it has happened *at the expense of Christianity*.

For instead of the educational authorities taking advantage of the situation by teaching overseas children faith in Christ, our own British children are being taught and encouraged to believe that the Christian faith is just one of many faiths, that there is good in all of them, and that it is a matter of choosing what is best from each of them. So the educational policy is that all faiths and religions must be given an equal place in the teaching syllabus.

In fact, a study of the syllabuses used in schools will show that the Christian faith, our national faith which, by our British Constitution, marks us out as a Christian country as distinct from a Muslim, Buddhist, or Hindu one—that Christian faith is often relegated to third or even fourth place in relation to the others. Indeed, in some cases, the teaching of the Christian faith (if 'teaching' is what it can rightly be called) is left until the children have passed into the more senior classes; by which time, of course, it is inevitable that they will have already imbibed much of the teaching of the other world religions. And that is to say nothing of such subjects as witchcraft and the occult, which are also included in some religious syllabuses. It is to say nothing of communism, which was introduced into the schools syllabus in Birmingham a few years ago, and is being taught in many schools elsewhere.

All this has happened, because this method of mixing all these beliefs and ideas has now become the educational policy of the country. It again points to the way things are going.

As if that is not disturbing enough, I discover on very

good authority that there is a pressure group working within Parliament at the present time, whose stated aim is to introduce an overall policy of education which lays down that the various other creeds and faiths of the world shall be taught in schools *'with the minimum reference to Christianity.'*! In fact, this is now the generally accepted overall attitude towards religious education in schools, no matter what political party is in power.

The intention is to introduce that policy at some time in the very near future, when, according to this Parliamentary group the 'climate of opinion' is considered to be favourable. That could be at any moment.

Meanwhile, the British Humanist Association has, as its stated aim, the phasing out of Christian teaching in schools altogether, and it is working hard, both in the country and in Parliament, to achieve that end.

All this is going on, despite the fact that, as I have pointed out, it is the Christian faith which has been recognised as the historic faith of the nation, and which is still, by the Constitution, our official national position.

Why do I get so worked up about this? Because, in this urgent matter of continuing to teach the Christian faith, it is the eternal salvation of every child which is at stake.

The issue is one of salvation. For far from the Christian faith being just one of many faiths, Jesus—the greatest teacher the world has ever known—taught, that he is the *only* way to the Father (John 14:6). 'Come unto *me*', he said, 'and I will give you life.'

It cannot be stressed too strongly that, when he said '*I* am the way, the truth, and the life: no man cometh unto the Father, but by *me*' (John 14:6), he was not saying 'I am one of many ways'. Nor was he saying, 'I am but *one aspect* of the truth.' Instead, he said 'I am *the* way,' meaning 'the *only* way'; 'I am *the* truth,' meaning 'the *only* truth.'

Therefore the Lord Jesus Christ himself declared the Christian faith to be *unique*, and showed that it is set apart in a place by itself among all the other religions of the world as the *only* way of salvation. By declaring himself to be the *only* way to the Father, he automatically rules that all *other* ways and all *other* faiths are *false*, and therefore misleading.

The rest of the New Testament bears this out, of course, when it says: *'Neither is there salvation in any other*: for there is *none other name* under heaven given among men, *whereby we must be saved'* (Acts 4:12). And further: there is 'one mediator between God and men [meaning *only* one], the man Christ Jesus; who gave himself a ransom for all' (1 Timothy 2:5, 6).

With all the other religions of the world in mind, it needs to be firmly stated that the Bible declares that 'The gods that have not made the heavens and the earth...shall perish from the earth, and from under these heavens' (Jeremiah 10:11) and that 'The Lord will reduce to *nothing* all the gods of the earth' (Zephaniah 2:11, RAV). *All* of them, it says, and to emphasise the point: 'The graven image...is falsehood...they are futile—a work of errors. *In the time of their punishment they shall perish'* (Jeremiah 10:14–15, RAV). Or again, God says: 'the idols he shall utterly abolish' (Isaiah 2:18).

That is what God thinks of them. So infuriated is he with all false religions that when he visits in judgment he utterly destroys them. They are no more. He did so when he visited Egypt with judgment at the time of Moses. Indeed he said, 'against all the gods of Egypt I will execute judgment: I am the Lord' (Exodus 12:12).

Later, he destroyed all the false gods of the Amorites. He did the same again with the gods of the Assyrians and of the Babylonians. And when Judah, under wicked Manasseh, turned to false gods, and God said in consequence that he would visit Jerusalem in judgment, he also declared, 'the houses of Jerusalem, and the houses of the kings of Judah, shall be defiled [in judgment]...*because* of all the houses upon whose roofs they have burned incense unto all the host of heaven, and have poured out drink offerings *unto other gods'* (Jeremiah 19:13).

That is God's attitude to all these false gods which deceive people and lead them astray. He eventually removes them in judgment. It has been his attitude all down the years of Bible history.

When the great and terrible Day of the Lord comes, when the Lord shall come forth to punish the inhabitants of the earth for their iniquity, that will again be his attitude. He will utterly destroy all false and misleading gods. God will have no challenger *then*!

That is what is meant by the strong declaration, 'The gods that have not made the heavens and the earth...shall perish from the earth and from under these heavens' (Jeremiah 10:11). They will have been utterly removed— made totally non-existent. It will include all Hindu gods, Buddhas, the gods of Shintoism, and any other foreign gods that could be mentioned. Why? Because the God who commanded, 'Thou shalt have no *other* gods before me.... Thou shalt not bow down thyself to them, nor serve them; is so infuriated against them because they have deceived and led astray literally billions of people.

I say again: 'There is only *one way of salvation*.' That is through faith in Jesus Christ. 'I am the way', Jesus said, 'the truth and the life. *No* man cometh unto the Father *but by me*'. Not *one* person can.

British ministers of education, policy makers, and all members of Britain's teaching profession should take particular note of this. For of all people, educationalists should know that, once it has been established that there is only *one* way of salvation (and it has), and that the *one* way is by faith in Jesus Christ, then it follows that to teach children, or anybody else for that matter, otherwise, is grievously to mislead them. For when it is their eternal salvation which is at stake, to teach them falsely could result in their being eternally *lost* rather than eternally saved.

So vital a matter is this, that what is taught in the syllabuses for religious education in schools and elsewhere, needs to be safeguarded. And, of course, in this country it *was* safeguarded until only recently, by that written part of our British Constitution which is embodied by act of Parliament in the Coronation Oath which, I repeat, is a solemn undertaking, *on oath before Almighty God himself*; 'to uphold to the utmost of our power...the True Profession of the Christian Gospel' in the United Kingdom. That, according to the wording of the Coronation Service itself, means 'the Protestant Reformed religion'.

It was indeed safeguarded when, on 2 June 1953, Her Majesty the Queen stood before the altar in Westminster Abbey, with her right hand on the open Bible, and having taken the oath, promised, in the sight and hearing of all her peoples: 'The things which I have here before promised, I will perform and keep. So help me God.' And it was further safeguarded when she publicly *signed* the oath in her own hand, with the whole world watching on television.

Nothing could be more binding.

There is no question, therefore, but that it is the Christian faith, and *not* the faiths and creeds of the other world religions which should be taught in our British schools, for it is embodied and safeguarded in our Constitution.

The solemn undertaking into which Her Majesty so sincerely entered cannot be deliberately set aside or ignored by anybody—be it Parliament or anyone else—without their being guilty, before Almighty God, of betraying a sacred trust.

And yet it *has* been deliberately set aside and ignored, which is why I say that the Christian position in this country was safeguarded 'until only recently'.

I can substantiate this in the following way.

In the last chapter I said that I had engaged in correspondence with the Home Secretary and the Lord Chancellor to try to establish what is the present position of Parliament in relation to the Constitution, and in particular to that Christian part of it which is embodied by Act of Parliament in the Coronation Oath and which the Sovereign solemnly undertook to fulfil. A learned QC in the House of Commons had told me that he could see a very real inconsistency between the Coronation Oath and the kind of thing that I had seen in Trafalgar Square and which had been authorised by a Government department.

I could get no peace about it, so eventually I sought an interview with Lord Denning, who was then the Master of the Rolls. This he graciously granted me in May 1976. I asked him point blank if the Coronation Oath was now being ignored. 'Yes, it is being ignored', he said. I asked him, 'Is it even being ignored or set aside by Prime Ministers?' 'Yes, it is', he said. I went on, 'Is it being ignored, set aside, or being swept under the carpet by Parliament?' 'Yes, it is', he said. 'The answer to all your questions is Yes—unfortunately Yes.' I asked, 'Does what is embodied and was undertaken in that oath count for anything now?' 'Very little,' he replied. Then he added, 'But the courts, unfortunately, cannot do anything about it. It is the responsibility of Parliament.'

I explained to him why I was so disturbed and exercised about this tragic situation. In response he said, 'I quite agree with everything you say, and I understand you have been speaking out about it. I am very glad you are making your views known as widely as you can. And I hope you will continue to speak out about it in the way that you have been doing. I would like to come and hear you sometime!'

Now Lord Denning is an outstanding Christian. He was also Master of the Rolls. Therefore one could not have had a higher authority as to what is happening with regard to this deeply disturbing situation, apart from the Queen herself. So I had established that the Coronation Oath and everything that was embodied and undertaken in it, *is* being ignored, set aside and swept under the carpet by Prime Ministers and by Parliament.

Yet only a month later it was made clear in the House of Lords that precisely the opposite attitude ought to be taken. For this whole question of the obligation which Parliament has towards the Coronation Oath was raised by Lord

Lauderdale in the House of Lords during a debate on the family on 16 June 1976. I had been invited to listen, and to cover the debate in prayer.

Lord Lauderdale, in the course of his speech, had been referring to 'the most solemn pledge which was involved in the British voice among the overwhelming majority that voted for the Universal Declaration of Human Rights in 1948.'

But then he went on to say: 'I should like to ask the Government a further question, and that is, whether the Government will recognise that there is an obligation which overrides all that; something that overrides the context in which any Prime Minister takes office and forms a Cabinet at the hands of Her Majesty. Something that is done in the light of Her Majesty's anointing, consecration and coronation as Head of State after she has taken a series of oaths. *If those oaths are binding on Her Majesty, I submit that they are binding on Her Majesty's Governments* [my italics]. One of the oaths, to which I should like to draw attention is this one.

'She swears: "To maintain the laws of God and the profession of the Gospel." My Lords, it is difficult to find anything more categorical than that, and I repeat it.

'She swears at her Coronation: "To maintain the laws of God and the profession of the Gospel."

'It is in the context of that oath that Governments take office. So no matter what Governments take office, no matter what their ideas may be, no matter how Governments are composed, surely they will admit that they take office within the context of that oath and therefore in support of it. It is an oath solemnly given and solemnly subscribed by the Queen, at the instance, ultimately, of the State. It is binding, it is mandatory, it is categorical: and I ask the Government to affirm that that is so.'[1]

I could hardly believe my ears! This was the very thing I had been trying, for so long, to get established and have clarified. I felt it was of the Lord that I should be listening to that debate on that day, and that God had brought me there in order to hear this.

When Lord Wells-Pestell, Lord-in-Waiting to the Queen, stood to reply for the Government at the end of the evening, he said: 'I come to the noble Earl, Lord Lauderdale. He asked about the obligation of the Government. I think the answer to that is that what applies to the Monarch and the Constitution as a whole applies no less to the Government. I think one must follow the other.'[2]

On hearing this, I felt that the question had at long last been nailed. The position could hardly have been stated more clearly. And Lord Wells-Pestell, as Lord-in-Waiting to the Queen, could not afford to be wrong.

Yet succeeding governments, Prime Ministers, and even Parliament itself, have not, for years now, been fulfilling these obligations to the Coronation Oaths. All that I have written testifies to this fact. I say that they are therefore guilty before Almighty God of betraying a sacred trust. There is no doubt about it.

In respect of this matter of religious education in schools, the solemn undertaking made by the Queen has repeatedly been set on one side, and Parliament has turned a blind eye to it. And it has been done as a matter of 'convenience'. For on account of all the children from *other* countries who are now attending our schools, it is apparently considered to be 'no longer tenable' and indeed an 'embarrassment' for a Government department to authorise that it must be the Christian faith which is taught in British schools today. For the sake of convenience, the Christian faith must now be set on one side, even in favour of teaching other faiths, creeds, and world religions.

Do you see what a mess we have got ourselves into by becoming a multi-religious society? And what an affront it all is to Almighty God!

What a monstrous thing it must be to him for *anyone* to set aside the faith of a nation on such a flimsy and contemptuous pretext, let alone for a nation's Parliament to do it.

Do we for one moment imagine that the God who has worked so marvellously in our history to ensure that it was the Christian faith which became firmly established in these islands, can possibly treat such a betrayal of our historical and constitutional Christian position lightly?

Do we imagine that he can in any way be tolerant towards it?

Notes

1. *Hansard*, Wednesday, 16 June 1976, pp. 1329–30.
2. ibid., p.1361.

Chapter Five

Crumbling Within

When King Solomon was guilty of introducing false religions, God Almighty was by no means tolerant of what he did. Neither was he tolerant of the consequent landslide which Solomon's retrograde step brought about.

He was grieved, deeply grieved.

His indignation and the fire of his fierce anger was aroused and, in consequence, God began to visit Solomon's kingdom with judgment. So similar were these judgments to what we are experiencing in Britain today that I believe Britain *has* indeed gone as far as, if not further than, committing the sin of Solomon.

In Solomon's case, the first thing that happened was that *his kingdom began to crumble from within*. A process of disintegration set in. Over a period of time, his kingdom fell apart. First one part of it became independent, and then another.

Is not this precisely what has happened in Britain's case during the past thirty-five years?

Look at what has happened to the once proud British Empire. Soon after World War II, first one, and then another, of the countries within the empire began to ask for independence. What was that but the empire *beginning to crumble from within*? The result was that the Crown in Parliament was obliged to renounce its authority over one territory after another. Within a comparatively short space of time the empire disintegrated.

Why was it that we lost our empire so soon after World War II, when—as a result of all the mighty miracles of deliverance which God had wrought on Britains' behalf—our national leaders were all saying, 'We have been saved for a purpose, and now we need humbly to seek what that purpose is and then to be faithful to it?'

Why was it that Britain, which at the time of the preaching of Whitefield and Wesley had been raised by God to a height of glory and prosperity never known in any former age, and had become a Bible-loving and Missionary-hearted nation, sending missionaries to the far corners of the earth—why was it, I ask, that she began to decline and fall so rapidly? Surely this demands more than just a superficial explanation. Had Britain, for instance, taken yet another step to bring her on to a direct collision course with God?

I believe that she had, and that this was the reason why, in the purpose of God, there were demands for independence and the consequent break-up of the empire began.

Something very significant in the history of the world was beginning to happen just at that time—something which was related to the ancient Bible prophecies. And Britain decided to resist it.

Just after World War II, European Jews, in their thousands, began treking away from the regions of the Nazi concentration camps, over the mountains of central Europe, until they reached the coast of the Mediterranean. And the way in which Britain, of *all* Nations, treated this mass Jewish migration of refugees, was appalling.

A major prophecy of the Bible was beginning to be fulfilled, which heralded to the world that the return of our Lord Jesus Christ must be getting very near. For God had said, as far back as the time of the prophet Isaiah in the Old

Testament, concerning his widely scattered ancient people, the Jews:- 'Fear not, for I am with you: I will bring your descendants from the east, and gather you from the west: I will say to the north, "Give them up!" And to the south, "Do not keep them back!" "Bring my sons from afar, and my daughters from the ends of the earth."' (Isaiah 43:5,6 RAV). And there are many other similar prophecies. They all refer to what will happen 'in the last days' or 'the latter days'. And here, in 1946, it was all beginning to take shape!

World War II had indeed sparked off the fulfilment of some of these prophecies, and particularly those which refer to God bringing the people of Israel back to their own land from the countries where he had scattered them.

The Jewish survivors of those Nazi concentration camps came from the north and from the west. They had no other home to go to but Palestine, and now they were making for it.

On reaching the Mediterranean coast they boarded anything that floated and would transport them to Palestine, which, at that time, was a British responsibility, being held under mandate. All these heavily congested vessels—some of them quite unseaworthy—were proudly flying the Israeli flag.

The trickle of pathetic human beings quickly became a flood. Very soon they found themselves confronted with the might of the British Empire. For the British Government, and her then Foreign Secretary, Ernest Bevin, callously withstood this flood of desperate Jewish refugees, and issued instructions that none of these 'illegal immigrants', as the British Government and Foreign Office called them, was to be admitted into Palestine. Thousands, therefore, were either interned in Cyprus or sent back to Europe to the very concentration camps from which they had come—albeit the camps had been cleaned and the conditions improved.

This was going directly against the prophecy. The voice of God was saying 'Do not keep them back!' (Isaiah 43:6

RAV). And Britain was keeping them back. In doing so, she was resisting the will of God.

But the tide of these very determined and desperate survivors became so strong, and the measures imposed by the British Government and its authorities became so unpopular with world opinion, that finally, in 1947, the British Government gave back the mandate to the United Nations.

'Now also many nations have gathered against you [Israel]...but they do not know the thoughts of the Lord, nor do they understand his counsel' (Micah 4:11,12, RAV). No doubt the British Government did not know the thoughts of the Lord as he was bringing about this mass Jewish immigration to Palestine. Yet the fact remains that Britain's Government and Foreign Secretary brought the British Empire into direct collision with the long-declared will and purpose of God, so blind were we to spiritual things, and so totally bereft of Bible knowledge, particularly of prophecy. As was bound to be the case in such a confrontation, it was the purpose, the will, and the Word of God which prevailed, and judgment fell upon the British Empire in consequence of the British Government's resistance. For it is impossible to ignore the fact that it was precisely from that time that the eclipse of the British Empire began.

The British Parliament and people must never forget, as they seem to have done from 1946 to 1947, that at the very beginning of the history of the people of Israel—before they ever became a nation—God promised to Abraham 'I will bless them that bless thee, and him that curseth thee I will curse' (Genesis 12:3 RV). That promise still stands for Abraham's descendants today, and Britain paid the penalty for not blessing them in 1947.

In a prophecy of Isaiah, God also said, 'For that nation or kingdom that will not serve thee [Israel] shall perish, yea, those nations shall be utterly wasted' (Isaiah 60:12, RV).

It is a most amazing fact to me that, in 1946 and 1947, Britain, which had enjoyed such a rich Christian heritage and had once been a missionary-hearted nation, was given a golden opportunity to serve Israel—the nation to whom was committed the oracles of God and from whom, according to the flesh, Christ the Messiah came, and to which nation, in that sense, she owes the Gospel—yet did the exact opposite.

She could have served Israel marvellously by throwing the door of Palestine wide open to this God-motivated mass migration of thousands of Jewish refugee people, and she could have welcomed them there with open arms. She could have supported this movement with the full backing, wealth and resources of her empire. Had she done so, she would have been blessed indeed.

Britain adamantly refused to serve Israel in that way. Instead of throwing the door of Palestine wide open, she shut it firmly against them.

The consequence was that she soon lost her empire and saw the ancient promise given to Abraham, and the prophesy made through Isaiah, being fulfilled in that loss.

The British Empire disintegrated, and there was formed, from the pieces, what came to be called the British Commonwealth of Nations. But shortly afterwards certain artificially created federal states within the main body of the Commonwealth, and who were never really in agreement, began to break up, revealing the whole of the Commonwealth to be somewhat unstable. A leading politician, Enoch Powell, is now describing the Commonwealth as 'a humbug', and our British view of it as mere 'make-believe'— 'a fiction British-made and for British consumption'. The whole structure seems to be very precarious.

Again, it is a case of the commonwealth, like Solomon's kingdom of old, *beginning to crumble and go to pieces from within*. Enoch Powell predicts that internal disruption, secession, external interference, aggression and absorption, are likely to be more and more the fate of these 'often unstable, and highly artificial British ex-dominions', as he calls them.

He describes the present situation as, 'The Common-wealth morning after the imperial night before.'[2]

So, within the Commonwealth, the seed germs of disin-tegration are undoubtedly present, a fact which has been manifesting itself for some time and no doubt will continue increasingly to do so.

Australia, under its present Prime Minister, has mur-mured about freeing itself from the Crown; the status of Hong Kong has recently been negotiated, and the position of Gibraltar is, to say the least, questionable. So it goes on!

Within the British Isles themselves the seeds of disinte-gration have also been revealing themselves since World War II. Scotland was pressing for its independence at one time. So also was Wales. The Shetlands were also doing it! That is what the debates in Parliament and in the country on devolution a few years ago were all about. Warnings about the dangers of separatism—reverting to a state of independent control—were regularly being sounded.

The fact that the United Kingdom did not break up at that time into separate, independent parts, does not mean that those seeds of disintegration are no longer present. They could surface again at any time, given the right con-ditions.

Since we seem to have been putting back the clock of our own British history in so many other respects, is it altogether beyond the bounds of possibility that we shall see the British Isles reverting once more to its early form—that of once again being divided into a number of small indepen-dent kingdoms and realms? I don't believe it is.

Let us not delude ourselves. Were that to happen, and in the light of the way King Solomon and his nation went, and of all that 1 Kings 11 has to teach us about the consequences that followed, it would have to be seen as part of the judgment of God of the nation because of the way in which we have departed from him.

The next thing we find is that the Lord stirred up adver-saries against King Solomon. Notice that the *Lord* did so.

(1 Kings 11:14, 23–25). There was first one, and then another. From that point onwards, this kind of thing continued all the days of Solomon. His kingdom was really shaken. And we read that it was *God* who stirred up these adversaries against him.

These were agitators, trouble-makers, disruptive elements with which he had to contend. Today we would refer to them as 'the enemies within'. They were *internal* enemies. And is it not significant that we have been seeing exactly the same thing happening in Britain today?

For a number of years now, there have been trouble-makers, agitators and stirrers-up of strife in almost every department of our society. Leading national figures have warned that these enemies are in industry, in the civil Service, in the professions, in schools, colleges and universities, in Government circles, in the intelligence services, and working within the media.

We see thousands of massed pickets on our television screens, and witness the violence that often takes palce. We even see Fleet Street brought to an abrupt halt by an industrial dispute in which the papers themselves are in no way involved.

In short, these trouble-makers and agitators are *everywhere*. In Solomon's case there was first one adversary and then another. In Britain's case that can be multiplied by thousands!

The alarm has been sounded about those who are seeking to break up the United Kingdom, or even to take it over. We have seen it in politics, but it now appears that there are those within the Unions who are prepared to lift up one finger against Parliament and another against the Courts, and ask for the backing of thousands as they do so. Of course they claim that they are not seeking a confrontation with the Government, but that is, in fact, what they *are* doing. Who are they kidding?!

The impression created is that of a boiling cauldron lying underneath the surface of our industrial society, which could erupt like a dangerous volcano at any moment.

To cap it all, there are spies who keep cropping up in our Nation's security establishments, who are selling defence secrets to foreign powers and thus putting the nation's security seriously at risk.

No wonder that Doctor Coggan, the former Archbishop of Canterbury, said when he was still in office, and as he issued his 'Call to the Nation': 'There are enemies *within the gates*'.

In King Solomon's day, it was specifically stated that *God* stirred up the adversaries, and therefore it was all part of the judgment of God upon the nation. Make no mistake about it, it is *God* who is shaking our nation today through these agitators, spies, and trouble-makers, by national scandals, and in many other ways. In fact, I believe Britain is being severely chastised at this time.

We also find that in Solomon's day there were those who began *to lift up their hand against the monarchy* (1 Kings 11:26). And who can say that this is not happening in Britain today?

The brutal and callous assassination of Lord Louis Mountbatten was exactly that. It was a blow struck directly at the monarchy and was meant to be interpreted as such. He was a highly influential member of the Royal Family.

We have experienced the incident of shots being fired at the Queen whilst she was riding on horseback towards Horse Guards Parade on her way to the Trooping of the Colour followed very soon afterwards by an intruder successfully evading all the security precautions in Buckingham Palace and penetrating right through into the Queen's bedroom. The effrontery of it all! People lifting up their voices, and now their hands, against the throne, and against the Sovereign.

We have even had the case of a Member of Parliament going as far as taking the Oath of Allegiance to the Queen, and then stating, within hours of having done so, that he didn't mean a word of what he said!

More recently, it was reported in the *Daily Telegraph*[3] that less than ten days after Mr Wedgwood Benn had returned to Westminster as a Member of Parliament, he joined the Campaign Group of Labour MPs at the launch of their pamphlet *Parliamentary Democracy and the Labour Movement*, which includes a proposal to *deprive the Queen of her remaining powers over Parliament*. Mr Kinnock had already stated during an interview on TV AM on Sunday, 29 August 1983 that the Royal Family would be safe in 'Kinnocks Britain', and that although the Labour Party is committed to a number of radical policies such as abolishing the House of Lords, he wanted to make it clear that a future Labour Government *under his leadership* would safeguard the role of the Royal Family. But that, apparently, is not what Mr Wedgwood Benn and some others would have in mind in a future Labour Government under Wedgwood Benn's leadership! Not according to their pamphlet. For Mr Kinnock even to have to make such a statement as he did, implies that the monarch is by no means secure in the eyes of some.

As a strong monarchist I utterly deplore all this anti-monarchist activity. It is totally abhorrent to me. But when things like this began to happen in King Solomn's day, God said it was part of his judgment of the nation.

It was all part of a *process* of judgment, in fact. For we need to realise that there is a kind of judgment which God does not visit upon a country suddenly, or at a stroke, as it were. It is something which does not come all at once. Rather, it is the kind of judgment which God first prepares, and then announces that it is coming. He then allows it to develop gradually, and during that time he is repeatedly issuing warnings and urgent calls to repentance. Then, if the nation which has incurred his wrath and upon which he is bringing that judgment still fails to repent and turn back to him, despite his repeated warnings, he suddenly causes judgment to fall. Then the consequences are too terrible to relate.

It was this kind of judgment which was building up in King Solomon's day. It is this which was being described when God said to him: 'Notwithstanding in thy days I will not do it [punish you] for David thy fathers sake, but I will send [the Kingdom] *out of the hand of thy son*' (1 Kings 11:12). This was to be the punishment for having forsaken the true God, worshipping other gods and refusing to walk 'in [his] ways, to do that which is right in [his] eyes, and to keep [his] statutes and [his] judgments, as did David his father' (1 Kings 11:33).

That was the kind of judgment which was hanging over the nation. But eventually God caused it to fall. It happened within a generation.

In all these ways God judged Solomon's sin of national apostasy in *those* days. So I ask, 'since Britain seems to have gone exactly the same way as Solomon and his nation went, and since God himself has said 'I am *the Lord*, I *change* not' (Malachi 3:6), have we any right to expect God to judge Britain any differently?

The God of the Bible is the same God today.

Notes

1. See *The Trumpet Sounds for Britain*, Volume 2, ch. 16.
2. Leading Article in the *Daily Telegraph*, 22nd November 1983.
3. The *Daily Telegraph*, 16 March 1984.

Chapter Six

Reformation in Reverse

Now what about this matter of committing the Sin of the notoriously wicked Manasseh? What did *he* do?

There is a whole catalogue of his grim and grievous sins set out in 2 Kings 21, and other references to them are to be found in 2 Chronicles 33 and Jeremiah 19. We have only to read these chapters to see that Britain today can be likened to the days of Manasseh in a frightening number of ways.

The divine record states that 'he did that which was *evil* in the sight of the Lord' (2 Kings 21:2); that he 'seduced [his people] to do more evil than did the nations whom the Lord destroyed before the children of Israel' (2 Kings 21:9).

The same divine record makes it plain that Manasseh wrought so much wickedness that he aroused the wrath of Almighty God against him and against his nation irretrievably. We, in this modern age, need to be reminded that this is something which it is terribly possible to do today. In other words, Manasseh took his nation so far away from God that it went beyond the point of no return.

God eventually had to say, through his servants the prophets: 'Because Manasseh king of Judah hath done these abominations, and hath done wickedly above all that the Amorites did, which were before him, and hath made

Judah also to sin with his idols: *therefore* thus saith the Lord God of Israel; "Behold I am bringing such evil upon Jerusalem [the capital] and upon Judah [the nation] that whosoever heareth of it, both his ears shall tingle.... I will forsake the remnant of mine inheritance, and deliver them into the hand of their enemies; and they shall become a prey and a spoil to all their enemies; *because* they have done that which was evil in my sight, and have provoked me to anger'" (2 Kings 21:11–15). And 2 Chronicles 33:11 tells us specifically what that meant: 'wherefore the Lord brought upon them the captains of the host of the king of Assyria.'

In other words, it was judgment at the hands of a foreign power—the armies of the then king of the North.

But what did Manasseh do?

Manasseh's sins included much of which Jeroboam and Solomon had already been guilty, but also far more. In the first place, he reversed his father's (King Hezekiah's) religious reformation.

So have we been reversing ours. King Hezekiah, it will be remembered, had been a most godly king. As such, he had initiated one of the greatest religious reformations and revivals in the history of Israel. We can read all about it in 2 Chronicles 29–31.

The whole nation seemed to be turning to the Lord under his inspiring leadership and, as a result, the spiritual life in the land had reached a very high peak. There were many outward signs of this, and not a few inward evidences, as a reading of the chapters from 2 Chronicles will show. Call it a national return to religion, if you like, or a spiritual reformation. It was certainly something very akin to that.

Our British nation has experienced such times. I have referred to some of them in the first two volumes of this book. The Reformation of the sixteenth century, for instance, and the spiritual awakening which took place under Whitefield and Wesley, are but two of them.

We read of the man who was at the head of the nation at

the time of Judah's spiritual reformation that 'he did that which was right in the sight of the Lord...' (2 Kings 18:3); 'he trusted in the Lord God of Israel...he clave to the Lord, and departed not from following him, but kept his commandments, which the Lord commanded Moses' (2 Kings 18:5, 6). Is it any wonder, therefore, that we read 'And the Lord was with him; and he prospered whithersoever he went forth' (2 Kings 18:7) and 'so that after him was none like him among all the kings of Judah, nor any that were before him' (2 Kings 18:5)? What a testimony to his spiritual calibre! He towered head and shoulders above them all.

What a wonderful example and illustration Hezekiah provides, too, of the kind of leadership we need in Britain today!

But then, after giving his nation twenty-nine years of strong, godly leadership, King Hezekiah died. Almost immediately, his son Manasseh, promptly began to undo all that his saintly father had done.

First, he forsook the Lord. Having done that, he proceeded to put the great religious reformation into reverse. He had inherited a rich spiritual heritage, as we in Britain have done. Yet instead of continuing the policy of reformation from where his father had left off, Manasseh proceeded to overthrow it, and to go back on it all. So he struck a tragic and fatal blow from which that nation was never to recover. A terrible moral and spiritual escalation was bound to result—and it did. As a result, the entire nation was plunged into awful spiritual darkness.

The tragedy is that we, in Britain, have gone back on our own Reformation and have been dismantling it all, and so have gone as far as committing the sin of Manasseh.

This time, it is the church within the nation, and the leaders of that church, who are guilty. What is more, it has been happening with scarcely a voice in any place of authority being raised against it. Indeed, many church members have done much to encourage, and even help

77

forward, the present trend of reversing our Reformation. Others are silent, because they do not seem to realise what is going on.

Now what I am talking about is the glorious Reformation which took place during the sixteenth century and eventually came to this country from the Continent.

I can never repeat sufficiently that the Reformation was a movement initiated by the Holy Spirit of God. How else do you account for Martin Luther's dramatic conversion on the steps of St Peter's, or the conversions of Calvin, John Knox and other leaders of the time? Any such conversion is the work of the Holy Spirit.

Moreover, at the heart of the Reformation was a rediscovery of the original, basic, and dynamic New Testament form of Christianity which God had brought to these islands from the very earliest times and which had later so tragically become lost. But a dramatic return to that purer form of Christianity followed. It was a rediscovery of the basic and fundamental biblical Christian truth that the only way for a man to be reconciled to God is by faith in Jesus Christ, and in Jesus Christ alone.

Martin Luther was deeply conscious of the great chasm which existed between himself and a holy God, which he knew was caused by his sin. He was desperately trying to earn his salvation through all kinds of religious duties and works. Then, as he was going up those 'holy stairs' of St Peter's in Rome, on his knees, so as to try and gain more favour from heaven—when he was in the middle of the stairs, he heard a voice say, 'The just shall live by faith.' It startled him. He proceeded a step or two further, and the voice resounded again in his ears, 'The just shall live by faith.' Again there was no one to be seen. But those words brought a real revelation to his soul.

For the third time the voice seemed to sound in his ears, 'Therefore, being justified by faith, we have peace with God.' Luther rose from his knees, but still there was no one—no human voice. The Scripture was re-echoing in his heart, and it was the voice of The Holy Spirit calling Luther. He rose, went down the stairs and out into the open, a new man in Christ. The gulf had been bridged. Luther had been immediately reconciled to his Maker and a great peace had entered into his heart and soul. That was what the glorious Reformation was all about. That is how it started.

It was the rediscovery of the *only* way of salvation, and of the new birth.

Others followed Martin Luther's lead and took the same step of faith. They, too, became similarly transformed. It was unquestionably a movement of The Holy Spirit. That was why there were all these conversions—God was moving. Consequently a new spiritual awakening suddenly began to dawn, and thousands of people were brought 'from darkness to light, and from the power of Satan unto God' (Acts 26:17, 18).

As more and more people entered into this new dimension of life in Christ, the whole church in the West, first on the Continent, and then in Britain, began to vibrate. Its members were suddenly set free from the old shackles with which they had long been bound by papal Rome, and an entirely new era began to dawn.

At the heart of the Reformation, too, was the rediscovery of the authority of the Bible. It was the authority and teaching of the Word of God which now determined all matters of faith and conduct, not the authority and teaching of 'mother church'.

In this country, the inevitable result of the reformation was that the church broke away from domination by the Church of Rome. As everybody knows, that took place during the reign of Henry VIII. Oh yes, I know that politics inevitably became involved, but the Reformation was predominantly a work of the Holy Spirit. It was due to the Holy Spirit that, during Henry VIII's reign, this country became predominantly a *Protestant* Christian country, and her people a Bible-loving people. Eventually she became known all over the world as such. Furthermore, it was due to the continued work of the Holy Spirit that, early in the reign of Queen Elizabeth 1, this country became a Protestant Christian country *by law*.

We know, too, that God set his seal upon the fact that it was clearly his will and purpose that we should be, and should *remain*, a Protestant Christian country, by intervening in our history to bring about the defeat of the Spanish Armada.

Just 100 years later, when James II sought, against the will of the people, to uproot the Protestant Christian religion and bring about a forcible reconversion of England to the Roman Catholic faith, God intervened again in a most miraculous way by bringing William of Orange and his sea-borne armies here, on a favourable wind, and at the request of an influential body of English citizens, to secure the Protestant position of England. There were at least two mighty miracles involved which space does not permit me to relate here. And when William of Orange marched from Torbay to London, he carried a banner on which was written, 'The Protestant religion and the liberties of England I will maintain.'

At the end of the same century, when the Protestant position in England was yet again being threatened, God intervened once more in our history. This time he gave us a Marlborough, and a Sarah Churchill, whose strong Protestant influence—together with that of the then Princess Anne, herself a Protestant who later became Queen Anne—did much to cause Parliament to take the initiative and pass the Act of Settlement in 1701. This excluded a Roman Catholic from the throne, and also vested the succession in the Protestant Royal House of Hanover after the reigns of William I and Queen Anne were over. This brings us eventually to George III, whom I have mentioned in a previous chapter.

So the Protestant Christian position in England was made safe and secure, and it was the sixteenth-century glorious Reformation which led to all this.

The tragedy today is that we have been going back on, and have been undoing it all. We have been wanting to sweep it under the carpet.

During the last two or three decades at least, many of the leaders of the church have been declaring that the Reformation was a mistake. Even evangelical leaders have shifted their position in that direction during the last fifteen years. One leading evangelical even went so far as to say that the Reformation was the greatest tragedy ever to take place in the history of the church!

A work of the Holy Spirit a mistake! A work of the Holy Spirit the greatest tragedy that has happened in the history of the church!

For a number of years, the subtle schemes of successive archbishops and other church leaders, in pursuing their policy of endeavouring to unite all churches and denominations together in a false and non-biblical form of 'unity', have been setting a trend in motion which is aimed at dismantling all that God brought about through the Reformation so as eventually to reintroduce the universal supremacy of the Bishop of Rome over all the main-line churches. That is the language which is being used. Furthermore, there seems to be a strong but subtle conspiracy at work behind the scenes in order to achieve this aim. In other words, it is reunion with Rome which is being aimed at. That is what the ecumenical movement is all about, and it is astounding to see the number of true Christians who are being taken in by what is going on.

All this is being done at the expense of essential and basic biblical doctrine. The instigators of the ecumenical movement knew full well that they could never achieve their kind of so-called 'Christian unity' whilst basic Christian truth stood in the way, like some great barrier looming up in front of them, preventing them from achieving their objective. So they decided they must set many of the cardinal Christian truths on one side, and even ignore them totally. Essential New Testament doctrine no longer mattered.

Articles of faith, like the Thirty-nine Articles of the Church of England, must now be relegated to some remote 'ecclesiastical archive' as if they were just so many museum pieces. Service books must be altered to bring their wording more and more into line with the teaching of Rome, but it must be done very gradually, so that an increasingly doctrinally illiterate and untaught laity would scarcely detect what was going on. Hence the Series I, II, and III services in the Church of England. This is referred to as 'a process of gradualism'.

Evangelical leaders at the Keele Congress in 1967 had now, if you please, to put their main emphasis on baptism as the way a person enters the church (*infant* baptism at that), and no longer on the new birth—thus subtly making the teaching appear to be akin to that of Rome! Double-speak language must now be introduced into the wording of the Communion service (or administration of the Lord's Supper) to make it appear, to those who want to interpret it that way, that it is the actual body and blood of our Lord which is received at that service, not just the symbols of it. In other words, a subtle form of the doctrine of transubstantiation, as taught by the Church of Rome, was now being reintroduced. This is sheer deception.

The result of departing from the real truth in so many ways is that the church has become apostate. The age-old battle is still on. For the original, dynamic, New Testament form of Christianity which God brought to these islands in the first place, has once again, to a very large extent, become submerged in confused and false teaching, if not indeed been almost lost. And the church in this country is fast being taken back to where it stood *before* the Reformation. It is obviously the deliberate intention of some people that this should be so.

If you do not believe it, listen to the great capital which the BBC and the national press made out of what happened immediately after Cardinal Hume had been installed in Westminster Cathedral as the new Roman Catholic Archbishop of Westminster. They declared: '*For the first time since the Reformation* the new Archbishop and his Order of monks were able, on that same day, to chant their chants in Westminster Abbey, which *before the Reformation, used to belong to them*' (my italics.).

Or listen to what a well-known Roman Catholic-controlled national daily newspaper declared a few days later: 'A New Era has dawned for the Roman Catholic Church in England…the Roman Catholic Church is gradually becoming a "*national*" instead of a "local" and "community" church', and 'the aim of the new Roman Catholic Archbishops of Liverpool and Westminster is to foster and develop this process by creating more and more Roman Catholic dioceses throughout the United Kingdom.'

Or listen yet again to what the *Daily Telegraph's* church affairs correspondent stated at the same time: 'The need to restore Westminster Cathedral completely, is regarded by the Roman Catholic authorities in Westminster as a first priority, because Archbiship Hume is known to be anxious to see Westminster Cathedral used for *national* as well as diocesan occasions' (my italics).

Does the Archbishop mean future Coronation Services, I wonder? No doubt that is what he, and Rome, have got their eyes on. Bearing that possibility in mind, is it not true that certain members of the Church of England General Synod recently made attempts to bring about changes in the Act of Settlement of 1701, which, if the Act were to be amended, would be in order to enable any heir to the throne to marry a Roman Catholic? These are all subtle and crafty moves in the same direction, I would suggest!

Is it not very noticeable, too, that no religious service on state occasions ever takes place now without the Church of England and Roman Catholic hierachies *jointly* taking part in them? Surely that is to reverse and to dismantle the Reformation, just as Manasseh did with his father's reformation. It is also to set back the clock of our history. Jeremiah called it 'going away backwards.'

Chapter Seven

'Pioneer of Reunion'

Whilst this book was being prepared, Lord Ramsey, a former Archbishop of Canterbury (1961–1974), and the *Church Times* brought out into the open how this more recent movement towards reunion with Rome first started. Up to now it has been quietly hushed up, but suddenly, for some reason, they decided to 'go public'. It is a remarkable fact that this was all brought to light in January 1984, not two months after Bible-believing Christians everywhere had been celebrating the 500th anniversary of the birth of that great saint of the Lord, Martin Luther. The anniversary was celebrated throughout the world, and particularly in the West, during November and December of 1983, with special sermons, radio and television programmes, conferences, preachings at Wittenberg, special lectures at Wörms, and such like.

Scarcely had the sounds of these rejoicings, and the thunderings of this preaching died away, when many leading members of the church of England began to celebrate the fiftieth anniversary of the death of the man who, in their minds, has gone down in recent church history as 'a pioneer of Anglican—Roman Catholic reunion' and 'a prophet of church unity'. I refer to Lord Halifax, and these anniversary celebrations have brought a number of very interesting things into focus.

Lord Ramsey, for instance, has revealed in an article in *The Times*[1] that this recent move towards reunion with the church of Rome started near the end of the nineteenth century. Both he and the *Church Times*[2] describe how, on the Continent at the time, a certain French Roman Catholic priest named Etienne Fernand Portal (or Abbe Portal), and a man named Duchesne, published certain works advocating a reconciliation between the Roman Catholic Church and the Church of England, defending at the same time the validity of Anglican orders.

Lord Halifax, an Anglican churchman, had been dismayed, as the *Church Times* puts it, at the deep Protestantism of his own church, and was speaking very strongly for the Catholic Party in the Church of England—he continued to do so for over sixty years from 1869 to 1934.

When at the end of the nineteenth century he heard of what the Abbe Portal was advocating, he formed a close friendship with him, and together they talked with leading Roman Catholics and Anglicans, both on the Continent and in Britain, encouraging discussions between the two churches. They even begged the then Archbishop of Canterbury, Edward Benson, to initiate discussions which would have Vatican auspices. Lord Ramsey very proudly and quite unashamedly recounts all this.

Halifax thus set in motion the *first* Anglican—Roman conversations in the 1880s.

A strong body of Roman Catholic opinion on the continent was willing at the time to open exploratory talks, but the then Roman Catholic Archbishop of Westminster, Cardinal Vaughan, was not. Nor were the majority of Anglicans, significantly enough. Then in 1896 Pope Leo XIII slammed the door to reunion when he issued the papal encyclical declaring Anglican orders void.

But Halifax did not give up.

The Church Times, in its article about him, said that he

was always certain of three things:
1) The Church of England was part of the Catholic Church (by which I take it, he meant the *Roman* Catholic Church);
2) A healing of the schism between Rome and Canterbury was inevitable sooner or later;
3) Individual 'conversions' to Roman Catholicism or individual submissions to Rome did nothing to advance the reunion between the two churches. Something more was needed.

He never lost his belief that the reunited churches would find their leadership in a future papacy.

I will return to these three points later.

So we can see very clearly where he was heading—to bring the Church of England once again under the papacy, which is a deliberate resolve to reverse the Reformation.

The *second* part of this new drama took place when the bishops of the Anglican Communion in the Lambeth Conference of 1920 issued the 'appeal to all Christian people inviting every Christian church in the world to take some steps in the path of unity.'.

Not, you notice, to take strong steps to proclaim to the whole world 'the faith which was once delivered unto the saints' (Jude v.3), and so to fulfil the Lord Jesus' commission to 'preach the gospel to every creature', which is the *real* task of the church! Had *that* happened, it could have changed the whole course of world history, especially had it been done by every true Christian the world over, through the Holy Spirit and with power. It might even have prevented World War II!

It was an appeal to take *some* steps in the path of unity—and 'unity' has become *the* Gospel ever since.

I was not yet born at that time, but as one of the 'all Christian people' today, I have a right to ask: Unity, yes—but on what basis? At the expense of what? Could it be at the expense of essential, cardinal, Christian doctrine and biblical truth? What about the millions, indeed billions, who are perishing without the Gospel, outside the churches (and within them, too, because of the stifling of true preaching)?

However, Halifax was so encouraged by this appeal that he and the Abbé Portal set out on a new quest. The Abbé took Halifax to meet the Roman Catholic Cardinal Mercier of Malines in Belgium.

This led to the *third* part of the drama, and to what has since become known as the Malines Conversations which, incidentally, eventually provided the answers to my questions above. Here at Malines, two strong parties met to confer in private.

One party, from England, consisted of Lord Halifax, Armitage Robinson (Dean of Wells Cathedral) and the Roman Catholic Father Frere of the Community of the Resurrection. The Continental party was made up of the Roman Catholic Cardinal Mercier, the Abbé Portal, and Cardinal Mercier's own vicar-general, Monsignor van Roey.

Their meetings were described as 'private', and there were no official appointments, neither was there any official agenda. But both Randall Davidson, then Archbishop of Canterbury, and the Vatican, had given these meetings a certain amount of encouragement. And so, as Lord Ramsey says in his *Times* article, they were, in fact, a little *more* than private. Perhaps 'secret' would be a more appropriate description?

Initially two conferences were held at Malines. One was in December 1921, and the second in March 1923. At these, the deep doctrinal differences between the church of Rome and the Anglican Church were very significantly indeed *deliberately* set on one side. Ramsey says that 'there was no attempt to go into them.' This was to ignore completely the New Testament pattern and principle, which is always doctrine first, then deductions from doctrine. But you see, doctrine to these people is not the important thing. It only hinders what they are trying to bring about. So according to Ramsey, the method (note the term) was to say in effect: 'Suppose that the deep differences were solved, what might the position of the two churches be?' *That* became the question under discussion—*not*, I notice, 'What is the Gospel we should be proclaiming?'.

Here the Roman Catholic Cardinal Mercier's party came up with the answer in the form of a picture for the future. It was this: The Pope would be universal primate, the Archbishop of Canterbury would be provincial primate, and the Church of England would continue with its own liturgy in the vernacular (English), still continue its use of married priests and the receiving of Communion in two kinds together with many other existing Anglican customs.

This was seen, by those conferring, as a beginning. Many were alarmed that these conversations were going on at all, but Archbishop Davidson wished for their continuance. and so strongly did Cardinal Mercier want them to continue that there was a strengthening of the two discussion teams. It is quite obvious that a lot of pressure was coming from the Roman Catholic side!

Bishop Gore, an extreme high churchman, and Dr Kidd, the warden of Keble College, Oxford, were added to the English side, and two formidable Roman Catholic historians, Monsignor Batiffol and Monsignor Hemmer, joined the continental team. With this added weight, the talks continued at two further conferences, one in November 1923 and the other in May 1925.

There was a clash between Bishop Gore and Monsignor Batiffol about the role of the Pope in the early church, whilst Dr Kidd expounded a role of leadership for the See of Rome '*as in the early church*' (as he put it, but my italics), although very limited in scope.

Gore also made a powerful plea that nothing should be required as *de fide* (of the faith) except what belonged to the agreed consensus of East and West in the early centuries.

All this exposes at least three fallacies. First, why should there have been this argument about 'the role of the Pope in the early church!? There *was* no Pope in the early church, if 'early' really means *early*.

Up until AD 610, the heads of the Christian church in the

city of Rome had been content to call themselves simply 'Bishops of Rome'. In fact, the one referred to by the early church historians as the *first* Bishop of Rome' was Linus, who assumed or was given the title 'first Bishop of Rome' after the deaths by martyrdom of the apostles Peter and Paul at the hands of the Emperor Nero. Peter was *never*, known in his own day as 'Bishop of Rome'. He was always referred to as the apostle Peter.

Leo the Great (Bishop of Rome from 440 to 461) developed the idea of a universal primacy but, even so, the title of 'Pope' was generally unknown until it was offered to Gregory the Great, then Bishop of Rome, by the Emperor Phocas. Gregory graciously refused the title, claiming that he was no more than 'first among equals'. So even Gregory should never be referred to as Pope Gregory the Great, but merely as Gregory, Bishop of Rome.

It was Gregory's successor, Boniface III, who first assumed the title of 'Pope' in AD 610. So what were Bishop Gore and Monsignor Batiffol arguing about when they discussed the role of the Pope in the *early* church?

The Christian church was nearly 600 years old before any 'Pope' appeared on the scene, if we date the beginning of the church from the time when the Lord Jesus Christ called his original twelve disciples. It is well over 550 years old if we date its beginning from the Day of Pentecost. This means that the church had existed and had been rapidly spreading and thriving for well over half a millenium before any 'Pope' emerged. Is that to be called *early*? When Bishop Gore and Monsignor Batiffol argued so strongly, it would seem to imply that, to them, the history of the Christian church began with the Popes! If that is so, then they were ignoring entirely the history of the *New Testament* church. Search the pages of the New Testament as much as you like, but you will find no reference to a Pope, let alone a role!

The second fallacy was exposed by Bishop Gore making his strong plea that nothing should be required as *de fide*, except what belonged to the agreed consensus of East and West in the early centuries.

Amongst true believers, who ever heard of basing the faith on an agreed consensus of the churches? Any true believer, and any Christian leader who is faithful to his Lord, knows full well that nothing should be required as 'of the faith' except what is found in the Bible. The unalterable rule is 'Whatever I find in The Bible I accept; whatever I cannot find in The Bible I reject absolutely', because it is the Bible which is our authority.

Furthermore, the New Testament epistles teach us that the Christian church was built on 'the foundation of the apostles and prophets, Jesus Christ himself being the chief corner stone' (see, for instance, Ephesians 2:20). That means it was founded on the teachings of the apostles and prophets, with Jesus Christ himself, in person, as its chief foundation. It was not founded on any 'agreed consensus between East and West'.

In any case, nobody started talking about 'the Eastern Church and the Western Church' until at least the fourth century. It follows, therefore, that East and West could not possibly have come to any 'agreed consensus' for quite a number of years beyond that point. Once again Bishop Gore and the two powerful Romanising conference teams were not going back far enough in early church history. They were certainly not going back to the days of the New Testament church, nor to the teaching of the Bible. They were, it would seem, deliberately turning a blind eye.

What Bishop Gore was doing, therefore, when he issued his strong plea, was deliberately attempting to build the structure of 'the two reunited churches', which he and his confederates envisaged, on what was, in fact, a faulty and quite false foundation, and one far removed from the foundation as revealed in the pages of the New Testament. That is a fact which comes out perfectly clearly. In doing so, all of them must have been deliberately refusing to appeal to the Bible as the only authority and court of appeal on such matters.

When he and others talk about nothing being required as *de fide*, except what belonged to the agreed consensus of East and West in the early centuries—as if *that* is where you begin—the question I would like to put to them is this: 'If you insist that the apostle Peter was the first Bishop of Rome, why do you not accept that Peter said in the opening two verses of his second epistle—"Simon Peter, a servant and an apostle of Jesus Christ, to them that have obtained *like precious faith with us*..." (2 Peter 1:1)?

The apostle is writing to Christian people who were scattered amongst various Roman provinces (see his first epistle, chapter 1:1). Some of them were Gentiles, some were Jews, and yet Peter is saying that the faith they have— the faith they have obtained—is the same. It is a precious faith, like that which he and his fellow apostles, and all believers everywhere, have obtained. He is emphasising, therefore, that *there is only one faith*.

But the apostle Peter, in addition to saying that there is only one faith, is asserting that the only faith is the *faith of the apostles*. For he tells them that they have obtained a 'like precious faith *with us*.' Therefore the only faith is *the apostolic faith*. And that is as true today as it was in the days when Peter wrote this epistle.

If such people as Bishop Gore and his successors *will* insist that the apostle Peter was the first Bishop of Rome, why will they not accept and hold to the fact that Peter made it plain that there was only *one faith*, and then build on that? For to build on 'only that which belonged to the agreed consensus of East and West in the early centuries' is to build on another foundation.

When Dr Kidd expounded a role of leadership for the see of Rome 'as in the early church, and very limited in scope', he introduced the *third* fallacy into the discussions. He was, in fact, begging the question. For there *was* no see of Rome in the early New Testament Church.

There is no mention of 'a see of Rome' in the later

chapters of the Acts of the Apostles, for instance, where we have the clear account of the apostle Paul arriving there, and of the Christians who met him. Nothing could be further removed from that scene. Neither do we find Paul making any reference to 'a see of Rome' in his epistle to the Romans, or in any of his other epistles. Nor do we find reference to any such a 'see' in the last book of the New Testament, the book of the Revelation. And all these New Testament writings cover almost the first one hundred years or so of the history of the early New Testament church. The whole idea of 'sees' and of 'popes' is entirely foreign to the spirit and teachings of the New Testament.'

'Sees' came much later. But even then, such an idea was extremely questionable. It is highly debatable, for instance, whether the Lord Jesus Christ, as the head of the church, ever had it in mind that such things as 'sees' should exist. They are merely part of a later man-made ecclesiastical structure.

Then Cardinal Mercier read a paper at the May 1925 conference entitled 'United, but not Absorbed'. Significantly, this paper was not his own, apparently, but had been written by a certain Roman Catholic monk by the name of Dom Beauduin, of the Benedictine monastery at Amay in Belgium. 'That monastery', says Lord Ramsey, 'which later moved to Chevetogne, *was a continuing centre for ecumenical interest* not least towards the East' (my italics).

And this is the point at which '*ecumenical* interest' and an 'ecumenical movement' is first mentioned. Referring to the paper, Lord Ramsey says 'And the title "[United, not Absorbed"] told its own story'.

Lord Halifax died before he saw the fruits of all his efforts towards reunion between Canterbury and Rome. So did the Roman Catholic Cardinal Mercier. But thirty years after Halifax's death, the fourth drama of this new move towards Anglican-Roman Catholic reunion took place.

93

The Second Vatican Council was held, where the Decree on Ecumenism declared that the Anglican Communion has a special place among those in which Catholic tradition and institutions in parts survive. So the door to Rome was now more than ajar. This declaration was a real major step towards the Roman Church receiving the Anglican Church back into its fold.

Not long after this, and only forty years after the deaths of Mercier, Portal and Halifax, Pope Paul VI was receiving an Archbishop of Canterbury in the Sistine Chapel in Rome. And that Archbishop was Lord Ramsey!

There, in the Chapel, the Pope placed his own pastoral ring on Archbishop Ramsey's finger, with the words, 'This is not yet the marriage ring between our two churches but it is the engagement ring' (I quote the *Church Times*). Lord Ramsey himself relates, in *The Times*, that the Pope added these words: 'Surely from heaven, St Gregory the Great and St Augustine look down and bless.'

We need to know what goes on. For what is all this but blatantly and unashamedly to take major steps deliberately to reverse and undo our own Reformation? It is reversing even earlier history. When Gregory the Great sent Augustine to England in AD 596, it was in order to bring the already existing, thriving, actively evangelistic, and very lively Christian church in Britain under the one earthly headship of the Bishop of Rome, when it had been free of all outside domination and control for well over 500 years.

The sending of Augustine was, in fact, the first step Rome was to take towards making this country a Roman Catholic one. That original step failed. But a further step was taken by Rome in AD 663 which was more successful, when, as the result of a lamentable decision taken at the Synod of Whitby, by far the greater and more powerful part of the Christian church in these Islands was now to become associated with the papacy, whereas it had been entirely free before. This second step therefore, was a major one. It was a development which eventually plunged the country into centuries of appalling Roman Catholic darkness, right up to the Tudor period, until the darkness was eventually broken by the glorious Reformation.

So are we not now in the process of turning the clock of our history right back to the time of the Synod of Whitby?

Just two days after Pope Paul VI had placed this 'engagement ring' on Archbishop Ramsey's finger, the two of them, on Lord Ramsey's own admission, were signing a Common Declaration calling for serious dialogue which should lead to further so-called 'unity' between the Church of England and the Church of Rome, with the Church of Rome predominant.

To crown all this, of course, the fifth drama in the whole subtle movement towards reunion took place when, in the summer of 1982, there was the visit to this country of Pope John Paul II. In Canterbury Cathedral, amidst certain ceremonies where even representatives of some of the Free Churches were present, 'the heart of ecumenism' was expressed in an affirmation made by the Pope in the presence of the Archbishop of Canterbury and of the heir to the British throne, revealing that what was really afoot was the ultimate embracing of *all* the Churches, not just the Church of England, under one supreme earthly head, the Pope. That is how it all evolved. That is the direction in which things are now fast moving. It was what the Archbishop of Canterbury and the present Archbishop of York are now constantly referring to as 'reunion by stages'. The frequent 'united' and 'amalgamated' services and functions which are now constantly being held, all testify to that fact.

What needs to be stated clearly and strongly is that when Lord Halifax, as a so-called 'pioneer', took such strong strides towards reversing and undoing our Reformation, he was not only flying in the face of history, and in the face of the New Testament, but in the face of *God*. He was flying in the face of what God did to bring about the defeat of the Spanish Armada, which was the first major attempt, after the Reformation, to overthrow our Protestant Christian

Sovereign and bring this country back under Roman Catholic domination. When God brought about this defeat he made it abundantly plain that we were meant to be a Protestant Christian country. Halifax was also disputing what God did at a later stage when he brought William of Orange here to preserve the Protestant succession to the English throne.

And he was in contention with what the Duke of Marlborough and Sarah Churchill did at a still later stage in our history, in bringing the Royal House of Hanover over to this country from the Continent, once again to secure the Protestant succession to the English throne.

As to Halifax being certain that the Church of England was part of the Catholic Church, our English history shows that it never has been so, since the Reformation. Rather, there have been constant attempts, ever since the time of Augustine, to bring the Christian church in Britain under Roman Catholic domination.

Notes

1. *The Times*, 21 January 1984.
2. The *Church Times* 20 January 1984.

Chapter Eight

Early Christianity

In order to refute his claim still further, I will restate what I have already written in volume 1, that all the evidence suggests that Christianity must have come to Britain extremely early, and certainly well over 500 years before the arrival of Augustine in 596–7; and that the Christian church which existed throughout that long time was a church which was quite free of any control or domination from Rome.

I gave reasons why I am persuaded that there is no reason whatsoever why personal faith in Jesus Christ could not have been brought to Britain direct from Pentecost, or at least shortly after it. If this was so, it must have been the *New Testament* form of faith in Christ that was brought here.

I pointed out that any history book will tell you that, within the period of the Roman occupation of Britain between AD 43 and 407, there arose a British Christian church which sent its bishops to the early church councils. And I said that early Christianity would have had to be quite strongly established to be in a position to do that!

I have since discovered that Gildas, who was a Celtic priest, and one of the earliest historians on the conquest of Britain, testified that Britain received the Gospel *in the latter part of the reign of the Emperor Tiberias*.

This is the Emperor Tiberias to whom Luke refers in his Gospel when he says that it was in the fifteenth year of Tiberias Caesar that John the Baptist first arrived on the scene to begin his public ministry of heralding the arrival of Jesus Christ, the long promised Messiah (Luke 3:1–2). It is a known fact of history that Tiberias Caesar reigned as Emperor from AD 14 to 37. If Britain therefore received the Gospel *in the latter part of the reign of Tiberias*, it must have been shortly after the crucifixion, resurrection and ascension of our Lord, and the coming of the Holy Ghost on the 120 disciples on the Day of Pentecost, even if not before. We can say this, since Luke tells us that Jesus himself was about thirty years of age when he began his public ministry (Luke 3:23). It would certainly have had to be before AD 37, if it were in the latter part of the reign of the Emperor Tiberias.

But I find that the Venerable Bede also speaks of an early Christian mission to Britain, dating from AD 37.

Another historian, Eusebius (264–349), who is sometimes known as the 'Greek father of ecclesiastical history', who was at the Council of Nicea in AD 325, and who would therefore have had the opportunity to meet and confer with the bishops from Britain who attended that council and thus learn from them, makes this very significant statement: 'The *apostles* passed beyond the ocean to the isles called the Britannic Isles.'

The apostles did!

If this is so, it follows that the Gospel which they brought with them was the *apostolic* Gospel, and was what they preached here! It certainly was not in anyway Romanised or Catholic, as Lord Halifax would have us believe!

Then Tertullian, who was a trained advocate, which ensures his accuracy in the examination of records, writing in 190 *circa*, said: 'The extremities of Spain, the various parts of Gaul, *the regions of Britain,* which the Roman arms have failed to penetrate, *have received the Christian faith*' (please note 'The Regions of Britain').

I have also discovered that several other early church historians have identified who these apostles were who 'passed beyond the ocean to the isles called the Brittanic Isles.'

Theodoretus, for instance, who as Bishop of Cyrrhus from 393–466 had attended the General Council of Ephesus in 431 and of Chalcedon in 451, wrote in a book dated 435: 'Paul, liberated from his first captivity at Rome, *preached the gospel to the Britons* and others in the West' (please note 'to the Britons').

Then Sophronuis, Bishop of Jerusalem in 600, says: 'Paul, doctor of the Gentiles, passed over the ocean to the island that makes a haven on the other side, *even to the lands of the Britons,* even to Ultima Thule.'

Once again, Arnoldus Mirmannus, yet another early church historian, stated, 'Paul passed *to Britain* in the fourth year of Nero, AD 59, and there preached, and afterward returned to Italy.'

In addition, there were early historians and writers such as Eusebius and Metaphrastes, who stated that Peter *went to Britain* during the expulsion of the Jews from Rome under Claudius (see Acts 18:1–2). *Peter* did! According to the most reliable dating, this expulsion of the Jews from Rome under the Emperor Claudius was in AD 54. This means that Peter would have come to Britain in AD 54 or soon after, if this statement is true. But there was also another expulsion of the Jews from Rome under Nero in AD 59, so he might have come soon after that.

I discover that *all* these early church historians speak of the apostles and others as *preaching in Britain.* And in considering what they say, it should be realized that they were all careful scholars who had available to them documents which have long since perished. Their statements therefore should not be cast on one side. From what they all say, therefore, it can be established that the apostles who 'passed beyond the ocean to the isles called the Brittanic

Isles' included Paul and Peter.

That being so, we also know what Gospel they would have brought with them. Paul would have preached what is recorded in the Acts of the Apostles—the kind of sermon that he delivered on Mars Hill, for instance (Acts 17)! He would have preached what he had already expounded in writing to the Romans, Ephesians, Philippians, Colossians, Galatians, Corinthians and Thessalonians, and in his other epistles. Peter would have given sermons similar to those we find in the Acts, and which he had already committed to writing in his two epistles. If, as many authorities claim, he dictated to Mark the contents of the latter's Gospel, he would no doubt have shared with his hearers in Britain the events and details of the Lord's life which are recorded there. And nowhere, in all this teaching and preaching, do we find any Roman Catholic doctrine!

There is all this accumulated evidence, therefore, by which to substantiate that the original Christian church in England was not only founded very early, but that it was founded by the apostles, and upon their teaching and preaching as it is to be found in the pages of the New Testament.

As the apostle Jude would have put it, it was 'the common salvation' which the apostles would have taught and preached here in Britain (Jude v.3)—in other words, the faith which was common to them all, and common to the New Testament churches everywhere, the faith as it was once delivered to the saints. This early Christian church in Britain could rightly claim to have *apostolic* foundations. Nobody could claim that it was Roman Catholic!

I discover that Eleutherius, Bishop of Rome (*circa* 175– 190), who according to the early church historians was twelfth in order from the apostles, said in a message which he sent to King Lucius, one of the strong tribal kings in Britain: 'Ye have received of late through God's mercy *in the realm of Britain* the law and faith of Jesus Christ. Ye have within your realm *both parts of Scripture.* Out of them by God's grace, with the Council of your Realm, take ye a law that can, through God's suffrance, rule your Kingdom of Britain.'

If by '*both* parts of Scripture' he meant the Old and New Testaments, then somewhere between AD 175 and 190, not only was it widely known overseas and in the Middle East that the faith of Jesus Christ was well and truly established *in the realm of Britain*, but it was known to be a truly *Bible*-based faith in Jesus Christ.

Furthermore, the Venerable Bede adds this important information concerning the same period: 'The Britons preserved the faith which they had *nationally* received under King Lucius, *uncorrupted* and *entire*, and continued in peace and tranquility until the time of the Emperor Diocletian' (AD 303). Please notice that they preserved that *Bible*-based faith of Jesus Christ *uncorrupted* and *entire* right up to that time.

Eventually darkness fell on Britain, which brings us to the period in our history called the Dark Ages. But then, in AD 432, Patrick, and later Columba in 563, were used of God to bring about the return of Christianity to Britain. Augustine was not to come for another thirty-three years!

It is important to note that Churchill, in his *History of the English-speaking Peoples*, says that the form of Christianity which Columba brought had travelled from its original source in the Middle East (from Jerusalem and Judaea), through Northern Ireland, to its new home in Scotland and in Northern England '*without touching at any moment the centre at Rome*' (my italics). It was also a different form of Christianity from that Romanised form which, by then, existed throughout the Christianised countries of Europe. It is vitally important to make that distinction.

No wonder that when Augustine did eventually arrive in 596, he found that there was already on the far side of Britain, and to the north, a thriving Christian church which had a long and proud tradition of its own, quite free from outside domination, and which *persisted in claiming apostolic* foundations!

How then could Lord Halifax possibly claim that the Church of England was part of the Roman Catholic Church? The church of God in England, and in Britain as a whole, most certainly never had been part of the Catholic Church, right up until the arrival of Augustine. It was not until Gregory the Great sent Augustine as a 'missionary' that the Roman form of Christianity which had come to dominate Western Europe was introduced into Britain.

It is high time we got the record straight!

Thereafter, *two streams of Christianity* flowed through the land—the one which had been brought by Columba, and the Roman form which had come with Augustine.

As time went on, the Roman form sought to exercise a position of supremacy over the other. And this, of course, is what Lord Halifax and his Romanising confederates, assisted by Archbishops of Canterbury from his time onwards, have been seeking to bring about once again.

It has all been happening in the interests of a false form of Christian unity, because the New Testament teaches quite clearly that all true believers in Jesus Christ already are one. They do not have to be *made* one. And by true believers, I mean all those who are born again of the Holy Spirit of God, because you cannot be a Christian if you are not born again of God's Spirit. That is the teaching of the Bible.

It is because they already *are* one, that the Scripture says '[Endeavour] to *keep* the unity of the Spirit in the bond of peace' (Ephesians 4:3). The unity is already there. True Christians are called to *keep it*, not to create it. In any case, it is impossible to create unity by trying to amalgamate and bring together all the various denominations and churches under one umbrella, because many of the adherents to these various denominations are not born-again believers.

It is impossible to bring about unity on that basis, because there would not be a oneness of spirit between everybody. The matter is so obvious that it hardly needs to be stated.

Therefore the result of such endeavours is bound to produce something which is false.

How blind must these ecumenical enthusiasts be, not to understand that! But they don't want to see it, because they blatantly and wilfully intend to continue pursuing their policies. The tragedy is that their policy of trying to amalgamate all churches, denominations and theological viewpoints has had at least two disastrous effects on the church's witness to the nation.

First, it has seriously affected the teaching and preaching of the Christian message throughout the land and has led to utter confusion: for no longer is the church's message pure; no longer is it crystal clear and forthright; no longer is it a message based on the Bible and *only* on the Bible.

It is now a 'mixed' message, representing a variety of mere men's opinions, and is the product of various schools of thought. Therefore the church no longer speaks with one voice, and its message no longer carries conviction. No longer does the authoritative declaration, 'Thus saith the Lord', or 'The Bible says', ring throughout the land.

As the nation has been debasing its coinage, so has the church been debasing its message. Consequently the original Christian message of the New Testament has become hopelessly obscured. So much so, that when you compare what is preached over the radio or on television, or from many pulpits, with the Christianity of the New Testament, the two are found to be poles apart. They defy comparison with one another. They are as different as chalk is from cheese.

Therefore there is an urgent need to proclaim forthrightly all over again, throughout the length and breadth of the land, 'the faith which was once delivered to the saints'. And not only to proclaim it, but to *preserve* it, because it is fast becoming lost.

Secondly, this ecumenical policy of attempted amalgamation at the expense of essential Christian doctrine has had a paralysing and totally confusing effect upon the church's evangelistic strategy and outreach. For instance, it has had a disastrous effect on the launching of national or city-wide missions and crusades.

It seems to have been forgotten, or carefully overlooked, that when the Lord Jesus commissioned his original disciples, by saying 'Go ye into all the world, and preach the Gospel to every creature' (Mark 16:15), what he meant was the proclaiming of one clear message. For so far as preaching the Gospel is concerned, there is only *one truth*.

But the organisers of these crusades say that it is necessary to cater for *all* denominational outlooks, for *all* theological and doctrinal schools of thought, for *all* shades of ecclesiastical opinion, by having a widely representative body of speakers. This results in a 'mixed platform', which in turn inevitably leads to a mixed message, and all with the idea that they 'must please everybody'.

The net result is chaos—utter chaos. What is preached is not the Gospel of the New Testament.

And all this at a time when the nation could not be in more need of the clear, dynamic, forthright, New Testament Christian message of salvation.

Chapter Nine

What is the Church?

To add to the confusion, the Church of England has, at the local level, been pursuing a policy of closing down many of its churches, and of introducing, for the remainder, what it describes as a 'group ministry' which inevitably and intentionally is designed to be predominantly ecumenical in character, and based on this false conception of 'unity'. Under this system, a number of clergy, who are often referred to as 'a team', visit the various churches in their group on a kind of rota system on Sundays. Sadly, some of them have never experienced the new birth and have no experience of personal salvation. They may well all hold different theological and doctrinal views, and many, too, would not appeal to the bible as the supreme authority in deciding matters of faith and conduct.

What they do, in the first place, is to conduct a 'round' of Communion Services in the various churches in their area as if that were the most important part of their ministry. To their minds a constant round of Communion Services, often read at break-neck speed, and in a mumbled voice which can scarcely be heard by those present, is all that is necessary to cater for the souls of the people in the area.

Many of those who attend have no knowledge or

experience of personal salvation. They are, therefore, unregenerate, can only be classified as unrepentant sinners, and will remain in that state until the Gospel is preached amongst them in the power of The Holy Spirit so that many of them are convicted, repent, and are saved. The point is that whilst they remain in their present unregenerate condition they do not in any way qualify for partaking of the Lord's Supper. The Lord's Supper is only for those who have been born again of the Holy Spirit; it is for those who, by their faith in the Lord Jesus, and in the efficacy of his blood to cleanse them, have been brought under the New Covenant. It is for nobody else.

I know of one area in England where there are three churches for which the local rector is responsible, and in one of which, at least, there is not one converted person to be found. Yet as he 'goes his rounds', he gives Communion to all these unregenerate people without distinction. As I travel the country I find that this kind of situation applies countless times.

The implication which lies behind the holding of all such Communion Services must surely be that salvation is by means of the sacraments. It is, in fact, to introduce another Gospel, for nowhere in The New Testament do we find this teaching. Rather, the Bible clearly states that 'it pleased God by the foolishness of *preaching* to save them that believe (1 Corinthians 1:21). There must be the preaching, and then there must be the *believing*. Preaching, therefore, should be held by clergy to be paramount, as they visit churches Sunday after Sunday, not the holding of Communion Services.

It should be preaching in the power of the Holy Spirit, so that those who hear the Gospel, believe and are converted. Then they become qualified to be partakers of the Lord's Supper. 'Group Ministries' need to get things into the right perspective.

The fact is however, that if a clergyman does engage in any preaching under these conditions, it is never for more than ten minutes, because he needs to keep looking at his watch in order to ensure that he reaches his next church on time! In many cases such preaching lacks a clear, and forthright declaration of the way of salvation. Instead, unfortunate congregations find themselves hearing first one theological viewpoint, and then another, so that in the course of time these visiting clergy are seen to be preaching different, and often quite contradictory, views, instead of proclaiming the one, clear, message of the Gospel as it is found in the Bible. So what kind of instruction do these congregations get? What firm grounding do they have in the Christian faith?

The idea of such 'ministries' is mad! Since this practice goes on in many parts of our country, it inevitably results in the nation having many totally uninstructed and un-regenerate congregations, with very little knowledge of what true Christianity is all about.

No wonder the church no longer counts for much in the life of the nation! No wonder that numbers of people who attend church are not making any impact for Jesus Christ on the area around, let along on the country as a whole. Often they don't even *know* him!

Many have been utterly deceived and misled. They go into a church, for instance, where there is a mixture of unregenerate and regenerate people present, and hear *everybody* who is there being invited by the officiating clergyman to recite the words 'We are the body of Christ', which is just not true. How can those who are unregenerate and still dead in their trespasses and sins, possibly be the body of Christ? It is sheer deception to invite such people to say, with others, that they are, and an affront to Almighty God. To do such a thing is utterly abhorrent in his sight, and is also to mislead everybody present, including any strangers who may come in.

Another consequence is that people may go into such a church and hear a minister say to the same mixture of unregenerate and regenerate people, '*You* are the church', which, equally is just not true. For the church is comprised of only those who are regenerate, born again of the Holy Spirit of God.

Not only are such things taking place in churches with a liberal or modernist theology, or where only a social gospel is preached, but I have been present in leading Anglican evangelical churches where I have been appalled to discover that, in front of a large congregation of mainly born-again Christians, the officiating clergyman has taken a baby in his arms and has proclaimed, with no qualms whatsoever, 'I baptize this child into the faith of the church'. I ask you, wherever in the New Testament do we read about *anybody* 'being baptized into the faith of the church', let alone babies? Scripture makes it perfectly plain that entry into the church is *by believing in Jesus*, as a result of hearing the glorious Gospel about him. That *believing* results in the believing person being born again by the Holy Spirit of God. Baptism should then follow, to give public testimony to the belief in Jesus Christ as Saviour and Lord which has already taken place in the heart. That is the New Testament teaching on how a person enters the church of God. These leading evangelical churches, are supposed to be committed to upholding the teaching of the New Testament, indeed of the Bible as a whole. So how inconsistent they are, in saying 'I baptize this infant into the faith of the church'. It is going completely against the teaching of the New Testament and therefore *denying* that teaching.

How widespread has this erroneous and deceitful practice become? God only knows. But it is another serious contribution which has been made to the apostasy of the church in the nation, and it needs urgently to be repented of. It is the teaching of the New testament that needs to be recovered.

It is the teaching of Scripture that needs to be recovered in the free Churches throughout the land as well. For there, also, we regretably find much false teaching. Some of them are found to be totally dead and lifeless because they deny the need of the power of the Holy Spirit today. Some even go so far as to say that miracles, signs and wonders, and all the New Testament gifts of the Holy Spirit, were withdrawn at the end of the apostolic age. They have no authority whatsoever for saying this. The preaching in New Testament days was always accompanied by mighty acts of power. God Himself bore witness to this preaching by mighty signs and wonders, by many miracles which he wrought, and by gifts of the Holy Spirit sent down from heaven. The faithful preaching of the Gospel is always meant to be accompanied by such mighty acts of power today.

For Jesus himself said, 'Verily, verily, I say unto you, he that believeth on me, the works that I do shall he do also; and greater works than these shall he do; because I go unto my Father' (John 14:12). When he said, 'he that believeth on me', he meant anyone, of *any* generation. The same is true when he said, 'Go ye into all the world, and preach the gospel to every creature. He that believeth and is baptized shall be saved; but he that believeth not shall be damned.' When he added, 'And these signs shall follow them that believe; In my name shall they cast out devils; they shall speak with new tongues; they shall take up serpents; and if they drink any deadly thing, it shall not hurt them; they shall lay hands on the sick, and they shall recover' (Mark 16:15–18), he meant 'these signs shall follow them that believe' *in any generation*. Testimony has been given to that effect in the revivals which have taken place in recent years in such countries as Indonesia, Korea, Cambodia and elsewhere in the Far East. In all these places, the miracles that took place in the New Testament have been repeated all over again, and in most remarkable ways, and still are being repeated.

Moreover, just as Jesus' command to 'go…into all the world and preach the gospel to every creature' applies to *every* age and generation, (and no Christian could possibly deny that!), so the Lord Jesus' following words, 'and these signs shall follow them that believe', must equally apply to *every* age and generation. You cannot have one without the other.

A preacher from Germany challenged the congregation in a London church recently by beginning his sermon with the words, 'The mark of a truly regenerate church in New Testament days should be the mark of a truly regenerate church today, namely, that it is "a supernatural people who believe in miracles, because they are constantly seeing miracles happen."'

The tragedy is that so many preachers and ministers today, both in the Free Churches and in the Church of England, have been guilty of quenching the Holy Spirit, and have therefore deprived their churches, and the church in the land, of supernatural power. Therefore, people at large no longer see God working in power. No wonder that many have long since become disillusioned with the church and have left it!

They can see that the glory has departed. 'Ichabod' is written large over so many of our churches and cathedrals. The church, as she is seen by most people today, no longer knows what she believes. Bishops are to be heard publicly stating on television and radio that they do not now believe in the main tenets of the Christian faith which have been held for centuries: the virgin birth, the literal and bodily resurrection of the Lord Jesus, and the authority of the Bible.

As a result of this terrible morass and state of apostasy, the church in the land has lost her true sense of vocation. For what, *really*, is the task of the church? What is her supreme calling?

It has to do, first and foremost, with the salvation of people's souls. It has to do with saving them from hell and preparing them for heaven. For the Christian message is all about salvation—eternal salvation (Hebrews 5:9). In these perilous times in which we live, when all the signs show that we are fast approaching the end of the age and the coming great day of God's judgment (Revelation 6:12–17), it is the task of the church to warn people everywhere about it, to call them to repentance, to make people anxious about the salvation of their souls, and to proclaim to the world what is the way of salvation.

In the light of all that, and of the appallingly godless and iniquitous state in which we find our nation, I make bold to put this question: When did we last hear an Archbishop proclaim *the* way of salvation to the nation? When did we last hear it, with television and all the other modern means of communication at his disposal?

When did we last hear diocesan bishops doing so, *to their entire diocese?* It is their primary task, isn't it? I must put another question. Supposing we were to ask the 56 million or so inhabitants of the British Isles to tell us, quite clearly, what is the way of salvation. How many of them could give the right answer?

Supposing you, the reader, were to put that question to all the people living in the area where you live, in your street, at your place of employment, in your school or college. How many of them could give you the right answer?

Or to bring the question still nearer home. Supposing you were to put that question to everybody who attends your place of worship, whatever its denomination. How many of them could give you the scriptural answer?

These are very challenging questions, they need to be asked. They should confront us, point blank, with exactly where the masses of the people in our nation stand, so far as any knowledge of personal salvation is concerned. Were they asked, I am convinced that it would be revealed that a very high percentage of the nation's population would have to admit that they are *lost.* And they will be *eternally* lost unless something is done about their salvation.

Instead of the church being used as an instrument in the hand of God to rectify this situation, the tragic consequence of the policies to which I have been refering, is that very many people, young and old alike, have no idea what genuine New Testament Christianity is all about. Such is the tragic and terrible result of the church in the land falling into apostasy. A frighteningly high proportion of our people find themselves totally confused. They are stumbling around, in a godless state, engulfed in materialism, and in a totally humanistic and largely sensual maze, utterly lost.

Even if they want to find the right way—the way that leads to life—and to follow it, there is so much confused and contradictory teaching being put across in so many of the churches, and on television and radio, that it is some-times well-nigh impossible for them to know where to go to have that way pointed out to them. There are so many 'versions' of Christianity in society today, that there is an urgent need for true Christians everywhere to proclaim, all over again, the New Testament answers to such vital and basic questions as 'What really is a Christian?', 'What really is the Church?', 'What is the Gospel?', and 'What is the true and only way of salvation?'

If there is still time, before the Lord Jesus Christ returns, our urgent need is for the original, basic and dynamic New Testament form of Christianity, which God brought to these islands at a very early stage of our history, to be proclaimed once again in the full power of the Holy Spirit all over the land.

Chapter Ten

One World Faith

I have already said that one of the aims of the ecumenical movement is ultimately to unite all the main-stream denominations together under the control and supremacy of the Bishop of Rome, and that the process is already far advanced. In other words, *one world church* is the goal of the ecumenical movement.

But that is not its only goal. There is something far more sinister afoot—to incorporate into this one world church all the other faiths and religions of the world, with the object of arriving at *one world faith*. And this movement, too, is already far advanced. There have been services in Westminster Abbey in the presence of the Queen, the aim of which has been to bring all the faiths and religions of the world together under one roof and to get royal sanction for it. There has been a service in St Paul's Cathedral—often described as the mother church of England—where, in the presence of the Queen and the Duke of Edinburgh, members of other religions and faiths, including a Hindu, a Buddhist, a Muslim and a Jew, took part in the service. I have heard prayers being uttered in Westminster Abbey asking God so to unite the peoples of all the various faiths of the world, that ultimately they may become the one

113

great family of God. This is an absolute denial of the Gospel. The family of God can only, and ever, consist of those who believe in Jesus Christ and are born again of his Holy Spirit. It is a complete denial of what the Saviour said quite categorically: 'I am the way, the truth, and the life: *no* man cometh unto the Father, *but by me*' (John 14:6).

The process which is being used to bring about this false 'unity' is called 'syncretism'. There are many conferences and dialogues going on at the present time aimed at the syncretization of all the faiths of the world. The term 'syncretism' is a word which, interestingly enough, according to the English Dictionary, means 'the *attempted* union of principles and parties, various religious beliefs and deities, which are *irreconcilably* at variance with one another' (My italics)! It reminds me of something which is included in the vision which Daniel had concerning events which would take place at the end of this present world system. It was told to him, '... they shall mingle themselves with the seed of men: but they shall not cleave one to another, even as iron is not mixed with clay' (Daniel 2:43). Is what we see happening in this respect part of the fulfilment of Daniel's prophecy? I don't know. I just wonder.

However that may be, this sinister process of syncretisation must, inevitably, be inspired by the spirit of antichrist. There is no other explanation. For in this process, the bringing about of one world church, and ultimately one world faith, is operating hand-in-hand with a movement which itself is already far advanced—the establishment of *one world government*. And that, inevitably, will ultimately mean having *one world ruler*. We know that is going to happen, because one world ruler is prophesied in Revelation 13 as someone who is to emerge on the stage of history towards the end of the age, and he is referred to as the antichrist, or the beast. All that we see happening in terms of syncretisation is preparing the way for this world ruler—this beast.

So what we are witnessing is not a movement of the Holy

Spirit. Far from it. It is the direct opposite. We are seeing a movement of the spirit of antichrist, and woe betide anyone who is caught up in it. It heralds, to all of us who believe, the nearness of the end of the age and therefore the nearness of the return of our Lord Jesus Christ. One world faith is the ultimate aim of the ecumenical movement, and one world church is but a step towards that ultimate goal. The cry of the hour to all true believers therefore needs to be: "come out from among them, and be ye separate", saith the Lord.' (2 Corinthians 6:17). The trumpet needs to be sounded out to the true church in the land!

Those who have set these trends in motion here in Britain, have launched this nation along a path which leads, not to more enlightenment (not with the light of the glorious Gospel of Christ terribly obscured and almost obliterated) but to darkness—dreadful darkness. Unless there is a miracle of divine intervention in terms of a mighty, heaven-sent, Holy Spirit generated, nation wide revival, which results in nation-wide repentance of sin amongst our people and a turning of the tide in our land, I fear that we in Britain are heading for a new dark age before, finally, the Lord Jesus Christ returns.

Were that darkness to fall, I believe that all history would have just cause to proclaim: 'This is the finger of God, in judgment', and all as a result of Britain putting back the clock of her great national history in the same way as the nation of Israel did in the Old Testament.

In that sense, also, then, has Britain gone as far, if not further than, committing the sin of Manasseh.

Manasseh, too, brought back into the land all the foreign religions and practices which Hezekiah, his father, had driven out.

Solomon had been guilty of doing precisely the same thing, and God was so angry that he had said: 'Forasmuch as this is done of thee ... I will surely rend the kingdom from thee, and will give it to thy servant. Notwithstanding in thy days I will not do it ... but I will rend it out of the hand of thy son' (1 Kings 11;11, 12).

But God said something far worse to Manasseh. For Manasseh understood full well what was the commandment of God: 'Thou shalt have no other gods before me.' (Exodus 20:3). He also knew that God had warned his people that if they *did* go after the gods of the nations round about, those gods would become a *snare* unto them (Deuteronomy 7:16), because their hearts would be turned away from him, the one true God.

Manasseh knew, too, that God had issued a strong warning that if the nation of Israel *did* begin to serve other gods, then the anger of the Lord would be kindled against them, and he would destroy them suddenly (Deuteronomy 7:4). God had persistently warned them about this from the time of Moses onwards. But Manasseh deliberately flew in the face of all that, and became guilty of leading his nation into the most appalling apostasy. For we read: 'So Manasseh made Judah...to err, and to do worse than the heathen, whom the Lord had destroyed before the children of Israel' (2 Chronicles 33:9)—worse than the heathen and notoriously wicked nations which the Lord destroyed at the hand of Joshua and his armies, when Joshua had first led Israel to occupy the land of Canaan.

God had constantly said that such direct and deliberate disobedience to his specific command never to go after other gods, was bound to arouse his indignation and anger, and would bring in its wake the direst consequences. In Manasseh's case, it *did* arouse that anger.

Furthermore, God called these other gods 'abominations', just as he had done in Solomon's day. So it is recorded, '[Manasseh] did that which was evil in the sight of the Lord, after the *abominations* of the heathen, whom the Lord cast out before the children of Israel' (2 Kings 21:2). And what was the dire consequence? It was far more severe than the judgment which God had pronounced on Solomon.

'And the Lord spake by his servants the prophets, saying, "because Manasseh king of Judah hath done these *abomi-*

nations, and hath done wickedly above all that the Amorites did, which were before him, and hath made Judah [his people] also to sin with his idols: *therefore* thus saith the Lord God of Israel, Behold, I am bringing such evil upon Jerusalem [the capital] and Judah [the nation] that whosoever heareth of it, both his ears shall tingle"' (2 Kings 21:10–12).

Do you suppose God is less angry today? This is the searching question which we, the British people, need to ask. God calls such gods 'abominations', today. He is the same God. He has the same outlook now as then. He views things the same way now as he did then.

God doesn't change.

God doesn't suddenly 'go modern'.

The tragedy is, that by creating a multi-racial and multi-religious society, we have brought back into the land, which was once freed from such practices, all kinds of foreign religions and heathen cults and thus have seriously beclouded the nation's outlook about the need to be worshippers of the one and only true God through the Lord Jesus Christ, his Son. It is being said in some circles today that we must not refer to the Lord Jesus Christ as being the only way of salvation, or the way to God; nor must we refer to the Christian Gospel any more, for fear of upsetting and offending the people of other faiths who are in our midst. We must learn to suppress all this, when those of other faiths are present. Or so it is being said.

In the Britain of which it was once said, 'The whole Island had become Christian', we have reached the sorry pass where the hearts of a considerable number of our people, and not only of the young, have been caused to go after these other gods—the eastern religions, and Islam in particular.

Chapter Eleven

Powers of Darkness

We find that when Manasseh had got rid of true religion, he had to put something else in its place. So he turned to such things as 'dealing with mediums', to witchcraft, to contacting the spirit world through the use of familiar spirits and trying to get in touch with the dead. He also practised necromancy, soothsaying, and the 'observing of times'. He resorted to sorcery, magic, the use of enchantments, dealing with wizards, and astrology (2 Kings 21:5–6, and 2 Chronicles 33:5, 6).

In other words, Manasseh turned to all the dark practices which have to do with Satan, the occult and spiritism.

God denounced all this in terrible terms, by saying that [Manasseh] wrought much wickedness in the sight of the Lord, to provoke him to anger (2 Kings 21:6), and by describing it in 2 Chronicles 33:6 as 'much evil'. We need to be told in the strongest of terms today that this kind of thing is evil and provokes God to anger.

Manasseh was now trafficking with all the powers of darkness. Furthermore, he was indulging in some of the most strongly condemned practices in the Bible, all strictly forbidden by God. To be involved in this evil realm is to be trespassing far into forbidden territory. For anyone to indulge in such evil practices can often lead to demon-possession.

This sort of involvement always happens in a time of apostasy. In fact, it is a sure indication that serious apostasy has taken place. When individuals or nations no longer look to God for guidance, they inevitably resort to other ways of obtaining the help that they need. And it is not long before they begin to turn to the positively dangerous and devious. Before they know where they are, they are caught up in the realm of evil spirits and become hopelessly involved.

It is all part of the escalation that takes place as a result of a departure from God and from *trusting* God. This is where such apostasy as Manasseh's leads. Yet Britain today is riddled with it.

Nor is the cause hard to find. In the days when the Word of God was penetrating the nation, and when the glorious Gospel of Christ was being preached in the full power of the Spirit all over the land—as at the time of the Reformation and the Great Awakening—the evil powers were obliged to fall back. Things like spiritism, witchcraft and demon-possession are obliged to retire before an aggressive, Holy-Spirit-inspired evangelism, and consequently the manifestation of the powers of darkness becomes less frequent. It always happens in a period of spiritual revival.

Now that Britain has departed from God and refuses to turn to him for help, and now that the church in the land is in such disarray and has become so ineffective, the inroads that are being made by the evil powers of darkness into the lives and homes of individuals and into every section of our society are dreadful to behold. Dark forces from the unseen world are flooding in upon us as a nation. As we revert more and more to a pagan, humanistic and materialistic way of life, so these evil powers, of which we had largely been rid in our more Christian days, are pressing in hard.

One single evidence for this is the tremendous advance that spiritism is making among all classes of our people. It has even got into the church in a big way. One leading bishop, for instance, has written about his spiritist experiences. Other bishops have penned articles for our national newspapers on such subjects as 'spiritism' and 'the use of mediums'. By describing their own personal contacts with 'the spirit world' and 'the departed', they have clearly shown that they have become deeply involved in such practices, when they should have been warning people against the dangers.

All over the nation, there has been an alarming proliferation of books and magazines dealing with all kinds of evil and devilish subjects, and they are to be seen in their abundance on almost every bookstall. We are confronted with it on boardings. Wherever you go, there are evil and sinister posters advertising films which have to do with the Devil, the occult and exorcism, each poster seemingly setting out to be more horrific than the previous one.

Penetration of our homes has been further achieved by a succession of television programmes and radio broadcasts discussing such evil and dark practices as black magic, Satanism, devil-worship, witchcraft and the like, even when it is known that children will be present to watch and listen. A widespread interest in such evil things has been created, which has spread to schools, colleges and universities—in fact, these subjects are even being *taught* in schools. Such an intense interest in these foul subjects has been engendered, that dangerous experimentation has frequently been taking place, often with alarming and frightening results. One hears of public schools where real terror has been manifest amongst boys in dormitories as a result of experimenting in this forbidden realm.

It is also a well-known fact that, for years now, Satan worshippers have met after dark in graveyards, cemeteries and woods in different parts of the country, and have practised their grisley rites and ceremonies. Highgate Cemetery has perhaps been the most publicised example of this, but I have good reason to believe that it is happening in every county in England. I was once travelling on a train from Brighton to London which was stopping at several stations at a time when children were coming out of school. Some schoolboys got in, and one of them began asking the others if they would take him to watch a witches' coven in operation one Saturday night. The others warned him that it would be dangerous. So he said, 'Where does this go on?' One boy immediately burst out in reply, 'Oh, it happens regularly on Saturday nights in graveyards and cemeteries all over Sussex.' Apparently he knew!

But not only does it happen in graveyards. Church buildings in different parts of the country have often been revoltingly desecrated by Satanists who have performed their evil sacrificial rites after dark, the results of their visit being discovered next day. I know of one vicar in the Midlands who even caught one of them in his church in broad daylight. The intruder was a young man, and what he had been doing had included inverting the cross and performing some wicked rites on the Lord's table. He was challenged and questioned, and had apparently been sent there by other people. Was it on behalf of a witches' coven? We don't know. What we *do* know is that his body was found later, on the nearby moors, in suspicious circumstances. It was believed locally that those for whom he had acted, might have suspected that he had betrayed some of their secrets whilst he was being questioned, or that they were frightened that he would do so later and that they had decided to silence him.

This is the Britain in which we live today. It is an established fact that Satanists and occult forces are actively engaged in calling down curses on any evangelistic crusade, campaign, or live church work that they know about. It is a fact that the Satanists were praying to the devil for the death of the late David Watson. Christians everywhere need to realize that they should stand against all these evil forces in the name of the Lord Jesus and overcome them by the power of his precious blood. In other words, they should be engaging in spiritual warfare in order to repel them and to throw them back, using the spiritual weapons that God has made available. The tragedy is that so few Christians in Britain today even know what these weapons are, let alone know how to use them. Some of them, alas, even in evangelical leadership, don't want to know, and refuse to believe that there is any need to engage in such spiritual warfare.

I have only uncovered the tip of the iceberg. Nobody really knows what terribly dark deeds are being done below the surface. So widespread has this revived interest in the occult become, and so harmful have been the dire results where people have become involved in it, that various dioceses in the Church of England have appointed official exorcists to go to the rescue of those who have become demon-possessed as a result of such involvement and experimentation. The Free Churches, too, have their qualified people who engage in this deliverance ministry, and it is a very arduous task.

We should make no mistake about how serious this realm of evil indulgence is, in the sight of a holy, Almighty God. He regards it as extremely iniquitous, and the Bible names dark practices such as 'resorting to spiritist mediums', 'dealing with familiar spirits', 'necromancy', 'resorting to wizards and witches' and 'using sorcery and enchantments' as *abominations* in the sight of the Lord'.

Isaiah faced the people of his day who were involved in such dark practices with this devastating challenge: 'And when they shall say unto you, 'Seek unto them that have familiar spirits, and unto wizards that peep and mutter', should not a people seek unto their God?' (Isaiah 8:19).

Oh, that we had a prophet like Isaiah in Britain, today! He would need to issue an equally strong challenge to us!

I sometimes have to ask myself whether God has had to hand us over to this kind of thing because we have so tragically turned away from him. Or, whether *this* is what we have chosen, to take the place of Christianity. I rather think he may well have had to hand us over to it, in order to chastise us severely.

However that may be, there is no doubt that, by reversing the work of the Holy Spirit which God wrought at the Reformation, by reintroducing heathen religions and false faiths into the land, and by fostering such an interest in Satanism and the occult, Britain is having once again to grapple with the problems of demon-possession, spiritism and witchcraft, from which she was freed so many years ago.

In that tragic respect, also, has Britain gone as far, if not further than, committing the sin of Mannasseh.

Chapter Twelve

The Worship of Baal

Manasseh went even further than turning to mediums and dealing with the occult.

For the next thing that he did was to substitute *the worship of Baal for the worship of the one true God*. And it is only when our eyes have been opened to what *this* involved, that we realize the enormity of this aspect of Manasseh's sin.

To turn to the worship of Baal involved doing at least *five* things. And I want to deal with each of these in turn in order to show that similar practices are happening in Britain today.

In the *first* place, 'Baal' means 'Lord.' So when Manasseh 'reared up altars for Baal' in different places throughout the land, and even in the temple itself (2 Kings 21:3), he was proclaiming publicly that Baal, not Jehovah, was now Lord.' In effect, he was dethroning God Almighty and enthroning Baal. Therefore he was challenging the authority of God Almighty, for by definition, there cannot be *two* Lords.

Such was the issue with which Elijah had had to confront Israel on Mount Carmel in an earlier age, when he proclaimed, 'If the Lord be God then follow him: but if Baal, then follow him (1 Kings 18:21). It had to be one or the other. Elijah had had to force Israel into making a choice. Manasseh had now brought Israel right back to where they were then, and so had created the need for the challenge to be issued all over again.

But the name 'Baal' also means, 'my master.' So the *second* implication was that Manasseh and his people were subjecting themselves to Baal as master.

The *third* features is seen clearly when we consider the meaning of some of the *composite names of Baal*, for then the real horror of Baal-worship really should begin to dawn! Take for example, the name Baal-zebub, and compare it with its New Testament equivalent, Be-elzebub (the prefix 'Be-el' is the same as 'Baal').

When Jesus used this name, he spoke of Be-elzebub as the prince, or lord, of the demons. And when the Pharisees accused Jesus of casting out devils by Be-elzebub, Jesus immediately identified Be-elzebub with Satan by saying, 'How can Satan cast out Satan?' (Mark 3:23). He therefore made it plain that Satan and Be-elzebub were one and the same.

In the light of this, what really is Baal-worship?

It is *Satan* worship.

It is, in effect, to dethrone God, to susbtitute Satan, and then to worship him in God's place. And what does that lead to? To being mastered by Satan, of course. When an individual sets up Baal's image and submits himself in worship to it, saying 'Baal is my master, my *lord*', he lays himself wide open to being mastered by Satan; to being brought into subjection to Satan; to being taken over totally, possessed totally, by Satan. Do we *now* see the consequences involved in proclaiming that 'Baal is my master'? Manasseh was not just an individual. He was the king, and therefore the head of his country. For the king of a country to *de*throne God from his sovereign position of rulership over that country, and to *en*throne Satan in God's place, is to put the entire nation in danger of being totally taken over by Satan.

What Manasseh did as head of his country was likely to have a disastrous effect upon the nation's religion. Setting up the image of Baal in the temple at Jerusalem, thus symbolically dethroning God and enthroning Satan was to turn everything in the nation's religious life upside down. It was to substitute the worship of Satan for the worship of the one true God at the highest possible national level—the temple. (Britain's nearest equivalent is St Paul's Cathedral or Westminster Abbey.) And so it would appear in the eyes of his people. Manasseh had, in consequence, set his nation and people well and truly on the course of being taken over completely by evil and by Satan himself. The horror of it!

When he set up that image in the temple, God's indignation was so aroused that he declared in his great wrath that it was something done by the house of Israel to drive him from his sanctuary (Ezekiel 8:6). We would do well to ponder over the implications of this declaration, in view of the widespread Satan-worship which is going on in this country. For when Satan-worshippers, and those who indulge in black magic rituals and ceremonies, perform their sacrificial rites in Christian churches, they do, symbolically, precisely what Manasseh did. The rites include turning the cross of the Lord Jesus Christ upside down. This is done to symbolize the inverting of the Christian religion and the replacing of Jesus with Satan. They are saying in symbolic form, but very meaningfully: 'Satan is now Lord'.

Think of the implications of this! Were it to spread on a large enough scale, these worshippers of Satan would eventually be able to declare, 'Satan is now Lord over the whole of the United Kingdom!'

The *fourth* aspect of Baal-worship is closely related, and so increases the frightening nature of it all. The devotees of Baal strongly believed that the 'spirit of the Baal', and the 'spirit of the Ashera'—which is the female counter-part of Baal—actually resided in these carved images and it was these spirits indwelling the images which the Baal-worship-

127

pers went to worship, not just the images themselves. So spirit-worship and the worship of demons were involved, and the worshippers laid themselves wide open to becoming demon-possessed. There is ample evidence to suggest that demonology lay behind all forms of Baal-worship, which again explains why God described going after the Baals as 'doing great wickedness'.

There are alarming signs that this country is fast going the same way. For the trend in Britain, for a number of years, has been to get rid of every idea of God. So we have already taken the *first* step of the Baal-worshippers. Rarely, if ever, do we hear his name mentioned during debates in Parliament. If there *is* any mention of his name, that part of the speech is often carefully omitted by the press and the BBC. As for the country being asked to turn to God in times of national crisis, that kind of suggestion has been rejected over and over again. Instead of turning to God, we are turning increasingly to things like the black arts, spiritism, Satan-worship and the occult. It is certainly true to say that the interest which is being shown in Satan and the things of Satan is far in excess of that being shown in God and the things of God, in Jesus Christ, and in the way of salvation.

God is being more and more dethroned, and Satan is being more and more enthroned. The result of interest being awakened in the powers of evil seems to be that of plunging the country further and further into the realms of darkness. It has certainly affected the capital. A visitor from overseas said recently, 'I felt such a pall of depression and general evil over London when I came this time that I really felt I did not ever want to come back again.'

My fear is that, if this trend continues unarrested, it will not be long before the whole country comes under the mastership of Satan and evil, just as Germany was during the days of Nazism. So in this sense of dethroning God, throwing away our Christian heritage, and turning to things of Satan, we are committing the sin of Manasseh.

But there was still a *fifth* feature of Baal-worship, and that had to do with its highly *sensual*, seductive, and *degrading* nature. By bringing back the worship of the Baals and the Ashera, Manasseh also set his people well on the road to becoming obsessed with, and mastered by, sex. For the Baals and their feminine counterparts, the Ashera, were 'fertility gods', set up and worshipped for the express purpose of encouraging and increasing 'fertility'. Included in the rites and ceremonies was all that unregenerate mankind is attracted to, and titillated by. Everything about Baal-worship, therefore, was extremely sensual.

Their initiation ceremonies involved ritual prostitution, public nudity and open rape. Lewd and licentious 'religious orgies', sexually stimulating dances, and vice of every description, were involved. There was everything which debases, depraves, and appeals to the baser instincts of mankind, for the very nature of 'fertility-worship' is to promote everything which is sexually stimulating.

Perhaps it was this aspect of Baal-worship, more than any other, which Manasseh found so attractive and which created a desire within him to bring back these heathen practices into the land. It is significant that he did all this in his youth, for he was only twelve years old when he inherited the throne. When the Bible describes the way in which his actions affected his people, it uses the word 'seduce': 'Manasseh *seduced* them to do more evil than did the nations whom the Lord destroyed before the children of Israel' (2 Kings 21:9).

Baal-worship, in short, could be described as 'the worship of sex'. It was that aspect of it which dominated the scene, and the various performances involved what so-called 'modern' Britain's alternative, permissive, and 'gay' society would call 'free-love'. The Bible calls it licentiousness.

No doubt some of today's perverted assessors of such activities would describe the scenes as 'the revellings of Manasseh's Gay Liberation Front', but Romans 1:24 describes them as 'being given over to sexual impurity', 'dishonouring their bodies amongst themselves', and 'worshipping and serving the creature, rather than the Creator' (Amplified Version). It was to make the human body the focal point of worship, instead of its Creator, God. So it was to 'invert' everything again, both in the realm of religion and morality. As Romans 1:23–25 puts it, this was 'exchanging the glory and majesty and excellence of the immortal God for *images*'—exchanging 'the truth of God for *a lie*.'

Is there any need to ask if this kind of behaviour bears any resemblance to Britain's situation today, with all the emphasis on sex that we find around us? It not only has a familiar ring in the present-day life of Britain, but in western society as a whole. It is certainly true that, today, the human body has become more and more the focal point of worship. Is it not about time, therefore, that we realized that God called this kind of behaviour *iniquity*, and that the Bible also calls it *evil* in the sight of the Lord'?

Scripture certainly does not give it the cloak of respectability which we do. In Manasseh's day, God spoke in the severest terms concerning this whole range of sins. He called them '*abominable practices*' (2 Corinthians 33:2). Neither was there any haggling over definitions as to what does or does not deprave and corrupt—not as far as God was concerned. When God described what Manasseh and his people were doing as something 'more evil than did the nations whom the Lord destroyed before the children of Israel' he was issuing the strongest possible indictment.

To bring out the full force of that, I need only to ask, 'Who were these nations whom God destroyed and to which he is referring?' The people whom the Lord drove out included first of all the notorious Amorites, who occupied the land of Canaan even before the time of Abraham, long before Israel possessed it, and whose iniquity God referred to in a vision which he gave to Abraham in Genesis 15:16. At that time, God said, 'The iniquity of the Amorites is not yet complete' (RAV). The judgment of being driven out of their land and destroyed, fell upon the Amorites when ultimately that iniquity had come to the full. God used the armies of Israel under Joshua's leadership as his instrument of judgment against them. That is partly what the invasion of Canaan by Joshua and the children of Israel was all about.

It was a judgment of *God*, judgment by annihilation, judgment by extermination—so serious a view did God take of the Amorites' sin. You have only to read the books of Joshua and Judges to understand it more fully.

That is how God, ultimately, has to deal with sin. He destroyed the Amorites. But, in his devastating indictment, God was also referring to the people of Sodom and Gomorrah. And their judgment came more speedily.

God was saying that the sins of Manasseh and his people were far in excess of the sins of Sodom and Gomorrah, yet their sin, as everybody knows, was appalling. Their sordid behaviour included committing all the gross sins which are being committed around us in our permissive and immoral society today. Adultery and fornication were rife, and so were all the effeminate and abhorrent practices of today's 'Gay Liberation Front' and of similar associations for sexual freedom. A study of the divine record shows that homosexuality was present in the most appalling forms. So depraved, perverted and corrupt were these people, that they even had lustful desires towards visiting angels. Lesbianism and all manner of other forms of bestial behaviour were there. Since there was widespread adultery, it follows that wife-swapping and husband-swapping were practised. This kind of behaviour is not something new. It was all being practised in Sodom and Gomorrah. And how does the Bible describe it? Not by giving it a cloak or respectability as we do today, but by 'calling a spade a spade'.

The New Testament says, for instance: 'They acted immorally and indulged in unnatural lust' (Jude 7, RSV), or, as the AV puts it, they were 'giving themselves over to *fornication*'.

But what does God say about it in the Old Testament? 'Their sin is very grievous' (Genesis 18:20)...'The men of Sodom were wicked' (Genesis 13:13)...'[They were] sinners before the Lord'.

We need to allow that to register in this modern and permissive age. We are reminded that it is not so much *what* is done, but against *whom* it is done, which determines the heinous nature of sin. *This* is the yardstick by which all such immoral behaviour must be measured. But the verse does not stop at that. It says they were 'sinners before the Lord *exceedingly*'. So the emphasis on the serious nature of their sin increases.

A modern age needs to be told, over and over again, that that is how God sees such sin *today*. What frightens me is that this kind of sordid behaviour in Britain today is likely to suffer the same consequences as that of Sodom and Gomorrah, because God has specifically warned us that he has made Sodom and Gomorrah an example to those who later would decide to live in the same ungodly and debased manner (see 2 Peter 2:6, Jude 7). Jude says, 'Sodom and Gomorrah and the surrounding cities which likewise acted immorally and indulged in unnatural lust serve as an *example* by undergoing a punishment of eternal fire.' Peter confirms that God turned 'the cities of Sodom and Gomorrah into ashes [and] condemned them with an overthrow, making them an *ensample* unto those that after should live ungodly.' And in referring to an incident in Israel's history, Paul writes: 'Now all these things happened unto them for *ensamples*: and they are written for *our* admonition, upon whom the ends of the world are come' (1 Corinthians 10:11).

So we are left in no doubt how God dealt with such debased behaviour. He brought it all under fearful judgment. It was judgment by annihilation, and the people perished. In the case of Sodom and Gomorrah 'God rained down fire and brimstone from heaven', such was his indignation towards them.

Who did this? *God* did it, on account of all this grossly immoral and unnatural behaviour.

It should be a very sobering challenge indeed for a loose sex-obsessed society such as our own,—living in an age in which its own cities and towns could so easily be reduced to dust and ashes by a nuclear attack. If God had to do that kind of thing to nations who had never enjoyed the privilege and benefit of the Christian Gospel, what is he likely to do with a nation such as Britian, which *has* enjoyed the full benefits of Christianity for almost 2,000 years, yet, despite what God has done for her throughout those centuries, has thrown it all away, and is found today to be fast going in the same abhorrent direction as Sodom and Gomorrah?

And what, for that matter, is God likely to do with the western world as a whole?

These are questions which, I believe, we need to face, no matter how unpalatable may be the answers. We need to do so because of the naivety which exists in some circles.

For instance, I had a letter from a leading Christian industrialist, just after the first volume of this book was published, raising an objection to what I was saying about what might well be Britain's forthcoming judgment. This is the only objection I have received out of the thousands of letters which have been written to me, but I want to deal with it now.

The letter said: 'I would in no way gainsay what you draw so forcibly to our attention about the terrible decline in moral values and standards....However, to try to deduce from this that we in Britain are going to have a special and exclusive judgment meted out on us, I find it extremely hard to believe. I certainly cannot accept that God is likely to use godless, sinful Russia as his method of just retribution.'

Why not, indeed?

God has used godless, sinful nations, as his instruments of judgment in the past. That's the whole point! A man who writes like this just does not know his Bible. God used

133

godless, heathen, sinful Assyria against the nation of Israel in judgment, when Israel had departed so far away from God and sunk into gross iniquity. So why cannot he use godless, sinful, atheistic Communist Russia as his instrument of judgment against Britain, the United States, and the whole of the western world?

As to the industrialist's other statement that I was trying to deduce that Britain is to have a special and exclusive judgment meted out on her, I did not say it was *exclusive*. I have included the United States and the whole of the western world as well, because I see judgment hanging over them all. In fact, Luis Palau, who told me as he began his Mission to London in September 1983 that he considered I had made an accurate assessment of Britain's present situation, said at the same time, 'Somebody needs to write a book called *The Trumpet Sounds for America* as well'!

The industrialist, and everybody else, for that matter, needs to be reminded that Jesus once said: 'Unto whomsoever much is given, of him shall much be required' (Luke 12:48). It applies to the individual, but I believe it applies equally to a nation. And I am sure it applies to Britain, as a nation, in particular. For consider how God has singularly blessed us in past days.

We had had the Gospel for centuries. Then God took great pains to ensure that we became a nation founded on Christian laws moulded on the Bible. He brought about the Reformation, and the Great Awakening under the preaching of Whitefield and Wesley. God caused us to become known, the world over, as a Bible-loving, Bible-believing nation, and to send missionaries to preach the Gospel in the far corners of the earth. As a direct result of the influence and impact of the Great Awakening, 'Divine providence exalted Great Britain to an height of prosperity and glory unknown to any former age.' That fact has been engraved in marble, for all to see, on the huge memorial to William Pitt just inside the north doors of Westminster Abbey, and on the right-hand wall as you go in.

It was then, let us never forget, that, under God, Great Britain reached her highest spiritual peak. But God has also repeatedly intervened in our history to save this country from imminent invasion. At the time of the Armada; again in Napoleon's day; then more recently in 1940, after the evacuation from Dunkirk, and during the Battle of Britain.

'Unto whomsoever much is given, of him shall much be required.'

In more recent years, God has sent us Billy Graham, with his Harringay, Wembley, All Scotland, and Manchester Crusades.

There has been the All Britain Crusade led by Tom Rees, and other evangelistic campaigns too numerous to mention by name. All of these were vast and expensive endeavours to try to turn the spiritual and moral tide in the nation, and to bring the British people to a real faith in Jesus Christ.

Coming right up to date, we have had Luis Palau's Mission to London, and the three-year Mission England with Billy Graham.

We can *never* say that God has not given us an opportunity. I believe that, if the truth were fully known, we would find that God has given Britain more attention than most other Gentile nations so far as opportunities to hear the Gospel are concerned. I believe that if Jesus were to visit Britain in person today, he would say of her: 'If the mighty works which have been done in you, and for you, had been done in Sodom and Gomorrah, they would have repented long ago, in sackcloth and ashes.' Sodom and Gomorrah did not have the Bible. Sodom and Gomorrah did not have evangelistic crusade after evangelistic crusade. Sodom and Gomorrah did not have mighty revivals such as Britain has had. Sodom and Gomorrah did not have all these mighty blessings of God which we, in Britain, have enjoyed.

So I believe that Jesus would go on to say: 'Woe! woe!

woe! unto you, proud Island, situated in the North Sea. You shall be brought down to hell.'

When we see the enormity of what we have done in casting away all this glorious and rich Christian heritage, in order to go our own iniquitous way, I believe that a very severe form of judgment on Britain is inevitable.

That is the message for Britain today—and that is why this book, *The Trumpet Sounds for Britain*, is so necessary.

Chapter Thirteen

Innocent Blood

Manasseh had thrown away the rich spiritual inheritance handed down from the past, reversed his father's reformation, and pursued the worship of Satan and sex. Yet God had a further charge against him: 'Moreover Manasseh shed innocent blood very much'. So much so, that God said he did it until 'he had filled Jerusalem [with this blood] from one end to another.' And God said he did this *beside* his sin [that is, *in addition to* his sin] wherewith he made Judah to sin, in doing that which was evil in the sight of the Lord' (2 Kings 21:16).

It would seem that in doing this, Manasseh aroused the wrath of Almighty God against the nation *irretrievably*.

For God said: 'Because Manasseh...hath done these abominations, and hath done wickedly above all that the Amorites did, which were before him...*Therefore*...I am bringing such evil upon [his nation and upon his capital] that whosoever heareth of it, both his ears shall tingle.... I will wipe Jerusalem [clean]...turning it upside down. And I will forsake the remnant of mine inheritance, and deliver them into the hand of their enemies...' (2 Kings 21:11–14).

So Israel had passed the point of no return, and this was God's final pronouncement of judgment—at the hands of a foreign power. It was not withdrawn, and that judgment finally fell.

What was this innocent blood that Manasseh was guilty of shedding in the land?

We find the explanation in Jeremiah 19, verses 4 and 5: '[they] have filled this place with the blood of innocents... [they burnt] *their sons* with fire for burnt offerings unto Baal'. It was babies—little children—which were involved. That is why they are referred to as 'innocents'. The place had been filled with the blood of their *own* children. They were offering them up as sacrifices to a false god.

But it says that Manasseh and the people of his nation were guilty of shedding innocent blood *very much* in the land. They were doing it on a vast scale. They were guilty of wholesale baby- and child-slaughter. And they were doing it in a most abhorrent and revolting manner. They were burning their own sons in the fire as burnt offerings to a false god—something which was so abhorrent to God that he said it was a thing 'which I commanded not, nor spake it, neither did it even come into my mind' (see Jeremiah 19:5).

To put it quite bluntly, these innocent ones were being incinerated. They were being cast into the fire to meet the insatiable demands of a false god. And this so aroused the wrath and indignation of Almighty God, irretrievably, that finally, he was moved to bring down his judgment upon the nation.

So the Lord began to speak through his prophets to the nation, to warn the people of what was coming. And he began to speak in a most devastating manner.

He used the word 'because' many times over, followed by the word 'therefore'. Listen to what he said: 'Because the people have forsaken me, and have profaned this place by burning incense to other gods... *Because* they have filled this place with the blood of innocents, and have built the high places of Baal to burn their sons in the fire as burnt offerings to Baal which I did not command or decree, nor did it come into my mind... *Because* Manasseh, King of

Judah, has committed these abominations and has done things more wicked than all that the Amorites did, who were before him...*Because* Manasseh shed very much innocent blood, till he had filled Jerusalem from one end to the other, besides the sin which he made Judah, his people, to sin, so that they did what was evil in the sight of the Lord...*Therefore*, thus says the Lord, the God of Israel: Behold I am bringing upon Jerusalem [the capital] and upon Judah [the country] such evil that the ears of everyone who hears of it will tingle.'

And then God stated in no uncertain terms what he was going to do: 'I will forsake the remnant of mine inheritance...And I will deliver them into the hand of their enemies...And they shall become a prey, and a spoil to all their enemies...*Because* they have done that which was evil in my sight and have provoked me to anger,...*Therefore*, behold, days are coming, says the Lord, when this place shall be called, the Valley of Slaughter' (extracted from 2 Kings 21:10–16; Jeremiah 19:1–6 RSV).

It was to be a judgment at the hands of an invading army. This is what God brought upon the nation; and let us make no mistake about it, this is what he could bring upon the nation of Britain now.

In Manasseh's case, that kind of judgment came because he and his people were guilty of shedding very much innocent blood in the land.

'Oh', you say with horror, 'Surely we in Britain are not guilty of doing anything as abhorrent and repulsive as Manasseh?'

My reply would be: 'What about all those babies who have been slaughtered wholesale every day, and cast into the incinerators in hospitals and clinics all over Britain?'

I am speaking about abortion. Is not *that* 'shedding much innocent blood in the land'? Is not that 'burning their sons [their own children] with fire'?

Remember, this has been done all over Britain *with the full sanction of Parliament*. So it is not going far enough to say it is child-murder. It is *legalised* child-murder, for which Parliament not only sought, but obtained (incredible as it may seem) *the Royal Assent*! And let us make no mistake whatsoever about it, these are *live* human beings which are involved. I have already shown that this fact can be well and truly established *biblically*.[1]

But it has been equally well established *medically*. Surgeons, doctors, ward sisters, nurses and other hospital staff testify to the same fact, that many of these embryonic children are capable of whimpering, struggling and crying. One superintendent of a hospital theatre has said: 'The nurse faces the dilemma of whether she should send for the incubator to prolong the baby's life, or whether she should look the other way'. He is describing an all-too familiar scene in any hospital theatre where an operation for abortion is being performed. Oh yes, they are living human beings alright, and in the majority of cases they are being cast into incinerators and offered for burnt offerings to a false god, the god or goddess of *sex*.

For the real truth is that this terrible slaughter of innocent children is being deliberately and legally perpetrated, with the connivance of Parliament, in order to get rid of the consequences of human *sin*—the sin of sexual intercourse outside marriage, which God calls fornication, but which a permissive society calls 'free love'. For it happens to be true that so many of these abortions are taking place in order to enable the culprits to escape the consequences of having indulged in such sexual misbehaviour and widespread promiscuity.

Sir John Peel, president of the British Medical Association, and the Queen's gynaecologist, has stated that 'the Abortion Act has had the effect of increasing the irresponsibility of young men. More and more men are in favour of abortions to shed their responsibilities.' He goes on: 'In the last four years there was a rapidly escalating number of unplanned pregnancies, especially in girls under 20. The extent to which easy access to abortion affects the sexual behaviour and attitudes of couples, especially the young, is something which requires very urgent study today.'

It is well known that when the Lane Committee was sitting, thirty-seven hospitals contributed evidence, and that the report submitted to that committee stated that '13 year-olds are attending National Health Service Hospitals for second abortions, and 15 year-olds are attending for their third.' So it is not with the results of intercourse within marriage that this brutal practice of abortion has to do—not in the majority of cases. In fact, it is quite to the contrary.

All that I have quoted is but a small part of what is happening. Were it possible to see the situation as it really is, I fear that it would be alarming in the extreme. Parliament, by passing the Abortion Act, is therefore not only aiding and abetting the sin of indulging in sexual intercourse outside marriage, but is making it more easy. In consequence, it is causing this terrible slaughter of unborn children to be carried out in order to get rid of, and cover up, the results.

As for the scale of this atrocious slaughter, the numbers of victims involved is astronomical. The figures soar at such a rate that it is difficult to keep abreast of them. For instance, as far back as March 1972, Sir John Peel produced figures to show how they had been rising between 1970 and 1972. In 1970 there were 83,000 legal abortions; in 1971 the figure had risen to 120,000; and in 1972, he said there would probably be more than 150,000 that year, without the slightest evidence that the trend would level off.[2]

The numbers continued to rise at an alarming rate, so that, in 1973, they passed the 180,000 mark. Since then, the figure has reached at least 300,000 per year, and the latest total available shows that no less than 2¾ million little lives have been destroyed in Britain since this atrocious Abortion Act was passed.

What is the casting of such little ones into hospital

incinerators, but the modern form of 'causing their sons and their daughters to pass through the fire'? Certainly it is their *own* children, their own offspring, that people are feeding to the flames. And is it not true, therefore, to say that they are offering them for burnt sacrifices in order to meet the insatiable demands of the goddess sex?

So what is this, but to commit the sin of Manasseh? By committing this outrageous and dastardly crime against the unborn, the country has become guilty of a sin equally as grievous, if not more so, in the eyes of God, than that sin of Manasseh.

For it is not just a case of *one* life being terminated. That, in itself, would be heinous enough a crime against the Creator God. Especially when it is remembered that he has been moulding that life ever since the moment of conception, and that he had a purpose for that life even *before* conception took place (Psalm 139:16).

No, we are talking in terms of thousands, *tens* of thousands. We are talking in terms of nearly 300,000 lives per year.

This is not something which is going on *illegally*, behind the scenes. Instead, it has been made legal by Parliament. The enormity of what Parliament has set in motion can only be seen in its true light when we realize that, if this rate of destruction continues, in about ten years' time the total will probably have reached 6 million, which is equal to the number of Jews that Hitler liquidated in the gas chambers of Nazi Germany during his wicked and devilish regime. And they called that the Holocaust!

That is the enormity of Parliament's crime, and of the country's too, for going along with Parliament's legislation. I believe that, because of this sin alone, God has been outraged and will require all this innocent blood of us. I believe that judgment, therefore, must inevitably fall.

Blood-guiltiness is a terrible thing in the sight of a holy, almighty God, and we have become a blood-guilty nation. Terrible judgment fell on Nazi Germany in 1944 and 1945 on account of what she did in exterminating 6 million Jews. And I say without any hesitation whatsoever, that Almighty God is going to require, at our hand, all these innocent lives that *we* have so callously taken. That is to say nothing of all the unrequited blood that Britain has on her hands from lives brutally taken in Northern Ireland almost every day, in calculated, cold-blooded murder, without the murderers ever having to forfeit their own lives.

It is to say nothing of all the unrequited blood shed in this country during bank robberies, muggings on the streets, burglaries and other crimes of violence since capital punishment was abolished, when the lives of brutal murderers have never been required of them in return.

And it does not take into account the way in which nearly 3 million Russian civilians and soldiers were repatriated to the Soviet Union, against their will, by the Western Allies between 1944 and 1947, with this country playing the leading part, in the sure and certain knowledge that many of them would be brutally executed on arrival. That was a sordid case of blood-guiltiness by British leaders, and it has left a crime on Britain's conscience which can never be removed, apart from deep and heart-felt national repentance.

The stain on her conscience can certainly never be expunged by erecting a monument to these millions of victims, as some have suggested. Nothing short of national repentance will suffice. And that repentance must be led by the very highest in the Realm. God does not allow such gross injustices as these to continue indefinitely without intervening in judgment in some way, although the judgment may be long delayed.

With all the blood-guiltiness which she has upon her, unless Britain repents, she will have to learn the lesson the hard way, as Manasseh and his people did, that Almighty God is by no means a God to be fooled around with, and that when the fire of his fierce anger has been aroused, it cannot easily be appeased. Something needs urgently to happen to turn that fierce anger away.

In the debates which took place in 1983 in the General Synod of the Church of England, archbishops, bishops, clergy and laity should not have been discussing the rights or wrongs of deploying Cruise missiles, or the issue of nuclear Deterrence. Instead, they should have been debating how to avert the coming judgment of God upon the nation.

Christians and others who are involved in the Campaign for Nuclear Disarmament marches and demonstrations, including the Greenham Common women, should be asking: 'What steps are being taken to turn away God's fierce anger from our country?' For these are the two most urgent issues which need to be raised, as the following chapter will show.

Notes

1. *The Trumpet Sounds for Britain*, Volume 2, pp. 143–8.
2. See the *Daily Telegraph*, 21 March 1972.

Chapter Fourteen

Instrument of Judgment?

Is there any evidence to indicate that God might be preparing a devastating form of judgment for Britain such as that which Israel ultimately underwent—by being invaded and taken over by foreign armies?

I would suggest that we are seeing it in terms of the alarming Soviet military build-up on the continent,[1] and about which Britain and the West are constantly being warned—even by China.

The Bible teaches very clearly that as God sees sin and wickedness going on, he is at work shaping his instrument of judgment against it. Scripture shows that he is often preparing judgment over a long period of time and that, when iniquity has reached its peak, he brings the chosen instrument against it. And the Bible makes it unquestionably plain that he often uses *nations* to effect judgment. We have already seen how, in the early days of the Old Testament, God used the nation of Israel as his instrument against the Amorites. But when the iniquity of Israel itself had come to the full, God began to use other nations as his means of judgment against *her*. God is no respecter of persons—nor of nations—where sin is concerned. In Isaiah's day, he used Assyria against the northern kingdom of Israel. In iniquitous Manasseh's day, because the southern kingdom of Judah had so seriously gone astray, he used the armies of Babylon. And Jeremiah constantly referred to what God was bringing against them as 'an army from the north'.

It is clear that, in both cases, God had been preparing these invading armies over a long period. Meanwhile, he issued repeated warnings through his prophets, and urged Israel and Judah to turn to him in humble repentance. But they refused, and when, under Manasseh, the nation's iniquity reached its climax, God brought these armies of the north against his land. It all happened in Jeremiah's day, with the land and the capital being besieged. They were confronted with such a grave situation that there was no alternative left but to surrender. The day of reckoning had arrived.

I believe that Britain is in a 'book of Jeremiah' situation today, and that we could be confronted with such a grave situation as to have no alternative left but to surrender.

This brings me back to the alarming Soviet build-up. I have already shown the danger which is threatening us on the central front in Europe, where, should a 'blitz-krieg' attack be launched, the Soviet forces are so formidable that they could reach the Channel ports in less than a week.[2] I have also pointed out the very real danger of the Soviets closing our sealines of communication in the vicinity of the Persian Gulf and around the Cape, thus causing us to be reduced to a state of siege.[3]

If we now examine what has been happening on another front, we shall be left in no doubt whatsoever that we are facing a similar kind of judgment to that which Israel ultimately underwent; a Day of God which, if it were suddenly to fall, would indeed be catastrophic, and of world-shattering proportions. It would certainly be one which would make both the ears, of everyone across the world who heard of it, to tingle.

The cold fact is that, in addition to the danger that

threatens from the central front in Europe, there has been emerging, during the last seventeen years at least, another overwhelming build-up of Soviet forces in the *northern* part of the Continent, in two very vulnerable and strategic areas which could form the two blades of a giant pincer movement reaching out westward across Europe, like two great arms, towards the North Sea and the Atlantic.

I would not hesitate to describe this development as the emergence of a modern 'army of the north'. I would also stress that it has been emerging over a long period of time. Therefore it could be interpreted as an instrument of judgment which God is preparing against us.

General Walker saw this situation developing when he was Commander-in-Chief of the Allied Forces in this Northern Area of Europe, and has kindly provided the details. He describes what has happened in one abrupt sentence: 'In 1967, during the Six Day War in the Middle East, when the eyes of the World were focused on the Arabs and the Israelis, a significant build-up of Soviet Forces began in the region of north Norway, and it has been increasingly rapidly ever since.'

A major shift in the whole balance of power quietly took place on NATO's northern flank under cover of the momentous events which were then taking place in and around Israel. It meant that the whole extent of northern Europe, stretching from the River Elbe to the Russian border near Kirkenes, suddenly became an area of key strategic importance to the North Atlantic Treaty Alliance and particularly since there was also a shift of power on that northern flank *at sea* (see p.159).

The General saw quite clearly that the defence of the entire northern flank area suddenly became vital to the survival of the *whole of the western world*. So let me describe what he says about those two build-ups which constitute the two blades of that giant pincer movement.

One of these military build-ups is in advance of the ice-free Soviet port of Murmansk, just behind the vulnerable borders of Finland, up in the Arctic circle.

The other is situated in the vicinity of the Baltic Straits, which lead into the North Sea immediately opposite the *east coast of Scotland*. So both constitute a direct threat to the security of this country. In addition to that, the Soviet Arctic fleet has extended its naval and air patrol area to beyond the Iceland-Scotland line.

Pincer Blade number one consists of a gigantic concentration of naval, air, land and sea-borne invasion forces—a veritable Colossus—in the Arctic regions, in the vicinity of Murmansk in the Kola Peninsula (see p.159).

The powerful units of the Soviet northern fleet are within about 300 miles, or less than ten hours steaming time, of the northern-most tip of Norway. They comprise some 500 surface warships, together with no less than 160 submarines, many of which carry payloads of long-range ballistic missiles and self-guided torpedoes—a truly formidable force which *is being strengthened each year*, and which has its own concentration of aircraft for reconnaissance and cover.

The land forces are greatly superior to the armies of NATO's Northern European Command, and are backed up by their own support aircraft. Then, in addition to these land forces, the Red Army has several more divisions standing northward all the way from Leningrad to Murmansk, all along the borders of Finland and Lappland (see p.159) and they are all facing in our direction!

Moreover, there has been a proliferation of fifty forward airfields and airstrips right across the entire region between Murmansk and Kandalaksha for the express purpose of increasing the scope for augmenting both ground and air forces in this entire region. Many of these airfields are within thirty miles of the Russian-Norwegian border. Still more ominous is the fact that these forces are backed up by greatly superior amphibious invasion forces, which are trained and equipped to make landings from the sea on the coasts of what the Soviets themselves openly describe as 'target countries'.

All these quite frightening and formidable forces are further backed by a follow-up lift, in merchant ships, comprising three divisions. So much for the moment, then, regarding the build-up in the region of Murmansk.

There is also the second threat, which we will call Pincer Blade number two. Here, in the Baltic, the strength of the Warsaw Pact forces facing the southern flank of NATO's Northern European Command is no less formidable. First there is the Soviet build-up at sea, where the combined Baltic fleet of the Warsaw Pact countries consists of no less than 1,000 vessels, including heavy and light cruisers and destroyers. These Warsaw Pact navies have a pronounced preponderance over the Baltic battle squadrons of the Federal German and Royal Dutch fleets. They have, for instance, a five-or ten fold superiority in respect of missile and torpedo-boats especially relevant to Baltic conditions. But then, as in the Arctic Circle off Murmansk, there is also a heavy concentration of missile-firing submarines. True, this immense Soviet and Warsaw Pact naval build-up is more or less bottled up in the Baltic, for a study of the map will show that in order for their warships to pass from the Baltic into the North Sea and beyond, they first have to sail through NATO's Northern European Command area. They have, for instance, to sail into the Kattegat, past the Danish islands, and then into the Skagerrak, before they can reach the North Sea. But all the evidence shows that this is partly the reason for the concentration of forces. If they intend to make that passage possible, the Warsaw Pact countries already have large numbers of mobile shore-to-ship missiles deployed all along the South Baltic coast, including the Baltic seaboard of East Germany. Moreover, in addition to deploying these missiles, there has been a marked increase in Soviet naval movements in these waters in recent years, and it is for ever increasing.

General Walker states that 'whereas, a few years back, Soviet warships were rarely seen west of the island of

Bornholm in the Baltic (unless they were individual ships on passage through the Baltic Straits on their way north to Murmansk, or west to the Mediterranean and the Black Sea), now their presence in Danish waters is a permanency. They station themselves off all parts of the Danish coast, including the Skagerrak and the Kattegat in a bid to dominate Danish waters.' 'The danger is', he warns, 'that by coming to regard their presence in these waters as a common-place, every day situation, we, in this Northern European Command Area, comprising Denmark, Schleswig-Holstein, and Norway, lay ourselves wide open to the danger of being taken by surprise and attacked.' But it is not just a naval build-up alone that menaces this area. For, as up in the Arctic north, there is, in addition, a very real threat from *overland*.

To appreciate the extreme danger of this threat, it should be realized that the forty-mile sector in the northern German province of Schleswig-Holstein, between the River Elbe and the Baltic, and which borders on East-Germany, is an exceedingly vulnerable one. It is only guarded by a single division of the West German Bundeswehr. Yet poised opposite that one division, stand several divisions of Warsaw Pact land forces. But these land forces do not stand alone. They are backed up by a follow-up lift, comprising four divisions of Russian and Warsaw Pact forces to match the three divisions already concentrated in the north, all ready to be transported by merchant ships, with an additional concentration of amphibious assault craft capable of being able to lift, simultaneously, a total of two or three brigades. All these forces are backed up by a heavy concentration of offensive aircraft just as are the forces in the Murmansk region. So, taken together, this mighty force, 'bottled up' in the Baltic, is very fearsome indeed. The danger is, that if that fragile sector between the River Elbe and the Baltic were breached, Warsaw Pact 'intruders' might progress rapidly down the relatively flat and open countryside between there and the Skaggerak. Were that to happen, Denmark would be overrun in the process, Warsaw Pact forces would reach the North Sea beaches, and a passage would consequently be opened for their vast armada of warships right through into the North Sea itself. And Scotland and the north of England are just opposite!

Meanwhile, 'spy-in-the-sky' satellites, and other highly sophisticated detection devices, have revealed that the Soviets are now using large earth-moving equipment (mostly acquired from the United States and West Germany!) rapidly to widen and deepen the White Sea Canal which stretches from the Baltic Sea city of Leningrad up through a series of lakes, including the Ladoga and Onega lakes, to the ice-free Arctic harbour of Archangel in the north (see p.159).

This canal was originally constructed between 1931 and 1933, and the widening and deepening of it would enable the rapid movement of either the Soviet Baltic fleet to the White Sea, or the much larger Soviet northern fleet, including its 160 submarines, to the Baltic. This direct canal route between the White Sea and the Baltic would shorten by more than 3,000 miles the distance that the Soviet northern fleet now has to travel. It would enable the Soviet northern fleet to move swiftly into the Baltic in support of military operations against any country or countries which border that sea, namely, Finland, Sweden, Norway, Denmark and West Germany. All this constitutes Pincer Blade Number Two.

In addition to these two blades, the Soviet Arctic fleet has pushed out its routine air and sea patrol-area into the Atlantic beyond the Iceland-Scotland line. General Walker says that at the same time they have erected or established 'a barrier at sea'. What does he mean by that? With the help of the map on page 159, I will endeavour to explain.

Our then First Sea Lord, Sir Michael Pollock, warned us a good eleven years ago that 'never has the Soviet activity round the shores of Scotland been so great'. A year later, Air-Commander E. M. Donaldson, air correspondent of

THE TRUMPET SOUNDS FOR BRITAIN

the *Daily Telegraph* reported that 'the sea area between Iceland and Scotland, which is called the "Icelandic-Gap", forms a natural gateway which brings Russian maritime movements comparatively close together, making it a most important operating area'. 'Russian warships', he said, 'from large cruisers to destroyers, are seen constantly in that Gap, keeping their eyes on Allied navy movements.'[4]

As long ago as 1 December 1968, a naval correspondent reported that the first permanent Russian naval replenishing anchorage for the North Atlantic area had been established off the *Shetlands*. He went on to explain that 'Russian electronic intelligence trawlers and other vessels, were already using an area near those islands as a regular rendezvous point for refuelling, revictualling, and changing crews.' But then Iceland, and its surrounding waters, has become a focal point of Soviet interest during the last fifteen or more years, including the long protracted period of the Icelandic 'Cod War'. Russian sea and air activity around Iceland has increased alarmingly ever since the Soviets began to enlarge their base complex around Murmansk in 1967. Hundreds of intercepts per year are now being made by the American Air Force fighter squadrons based at Keflavik, Iceland. A glance at the map on page 159, shows that such Russian air activity must be penetrating that area off Iceland known to all sea farers as the 'Denmark Straits'.

American maritime reconnaissance aircraft also report that Russian naval activity, as against their air activity, in Iceland's neighbouring sea areas, includes what appears to be replenishing, and possibly crew-changing, on nuclear-powered submarines, by depot ships on the high seas. If this is true, it means that Russia has now established naval replenishment anchorages off Iceland, as well as off the Shetlands. Pursuing the strategy further, it becomes clear that the Kremlin has been showing interest in using *Iceland* itself, as a kind of stepping stone from which to stride still further into the Atlantic. For the West has irrefutable evidence to show that Russian military aircraft, comparable in size to the giant American C-5s, *as a refuelling base have been using the Keflavik airfield on Iceland when flying arms to Cuba*, albeit under the guise at one time, of ferrying relief supplies to earthquake victims in Peru. The *Faeroes* have also become a focal point of Russian interest in recent years, for in addition to that which has been said above, the director of research of the Norwegian Political Institute, as long ago as November 1970, reached the conclusion concerning this increased Russian activity that 'it is the intention of the Soviets to push their naval defence line outwards to Iceland and the Faeroes.' 'If this is the likely development', he went on to say, 'then it indicates that the Russians would, to an increasing degree, come to regard the Norwegian Sea as a Soviet Lake, behind which, of course, Norway will lie.' That, from a Norwegian, is the language of 'Norway being outflanked or encircled—out at sea', for the Norwegian Sea lies between Norway and Iceland (please note the position of the Faeroes in relation to the Shetlands, the north of Scotland, and Iceland).

What has emerged so far, is that for many years there has been a considerable amount of disturbing Russian naval and air activity in the sea areas, running in a line from the north of Scotland across to the Shetlands, then to the Faeroes, then across to Iceland, and beyond that, into the Denmark Straits (and the Denmark Straits themselves are bounded by Greenland, which produces its own ice-barrier!). Notice that the whole of this sea area is under constant Soviet air surveillance, and that the Russians have also established naval anchorages or rendevous areas at points between the Shetlands, the Faeroes, Iceland, and possibly in the Denmark Straits, where their long-distance submarines can change their crews, refuel, and replenish their stores, so that they no longer need to return to Murmansk or the Baltic for those purposes.

This should enable us to appreciate what our senior naval, air and military authorities mean when they say that the Soviets have erected or established 'a barrier at sea'. The barrier is there in the most tangible of forms—cold steel hulls and superstructures of large Soviet cruisers, destroyers, electronic intelligence trawlers, formidable nuclear-powered submarines, some of them missile-firing— all sitting over the main sea supply lines of the free western world. And with no-one, apparently, to say them 'Nay'!

And it is there in the shape of long-range heavily-armed Russian aircraft, too, all connected directly with those two giant pincer blades.

So what is its aim?

In answer to that question, I quote General Walker: 'The aim of this Soviet strategy is to block the gap of Greenland, Iceland, Faeroes and Scotland, when they are ready.'

That means the closing, at sea, of the ends of those pincer blades, ready for the Russian occupation of the whole of Western Europe. With the closing of the blades, the slow strangulation of Western Europe will have begun. With powerful units of the Soviet Navy astride all our other main shipping routes throughout the world, and with more Soviet submarines prowling around in the Atlantic than Hitler had at the start of the 1939–45 War, the strangulation would very soon be complete.

Meanwhile, the Russians have nuclear-powered, missile-firing submarines deployed off all the coasts of North America, thus bringing 95 per cent of the American population and industrial centres within range. In addition, they now have at least seventeen Delta submarines in the Barents Sea, capable of hitting every city in the United States *from their own home waters*.

Their intention is to keep the United States at bay, and to prevent her from intervening, should they decide suddenly to move forward in Europe. That is the danger which is in prospect. So there *is* a devastating form of judgment threatening us similar to that which was overshadowing Israel in Manasseh's day! As in Jeremiah's day, there is the possibility of our being confronted with such a grave situation that there is no alternative left but to surrender.

Of these two things, there can be no denial. But how real, actually, is this danger and this possibility? Well now we come to the *real* crunch of all this Russian manoeuvring. General Walker asks: 'What does Russia need to do first, in order to guarantee success in fulfilling her aim of blocking the Scotland to Greenland Gap?' He answers his own question in one rapid sentence: 'It is to secure their sea lines of communication back to their bases.'

A further study of the map on page 159 will soon show what this means. It should be clear by now that it is from the strategic port of Murmansk that the Soviet fleets are pushing out into the Atlantic and beyond. The sea lanes of communication leading from Murmansk into the Atlantic, and beyond, pass over the North Cape of Norway. Thereafter, the most direct route into the Atlantic lies through the Denmark Straits between Iceland and Greenland. Alternatively, it will be seen that ships coming in from the Atlantic by this northern route to either Archangel or the main base at Murmansk must pass Iceland via the Denmark Straits or the Icelandic Gap before making their way round the North Cape. It should immediately become apparent, therefore, that both Norway and Iceland stand athwart those vital sea lanes. From the Russian point of view, Norway and Iceland hold the key so far as safe-guarding those lanes is concerned.

Once that is realized, something else becomes clear. Should the Russians suddenly decide to close the Icelandic Gap as the immediate prelude to expanding across Europe, their strategists would have reason to regard north Norway as a dangerous area, from which their vital lines of communication could be threatened by the forces of NATO's Northern Europe Command. Therefore, before moving to close the Scotland-Greenland gap, if that is what they are intending to do, they must first secure north Norway, and that inevitably means occupying it in some form or another. This is what the General is getting at when he says, 'they

155

must first secure their lines of communication back to their bases.'

The Soviets see so clearly what a vitally strategic position Norway holds for the protection of all Russian shipping which must pass round the North Cape, which is why they are giving particular attention to this region. It also explains why they already have a highly trained naval amphibious infantry brigade at a high state of readiness, equipped with sophisticated weapons and trained for assault landings, based at Pechenga, very near to Norway's northernmost borders. General Walker is particularly concerned about this brigade, saying that it is not defensive in nature, but offensive, that it could only be employed against NATO territory in this region, and that its whole existence must be to that end.

The Royal United Services Institute for Defence Studies, in its report entitled *European Security 1972–1980*, says that the possibility cannot be excluded of an attempt by the USSR to replace NATO's presence in the region with a presence of her own. The Report says, 'Most probably the assault echelon would be comprised of several brigades pushing overland, and this marine brigade based just across the border at Pechenga, moving in by sea. In readiness for such a move, a very substantial follow-up lift is already there at hand, in merchant ships, by way of back-up forces.'

Taking all these factors into consideration, therefore, it is beyond dispute that as far as *Norway* is concerned, Russia already has the necessary forces in position to provide her with the means of securing her lines of communication back to her base at Murmansk, when she considers the time is ready. She also sees what a vitally strategic position Norway holds with respect to her *global* aim, and that provides her with a further reason for wanting to take total control of that country.

General Walker reminds us that 'the long years of history have taught us that, whenever any great power has sought world empire, woe betide any country which stands in the way. And Norway stands in the way!

Strategists, therefore, hold that, from every point of view, in order for the Soviets to fulfil *all* their aims, Russian occupation of Norway, in some form, is *essential*. We can even go as far as to say that when they decide that the time is ripe to fulfil their *European* aims, Norway's occupation is *inevitable*.

The Soviets have an equal need to secure their lines of communication to their strategic base in the Baltic. We have already noted that the sea passage to the Atlantic, for Russia and the Warsaw Pact countries, passes through what is generally known as the Baltic Straits, the waters around Denmark called the Kattegat and the Skagerrak. The area of land which stands guard over these Straits includes Denmark, Schleswig-Holstein, part of southern Norway, and part of neutral Sweden. It follows, therefore, that to secure her sea lines of communication, Russia must, in some way, gain control of the whole of this region too.

If she failed to do so before moving to close the Scotland-Greenland Gap, or to roll forward in Central Europe, these southern sea lines would also be in jeopardy from the forces of NATO, as in the case of Norway. So occupation of the whole of this Baltic region would be necessary. We have already seen only too clearly how easy that would be, with only *one* West German division guarding the vulnerable forty-mile stretch of East Germany's border between Lubeck and the River Elbe.

Put both of these necessary Soviet moves together, and it should become quite plain that the occupation and control of the entire region from the North Cape, right down to Hamburg and the River Elbe below Denmark, is not only necessary, but would be inevitable. That comprises the whole land area between the two giant pincer blades. Should it happen, the immediate result would be that a major part of Great Britain's east coast would at once become exposed to the sea, air and land forces of the Soviet Colossus.

Notes

1. *The Trumpet Sounds for Britain*, Volume 1, pp. 104–7; 147–52.
2. ibid., pp. 105–6.
3. ibid., p. 150.
4. The *Daily Telegraph*, 23 May 1973.

Chapter Fifteen

A Question of Intention

Is this Russia's intention?

To answer the question, we can see from the map on page 159 how important it is to understand what has been taking place behind the Scotland-Iceland-Greenland line during the past few years.

The Soviets have been carrying out an ever-increasing number of ominous exercises along the entire Norwegian coastline in recent years. 'These exercises', states General Walker, 'have included convoys of Russian ships laden with tanks, lorries, naval infantry, and landing craft, making their way along the coast of Norway—right on the very doorstep of NATO's Northern Europe Command— heavily protected by missile-firing escorts, with larger landing-craft in company. And they have been making 'exercise-landings' on the Rybachiy Peninsula (USSR) just ahead of the massive build up, concentrated at the major base-complex around Murmansk' (this, the reader can see from the map, is very near to the vulnerable Finnish-Norwegian border.) To give an example of how sinister these exercises are, the Report of the Royal United Services Institute for Defence Studies said in 1980, 'Within the last four years, a couple of exercises have been carried out, in which amphibious task forces moved up from the Baltic to assault the Kola Peninsula' (the area of North Russia behind Murmansk). 'One of these exercises came shortly after the practice movement of a convoy from Murmansk to a point near Tromso, had coincided with land manoeuvres on a divisional scale right up against the Norwegian border'!

It clearly means that just after one 'exercise convoy' had rounded North Cape from Murmansk on passage *southward* along the coast of Norway, another such 'exercise convoy' steamed *northwards* from the Baltic in the opposite direction, along the coast of Norway and round the North Cape to Murmansk. And all the time, there were these menacing manoeuvres being launched *overland*, from behind Norway's northern border with Finland.

The Norwegian Defence Minister has given this warning to the Storting (Norwegian Parliament) about these 'exercises': 'An exercise pattern has now been created, which in future would make it possible for an amphibious force to set out, both from the Baltic and from the Kola Peninsula, without this necessarily having to be noted as unusual.' So what is the explanation of all this? Having seen the map on page 159, one can appreciate that the movement of these 'exercise convoys', both in a southerly as well as in a northerly direction, and whose object is to *make landings*, represent an *encircling movement* of Norway, along the whole length of her coast.

When General Walker states, as he has done, that 'the Soviet Baltic Fleet, by increasing its activity to the extent of pressing forward past the island of Bornholm into the Kattegat and Skagerrak, and by stationing itself off all parts of the Danish coast, thus dominating Danish waters with its permanent presence, whilst at the same time, the Soviet northern fleet presses forwards, and moves southwards, in an obvious attempt to dominate Norwegian waters; then, that in itself, represents a second encirclement of Norway out at sea.' It is obvious that whenever these two converging naval forces meet and pass each other at sea, they will have encompassed the whole of Norway. In fact, they have become like two outstretched arms, one protruding from the north, the other from the south (the Baltic), whose hands have been brought together, and have become interlocked, somewhere out there in the Norwegian Sea.

It is a picture of the 'Russian Bear-Hug' again. But this time, the long, hairy arms are hidden by the sleeves of a smart Soviet naval uniform! And this time, they have closed far nearer in to the coast than just beyond Iceland! Norway is therefore *already* being outflanked by the Soviets from seaward. Since their warships are steaming so freely, coastwise, from both north and south, the Russians already have Norway by the throat, albeit ever so loosely. It would not need much for them to tighten their grip.

Again, the Russians have also the means of striking Norway a sudden, cruel, stab in the back, for Norway is constantly being menaced by this further threat 'from behind', *overland,* up in the north, in the shape of the strong Soviet naval infantry brigade poised against Finnmark's northern-most border and only a few hours steaming distance from the North Cape. Since Finland has a common border with this part of Norway, the perilous nature of this particular threat should become apparent. 'It should never be forgotten that Finland could easily be crossed by an aggressor', says General Walker. 'For instance, Soviet forces have the capability to over-run Finnmark quickly, thus presenting NATO with a *fait accompli* unless the Alliance reacted with equal speed and resolution.' This situation from the landward side in the north, can therefore be likened to the Red Bear, crouched down, ready to strike, and already breathing down the back of Norway's neck.

Further south, the exercise pattern in the Baltic has increasingly been stepped up. In the large-scale amphibious exercises which the Soviets have taken to conducting in the area in recent years, their troop transports and warships have headed directly for the Danish coast, only to turn south at the final moment and then land on East German beaches, which bear a striking resemblance to the Danish beaches. On no less than 110 separate occasions in 1975, formation flights were made by Soviet warplanes to within a few miles of Danish territory. An intelligence report received by the Danish Parliament Defence Committee points out that between forty and fifty aircraft were engaged in some of these exercises. Then the Danish Chief of Defence was at pains to point out in February 1976 that since the beginning of that year the military activities of the Soviet Union and Warsaw Pact Countries had escalated substantially. Still later, on Saturday, 2 July 1977, it was the BBC who twice announced on its late-night Radio 4 news bulletins that Soviet and Warsaw Pact forces were currently engaging in the most massive amphibious exercises ever held in the Baltic. It reported that cruisers, heavier ships, and a large number of landing-craft were involved.

Of course, that is when it is all going to happen—on a Friday night, after Parliament has adjourned for the week-end, when the Prime Minister and most MPs are half-way between Westminster and their various constituencies, and when NATO officers and many of their troops are heading for week-end leave!

Commenting on this build-up of Warsaw Pact activity in the Baltic and in the airspace off the Danish coast, the Danish newspaper *Aktuelt*, on 13 March 1976, quoted official Danish Government sources as saying, 'the strategic aim of the Warsaw Pact countries includes plans to overrun Denmark, in order to secure a safe passage for the Baltic fleet to sail out into the Atlantic and marry up with the Soviet northern fleet.' According to a senior Danish official, 'Denmark, or a greater part of it, and Norway, are already behind the battle-front in the eyes of Soviet generals.' There you have it, straight from Danish Government sources!—the language of encirclement.

All this, then, has been happening behind the Scotland-Iceland-Greenland Line, close in to the coastline of Norway and behind her eastern border with Russia, and also down in the Baltic, off Denmark, ever since that extended naval defence line beyond Iceland began to be established.

So the question remains, 'Is it Russia's intention to occupy and take over control of the entire land-region between the two giant pincer blades, namely, the region from the North Cape right down to the foot of Denmark and the River Elbe?

Well, all the evidence which has been marshalled above shows that she has most certainly been getting ready for it! In fact, General Walker regards the establishing of that 'barrier at sea' as the advance preparations of 'outflanking the whole of that land area; and the blocking of the gap, Greenland-Iceland-the Faeroes-Scotland, as part of the Soviet's self-declared, long-term aim to establish Russian leadership throughout the whole of Europe.' He says: 'When I ask myself that question, "Is it Russia's intention to take over that whole area?" I am convinced that the answer is "yes".'

Perhaps we should add: *When the time is ready*.

In view of the theme of this book 'The Trumpet Sounds for Britain', what would be the effect of such an occupation of Norway, right down to Denmark, were it to take place? How would it affect the United Kingdom? What would be the military and spiritual implications?

To quote General Walker again: 'If the whole of Norway was over-run, outflanked, and neutralized, then the United Kingdom would be placed in a critical position of facing Soviet-occupied or Soviet-dominated territory, in the same way as she had to face German-occupied Norway across the North Sea in the last war. But this time, the threat, maritime, amphibious, air, missile, and land, would be far, far more serious.... Also by occupying the vast, sparsely populated area of Finmark in the north, Russia would secure some good arifields, some ice-free naval dispersal areas in the fjords, and easier access to the western shipping routes.'

That, once again, would immediately mean that our life-lines to and from the Atlantic would be in grave danger.

We have already seen only too clearly that in order to secure their lines of communication back to their northern and southern bases, the Soviets would need also to occupy Denmark and Schleswig-Holstein. This second move would bring the Russians right through to the Continent's North Sea coast, right opposite our industrial north, and Scotland, on the one hand (Hull is on the same longitudinal line as Hamburg), and to Norway's entire seaboard on the other.

NATO's airfields in north Norway, Jutland, and Schleswig-Holstein, which are temptingly close to the Norwegian Sea, on the one hand, and to the North Sea, on the other, would immediately fall into their hands. That would mean that Edinburgh and the Firth of Forth would be only a very short flying distance from air bases on Jutland; and that Humberside, Yorkshire, Lincolnshire, the whole of East Anglia, and even the Thames Estuary, would be about the same flying distance from the Schleswig-Holstein air bases.

And what about the missiles which would very soon be deployed all along that opposite coastline? Would not our cities immediately be in danger of being razed to the ground? In fact, the United Kingdom's eastern seaboard would immediately become exceedingly vulnerable and be exposed to anything that might be launched against it, from missiles, aircraft, and paratroopers to powerful amphibious landing fleets.

That is not the language of an alarmist; it is the language of a realist.

If the whole land-area between those two pincer blades were indeed occupied by Soviet forces, it would provide Russia with an easy air and sea approach to the enormous military and economic potential of the United States, which constitute the very foundations of the NATO Alliance. America's access to Europe would then be denied, and the United States' ability to come to our aid would be greatly curtailed if not altogether prevented. In addition to which, there is the disturbing fact that the United States is probably ringed by Russian nuclear missile firing submarines!

General Walker has been deeply disturbed at the number of these submarines which the Soviets have been constructing over the past fifteen years. Their numbers have increased over that period by fourteen times, and they now have more nuclear submarines than all the North Atlantic Treaty Organisation countries put together. And the Norwegian Navy's commander-in-Chief, Admiral Broadland, has given a warning that many of them are 'sailing' out, under water, from Murmansk, across the Atlantic in the direction of the United States.

'What, therefore, in view of this quite phenomenal increase, are the Soviet's intentions', asks General Walker. 'The Soviet Navy's intention, because of their submarines expanding range of operations, is to deploy long-range missiles—in submarines hidden under water—along the entire length of America's Atlantic and Pacific coasts, and in the Gulf of Mexico, thus bringing 95 per cent of the American population and industrial centres within range. .... It becomes obvious that the United States would be placed at a very great political disadvantage if the Soviet Union were able to ring the United States with a superior Polaris-type fleet off all their coasts.'

In any case, they can now achieve the same results from their own home waters in the Barents Sea by means of their Delta-type submarines.

All this means that should the Kremlin suddenly decide to order all her forces to roll forward in Europe with a view to establishing its leadership right through to the Channel and North Sea coasts, they have only to say: 'Don't make any move to come to their assistance, America—or else!'

The same would apply, of course, if the Russians were in a position to threaten the United Kingdom itself: 'Stay right where you are, Mr President! Our finger is already on the button!'

What we need to remember is that, *humanly* speaking, it is only the strength and power of the United States which, at the moment, is preventing Western Europe and ourselves from being over-run. As Robert Strausz-Hupe, the distinguished American diplomat, has said recently: 'Western civilisation exists because the United States exists. If the United States falls, Western civilisation falls with it, and goes under.... The overreaching issue of our times is the United States' struggle for its very survival against the formidable and ubiquitous challenge of the Soviet Union. The superiority of numbers in launches and mega-tonnage of the Soviet nuclear arsenal over that of the United States is no longer a matter of debate.

'The United States and the Soviet Union are now moving on a collision course and in a matter of a few years they are likely to collide.

'The West's best minds, and even most western statesmen, are troubled by this sensation of impending calamity. We need to heed the warning signals that now flare from every point along the perimeter of Western Defence.'

My own question is, what would happen if these two great world powers *did* collide, and supposing the United States *did* fall, or was rendered completely powerless to come to our aid in any move forward in Europe?

With no Churchill this time to stand in defiance and to open his lips to emit the lion's roar—'We will *defend* this Island; we will *never* surrender'—and cut off from all outside aid, what would our position in the United Kingdom be? Would we not be left with no alternative *other* than to surrender?

Isn't that to be in a book of Jeremiah situation?

But what are the spiritual implications of this?

It should be abundantly clear by now that it is no longer the case of *expecting* to see a day of God in judgment for Britain appearing over the horizon, if we have, indeed, gone the same way that Israel went at the time of Manasseh. Rather is it obvious that this is exactly what we *are* seeing.

It should never be forgotten that when Israel had gone so far away from God that she would no longer listen to his voice, or respond to his pleading to return to him, the time came when Almighty God had to say to her: 'Because thou servedst not the Lord thy God with joyfulness, and with gladness of heart...Therefore shalt thou serve thine enemies which the Lord shall send against thee...The Lord shall bring a nation against thee from far, from the end of the earth, as swift as the eagle flieth...A nation of fierce countenance, which shall not regard the person of the old, nor show favour to the young: and he shall eat the fruit of thy cattle, and the fruit of thy land, *until thou be destroyed*: which also shall not leave thee either corn, wine or oil[!], or the increase of thy kine, or flocks of thy sheep, until he have destroyed thee' (Deuteronomy 28:47–51).

But in saying that, God does not stop there. He goes on: 'And he shall besiege thee in all thy gates, until thy high and fenced walls come down, wherein thou trustedst, throughout all thy land: and he shall besiege thee in all thy gates throughout all thy land, which the Lord thy God hath given thee' (Deuteronomy 28:52).

Let us note that God utters the word 'besiege' twice—'Because thou servedst not the Lord thy God'.

What does it mean for Britain today? Surely 'gates' are the sea lanes leading to and from her ports. They are the passages through which her vital supplies are brought, and all these are already being threatened today.

For instance, the country has for a long time been deeply concerned about the Soviet navy's activities in the Indian Ocean, and about the possibility of a Russian naval blockade completely cutting off Britain's and the West's oil supplies from the Persian Gulf, thus causing the United Kingdom's entire economy to come grinding to a halt.

Our 'gates' also include the route from the Mediterranean through the Straits of Gibraltar, and the American Sixth Fleet is no longer superior in strength to the ever-growing Soviet fleet in that area. This fact was demonstrated as long ago as the Yom Kippur war against Israel. With the scales shifting all the time in their favour, the

Russians may soon gain complete control over the Mediterranean.

Spain is agitating for the possession of Gibraltar. The Russians already have bases very near to there, and should we yield possession of the Rock, it will not be very long before Russia obtains control of the Straits.

Then there are the Atlantic Approaches, the Western Approaches, and the Irish Sea. Speaking of the whole Atlantic, the American Admiral van Rees has said: 'If the strength and number of the North Atlantic Treaty Organisation Anti-Submarine and Escort Forces in the Atlantic continues to decline, there will come a moment in this decade when we will no longer be able to safe-guard our sea lines of communication in the Atlantic when challenged by the Soviets.'

Other vital 'gates' include the Denmark Straits and the Iceland Gap which, as we have seen, the Russians already plan to block. Nearer home, there are the English Channel, and the routes across the North Sea to the Continent. Russian electronic intelligence trawlers and other vessels operate an almost continuous patrol around Britain, and their surveillance trawlers with marines on board are almost permanently stationed off Plymouth.

In addition, the Soviets have recently issued another challenge. It has been revealed that the Russian Backfire Bomber—carrying the latest anti-ship missile, the AS-6 Kingfisher, which has a range of 380 nautical miles and is believed to be fitted with nuclear warheads—is capable of attacking ships in the Atlantic as far south as the Azores from bases in Northern Russia and of returning home without refuelling. The Russian philosophy, in planning the use of air or submarine-launched missiles at sea, means that provided a missile-carrying aircraft or submarine had some approximate indication of the whereabouts of a western fleet or convoy, probably from a reconnaisance space satellite, it would only need to launch missiles in the general area of the ships in order to be effective.

The verse in Deuteronomy says: 'And he shall besiege thee in *all* thy gates'. So we have to ask whether we are going to see that verse literally fulfilled as a result of the Soviets blocking the Iceland-Scotland Gap and then closing her tentacles around all the other main shipping routes around the world to effect the complete strangulation of Britain and the West. Are we about to see it fulfilled as part of a devastating form of divine judgment because of Britain's sin and departure from God? I say that the possibility is very much there, because there came a time when God had to say to Israel, 'The Lord shall bring a nation against thee from far... And he shall besiege thee in all thy gates'. God warned them (Deuteronomy 28:47–52) that it would happen if they forsook him.

That warning comes at the end of the long list of judgments in Deuteronomy 28 which we have studied elsewhere,[1] and which God said he would send upon Israel as signs to them that they had forsaken him.

We found that most of these other signs have been visited on Britain in recent years, which should cause us to take this warning of further judgment very seriously indeed.

It happened years later in the case of Israel, after she had gone so far away from God as to commit all those sins and to pass the point of no return.

God *did* bring a nation against them from afar. God *did* cause them to be besieged and confronted with such a grave situation that there was no alternative left but to surrender. All the available evidence suggests that the ingredients of that kind of judgment are present for Britain today, who has gone exactly the same way.

Isn't there a dire need, therefore, to sound the trumpet for Britain and urgently call all her people to repentance?

Note

1. *The Trumpet Sounds for Britain*, Volume 1, pp.118–134.

Chapter Sixteen

Prophecy Fulfilled

So far, I have placed the message of this book in a national setting, and even at times, referred to its relevance to the western, and free world.

But in view of everything which we see happening on a world-wide scale today, I believe there is an urgent need to put Britain's present situation in a global context as well. For we are undoubtedly living in momentous times.

We are living in a day when, on one hand, God is obviously paving the way for the restoration and spiritual revival of his ancient people of Israel, in fulfilment of all the Old and New Testament prophecies. So all eyes today are increasingly being forced to focus on the Middle East. All the evidence points to the fact that the coming again of the Lord Jesus Christ, the Messiah, must be drawing exceedingly near. On the other hand, it is a time when God is undeniably also preparing the Gentile nations for their long-predicted judgment. And Britain, today, whether she is aware of these things or not, is sandwiched between these two most momentous coming events. Furthermore, Britain happens to be one of those Gentile nations!

We need also to be reminded that Scripture clearly teaches that these two prophesied events—the spiritual revival of Israel, and God's judgment on the Gentiles, are due to coincide with one another.

My conviction that we should place Britain's situation in a global context, and not merely in a national one, is strongly reinforced by an equally firm conviction that Britain today is in a 'Book of Jeremiah' situation. That book is set against the background of a world-wide coming judgment of God upon the nations, because of their gross sin and iniquity, and because of their extreme blood-guiltiness. God is not going to let the nations of the world get away with the terrible violence and bloodshed throughout the world today. Of that we can be fully assured. But the same book is also set against the background of the coming spiritual restoration and revival of Israel in the last days. Many of its later chapters are devoted to that profound theme.

There is no doubt whatsoever that world events are shouting at us that we are now living in these 'last' or 'latter' days. So the nations of the world, and not only Britain, need to beware! The biblical prophecies are being fulfilled almost daily before their eyes.

One of the most relevant Scriptures concerning the coming judgment of God upon the nations, and about which the world needs to be warned, is to be found in Isaiah 26:21: 'For behold, the Lord cometh out of his place to punish the inhabitants of the earth for their iniquity: the earth also shall disclose her blood, and shall no more cover her slain.' Those last words, have to do with the coming judgment of God upon the terrible blood-guiltiness of the nations. All the blood which has been shed will then be disclosed to God, and those countless millions slain in violence will no longer be hidden. Their blood will all be required by Almighty God.

So far as Israel is concerned, it is a fact that, ever since the Balfour Declaration in 1917, the Jews have been returning to their ancient homeland in ever-increasing numbers from the many countries where they had been scattered—in fulfilment of the Old Testament prophecies. It is a fact too, that the State of Israel was established in 1948. It is also the case that, in 1967, Jerusalem came back into the hands of the Jews for the first time in nearly 2,000 years. Remember, Jesus said, 'Jerusalem shall be trodden down of the Gentiles, until the times of the gentiles be fulfilled' (Luke 21:24). Everybody knows that Jerusalem today is no longer 'trodden down of the Gentiles', but is in Israel's possession.

The fact that Jerusalem is now back in the hands of the Jews after all these centuries is a sure sign that 'the times of the Gentiles'; are fast running out, if, indeed, they have not already done so. That being the case, the spiritual revival of Israel itself must be very near, because God has said 'Blindness [spiritual] in part is happened to Israel, *until the fulness* of the Gentiles be come in (Romans 11:25). When the 'fulness of the Gentiles' has completely come in, God says that he has covenanted with his people that 'there shall come out of Sion the Deliverer, and shall turn away ungodliness from Jacob [the name for unregenerate Israel], (Romans 11:26b) 'and so all Israel shall be saved' (v.26a). To use the language of Scripture, they will be grafted in again into their own olive tree from whence they were broken off and cast away, and that will mean 'life from the dead' for them, and great spiritual riches for the world (Romans 11:11–24).

Early in January 1984, the *Jewish Chronicle*, in a single issue, published three very interesting items. The first was a report that oil had been discovered in the southern part of Israel in *considerable commercial quantities*. To me, that is very significant, because Ezekiel chapters 38 and 39 prophesy a coming invasion of the land of Israel by the armies of Gog and Magog, together with a group of confederate Middle-Eastern countries, and speak of those armies going up to that land with an evil thought in their mind 'to take a spoil' (Ezekiel 8:8–12). And the question has always been raised, 'What is this spoil?' If oil has now indeed been discovered in Israel in commercial quantities, that would provide at least part of the answer! The Soviet Union happens to be fast running short of oil and latest reports state that she will soon be in serious trouble in this respect. Since these chapters of Ezekiel state quite clearly that Gog and Magog are located in the most northern regions of the world, which is where the Soviet Union and the Warsaw Pact countries are situated when viewed geographically from Israel itself, this news that oil has been discovered in such quantities in Israel should serve to emphasise how near we are to seeing these prophecies being fulfilled. Especially is this so when it is already known in NATO circles that part of the Soviet Union's strategy in preparation for taking over the whole of Western Europe would be to seize all Middle-Eastern oil supplies and thus bring western and American industry, together with their armies, navies and air forces, to a grinding halt. The West would then have no alternative left but to surrender or 'come to terms'.

The second item which the *Jewish Chronicle* reported was that senior rabbis in Israel were now spending a great deal of time studying what should be the content of the temple services and ceremonies. This immediately raises the question as to whether these rabbis envisage the temple being rebuilt in some foreseeable future? If so, this also would be in line with those Old Testament prophecies. For several prophecies, and particularly Ezekiel 40–48, speak of a time when the temple in Jerusalem *will* be rebuilt. The studies by the rabbis are thus very significant.

The third item in the *Chronicle* was a report to the effect that 'an increasing number in Israel today are talking about the Messiah'. The same report stated that 'it is believed very strongly in Israel today, that the only answer to Israel's problems today, and the only answer to the world's problems today, is for the Messiah to come.' It is the *Jewish Chronicle*, which is saying this, not the Christian press! The paper admits that nobody in Israel who holds this strong belief or is talking in this way, knows who the Messiah is! Certainly they do not have in mind Jesus of Nazareth, now the enthroned Lord of glory, who is soon to come the second time.

It is very interesting that the *Jewish Chronicle* of all papers, should report that it is strongly believed in Israel today that the only answer to Israel's and the world's problems is for the Messiah to come. For if many is Israel believe that so strongly, then surely the time has come when somebody like Paul the apostle should go into the synagogues and into the streets all over Israel, and proclaim boldly: 'Jesus of Nazareth is the Messiah'. That was Paul's message to the Jews. That is the message that needs to be proclaimed throughout Israel *now*.

As the Jews were about to celebrate the seventeenth anniversary of the reunification of Jerusalem, during the week commencing 25 May 1984, the *Jewish Chronicle* actually published an article which discussed 'The Feasibility of Rebuilding the Temple'. At the top of this article was an aerial view of the temple platform in Jerusalem, pointing out possible ways in which this could be done without offending the Arabs! This was going much further than studying what the content of the temple ceremonies and services should be!

All these reports inevitably raise the question: How near are we to the greatest event which has yet to take place in the history of the world—the personal and long-promised return in glory of our Lord Jesus Christ, the Messiah?

The answer surely must be that we are far nearer than we think! So I believe that there is an urgent need to set Britain's desperate situation today against these momentous events which are happening in Israel and other Middle-Eastern countries, and also against all that we see happening on the global scale. I consider it is even more urgent to do so, when all the evidence gleaned from the Bible shows that it is an indisputable fact that Britain has indeed gone as far away from God, if not further, than wicked Manasseh's nation went; that she has therefore passed the point of no return; has aroused God's fierce anger against her; and, in consequence, a fearful and irrevocable judgment of God has already been pronounced.

All the evidence from the Bible, and from events today, suggest that world history has turned full circle to what it was, and to where it was heading, in Jeremiah's day. There are some most interesting similarities and parallels that we need to consider.

For instance, when wicked Manasseh and his nation went as far as they did, the Lord began to speak through his prophets to warn the people of what was to come in judgment. And at the time that their message began to be sounded forth, the signs of that judgment were already on the horizon, with the growing armies of the then king of the north. The same is true today.

God, in fact, said to Jeremiah, 'Out of the north an evil shall break forth upon all the inhabitants of the land' (Jeremiah 1:14). God even said to him, 'I have purposed it, and will not repent, neither will I turn back from it' (Jeremiah 4:28). This was because they had gone too far in their sin and iniquity. And when God said that, it needs to be understood that it was a *good twenty-two years* before that terrible judgment was finally to fall. In fact, the original pronouncement that the judgment was coming 'out of the north' was the beginning of a whole series of pronouncements of irrevocable judgment which God was to make upon that nation during those twenty-two years.

God made the coming judgment quite specific when he said in chapter 1:15, 'For, lo, I will call all the families of the kingdoms of the north, saith the Lord; and they shall come'. God says, '*I* will call'. So it needs to be clearly realized, in a day when the events related in the book of Jeremiah look like being re-enacted, that when God calls for such 'families of the kingdoms' to come, they have to come. They have no alternative. And does the phrase 'all the families of the kingdoms of the north' speak to the people of Britain and of the western world today of the Warsaw Pact countries, I wonder?

In Jeremiah 1, the form of judgment was already divinely decreed. Then in chapter 4 it had begun to move forward towards them: 'The lion is come up from his thicket, and the destroyer of the Gentiles is on his way (4:7).

Therefore they needed to sound the alarm in the nation—to blow the trumpet in the land; to man the defences (4:5, 6)! By verse 13 of that same chapter it is coming as swiftly as a whirlwind. 'Behold, he shall come up as clouds, and his chariots shall be as a whirlwind: his horses are swifter than eagles' (4:13).

So it is an army with chariots which is advancing at lightning speed. And it is worthy of note that General Walker has warned us that once the present-day armies of the north begin to roll forward, they would advance at the rate of seventy miles per day, which, so far as Western Europe is concerned, would bring them to the Rhine in less than forty-eight hours and to the Channel ports in less than a week. [1]

Jeremiah 4:11–13 describes the oncoming judgment as a person. '*He* shall come up as clouds'. It is a person with chariots and horses; a person with an army; and with a massive army. By chapter 8, the army is at the very northern borders of the nation. Verse 16 says very graphically, 'The snorting of his horses was heard from Dan: the whole land trembled at the sound of the neighing of his strong ones.' Dan is on the northernmost border of Israel, as John o' Groats is on ours. The reason for the coming onslaught of this massive army has already been given in chapter 4:18, 'Thy way and thy doings have procured these things unto thee; this is thy wickedness'. So let Britain and the western world beware, today! By chapter 13 the enemy is so near that he can actually be seen. Verse 20 says 'Lift up your eyes, and *behold* them that come from the north'. And verse 21, 'What wilt thou say when he shall punish thee?' You cannot 'behold' them unless they are in sight, can you?

It is not until chapter 20 that these massive oncoming armies are identified as the King of Babylon's. By chapter 21, they are at the very walls of the capital, Jerusalem, besieging it. And by chapter 39, the capital has fallen. The city walls have been broken down. Its houses and palaces have been burnt with fire, and the greater part of the inhabitants of the land have been taken away into captivity, with only the very poorest of the land left behind.

So the irrevocable judgment which God had pronounced, well over twenty-two years before, had finally fallen. It had all happened exactly as God had said it would, so Jeremiah said: 'what thou has spoken is come to pass; and, behold, thou seest it' (Jeremiah 32:24). He said again in Lamentations 2:17: 'The Lord hath done that which he had devised; he hath fulfilled his word that he had commanded in the days of old.'

The consequence was that the whole world was stunned and completely shaken by what had happened. For we read in Lamentations 4:11,12: 'The Lord hath accomplished his fury; he hath poured out his fierce anger, and hath kindled a fire in Zion, and it hath devoured the foundations thereof. *The kings of the earth, and all the inhabitants of the world, would not have believed* that the adversary and the enemy should have entered into the gates of Jerusalem'!

Will they be saying that of London, one day, I wonder?

A 'Book of Jeremiah' situation means, therefore, to have gone beyond the point of no return, and thus to have aroused God's fierce anger against the nation. It means that, in consequence, an irrevocable and irreversible judgment of God has had to be pronounced; that God has already prepared his instrument of judgment; and that the instrument of judgment could well be the armies of a rising and menacing super power. It means that, for years, warning after warning has been pronounced through God's servants the prophets; that those warnings have gone totally unheeded; and that when sin and iniquity have come to a head, the judgment of God will inevitably fall.

It means, *today*, that judgment on an individual nation such as Britain, or upon the western world, could well be visited in the context of a world-wide judgment on the nations, because we are living so near to 'the time of the end'. It means that the judgment, when it comes, will take place exactly as God has said it would, and that it will be total.

It means that judgment today could occur as a fulfilment of the Old Testament prophecies which predict that God's judgment on all the Gentile nations will take place in the context of the armies of the north rolling forward at lightning speed to invade the land of Israel and other Middle-Eastern countries in a kind of repetition of what took place in Jeremiah's day. Only this time, God himself will intervene on Israel's behalf with a mighty earthquake, great hailstones, fire, brimstone, and other terrible phenomena, which will devastate those northern armies completely on the mountains of Israel. God will also intervene with nothing less than the personal return of the Lord Jesus Christ on the Mount of Olives. A new age will then be ushered in—the Messianic Age.

So it needs to be stated very emphatically that God *is* indeed going to 'call all the families of the kingdoms of the north' at some stage soon, 'and they shall come'. And that is when there will be a re-enactment of what happened in Jeremiah's time. This time the armies will come like a storm, not from Babylon, but from the regions to the extreme north. For Ezekiel chapters 38 and 39 say that 'in the latter years' and in the 'latter days' God will say to the heads of these armies, 'I will... put hooks into thy jaws, and I will bring thee forth, and all thine army... and thou shalt come from thy place out of the north parts, thou, and many people with thee... a great company, and a mighty army: and thou shalt come up against my people of Israel, as a cloud to cover the land... it shall be *in the latter days*, and I will bring thee against my land, [Israel] that the heathen may know me, when I shall be sanctified in thee, O

Gog, before their eyes.'

God says repeatedly, 'I will do this'. *He* will put hooks into [their] jaws and bring [them]...and they shall come from [their] place out of the north parts. God even refers to this person called Gog as, 'he of whom I have spoken in old time by my servants the prophets of Israel, which prophesied in those days many years that I would bring thee against them' (Ezekiel 38:17). So it is bound to happen. It is divinely decreed. Jeremiah, Isaiah, Ezekiel and other Old Testament prophets all speak of this forthcoming event in terms of a world-wide judgment of God on the nations. They refer to it as the time when God 'will call for a sword upon *all* the inhabitants of the earth' (Jeremiah 25:29).

It seems from these prophesies, therefore, that *all the nations of the world* will be involved. As Jeremiah 25:30–33 goes on to say: 'Therefore prophesy thou against them all these words, and say unto them, the Lord shall roar from on high, and utter his voice from his holy habitation; he shall give a shout... *against all the inhabitants of the earth*'. Again: 'A noise shall come even to the ends of the earth; *for the Lord hath a controversy with the nations*, he will plead *with all flesh*; he will give them that are wicked to the sword'. And yet again: 'For thus saith the Lord of hosts, Behold, evil shall go forth *from nation to nation*, and a great whirlwind shall be raised up from the coasts of the earth. And the slain of the Lord shall be at that day *from one end of the earth even unto the other end of the earth*: they shall not be lamented, neither gathered, nor buried; they shall be dung upon the ground.' It happened in Jeremiah's day on this world-wide scale as the massive armies of the then king of the north and of the huge Babylonian Empire swept forward from the far distant horizon, over-running and taking over country after country, heading towards Israel and Jerusalem. And many of the prophetic Scriptures indicate that the same kind of thing will be repeated in these latter days by another great world empire centred far further north.

'But', someone may say, 'if it is true that Britain today has plunged herself into a "Book of Jeremiah" situation by going far further away from God in its extreme wickedness than the nation of Judah went under the notoriously wicked Manasseh, and if it is true that the point where she finally passed the point of no return was when her Parliament passed the United Kingdom Abortion Act on to her statute book, thus causing her to become an extremely blood-guilty nation, the passing of that Abortion Act was as long ago as 1967, and nothing by way of an irrevocable divine judgment has happened since then!'

To such an objection I would reply that it was precisely in the year 1967 that the Soviet Union began to make a very significant move forward on NATO's northern front in Europe under cover of the Six Day War in the Middle East. It was in that year that Russia began to push out her naval defence line towards the Greenland-Iceland-Faeroes Gap. In fact, it was at this time that General Walker first began to issue his warnings of the dangers of the massive Soviet build-up and of their intentions, from NATO's northern headquarters in Norway.

We have already noticed that it was some twenty-two years between the time when God first called Jeremiah to proclaim, 'Out of the north an evil shall come', and the point when judgment finally fell. On the basis of a twenty-two year measurement from 1967, we have got four years to go at the most, if we are to be guided in any way by the same time-scale as applied in the book of Jeremiah.

It *could* be said to be true that the time at which Britain passed the point of no return in her wickedness was when she introduced the permissive society and when her Parliament legalized sin. That particular trend had already set in by about 1945, which would mean that our time has already run out! For a study of the Scriptures will show that the time between God's *first* pronouncement of an irrevocable coming judgment on wicked King Manasseh and his nation, and the time when that judgment finally fell, was a good forty years. Throughout that long period, prophet after prophet—long before Jeremiah—was sent by God to warn that judgment was coming.

Let us now, therefore, consider some of the interesting parallels which arise.

Notes

1. See *The Trumpet Sounds for Britain*, Volume 1, pp.105,106.

Chapter Seventeen

Jeremiah Speaks Today

At the time when the wicked Manasseh forsook the Lord, did a U-turn, and proceeded to reverse his father's reformation, the instrument which God was preparing for his nation's judgment was already in existence—the rising and expanding Babylonian Empire.

The same was true in relation to Britain and the West between the years 1945 and 1950, which was approximately the time when we forsook God, overthrew our Christian heritage, placed anti-God and anti-Christian laws on to our statute book and began to reverse our own Reformation. Britain's catastrophical moral and spiritual landslide stemmed from that point, and the instrument which God was preparing for our judgment, was already there. The Russian armies had overrun Poland during their advance on the German armies at the end of the Second World War, and had occupied East Berlin and other areas of Eastern Europe.

In the case of Judah, by the time Jeremiah came on to the scene and pronounced his prophecy, 'Out of the north an evil shall break forth'—which was roughly fifteen years after the wicked King Manasseh's death—the ingredients of the coming irrevocable judgment were already presenting a serious threat.

And for Britain, as we have seen, the ingredients of judgment were already *on the horizon*, in the year when Parliament passed the United Kingdom Abortion Act. The threat to Britain and the West from the Soviet and Warsaw Pact build-up had, in fact, been seriously developing from 1945 onwards; but now, in 1967, came that significant shift. By October 1968, the British press announced that Russia's aim was to estabish a socialist commonwealth or empire, so the threat of territorial expansion was present. The first permanent Russian naval replenishment anchorage for the North Atlantic was established off the Shetlands, as Russia began to push out her naval defence lines from Murmansk.

In 1969 *A Warning to the Nation* was first published and eventually went into 120,000 copies. The booklet is still very much in demand, so the warning is still going out. From that point onwards, things began to escalate alarmingly almost year by year, as they did almost chapter by chapter in the Book of Jeremiah, and the threat drew nearer and nearer.

In 1970, for instance, Norway reached the conclusion that 'it is the intention of the Soviets to push their naval defence line outwards to Iceland and the Faeroes', thus establishing 'a barrier at sea' with the intention of blocking the Greenland - Iceland - Faeroes Gap right through to the northernmost point of the United Kingdom, and with the occupation of Norway in mind. The Norwegians know that the Soviets are seeking a world empire, and Norway stands in the way of their achieving that. So they see the occupation of Norway as essential to the Soviets, if ever the latter are to achieve their aim.

Two years later, in 1972, the First Sea Lord gave his warning that, 'Never has the Soviet activity round the shores of Scotland been so great. In 1973 came Air Commander Donaldson's warning that 'Russian warships, from large cruisers to destroyers, are seen constantly in the Icelandic Gap keeping their eyes on allied naval movements.'

During 1975, there were no less than 110 separate occasions when formation flights of Soviet warplanes were made to within a few miles of Danish territory, and the following year these flights increased and escalated considerably.

In 1976, a series of Soviet amphibious exercises began, with ships laden with tanks and troops sailing from the Baltic to Murmansk on the one hand, whilst others, similarly laden, sailed from Murmansk to the Baltic, thus outflanking Norway at sea. The aim, according to the opinion of the Danish Government, was 'to overrun Denmark', and General Walker issued his warning, 'Never has the situation in Europe been so grave. The Free World stands today in greater peril than at any time since World War II.' God was therefore warning through the voice of a *military* prophet, as he was constantly warning through prophets in Jeremiah's day.

Less than a year later, in July 1977, Soviet and Warsaw Pact forces engaged in the most massive amphibious exercises ever held in the Baltic, their sea-forces including cruisers, heavier ships, and large numbers of landing craft. So the threat was now getting very ominous indeed.

All the time, from 1969 onwards, Soviet nuclear-firing submarines have been sailing out from Murmansk, heading in the direction of the United States, to station themselves along the entire length of America's Atlantic and Pacific coasts, thus 'ringing' the United States and bringing 95 per cent of her population and industrial centres within range. In May 1975, the Kremlin announced that those nuclear-firing submarines had been increased in number. Meanwhile, Delta-type Soviet submarines can achieve the same results from their home waters in the Barents Sea.

Over Christmas 1979, alarm bells were set ringing all over Western Europe and the free world by Russia's sudden military occupation of Afghanistan. They were set off again in February 1981, when the Soviet Union doubled the rate at which it was installing SS20 multi-warhead nuclear missiles in Eastern Europe, bringing the total at that time to

200 targetted on Britain and other Western European countries. These have recently been increased.

The West was suddenly caused to hold its breath when, on 2 April 1984, the national press dramatically announced that a giant Russian armada had suddenly put to sea, but the press didn't know what for! One fleet was sailing from the Baltic, whilst another equally massive one was sailing from Murmansk to link up in the Iceland - Faeroes - United Kingdom Gap. The sudden sailing of this huge Soviet armada had apparently taken NATO by surprise!

With well-nigh two-thirds of the world now under communist domination, and with Soviet naval units stationed off, and under, all the major sea and ocean routes of the world, and with General Walker's book, *The Next Domino?*,[1] stating that 'The Russian programme for global domination is on schedule, and in the military sphere is moving towards the point of no return', who can say that the threat is not world-wide as it was in Jeremiah's day, and that all the nations of the world are not going to be involved as they were then? It raises the question: 'How near must the final move be?'

Dr Billy Graham is warning us now that the scientists are predicting that the final catastrophe will take place before the year 2000. We are nearer to the brink than we think. There can be no question, either, of Britain not being in a 'Book of Jeremiah' situation. If further evidence is needed, just consider the following statements, all gathered from the book of Jeremiah, concerning the condition of the nation of Judah, and compare them with the condition of our own nation now:

Chapter 2, v.5 They had gone far away from God; so have we.

vv.6,7 Nobody among them said, 'Where is the Lord that brought us up out of the land of Egypt, that led us through the wilderness, [and brought us] into a plentiful country'.

Not even the priests said, 'Where is the Lord?' And isn't this true of Britain today? No one in these days of serious trouble says, 'Where is the Lord that wrought the mighty miracles at Dunkirk; that saved us from invasion during the Battle of Britain; that brought us through the whole of the 1939–45 War; and gave us victory in Europe after D-Day?' Not even archbishops, bishops, clergy and Free Church pastors and ministers say, 'Where is *that* Lord, now?' What he did *then*, has all been conveniently forgotten, and he is certainly not appealed to by our national and church leaders to work miracles for us now.

Indeed, no mention whatsoever was made of any of these miracles during the VE Day Thanksgiving Service held in Westminster Abbey on 8 May 1985. The part that *God* played during the 1939–45 War did not even enter into the proceedings.

v.13 They had forsaken God; so have we.

v.27 They had turned their backs on God; so have we.

v.31 They said, '*We* are lords; we will come no more unto thee'. And that is what the national leaders of Britain are saying. '*We* are lords; *we* are the bosses; *we* are in charge; *we* can manage our own affairs, thank you very much. We don't need God anymore. We won't come any more to him for help.'

v.32 They had forgotten God; so have we.

Chapter 5, v.3 They had refused to receive correction; so have we.

v.6a Their transgressions were many; and so are ours.

v.6b Their backslidings had increased; and so have ours.

v.7 In consequence, their children, their offspring, had forsaken God; so have ours.

vv.7,8 This description could just as easily be applied today, 'When I had fed them to the full, then they committed adultery, and assembled themselves by troops in the harlots' houses. They were as fed horses in the morning: every one neighed after his neighbour's wife'. We, too have become an extremely adulterous nation. Britain has probably never been better fed in the whole of her history. Look at the well-stocked shelves in all our supermarkets. This is the *Lord* feeding Britain, as in Jeremiah's day. *He* feeds them. Yet Britain has, perhaps, never been more adulterous. Her daily newspapers testify to this fact, as do adulterous scandals amongst MPs and even Cabinet minsters.

v.9 Jeremiah warned; 'Shall I not visit for these things? saith the Lord; and shall not my soul be avenged on such a nation as this?' And by 'visit', he means visit in judgment. So it is not anymore a question of 'How can God pardon?' He cannot. He must now visit in judgment.

v.27 Many of them had become rich by deceitful means; and so have many in Britain today.

v.28 They overpassed the deeds of the wicked. And is not even this, happening, in our law courts today? So many are 'getting away with it'—in some cases, because the prisons are already over-crowded! And for the same reason the tendency is to lessen prison sentences. Certainly the deeds of the wicked are being overpassed in our schools and colleges, on the basis that we must not punish people anymore!

v.29 The warning continues, 'Shall I not visit for these things? saith the Lord: Shall not my soul be avenged on such a nation as this?' And the same God would put the same question to Britain today, and give the same answer, 'How shall I pardon thee, Britain, for this? Shall I not visit for these things, saith the Lord; and shall not my soul be avenged on such a nation as this?'

Chapter 6, v.16 God said to them, 'Thus saith the Lord, stand ye in the ways, and see, and ask for the old paths, where is the good way, and walk therein, and ye shall find rest for your souls'. But they said, 'We will not walk therein'. Which is exactly what the people of Britain are saying today.

v.17 God said to them, 'Also I set watchmen over you, saying, Hearken to the sound of the trumpet'. But they said, 'We will not hearken'. Again, this is precisely what the leaders and people of Britain are saying today.

Chapter 7, v.3 God even said to them, 'Thus saith the Lord of hosts, the God of Israel, Amend your ways and your doings, and I will cause you to dwell in this place', but they refused to listen or to respond. That also is what the leaders and people of Britain are doing.

v.10 God said to them, 'Are you going to come before me and say We were delivered to do all these abominations?' And God would say the same to the British people today. 'Were you delivered in 1939–45 to do all these evil things?' The answer is No—most emphatically, No.

v.16 Eventually God had to say to Jeremiah, 'Therefore pray not thou for this people, neither lift up, cry nor prayer for them, neither make intercession to me: for I will not hear thee' (see also 11:4 11–12).

Chapter 8, v.5a Theirs was a perpetual backsliding; and so is ours.

v.5b They refused to return; and so do we—despite much pleading.

v.6 They would not acknowledge their sin, 'No man repented him of his wickedness: saying What have I done?' This also is very much the condition of Britain's people today.

v.10 They had become a covetous nation in the extreme. 'Every one from the least even unto the greatest is given to covetousness'. And so have we. The more we have in Britain, the more we want.

v.12 'They were not at all ashamed, neither could they blush' when they had committed abomination. This is certainly the people of Britain's condition today. Murders, violence, rapes, robberies and such like were commonplace. The references to them abound. And so are they in Britain. These things are all part of everyday life in our nation now. *Their* sin was greater than that of Sodom, therefore their punishment was greater, (see Lamentations 4:6). So is *ours* greater. So will *our* punishment be greater.

Chapter 9 vv. 2–8 Few amongst them could be trusted. They had become a nation of liars. they even refused to speak the truth. And they were deceitful in every way, and full of 'sharp' and 'shady' practices. And isn't this true of Britain: in industry and commerce, in shops and offices, and even in families? Swindles, lies, sharp practices and deceit are on every side. Honesty, uprightness and truthfulness have long gone from us.
v.3 They proceeded from evil to evil; so have we.

Chapter 11, v.13 They had as many gods as they had cities; and so have we.
v.14 God told Jeremiah, a second time, 'Therefore, pray not thou for this people, neither lift up a cry or prayer for them: for I will not hear them in the time that they cry unto me for their trouble' (see also 7:6 and 14;11–12).

Chapter 14, v.10 'They [had] loved to wander, they [had] not refrained their feet', therefore the Lord did not accept them. He said he would now remember their iniquity, and visit their sins. That is our condition also.
v.11–12 For the third time, and even more strongly than before, God told Jeremiah, 'Pray not for this people for their good. When they fast, I will not hear their cry; and when they offer burnt offering and oblation, I will not accept them: but I will consume them by the sword, and by the famine, and by the pestilence' (see also 7:6 and 11:14). This was because they really had gone beyond the point of no return as a nation, both morally and spiritually. And I am obliged to ask if God is now saying, 'Pray not for Britain today' I fear he might be.

v.13 But there were false prophets and false pastors in those days. Therefore Jeremiah had to say, 'Ah, Lord God! behold the prophets say unto the people, Ye shall not see the sword—neither shall ye have famine: but I will give you assured peace in this place'. In other words, they were saying, 'All this can't happen to you.' Unhappily, there are plenty of false prophets and false pastors in Britain today who are saying the same thing. They even prophesy airy-fairy dreams.

Chapter 15, v.6 They have gone backward; so have we.

Chapter 17, vv.19–23, 27 They had been breaking and profaning the Sabbaths for a very long time. And so have we, in Britain, for years now. And Sabbath breaking is on the increase everywhere. On 21 May 1985, the House of Commons voted to take note of the Auld Report (which recommended the removal of restrictions on Sunday trading), and to look forward to the Government bringing forward the necessary legislation. The Debate caused the Press to say: 'Government favours mammon rather than God.'

Chapter 18, v.11 God still offered them the opportunity to repent, he even said, 'Thus saith the Lord, Behold I frame evil against you, and devise a device against you: *return* ye now, *every one* from his evil way: and make your ways and your doings good'.
v.12 But they said; 'There is no hope: but we will walk after our *own* devices, and we will every one do the imagination of his evil heart'. And I fear that that is exactly the attitude of many of Britain's leaders and people.

Chapter 19, v.15 They had 'hardened their necks, that they might not hear [God's] words; so have we.

Chapter 23, God had strong words, too, for the false prophets, pastors and teachers of Jeremiah's Day who were condemned as 'ye who have perverted the words of the living God' (v.36). There is plenty of that going on in Britain's churches today, in almost every denomination—the perversion of the word of God! They were also charged with causing 'my people...to err' by 'their lies and by their lightness' (vv.13, 32). And isn't 'lightness' in services and sermons the main modern trend today? Entertainment is the cry of the hour. God said of the false teachers in those days 'from the prophets of Jerusalem is profaneness gone forth into all the land' (v.15). How very true this is of Britain, including profanity going forth into the land in the name of Christianity and of religion by means of television and radio.

God said of that nation in those days, 'Their pastors are become brutish, and have not sought the Lord' (Jeremiah 10:21). And both these things can be said of many a pastor in Britain. How many of them, for instance, have really sought the Lord concerning all the troubles our country has been in? I fear the answer is not many. God said of them also, 'They commit adultery, walk in lies, strengthen the hands of evil-doers, that none return from his wickedness' (v.14). And surely the acid test, in the sight of God, of all pastors, ministers, clergy, bishops and archbishops today is whether, as a result of their ministry, there are those who are returning from their wickedness. We don't see it happening in Britain, do we?

So God said in Jeremiah's day, that he was 'against' the pastors: 'Behold I will visit upon you the evil of your doings' (23:2); 'both prophet and priest are profane' (v.11); 'behold I am *against* the prophets' (v.31); 'behold I am *against* them that prophesy false dreams, saith the Lord, and do tell them, and cause my people to err by their lies, and by their lightness; yet I sent them not, nor commanded them' (v.32); God was *against* those who said 'the Lord hath said, Ye shall have peace; and...No evil shall come upon you' (v.17). He made it perfectly plain that all such false prophets, priests, pastors, and teachers would be caught up in the coming judgment. And the same will be true of all false pastors, teachers, ministers, clergy, bishops and archbishops today. They will all be under judgment.

Here, then, are the indictments which God made against that nation in Jeremiah's day, and one is forced to admit that their similarities and parallels with the present condition of Britain are striking in the extreme. It is abundantly clear, therefore, that we, as a nation, are in a 'Book of Jeremiah' situation. There is no escaping from it.

All down the years that God was making these indictments, he was interspersing them with his warnings of the coming judgment at the hands of the on-coming, and fast approaching, armies of the then king of the north, and to the rest of the world as well. And God has been doing that, in Britain's case today, ever since 1967, and even earlier.

Note

1. General Sir Walter Walker, *The Next Domino?* Covenant Books, London 1980.

Chapter Eighteen

Point of no Return?

What, then, is the burden of the message for Britain? It is being suggested that the urgent need is to pray for revival—and I couldn't agree more.

The most urgent need today, is for God's people not just to pray for, but to cry out to heaven for, a mighty visitation of the Holy Spirit upon our country, and particularly upon our churches. This applies to the western world as a whole, including America. I am utterly convinced that there is now nothing that will turn the tide and reverse the trend but *that* kind of mighty intervention of God.

Evangelism won't do it any more. Preaching *by itself* won't do it any more. Neither will such large-scale efforts as Mission England and Mission to London, in and of themselves. Oh! yes. They will result in many conversions. There is no doubt whatsoever about that. But they will not, *by themselves*, reverse the trend or turn the tide. Only a mighty, heaven-sent Holy Spirit revival will do that—an act of God, without any man being involved. In fact, I am seriously beginning to wonder whether Billy Graham's large-scale preaching in England and Luis Palau's Mission to London are not the last great harvesting of souls in England before the return of Our Lord Jesus Christ takes place. However that might be, a heaven-sent, Holy Spirit revival is the only thing that will turn the tide in Britain and the western world.

When I talk about 'revival', I am not talking about 'renewal'. I am not talking about something which does not change people's direction or habits or outlook, radically. I am not talking about something that does not change the beliefs which people may hold and which do not agree with the Bible, or that will leave them still maintaining erroneous and false teaching and practices. I am not talking about something superficial. 'Revival' is quite different from 'renewal'; it is much more deep-seated and radical. When I talk about 'revival' I am talking about *God* coming down in such mighty power, and with such an overwhelming and awesome sense of his presence for miles around, that men, women, children and young people everywhere are so convicted of sin by this awesome sense of the presence of God around them, that they fall on their faces by their hundreds and by their thousands and cry out to God for mercy.

I am talking about such a visitation of the Holy Spirit upon our churches, upon their ministers and pastors, upon Christian workers of every description, and upon every true Christian believer everywhere, that they become anointed and infused with new life from God; that they indeed become vibrant with new life—with Holy Spirit Life. I cannot emphasize strongly enough that true Christians everywhere in these latter days all need to be endued with power from on high. Indeed, when Jesus issued his commission to his first disciples to 'Go...into all the world, and preach the Gospel to every creature', he made it abundantly plain that it is an indispensable necessity, before anybody can do this, that they be endued with power from on high (see Luke 24:49). True believers everywhere need to be filled with power by the Spirit of the Lord, as was John the Baptist, and as were the 120 in the Upper Room in Jerusalem, and as were the prophets of old, to declare to Britain her transgressions, and to the British people their sin, and to do that all over the free world as well.

It is not enough just to be Christians, or true believers in these latter days. We all need to be full of the fire of God. I repeat, only a mighty intervention of God in terms of such a heaven-sent, Holy Spirit revival—God coming down amongst us, and upon us, in mighty power in answer to his people's cry—can save our nation and the Free World now.

But suppose we *have* passed the point of no return both spiritually and morally? What then? Supposing God *is* saying, 'Pray not for this people'? Well, I am afraid such a revival will not stop the irrevocable judgment from coming, however many blessings it may bring. It did not stop judgment in godly king Josiah's day, after he eventually replaced wicked Manasseh, even though, for eighteen years, he devoted himself with tremendous zeal to sweeping out of his entire nation, and out of the northern kingdom of Israel, everything that was offensive to God and which provoked God to anger; nor even when he was used of God to bring about such a tremendous religious reform that it was tantamount to a nationwide spiritual revival.

For despite the finding of the Book of the Law in the temple; despite the fact that the young king, in his fiery and fervent zeal for God, commanded the priests to bring out everything that was idolatrous in the temple and ruthlessly burn it outside Jerusalem, thus completely to cleanse the temple; despite his clean sweep of all the offending heathen idols and images which were littering the land; despite the fact that he utterly put away the workers with familiar spirits, the mediums, the wizards, and everything to do with the occult; despite the fact that he held such a Passover to the Lord his God as had never before been held from the days of the judges onwards; and even despite the fact that God said of this godly young king, 'Like unto him was there no king before him, that turned to the Lord with all his heart, and with all his soul, and with all his might, according to the law of Moses; neither after him arose there any like him' (2 Kings 23:25). Despite all that, the judgment which

God had already pronounced on his predecessor, Manasseh, and on his nation, several years before, was not prevented from coming.

That judgment still remained irrevocable and irreversible. God even said, 'Notwithstanding [all that the godly king Josiah did] the Lord turned not from the fierceness of his great wrath, wherewith his anger was kindled against Judah, *because of all the provocations that Manasseh had provoked him withal*' (2 Kings 23:26,27); 'and also for the innocent blood that he shed: for he filled Jerusalem with innocent blood; *which the Lord would not pardon*' (2 Kings 24:4).

In other words, God said that despite all that King Josiah had done, and despite all that he was, the judgment which he had pronounced on Manasseh's kingdom well over fifteen years before, was still coming. It was on its way. God said it would not come upon King Josiah himself, or during his reign, because his heart was tender, but it would come, nevertheless, at a later time.

So what hope has Britain or the western world of a mighty revival stopping any irrevocable judgment from coming, if they, in their turn, have passed the point of no return? None whatsoever, I would suggest. We read in Jeremiah that, for those eighteen years during which Josiah was ruthlessly purging his nation of everything that was evil, and whilst he was engaged in bringing about a great spiritual reformation and revival, God was continually sending his prophets to the people, crying, 'Turn from your evil ways'. But they would not hear.

Jeremiah and the others were doing so for a good ten years; but always with the same adamant response. The people would not listen, neither would they turn. For we read that Jeremiah himself said to the people of Judah and to the inhabitants of Jerusalem, 'From the thirteenth year of Josiah the son of Amon king of Judah, even unto this day, that is the three and twentieth year [which is ten years], the word of the Lord hath come unto me, and I have spoken unto you, rising early and speaking; *but ye have not hearkened*. And the Lord hath sent unto you *all* His servants the prophets, rising early and sending them; *but ye have not hearkened, nor inclined your ear to hear*. They said, *Turn ye again now* every one from his evil way, and from the evil of your doings...Yet ye have not hearkened unto me, saith the Lord' (Jeremiah 25:3–7). As we read those words, we should note that (according to Jeremiah 1) it was from that thirteenth year of King Josiah that God told Jeremiah to proclaim, 'Out of the north an evil shall break forth...For, lo, I will call all the families of the kingdoms of the north, saith the Lord, and they shall come.'

It is very revealing to note, in this connection, that it was when the Soviet Union was beginning to become a major threat to the western world that God first sent Billy Graham to this country. Since then, he has conducted several crusades, as well as those led by Tom Rees, Dick Saunders, Eric Hutchings, Don Summers, Luis Palau, and others. So during at least thirty-four years, God has been sending his prophets to Britain, whilst the threat has been increasing!

We read, too, that during those eighteen years whilst King Josiah was cleansing his land of evil, Jeremiah was proclaiming, 'Thus saith the Lord of hosts, the God of Israel, Amend your ways and your doings' (Jeremiah 7:3). But they would not. He proclaimed, 'Thus saith the Lord... ask for the old paths, where is the good way, and walk therein, and ye shall find rest for your souls. But they said, We will not walk therein' (Jeremiah 6:16). Jeremiah also proclaimed that the Lord had said 'I [have] set watchmen over you, saying, Hearken to the sound of the trumpet [warning you that Judgment is coming]. But they said, We will *not* hearken' (Jeremiah 6:17).

Isn't all this exactly the attitude of Britain and of her people today? They proudly and confidently say, 'Oh, It will never happen to us'! 'We are British!' They shut their ears to preaching, saying, 'This is not my scene'! They just don't want to know.

We are truly in a 'Book of Jeremiah' situation in Britain today. There is nothing left for it, but to say that when you have got this kind of stiff-necked situation, another kind of intervention of God can be expected—not one of revival, but one of judgment.

When the world was so wicked just before the Flood, and before the destruction of abominably sinful Sodom and Gomorrah—in both these cases, Almighty God decided that a revival was not what was needed. He saw that he must judge, punish, destroy and wipe out, because that was the only way that sin and iniquity could be purged. Wickedness had gone too far. It had got completely out of bounds. It had passed the point of no return. This, therefore, was the only way in which it could be removed.

Britain and the western world need to be told today, what was said of those people's behaviour then—that such gross sin and wickedness comes up before God and arouses his fierce anger. God's servants—his present day prophets and preachers—need also to be told today that because God is against such sin and such wickedness, he calls them to cry out against it, because something needs urgently to be done to turn that fierce anger away. That is the teaching of the Bible.

Britain and the western world, including the United States of America, need also to be told that God always has his appointed time when his judgment is due to fall, and in every case it is when iniquity has come to a head. That is an extremely sobering thought, especially when I hear people asking, 'Can Britain's iniquity get any worse?' The answer surely must be, 'It must have almost reached its peak by now.'

At the time immediately preceding the Flood, God told Noah that judgment would come within seven days of the day that he and his family had entered into the ark. In the case of Sodom and Gomorrah, God said its judgment would fall as soon as Lot had got safely away to the city of refuge. In the case of wicked Nineveh in the prophet Johah's day,

God told Jonah to proclaim in its streets that the city would be overthrown by a terrible destruction within the next forty days. And I tell you, in Britain's case, judgment could fall within a very short time, and without warning. I need to state most emphatically that it was at least three Christmasses ago when members of the British Army on the Rhine were saying, 'It is no longer a question of *if* the Soviet and Warsaw Pact Forces will begin to roll forward across Europe. It is only a question of *when*!'

The massive Russian naval exercises which took place during the first week of April 1984, and which took everybody, including NATO, completely by surprise, may have been but a major rehearsal of, and prelude to, the real thing. There will be no warning when the real day arrives.

An article which appeared in *The Times* on Wednesday, 22 May 1985 emphasised this further when it said that NATO defence ministers were meeting in Brussels and had before them 'a secret report, agreed by the top military commanders of all members of the Alliance [in which it was claimed that] "Soviet conventional forces will be able with hope of success to launch a full-scale surprise attack on NATO within fifteen years".' According to Frederick Bonnart, reporting from Brussels, a senior NATO military source added that 'Such an attack could follow "an ambiguous or very short warning", making it impossible for the Alliance to mobilise its forces in time.'

In any case, were one of the Old Testament prophets to emerge from the pages of the Bible today, his message most surely would be, 'Within a given period of time those forces *will*, indeed, begin to roll forward, because it is both predicted and divinely decreed in the Old Testament prophecies concerning the end of time, and in the book of Revelation.'

As Daniel 11:40 says, for instance, 'At the time of the end...the king of the north shall come...with chariots, and with horsemen, *and with many ships*; and he shall *enter into the countries*, and shall overflow and pass over' (The

203

language of widespread invasion, maybe of whole continents). 'He shall enter also into the glorious land [Israel], and *many countries shall be overthrown*: he shall stretch forth his hand also *upon the countries* (vv.41,42). And as Ezekiel 38: 14–16 says, 'Thus saith the Lord God [to Gog— the chief prince of Meshech and Tubal]...in that day when my people of Israel dwelleth safely...[*in the latter days*] thou shalt come from thy place *out of the north parts*, thou, and many people with thee, all of them riding upon horses, *a great company*, *and a mighty army*, and thou shalt come up against my people Israel, as a cloud to cover the land... and I will bring thee against my land, that the heathen may know me, when I shall be sanctified in thee, O Gog, before their eyes.'

What is that but 'the Lord calling for 'all the families of the kingdoms of the north' in these last days, 'and they shall come' (Jeremiah 1:15)? And who are 'all the families of the kingdoms of the north' today, but the Soviet Union and the Warsaw Pact countries? Notice too, the phrases 'a great company, and a mighty army' 'and with many ships'.

As we consider all this, what we need to realise is that the prophecies of Isaiah, Jeremiah and Ezekiel all indicate that when this happens in the latter days, it will happen on a world-wide scale, as it did in the days of Jeremiah, and in the context of a judgment of God upon the nations.

These mighty forces from the north will indeed suddenly roll forward and head in different directions. They would quickly overrun Europe, whilst at the same time keeping America at bay. They would then, no doubt, turn and head in the direction of the Mediteranean, assisted by their amphibious transport fleets and massive naval squadrons. Contingents of their armies would also come from another direction through Turkey and Cyprus, and no doubt through Greece. According to Ezekiel 38:5, Persian, Ethiopian and Libyan armies are to be numbered amongst these mighty, united, advancing hosts. And according to Revelation 9:13–16, a vast and innumerable army from the

Euphrates area will also be involved, so there would also be an advance through the Gulf. From all these directions, the armies would converge on Israel and Jerusalem as their ultimate objective, to be dealt with there by God, who will intervene supernaturally on Israel's behalf.

Britain would have to be neutralised in the very early stages of such an advance, if the sudden move forward across Europe were to be effective. So what if Britain then is still going against God, and still wilfully flying in his face? What if she resists those oncoming forces under such circumstances?

I am afraid the result would not be the same as it was between 1939 and 1945. Instead, the position would be like that in Jeremiah's day, when the armies of the then king of the north, the king of Babylon, were at the very gates of the capital, Jerusalem, and when King Zedekiah sent messengers to Jeremiah, saying, 'Enquire, I pray thee, of the Lord for us; for Nebuchadrezzar king of Babylon maketh war against us; if so be that the Lord will deal with us according to all his wondrous works, that he [the enemy] may go up from us' (Jeremiah 21:1,2). The answer today would be the same as God gave to Jeremiah, 'Thus saith the Lord God of Israel; Behold, I will turn back the weapons of war that are in your hands, wherewith ye fight against the king of Babylon, and against the Chaldeans which besiege you without the walls...and I myself will fight against you with an outstretched hand and with a strong arm, even in anger, and in fury, and in great wrath' (Jeremiah 21:4–5).

That is what happens when a nation is deliberately, wilfully and consistently going against God and refusing to have anything to do with him. God fights against that nation 'with an outstretched hand and with a strong arm, even in anger and in fury, and in great wrath'. He turns back the weapons of war that are in its hands. It is all part of the judgment. There would not *then* be miracles of deliverance, as there were at the time of Dunkirk and during the Battle of Britain. There would only be disaster. Almighty

God was fighting *with* us then. This time, he would be fighting *against* us. Woe betide us, as a nation! The clarion call should therefore be sounded out, right up to the last moment, even as those forces are rolling forward, and just as it was sounded out right up to the last moment by Jeremiah. Indeed that was the reason why, after his prophet had been faithfully sounding out the warning of a coming judgment by armies for twenty-two years or so, God wanted him now to place all that he had been proclaiming in a book, 'It may be', said the Lord, 'that the house of Judah will hear all the evil which I purpose to do unto them; that they may *return* every man, from his evil way; that I may forgive their iniquity and their sin' (Jeremiah 36:3). It *may* be that each and every man will return from his evil way, when he hears about the coming awful judgment. It was a message for each and every individual.

It was for the same reason that Jeremiah commanded his scribe, Baruch, to read to the people all that he had written: 'It may be they will present their supplication before the Lord, and will *return*, every one [every individual] from his evil way: for great is the anger and the fury that the Lord hath pronounced against this people' (Jeremiah 36:7).

No doubt it is for the selfsame reason that God wanted this book to be written, and then read by every person in Britain, so that all may turn from their evil ways while there is still time.

Chapter Nineteen

Send out the Message!

A few years ago, when General Sir Walter Walker was Commander-in-Chief Northern Europe, I noticed for the first time that he was raising his voice about the Soviet build-up which he could see taking place at such an alarming rate.

Seeing these reports in the press, I wrote to ask him if a copy of what he had said was available so that I could study it for myself. I also asked if he was likely to be coming to this country to say the same things as he had been saying on the Continent.

Then I added, 'We used to be called a race of lions; now we seem to have become a race of ostriches with our heads well and truly buried in the sand.... It seems to me that we are in an "Ezekiel chapter 33" situation, and what we need is a watchman to sound the trumpet and warn the people.... The soldier needs to warn militarily, the politician needs to warn politically, but *the preacher* needs to warn *spiritually*, and a study of Ezekiel 33 will leave us in no doubt whatsoever as to whose is the greater responsibility.'

I enclosed in my letter a copy of *A warning to the Nation*, which by this time had run into several editions, and which the Lord was causing to be circulated very widely throughout the country, and overseas. To my amazement, not very long afterwards, a fat envelope from the General arrived by post, containing a copy of an address which he had given on the Continent to all ranks—an address which lasted for no less than three hours, albeit with two breaks!

Three hours, please notice—not just a mere twenty minutes, which is often the most a preacher is allowed when delivering a challenging address during a church service. On each sheet of that address was stamped: 'Unclassified NATO Material'. And the General said in his covering letter, 'You have my permission to quote this wherever and whenever you want to.' He also thanked me for the booklet, which he had read, and said concerning it, 'I agree with every word you say'.

He went on in his letter to inform me that he was coming to Norwich on a particular day in the June of that year, and that he would be addressing a meeting there. He also gave me the address of a brigadier with whom I could get in touch for all the details. So on the given date I made my way to Norwich, believing it was of the Lord that I should be there.

When I got to the doorway of the public hall where the meeting was being held, his staff officer was out in the foyer welcoming people. On seeing me, he said, 'Is this the Reverend David Gardner?' I hadn't a clerical collar on, so how he knew, I have no idea! Military Intelligence, I guess!

I said: 'Yes, it is. I am guilty!'

He said, 'The General wants to see you.'

I said, '*Does* he?'

He replied, 'Yes. And he wants to see you before the meeting starts.'

So he ushered me into 'the presence'! As I approached, the General said, 'Padre, I am going to quote tonight what you said to me in your letter, and I'm not going to ask your permission! 'What is it from my letter that you intend to quote?', I asked. 'You sit down and enjoy the meeting, and you will discover what it is I am going to quote!', he replied.

He had maps of Europe on the wall as a background, and various charts, together with a number of symbols on the maps indicating the size of the Soviet build-up which was taking place, in terms of numbers of tanks, aircraft, missiles, troops, warships, submarines, etc., and how they were deployed. Furthermore, he explained that there was this great pincer movement threatening the whole of northern Europe. He showed how one arm of the pincers was poised to come through the borders of Norway to her seaboard, whilst the other was reaching out through the Baltic, threatening to cut off the whole of that section of Europe from the rest of the NATO Alliance. Then he explained how Russian submarines had those refuelling bases from northern Scotland right up to Greenland, and how the Soviets were pushing out their naval defence line from Murmansk to well beyond Iceland. He then stated that the Russians had nuclear-powered missile-firing submarines off all the coasts of North America, thus bringing every town, city and industrial area within range, so that America could be 'held-off', should she be tempted to intervene in any Russian 'move forward' in Europe.

Having showed us all this, and a lot else besides, General Walker then said: 'We are in a 1939 situation; only for Adolf Hitler, substitute the Kremlin...the writing is already on the wall...time is not on our side.' He added, 'In fact, we are in an "Ezekiel chapter 33" situation!.... The soldier, like myself, needs to warn militarily. The politician, if he has got guts enough [and I am quoting the General!] needs to warn politically. And the *preacher*', he said—sticking out his hand and pointing to 'yours truly' sitting in the audience—'the *preacher* needs to warn spiritually. When you get back home, read Ezekiel 33 for yourselves, especially the first seven verses, and you will have no doubt whatsoever as to whose is the greatest responsibility.'

There was a time for questions afterwards, and when the General had answered several people's questions, he sud-

209

denly said, 'That man, *that* man'—pointing again to 'yours truly'—'needs to get this message out from every pulpit that is made available to him in the land.'

So we are in an 'Ezekiel chapter 33' situation. But what exactly does Ezekiel 33 say?

In the first place: '... the word of the Lord came unto me, saying, Son of man, speak to the children of they people, and say unto them, When *I* bring the sword upon a land...' (vv.1,2). So the first thing that we need to recognise is, that it is *God* who does it. and when he does it, he does it in judgment. In other words, it is to be recognised as a judgment of God.

The second thing that Ezekiel 33:2 goes on to say is that there is a man who is set for a watchman who 'seeth the sword come upon the land'. That word 'seeth' tells us that this man is 'a seer'. I need to ask the Christian reader, 'Can *you* see that sword coming upon *this* land?'

A prophet is a seer. He sees things that other people do not see, because he has a God-given gift of spiritual perception and discernment. And our nation desperately needs seers today. Samuel, in the Old Testament was a prophet, but he is also called a seer. A seer can see what is coming, long before it arrives. And God holds him responsible for proclaiming what he sees. When he sees the sword coming, for instance, he should blow the trumpet and warn the people. He should sound the alarm. That is why I believe that God wanted *The Trumpet Sounds for Britain* to be written. The 'sword' can already be seen on the distant eastern horizon—the previous chapters clearly point that out.

Then the third thing that Ezekiel 33 teaches us is that God sometimes uses *nations* as his instruments of judgment. I have said this several times before, but it needs to be stressed again. It is a theme which runs throughout the whole of the Bible.

As the iniquity of a particular nation, or group of nations, is coming to a head, God can often be seen to be in the process of raising up such an instrument of judgment in terms of an existing and growing world power. It is then the task of a prophet to sound forth the warning. Ezekiel 33:3–5 puts it this way: 'If when he seeth the sword come upon the land, he *blow the trumpet*, and *warn* the people; then whosoever heareth the sound of the trumpet, and taketh not warning; if the sword come, and take him away, *his blood shall be upon his own head*. He heard the sound of the trumpet, and took not warning; *his blood shall be upon him*.' This means that, thereafter, it is the individual's responsibility—verse 5 continues, 'he that taketh warning shall deliver his soul.'

On the other hand, proclaims verse 6, 'if the watchman see the sword come, and blow *not* the trumpet, and the people be *not* warned; if the sword come, and take any person from among them, he is taken away in his iniquity; but *his blood will I require at the watchman's hand*.' What a fearful responsibility for the watchman—for the prophet— for the preacher! And why such an *enormous* responsibility? Because it is the individual's *eternal* destiny which is at stake, not just his earthly life.

'If the sword come and take any person'—What a challenge! Hence the need to get this message out, from every pulpit and platform made available to the preacher in the land. Hence the need to get this book with its message, circulated as widely as possible, and into the hands of every person in the realm.

But to continue with the quotation from Ezekiel 33:7, 'So thou, O son of man, I have set thee a watchman unto the house of Israel; therefore thou shalt hear the word at my mouth and *warn them from me*.' It is a message of warning from God himself. Verse 8 is quite clear: 'When I say unto the wicked, O wicked man, thou shalt surely die; if thou dost not speak to warn the wicked from his way, that wicked man shall die in his iniquity; but his blood will I require at thine hand.'

Verses 9–11 continue: 'Nevertheless, if thou warn the

211

wicked of his way to turn from it; if he do not turn from his way, he shall die in his iniquity; but thou hast delivered thy soul. Therefore, O thou son of man, speak unto the house of Israel; thus do ye speak [at the present time], saying, If our transgressions and our sins be upon us, and we pine away in them, how should we then live? Say unto them [in answer], 'As I live, saith the Lord God, I have no pleasure in the death of the wicked; but that the wicked *turn from his way* [if Ezekiel had lived in New Testament days he would have added—*and turn to the Lord Jesus Christ* for forgiveness and salvation] *and live ... turn ye* from your evil ways; for why will ye die, O house of Israel?' It is the role of a prophet and of a preacher, therefore, to turn the wicked from his wickedness, and from his evil ways. That is the main message of Ezekiel 33.

It is important to notice that it is a message spoken first and foremost to a nation as a whole—to a land, and to the whole land: 'When I bring the sword upon a *land*'. So God says there is need for the watchman to blow the trumpet to warn the whole land. God speaks to nations; he speaks to cities (Nineveh is an example); he does not only speak to his church!

Then it is important to see that it is a message spoken to a nation which is facing coming judgment. And that judgment is to be at the hands of an invading foreign power. This was pending in Ezekiel's day. Hence the words, 'When I bring the *sword* upon a land'. The emphasis is on the word 'Sword'—invading armies.

That, I believe, is what is in store for Britain and the whole of the West. But a nation is made up of individual people. So it is a message spoken to the people—to warn *them*.

It is a *strong* message, the kind of message which we rarely, if ever, hear preached these days—not even in this violent, highly sensual, permissive, and extremely wicked age. But there is an urgent need to hear such a message being preached as the threat of enemy armies increases, because God says it is the duty of watchmen, of preachers, and of individual spirit-empowered Christians, to warn the wicked of his way so that he turns from it. Who is there, in Britain today, who is warning the wicked so that they turn away from their sin and look towards God?

For notice where the emphasis is placed in Ezekiel 33. It speaks about the terrible possibility of people 'being taken away *in [their] iniquity*'. If 'the people be not warned; if the sword [of judgment] come...[they are] taken away in [their] iniquity' (v.6). Further down, in verses 8 and 9, the emphasis is even more specific: 'if thou dost not speak to warn the wicked from his way, that wicked man shall die in his iniquity.' So it is twice repeated.

That is the issue at stake—people dying in their iniquity. It is not only a message to the people at large, but to the individual. It is to '*whosoever* heareth the sound of the trumpet, and taketh not warning; if the sword come, and take him away, *his blood shall be upon his own head*' (v.4). 'If the sword come and take *any* person from among them, he is taken away in his iniquity' (v.6). 'If thou dost not speak to warn the wicked man from his way, *that wicked man* shall die in his iniquity' (v.8).

How is it possible to express the utter solemnity of this? What this chapter is saying, and what the whole Bible says, is that if such an individual wicked person is taken away from this world suddenly, then he dies *in his iniquity*. And to understand the full force of this, we need to remember what Jesus said in the New Testament.

He put it another way: 'If ye believe not [on me], ye shall *die in your sins*' (John 8:24). It means to die with your sins unforgiven, and that immediately brings us face to face with the awful consequences which are involved should people die without believing on Jesus and thus having their sins forgiven. What happens after they have died? The Bible says: 'it is appointed unto men once to die, but after this the *judgment*' (Hebrews 9:27).

Not oblivion, please notice. Not extinction. Judgment!

After the Judgment, what?

After the judgment, the sentence is passed. That is what happens in any court of law, isn't it? The judge pronounces the sentence after the person's guilt has been established.

And after the sentence has been pronounced?

After the sentence has been pronounced, comes the execution of the sentence. In terms of judgment after death, it means that those who have died in their sin, are banished from the presence of a Holy God for ever, to a place which Jesus himself called hell, and 'the lake of fire and brimstone [which burns] for ever and ever', and into which everybody will be cast, after the Day of Judgment, whose names are not written in the Lamb's book of life (Revelation 20: 10–15). *That* is what makes the message so urgent. 'If the sword come [on Britain], and take any person from among them, he is taken away *in his iniquity*.'

The individual's eternal destiny is at stake. That is why the watchman needs to sound the trumpet and warn the people, lest any *one* person gets taken away in his iniquity, and dies in his sins, unforgiven, and so has to face that awful judgment. That is the *spiritual* implication behind this chapter 33 of Ezekiel, and behind the Soviet build-up or any other form of judgment with which Britain may yet be visited—even of the final day of Judgment itself. Any preacher, any watchman, ignores it at his peril. Because if he does ignore it, and fails to give out the warning, God says that he is going to require all these people's blood at the watchman's, or preacher's, hands.

So the clarion call needs to be sounded abroad: We are in an 'Ezekiel 33' situation; therefore, 'Sound the Trumpet for Britain'!

I must hasten to add that no person *needs* to die in his sins. Nobody *needs* to be confronted with that awful final judgment, because God has made provision for him to be saved from it. That is what the good news of the glorious Christian Gospel is all about.

There is hope for the individual—for the most wicked

individual. God says: 'I have no pleasure in the death of the wicked; but that the wicked *turn from his way*, and live' (Ezekiel 33:11). Or as the New Testament puts it, the Lord 'is longsuffering to usward, not willing that any should perish, but that all should come to repentance' (2 Peter 3:9). God has made provision for their salvation by what Jesus achieved when he laid down his life, and shed his atoning blood, on the cross.

There is something else which needs to be said. Ezekiel 33 makes it plain that there is a grave condition where people's sins are upon them. This seems to be what was troubling the people whom Ezekiel was addressing. For they were asking: 'If our transgressions and our sins be upon us . . . how can we live?' (v.10). It is obvious that they were deeply troubled by this.

Transgressions and sins *need* not be upon any one, any longer. That, too, is what the good news of the glorious Christian Gospel is all about. That is precisely where God has made the provision.

The Gospel tells us, first, that God Almighty took your sins and mine from us, and put them upon the Lord Jesus Christ, his Son, as he hung between earth and heaven, nailed to Calvary's cross by his hands and his feet. So they are not upon us any more, but on *him*. The prophet Isaiah tells us that, when he says, 'The Lord hath laid on him [the Lord Jesus] the iniquity of us *all*' (Isaiah 53:6).

And the second thing we learn is that, after God had taken our sin and laid it upon Jesus Christ, the Lord Jesus willingly took all the judgment of that sin upon himself as he hung there upon the cross. In other words, he assumed full responsibility for it, and bore the full punishment for it. This is what Isaiah means when he says, 'Yet it pleased the Lord to bruise him' (Isaiah 53:10). And again, he was 'smitten of God, and afflicted' (Isaiah 53:4). Or yet again, 'He was wounded for our transgressions, he was bruised for our iniquities' (Isaiah 53:5).

The Lord Jesus Christ went through all that, on your

215

behalf, in order that you might never have to face that other judgment after death. Therefore, as you visualise in your mind's eye all that took place at the cross during the crucifixion of the Lord Jesus, what you are seeing is God's judgment on *your* sin taking place.

He underwent your judgment *for you*. That is how much He loves you. 'The Son of God loved me, and gave himself for me' (Galatians 2:20).

As the hymn says:

> Bearing shame and scoffing rude,
> In my place condemned He stood,
> Sealed *my pardon* with His blood:
> Hallelujah! What a Saviour!

As that truth dawns on your heart and mind, what you also need to realise is that God can never judge your sin a second time, once you accept that God judged it on Jesus, on the cross of Calvary. It has been transferred from you to him, and been dealt with, on him, as he suffered there. It is in that way that God has made provision for your eternal salvation.

So another hymn says:

> Because the sinless Saviour died,
> My sinful soul is counted free;
> For God, the Just, is satisfied
> To look on Him and pardon me.

Thirdly, we find that the salvation for which God has made provision, is available *to all who believe*. That is the theme which runs throughout the whole of the New Testament. Jesus himself said that you need to *believe* to be *saved*, because salvation is by *faith*. Having faith in all that the Lord Jesus Christ has done for us, on the cross of Calvary, in taking the full judgment of God upon our sins, and in

216

shedding his blood to cleanse us and to atone for us, *is all that is necessary to save us.*

It is not anything we *do*, nor anything which God *requires* us to do, which will save us. It is simply trusting in what Jesus Christ has done, and resting in that.

One of our hymn-writers has applied it to himself, by putting it this way, and we each need to do so in order to be saved:

> I am trusting Thee, Lord Jesus,
> Trusting only Thee;
> Trusting Thee for full salvation,
> Great and free.
>
> I am trusting Thee for pardon,
> At Thy feet I bow;
> For Thy grace and tender mercy,
> Trusting now.
>
> I am trusting Thee for cleansing,
> In the crimson flood;
> Trusting Thee to make me holy,
> By Thy Blood
>
> I am trusting Thee, Lord Jesus,
> Never let me fall;
> I am trusting Thee for ever,
> And for all.

Immediately any reader applies such statements of faith as these to himself, with true faith in his heart, the Lord Jesus will hear, will honour that faith, and will save. We have his full assurance of that.

Immediately anyone turns from his sin and looks to the Lord Jesus Christ for salvation, he will find that a number of things will follow.

First, he will have the experience of knowing that all his sins have been forgiven.

Secondly, he will know that they are not there any more.

God has removed them: 'As far as the east is from the west, so far [have I] removed [your] transgressions from [you]' (Psalm 103:12). We can then say 'Thou hast cast all my sins behind thy back' (Isaiah 38:17).

Thirdly, having taken his sins and put them upon the Lord Jesus on the cross of Calvary, God now takes his own righteousness and puts it upon the believer. This is the other side, as it were, of what God does in this great act of transferrence. He transfers his own righteousness to the person who repents and believes on him. And it is on these grounds that he can now accept that person.

So fourthly, as that person turns from his sin and looks to the Lord Jesus for salvation, he will find that the Lord is waiting to receive him, and what is more, will accept him. For Jesus himself has said, 'Whosoever cometh unto me, I will in no wise cast out.' We can trust Jesus to keep his word. That is faith.

Furthermore, he will find that the Lord Jesus Christ will not only accept him, but will enter into him by his Holy Spirit, and that is what makes a person a Christian: 'Christ *in you*, the hope of glory' (Colossians 1:27). Jesus will pardon him of everything, cleanse him, and take full possession of him, causing him to become a new man in Christ Jesus—an entirely new creation, born again by the Holy Spirit. And the change will be seen by others almost immediately. God will also give him the unshakeable assurance that he will go to heaven, and that he is now, indeed, safe and secure in his hands for ever.

Even if God *does* bring upon the land that sword of judgment about which this book is sounding out the warning, even though the country *is* overrun and taken over, or even if God should visit Britain with any other severe judgment, *this* person will not be shaken by any of these events—not even by the knowledge of the final Day of Judgment itself. He knows, now, for absolute certainty, that his eternal salvation is secure, and he knows deep down within him that *that* is what matters in the long run.

So whatever may happen, his heart is now firmly fixed, trusting in the Lord.

Therefore, as the country continues heading towards a disaster of truly titanic and world-shattering proportions, and as the trumpet continues to sound loud and clear for Britain, it is this message—the glorious message concerning the way of eternal salvation, together with the urgent need to repent and believe—which needs to be proclaimed by radio and television, from every pulpit, and by every means at the nation's disposal, throughout the length and breadth of the land, to ensure that it reaches every individual, and gives them the opportunity to be saved for ever, while there is still time.

Acknowledgements

I list with grateful acknowledgements the various publications which I have consulted during the preparation of this book, and from which some of the material has been drawn.

Books

Winston S. Churchill, *History of the English-speaking Peoples*, Volume 1, Cassell, London 1956.

John Brooke, *King George III*, foreword by HRH The Prince of Wales, Constable, London 1972.

Lance Lambert, *The Uniqueness of Israel*, Kingsway Publications, Eastbourne 1980, ch.3, pp. 77–8.

General Sir Walter Walker, *The Next Domino?*, Covenant Books, London 1980.

The Revd David E. Gardner, *A Warning to the Nation*, eighth reprint, Christian Foundation Publications, 45 Appleton Road, Hale, Altrincham, Cheshire.

The Revd David E. Gardner, *The Trumpet Sounds for Britain*, Volume 1, Christian Foundation Publications,

221

Altrincham 1980, reprinted 1983; *The Trumpet Sounds for Britain*, Volume 2, Christian Foundation Publications, Altrincham 1981, reprinted 1983.

Leaflets, Booklets, Pamphlets and Addresses

The Coronation of Her Majesty Queen Elizabeth II, approved souvenir programme, Odhams Press, London 1953.

Hansard, Wednesday, 16 June 1976, pp. 1329, 1330, 1361.

General Sir Walter Walker's address to NATO forces in Europe (unclassified NATO material, with his full permission to quote).

The Royal United Services Institute for Defence Studies report, *European Security 1972–1980*.

Aktuelt, Copenhagen, 13 March 1976.